CHRONICLE

BY THE EDITORS OF  ConsumerGuide

pil

Publications International, Ltd.

Copyright © 2003, 2011 Publications International, Ltd. All rights
reserved. This book may not be reproduced or quoted in whole or
in part by any means whatsoever without written permission from:

Louis Weber, CEO
Publications International, Ltd.
7373 North Cicero Avenue
Lincolnwood, Illinois 60712

Permission is never granted for commercial purposes.

ISBN-13: 978-1-4508-2677-8
ISBN-10: 1-4508-2677-6

Manufactured in China.

8 7 6 5 4 3 2 1

Library of Congress Control Number: 2011925349

Photographers:

Mike Baker, Roger D. Barnes, Scott Baxter, Ken Beebe, Damon Bell, Les Bidrawn, Joe Bohovic, Arch Brown, Michael Brown, Chan Bush, Henry A. Clark, John Collier, Rick Cotta, Doug Dalton, Mirco Decet, Roland Flessner, Mitch Frumkin, Tom Glatch, Allan M. Grant, Sam Griffith, Mike Hastie, Jerry Heasley, Don Heiny, David Hogan, Jeff Johnson, Bud Juneau, Harry Kapsalis, Laurel Kenny Jr., Milton Kieft, Lloyd Koenig, Dan Lyons, Vince Manocchi, Medves, Doug Mitchel, Ron Moorehead, Mike Mueller, David Newhardt, Neil B. Nissing, Nina Padgett, David Patryus, Jay Peck, Rick Popely, D. Randy Riggs, Jeff Rose, Rob Van Schaick, Wm. J. Schintz, Tom Shaw, Rick Simmons, Gary Smith, Mike Spenner, Richard Spiegelman, Steve Statham, Jim Stewart, Rick Stiller, Tom Storm, Rich Szczepanski, David Temple, Gregory Thomas, Phil Toy, Dan Vecchio, Nicky Wright.

Car Owners:

A.A.M.A., James Adams, John B. Albert, Roy Albertson, Nick Alexander Imports, Carl & Mary Allen, Brian Altizer, Henry Alvarez, Thomas C. Amendola, Donald R. Anderson, Kim Anderson, Richard & Holly Anderson, Robert D. Anderson, Dan Armstrong, Arrowhead Water Company, Jim Ashworth, Art Astor, John Baker Sr., George Ball, Edgar Balsman, Art Bancucci, Joseph Barrera, Jack Bart, Ron & Ann Marie Batesole, John Roger Battistone, William Baumgartner, Rich Bayer, Michael Beandewburg, Nancy L. Beauregard, Carl J. Beck, Robert Becker, Karl Benefiel, David Berlew, Berry Motor Cars, Rod & Claudia Bjerke, Eugene & Sharon Blanc, Jeff Blind, Glen Bohannan, Joe Bombaci, Howard Bonner, Ken Boorsma, Norman & Joyce Booth, Ralph Bowermaster, Brad Boyajian, Mark Brandt, John Breda, Walt Brewer, Louis Broinac, W. Parker Brown, Tom Brunner, Jack Buchanan, Joe Burke, Ted S. Burleson, Ronald P. Butz, Dale & Ann Callen, Jerry Capizzi, Nelson Cardadeiro, Joe Carfagna, Castle Amusement Park, Rich & Pam Cathley, Jackie & Shana Cerrito, John Chandler, Jerry Charter, Sam S. Chastain, Chicago Car Exchange, Christine's Classic Continentals, Steve & Dawn Cizmas, Classic Car Center, Roger Clements, Bill Cline, Harley E. Cluxton III, Ron Colarossi, John Cook, Dr. Randy & Freda Cooper, Crawford Collection/Western, Dan Crossman, Fraser Dante, Ltd., Manuel & Ruth Darush, Dr. Edward & Joanne Dauer, T. Davidson, Betty Death, Ray Death, Richard Defendorf, Dells Auto Museum, Ray & Nancy Dietke, Terry E. Dinkel, Rocky DiOrio, Kim Dobbins, Paul R. Dobbins, David Domash, Dominoe's Classics, Tony Donna, J. Glenn Dowd, Robert Dowd, Ralph Dowling, Steve Drake, Jeffrey M. Drucker, Ken Dubach, Donald F. & Chris Dunn, Carroll J. & Marlene A. Dupriest, Richard Wayne Durham, Evan Eberlin, Ron Edwards, William B. Edwards, Jerry Emery, David & Karen Erschen, Finn Fahey, Vic & Cathy Falcone, Gordon A. Fenner, Don & Sue Fennig, Clarence E. Ferguson, Joel Ferris, Mark E. Figliozzi, Fred C. Fischer, Robert M. Forker, David Fortner, Ernest & Sheri Foster, Kenneth Freeman, Bob French, Bob Fruehe, Harry Fryer, Kevin Fuller, Stanley C. Fuller, Glen Gangestad, Ruben J. Garcia, Michell Garner, Gregory Gates, Brian Gatzow, Paul & Julie Gelinis, Bob Getsfried, Jerry Gibino, Richard C. Gise, George & Tony Gloriosa, Chris Golab, Frank Gonsalvez, Tom Griffith, Sigfried Grunze, Buzz Gunnarson, Lee Gurvey, Bill Halabrin, Dean Hammond, Mr. & Mrs. Robert E. Hannay, Nelson D. Hansen, Jack Harbaugh, Jim Hardy, William A. Harper, Shel Harriman, Rick Harris, Tom Hasse, Dennis J. Hauke, Michael R. Hausman, Ronald R. Hayden, Keith Hazley, Robert Heimstra, Bill Henderson, Jack Hendrikson, John L. Heinaman, Earl Heintz, A.W. Higginbotham, Russell Hoeksema, Philip & Nancy Hoffman, Roger Holdaway, James A. Hollingsworth, Tim Holsapple, David Holls, David Holmes, Rob Holmes, David D. Horn, Houston P.D., Tom Howard, Dennis L. Huff, A.W. Huffman Jr., Teresa & Doug Hvidston, Frank Iaccino, Leo Iniguez, Gary L. Ingersoll, Fred & Diane Ives, Vic Jacobellis, Cherie Jacobson, Blaine Jenkins, William Jenn, Dick Johnson, Tom Jones, Jack Karleskind, Lawrence Keck, Kelly's Classic Auto, Lee Keeney, Robert L. Keller, William Kipp, Edwin C. Kirstatter, Michael Kniest, David & Phyliss Knuth, Scott R. Koeshall, Darrell, Kombrink, Ken Kowalk, Christopher M Krueger, Richard Kughn, Alton Kunz, Sheldon Lake, Michael Lauren, Tony & Larry Lawler, Robert Ledbetter, Douglas Leicht, Jack & Cheryl Lenhart, Thomas F. Lerch, Libertyville Lincoln-Mercury, William R. Lindsey, Wayne Loomis, Los Angeles County Sheriff, Robert Lovato, Sherman Lovegren, Robert C. Lowry, George Lucie, The Wm. Lyon Collection, Frank R. Magyar, Larry G. Maisel, S.W. Mann, Bud Manning, Larry Martin, Bill May, Gerard & Lorraine May, Bob Mayer, Don McCormick, Michael Mennela, Marc Micale, S. Ray Miller, Amos Minter, Frank J. Monhart, Charles Montano, Al & Naomi Moore, Howard A. Moore, Don Morris, Roger Moser, Motor Cars Ltd., Milt Mouser, G. & Connie Moyer, Jim Mueller, William R. Muni, Richard Nassar, Greg Neffle, Terry Nelson, Carol Nesladek, Nethercutt's Museum, Rich Neubauer, Clay Nichols, Bob Niemann, Barry Norman, Larry O'Neal, Tom Orban, Mr. & Mrs. Rob Paino, Alan C. Parker, Patricia & Rexford Parker, Donald Passardi, Henry Patrick, Joseph A. Pessetti, Richard Perez, Jim Perrault, Marshall & Ellie Peters, William Peterson, Rob Petty, John Prokop, Charles Plylar, Bill Povero, Val Price, Priceless Classic Motorcars, Edwin Putz, Glen & Janice Pykiet, Dick Pyle, Richard T. Quinn, Ragtops Motorcars, Larry & Annis Ray, Roger Randolph, Virgil J. Recker, Bob Reed, Rader's Relics, Robert Reeves, Vince & Norma Rhodes, Charles Richards, Mark A. Rice, Gary Richards, Carl M. Riggins, Jeff Riley, John & Judy Riordan, Jerry Robbin, Gary D. Robley, Bob Rose, Dennis D. Rosenberry, Nino Rosso, H. Rohrman, Ed Rouge, Charles O. Roverman, Jess Rupp, Ron Russ, John Ryan, Wilbert D. Sackman, Allan St. Jacques, Stephen Salazar, David Sanborn, Col. J.L. Sanders, Homer J. Sanders, Rick J. Santelli, Phil G.D. Schaefer, Charles O. Scharpe, Art Schildknecht, Tom Schlitter, Schmerler Ford, Donald & Marlene Schmidt, Mike Schowalter, Sam H. Scoles, Ned Scudder, Robert J. Secondi, Bob Sejnost, Nelson & Evelyn Sembach, Steven Seneson, David Senholz, Rob & Dottie Sharkey, Elvin Sherman, Stephen & Teresa Shore, David Showalter, Robert Shulish, Ed Siegfried, J.W. & Barbara Silveira, Don Simpkin, Alan Simpson, Bob & Karyn Sitter, Ron Slater, Daniel P. Smith, Sherm Smith, Tony Smith, Michael A. Spaziano, Jerry C. Spear, Frank Spittle, Don & Wanda Spivey, Richard Staley, Bill & Collette Stanley, Rick Steiner, Richard L. Stevenson, Jack & Holly Stewart, Jim Stewart, John F. Stimac Jr., John Strewe, Johan Suerdrup, Edward Swoboda, Seth Swoboda, Tommy Taylor, David Temple, Michael Tesauro Jr., Times Collection, Gary Timmerman, Bret M. Traywick, James & Ellen Tremain, Gene Troyer, Frank Trummer, Dwight A. Tschantz, Unique Sports Cars, George P. Valiukas, Eugene Vaughn, Norman A. Vegely, Martin J. Vehstedt, Steve Verderber, James & Susan Verhasselt, John P. Vetter, Guy Viti Jr., Volo Auto Museum, Linda Wade, Larry & Beverly Wake, Brent Walker, Tom & Thelma Walters, Wayne & Terri Warner, Dr. Irv Warren, Larry Webb, John Webber, Geoffrey A. Weiner, Judge Lewis Weinstein, Dan Weiss, Charlie Wells, Don Wendel, Maurice White, Joyce & Jim Wickel, Vanetta Wilkerson, Al Wilkewicz, Lee Willer, Bud Williams, Sam Wilson, Durwood Winchell, Jerry Windle, Ron Wold, Steve & Sandie Wren, Gerald Wvichet, Ronald Youngman, Leonard Zannini, Charles Ziska, Harold E. Zulick. Special thanks to Bill Bailey for his collection of archival images.

Our appreciation to the historical archives and media services groups at Ford Motor Company.

About the Editors of Consumer Guide® Automotive:

For more than 40 years, Consumer Guide® has been a trusted provider of new-car buying information.

The Consumer Guide® staff drives and evaluates more than 200 vehicles annually.

Consumerguide.com is one of the web's most popular automotive resources, visited by roughly three million shoppers monthly.

The Editors of Consumer Guide® also publish the award-winning bimonthly *Collectible Automobile®* magazine.

CONTENTS

1910–1919
The World in Flux
Page 28

- Ford raises assembly line pay to five dollars for an eight-hour day
- One-millionth Ford vehicle built
- Henry Ford II is born

1920–1929
The Decade That Roared
Page 44

- "Tin Lizzie" replaced by Model A
- Ford market share reaches 65 percent
- Ford purchases Lincoln Motor Company

1930–1939
Depression!
Page 74

- Ford line goes exclusively V-8
- Henry Ford suffers stroke
- Management and labor clash at the "Battle of the Overpass"

1940–1949
War and Recovery
Page 106

- Ford factories build planes, jeeps, and tanks
- Ford of Germany falls into Nazi hands
- Edsel and Henry Ford die
- HF II takes helm

The Toughest Fords Ever Built!

CONTENTS

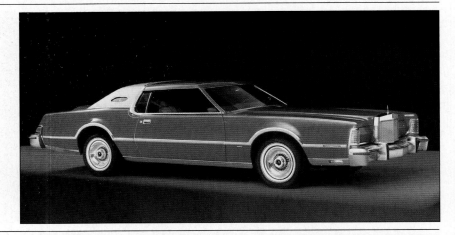

INTRODUCTION

As THE TITLE SUGGESTS, this book chronicles the fascinating story of the Ford Motor Company and its products from an American perspective, which is only right. After all, the Dearborn, Michigan-based automaker is a star-spangled institution that is inextricably woven into the fabric of American life and culture. Ask a friend or neighbor to name their favorite cars and/or trucks and chances are that person will name at least one FoMoCo model. Perhaps it's a Ford Mustang, F-150 pickup, Explorer SUV, or "Little Deuce Coupe." Perhaps it's Mercury's space-age Turnpike Cruiser, Cyclone musclecar, or the 1949 "bathtub" coupe immortalized by James Dean in the film *Rebel Without a Cause*. Some folks may think of Lincolns: the imposing Depression-era V12 K-Series, for example, or the elegant Continentals of 1940-41 and 1956-57.

No doubt about it: Ford Motor Company has built some memory-making vehicles—and still does. But it's important to observe here that Ford became a global enterprise quite early in its history, and it remains a significant force in many countries, not just the U.S. This is why the average Briton might mention a Ford Cortina, Capri, or Escort Cosworth as a favorite car; why a German may fondly recall a Ford Taunus or Sierra XR4x4; or why an Australian might name a Fairlane, a Falcon ute, or hot-rod Falcon XR. It's the same story in Argentina, Brazil, South Africa, and many other lands, with China, India, and Russia now further expanding Ford's global footprint and commercial impact.

In 2003, Ford threw itself a monthlong party in honor of its historic centennial. During the celebration, the company announced production of its 300-millionth vehicle. The figure was acknowledged as a global grand total and may or may not have been accurate, as it included outputs from four European automakers that Ford owned at the time. But no matter when number 300,000,000 was actually built, the sheer scale of that achievement highlights an indisputable fact: As the pioneer of vehicle mass production and marketing, Ford literally put the world on wheels, shaping the auto industry as we know it today and changing the lives of billions.

The Ford story is also a dynastic saga that began with a farm-bred Michigan tinkerer who was born soon after the Civil War and once declared "history is bunk." Henry Ford had a simple, homespun demeanor that belied a complex personality. He could be engaging, free-thinking, and public-spirited, but also grumpy, closed-minded, and bigoted. Blessed with innate mechanical gifts and a shrewd head for business, he conceived the landmark 1908 Model T as a simple, rugged little car that could be easily fixed and driven most anywhere at a time when mechanics and paved roads didn't exist outside major cities. But his true genius was developing the mass-production techniques and material resources that allowed selling the Tin Lizzie in ever greater numbers at ever lower prices. Public response was predictably enormous, and by 1920 Ford Motor Company was America's biggest automaker by far, its founder one of the world's richest, most influential industrialists.

As time passed, however, Henry became ever more eccentric, and the company suffered for it. He refused to retire the Model T even when demand began to wane, then inexplicably gambled everything on the 1928 Model A, which fortunately for him was a big hit. He then conjured America's first low-priced V-8 car, but only to one-up pesky six-cylinder competition. He resisted "modern" features like hydraulic brakes, yet pursued dubious ideas like making car bodies from soybeans. He made son Edsel, his one and only heir, company president in 1919, but consistently usurped his authority. By the time Edsel died in 1943, Dearborn had dropped to third in industry sales and earnings, behind General Motors and Chrysler. When the old man himself finally succumbed, in 1947, Ford was in utter disarray, its future uncertain.

It was left to Edsel's son, Henry Ford II, and some brainy "Whiz Kids" to secure that future, which they did with fair dispatch and no little luck. Helped by a boom market born of soaring post-World War II prosperity, Dearborn soon reclaimed title as America's number-two automaker. Though Lincoln, acquired in 1922, and Mercury, established in 1939, played a role, the recovery was owed almost entirely to the Ford brand, which steadily closed the sales gap with chart-topping Chevrolet—and occasionally outsold its perennial GM foe—thanks to ever faster and flashier cars and trucks.

Ford achieved even greater success in the 1960s, starting with the highly popular Falcon compact, then with America's first midsize car, the Fairlane. Ford also prospered with handsome "standard" cars and ever more elaborate "personal luxury" Thunderbirds. But its biggest triumph was the Mustang, a jaunty, affordable "ponycar" that was perfectly in tune with the freewheeling spirit of the times. Ford also captured the country's imagination with its "Total Performance" program, an all-out assault on motorsports from NASCAR to drag racing to international long-distance events. This effort not only spurred showroom sales but inspired a squadron of exciting driver-oriented street machines. These, too, have long been highly prized collectibles.

Everything changed in the 1970s, when Ford and its Detroit rivals were forced to deal with a suddenly sober public mood and stricter government standards for passenger safety, tailpipe emissions, and—after an unprecedented gas shortage—fuel economy. Many buyers, newly disillusioned with American cars, embraced a growing herd of Japanese-brand imports that not only offered better mpg but superior build quality. These trends continued into the 1980s, aggravated by the sharp recessions that bookended that decade. Even so,

A dapper Henry Ford stands next to one of 15 million Model Ts that would eventually roll off the lines. Not only did Ford bring affordable motoring to the general public, he forever changed the landscape of American industry.

the Blue Oval recovered market strength with striking "aerodynamic" cars like the 1986 Taurus and increased demand for its F-Series trucks, which to this day remain the nation's top-selling vehicles of any kind. Adding the Explorer sport-utility vehicle helped Ford to record sales and profits in the 1990s as light trucks began outselling cars for the first time.

Ford, GM, and Chrysler continued emphasizing trucks in the new millennium, spurred by their higher profit margins, less direct import-brand competition, and many forecasts that light-truck demand would go nowhere but up—much like home values were. This left Honda, Nissan, Toyota, and similar brands to dominate America's car market with more-appealing models than Detroit could muster. Meantime, U.S. automakers continued to put sales ahead of profitability by pushing out vehicles that could be tough to sell without hefty rebates, low-interest loans, and other dealer-sweeteners that consumers had grown accustomed to since the 1970s.

All this reflected a stubborn wishful thinking among Detroit managers that was dramatically exposed when buying patterns shifted 180 degrees with the end of the "dot-com" boom economy and the horror of September 11. Though the economy recovered by mid-decade, U.S. automakers found themselves in a seemingly unstoppable downward spiral, losing money and sales by the carload even as debt levels rose, due mainly to obligations for employee pensions and health care. The American companies were also unprepared for the sharp mid-decade spike in gas prices that sent consumers rushing to high-mileage cars, which chiefly benefited import brands. Ford had worsened its own

situation in 2000 by embarking on an ill-advised multibillion-dollar expansion that involved buying not only four European automakers (as mentioned; the heart of a new Premium Automotive Group luxury division) but all sorts of sideline businesses like "quick-stop" service centers and parts recyclers.

The stage was set for disaster, which duly arrived in late 2008 when America's housing boom went bust, triggering the most severe recession since October 1929. Vehicle sales tanked as millions of Americans lost their jobs and homes and lenders often refused to finance what buyers were left. By mid-2009, this situation had triggered a full-blown crisis at GM and Chrysler that forced those companies to accept government-ordered bankruptcy reorganizations in exchange for taxpayer-supplied emergency funding.

Ford was in better shape, thanks to a bold move in 2006 by then-new CEO Alan Mulally, recruited from airplane-maker Boeing by board chairman William C. Ford Jr. While moving quickly to dispose of money-losing non-core businesses, Mulally stunned the industry by mortgaging most remaining Ford assets—even the Blue Oval logo—to win $23.5 billion in loans for keeping the doors open and for funding a recovery plan based on fresh products and a vastly more-realistic business model. Avoiding the taint of "bailout" bolstered public confidence in Ford to the benefit of sales, and by 2010 the company seemed to have turned the corner, posting a $6.56 billion profit, its highest in 11 years. Significantly, Mulally's comeback strategy, labeled "One Ford," would marshal the company's global resources as never before to create vehicles that could be built and sold most anywhere, thus saving billions. Even the next generation of the all-American Mustang is to be designed with input from Ford's European and Australian operations, not just the home team in Dearborn.

Though the "One Ford" story is only just beginning, this book has been prepared at a time when the company's overall future looks brighter than it has in many years. Meanwhile, welcome to *Ford Chronicle*. We hope you enjoy it.

The Editors of Consumer Guide® Automotive
Lincolnwood, Illinois
March 2011

THE BEGINNINGS

- Henry Ford is born on July 30, 1863, in Dearborn, Michigan, to successful Irish-immigrant farmer William Ford and his wife, Mary

- Henry migrates to nearby Detroit in December 1879; having gained his mechanical apprenticeship, he returns to Dearborn in 1882 to farm

- Clara Bryant and Henry Ford are married on April 11, 1888

- The Fords move to Detroit in 1891; Henry serves as an engineer for the city's electric utility

- A son, Edsel, is born to Henry and Clara Ford on November 6, 1893; Henry builds his first experimental gasoline engine the following month

- Henry witnesses friend Charles King's test of the first "horseless carriage" in Detroit in March 1896

▲ A youthful Henry Ford casts a serious gaze from a portrait taken at a Detroit studio. Ford's first foray into the town he would eventually help transform into America's "Motor City" came when he was just 16. After working in a machine shop and for a ship-building company, in the early 1880s he returned to the farm community around Dearborn, Michigan, where he had been born. But machines held a greater attraction than farming and, in 1891, he headed back to Detroit.

▲ When Ford returned to Detroit, now with wife Clara, it was to serve as an engineer for Edison Illuminating, the city's electric utility company. In time, the Fords moved to Bagley Avenue. Behind their house was a shed—reproduced here at Greenfield Village—in which Henry built his first car in 1896.

▶ The shed behind the Bagley Avenue residence served as the laboratory for Henry Ford's homespun engineering. But it also quite unintentionally confined his creativity, too. The "Quadricycle"—as he called his first car—was too wide for the door; he had to knock bricks out of the wall to free the car for its first drive.

▲ The tiller-steered Quadricycle had a buggy-type chassis and rolled on wire-spoke bicycle wheels with hubs fashioned from gas pipe. Ford found it prudent to mount an electric doorbell to be rung as a warning to pedestrians when he began taking to the public roads. Later, he tacked on an oil lamp as a further safety precaution. Henry was wise to be cautious: As originally built, the car had no reverse gear and no brakes. The latter shortcoming was remedied when he worked up a transmission brake. The car employed chain drive.

▲ In the wee hours of the rainy morning of June 4, 1896, Henry Ford conducted the first virtually secret test of his car on the streets of Detroit. As the year wore on, he continued to field test the vehicle, eventually heading out to rutted country roads, sometimes accompanied by Clara and young son Edsel.

▶ Henry Ford's first automobile was powered by a water-cooled, four-stroke, two-cylinder engine. With a 2.5-inch bore and six-inch stroke per cylinder, the engine made approximately four horsepower, enough to propel the Quadricycle to a top speed of about 20 mph. A pulley acting on a transmission belt served as a clutch.

THE BEGINNINGS

▶ After about 18 months' work, Henry Ford completed a second, much-improved Quadricycle in 1898. Its wooden bodywork covered the two-cylinder engine and running gear. Other niceties included a leather dash, fenders, and running boards; a padded carriage seat; a carpeted floor; and twin front oil lamps. The next year, Ford demonstrated the car to a wealthy Detroit businessman, spurring formation of the Detroit Automobile Company.

▲ Ford got the capital to make his second car by selling his first—for $200. But, as he would repeatedly demonstrate, Henry had a nostalgic fondness for the artifacts of his life, not the least of which was the original Quadricycle. This photo is from around the time he bought it back about 10 years later (note the car reflected in the window).

▼ The Detroit Automobile Company was dissolved in January 1901, but some of Ford's backers were willing to try again. The result was the Henry Ford Company, established later that same year. This tiller-steered runabout was one of Henry's designs for that brief venture.

► Ford continued to attempt to perfect his ideas as he tried to meet his obligations to his backers to produce cars for quantity sale. His third handbuilt experimental car was this runabout from 1901 that featured wheel steering in place of a tiller and a return to equal sizes for front and rear tires.

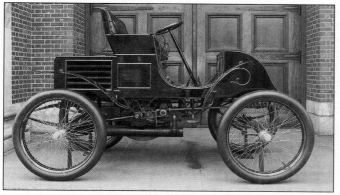

▲ Another prototype from the 1901 to 1902 period. Ford stayed with the Henry Ford Company only three months. Engine manufacturer Henry Leland was brought in as a consultant, but he and Ford clashed. After Ford left, the firm was reorganized, first as the Detroit Automobile Company (again), then as Cadillac.

► Though it was a ride in the second Quadricycle that convinced businessman William Murphy to recruit investors for the Detroit Automobile Company, runabouts weren't the only vehicles the budding firm hoped to make. In fact, the first type announced for sale was a delivery van, at least one of which was built in 1900. It featured tiller steering and solid-rubber tires.

▲ In 1901, Henry Ford decided to go racing. Seen here at the wheel of the 26-horsepower, two-cylinder special he built, Ford defeated Alexander Winton in a head-to-head 10-mile track race at Grosse Pointe, Michigan, on October 10. The victory gained him considerable publicity and led to formation of the Henry Ford Company, but a fixation with racing cars disturbed his backers.

1903–1909

A Company Begins

THE TWENTIETH CENTURY'S first decade produced Albert Einstein's Theory of Relativity, Sigmund Freud's *The Interpretation of Dreams,* and the Wright Brothers' miracle of powered flight at Kitty Hawk. Admiral Robert Peary reached the North Pole in 1909.

U.S. President William McKinley was shot and mortally wounded in 1901 at the Pan-American Exposition in Buffalo, New York; he was succeeded by Teddy Roosevelt. Czarist Russia was soundly trounced when it went to war with Japan over Korea and Manchuria in 1904.

The San Francisco earthquake of 1906 caused building collapses and fires that reduced most of the city to ruins, killed 2000, and produced 200,000 refugees.

Congress passed the Pure Food Act, and the National Association for the Advancement of Colored People was founded. An astonishing feat of engineering, the New York City subway, opened in 1904.

Britain's Queen Victoria died in 1901, a year before the end of the bloody, three-year war in South Africa between Dutch Boer settlers and the British. The Brits prevailed in a conflict predicated on disputes sparked by the discovery of gold.

And in Michigan in 1903, Henry Ford established the Ford Motor Company.

1903

- Ford Motor Company incorporates June 16, with $28,000 in capital

- Henry Ford holds 25.5 percent interest in the fledgling enterprise

- The Dodge brothers agree to supply completed chassis for $250 each

- First car sold in July, an $850 Model A runabout

- Company pays first dividend in November

- Model A available in any color as long as it's red

- Barney Oldfield pushes Henry Ford's massive "999" racer to a world record 64.5 mph

▶ Dressed in their Sunday best, a trio of early motorists brave the dusty unpaved roads of early twentieth-century America. The Model A runabout was ostensibly a two-seater, but three very friendly adventure seekers could squeeze onboard when necessary. Early production Fords had a hand throttle. Power for the ignition came from two sets of six dry-cell batteries. Frames for the Model A were supplied under contract from the Dodge brothers' machine shop.

▲ Rented for $75 a month, this Mack Avenue factory was the birthplace of the first salable Model A. Originally a one-story facility, the plant was the home of the Ford & Malcomson Company Limited, founded by Henry Ford, Detroit coal dealer Alexander Y. Malcomson, and a group of 10 investors. The organization eventually came to be known simply as the Ford Motor Company.

◄ Here, a restored 1903 Model A stands in front of the general store in Greenfield Village, Ford's tribute to early American life, located in Dearborn, Michigan. Passengers climbed aboard the high-off-the-road Model A by way of a small carriage step. A detachable rear tonneau, with seating for two extra people and back-door access, cost $100 extra. Red was the standard color, giving a flamboyant feel to the car's practical lines.

▼ Despite being billed in advertising as the "most reliable machine in the world," the Model A had its fair share of mechanical woes. Overheating and slipping transmission bands were among the most common maladies that faced early Ford owners.

▲ The Model A sold for $850 in runabout form, $950 as a four-seat tonneau. Storage baskets and other add-ons were typically used to accessorize early Ford cars. More than 1700 Model A Fords were built over a fifteen-month period. Refinements made during that period were applied to the next-generation Ford, the Model C.

1904

- Ford launches Models B, C, and F

- Ford produces almost eight percent of all cars built in America

- Ford Motor Company of Canada founded

- Ford opens first dealership, on Detroit's Jefferson Avenue

- Ford cars displayed at seven auto shows, including the Louisiana Purchase Exposition in St. Louis

- Henry Ford drives "Arrow" racer to world record 91.37 mph

- Ford models range in price from the $850 Model A to the new $2000 Model F tourer

▲ Henry Ford returns to drive the track at Grosse Pointe, Michigan, for the first time since defeating Alexander Winton in a 10-mile race in 1901. Here Ford, left, piloting the "999" racer keeps pace with Harry Harkess during a demonstration drive. Not only is Ford without goggles or helmet, he appears to be wearing a shirt and tie.

◄ Henry Ford's dream of building a $500 "family horse" was not furthered by the debut of the Model B, a well-equipped touring car on a 92-inch wheelbase. Though its 24-horsepower engine produced three times the power of the Model A's, sales never took off. The Model B was Ford's first four-cylinder car.

► Henry Ford's famous "999" racer was little more than a stripped-down chassis with a huge engine mounted to it. Powered by an enormous 1150-cubic-inch engine, the 999 set several land speed records. Steering was by tiller rather than wheel, and driver comfort was limited to a wooden "bucket" seat. Built at the same time was the 999's sister car, the Arrow, which Henry Ford piloted to a record 91.37 mph.

- Models B, C, and F are improved

- The first Ford "truck," a Model E commercial-delivery vehicle, is introduced

- Manufacturing moves out of the Mack Avenue factory to a bigger plant on Piquette Avenue

- Ford becomes member of the Society of Automotive Engineers

- Availability of windshields and headlamps grows, but they remain extra-cost items

- Price of Model F rises $200 to $1200, other prices are unchanged

- Ford sells slightly fewer cars than in 1904

▲ The Model C had 10 horsepower on tap for 1905, an increase of two over the previous year. This particular car was delivered without the optional windshield. Priced at $950 with tonneau rear seating, the Model C remained the most affordable car in the Ford lineup.

▲ Ford advertising of the day devoted much attention to dismissing the alleged qualities of more-expensive competitors. Later advertising would extol the virtues of purchasing a mass-produced car.

▲ Customers weren't clamoring to pay $2000, but the elegant, upscale Model B touring car returned with a slightly different radiator and more powerful four-cylinder engine. The Model B remained the only Ford with an engine of more than two cylinders.

1906

- New low-cost Model N introduced

- Henry Ford considers the $600 Model N his "crowning achievement"

- Plush new Model K is the most expensive Ford yet

- Model F is dropped

- Two-cylinder engines are phased out

- Ford production soars to almost 9000 vehicles

- Ford's market share reaches 26 percent

- A racing version of the Model K sets a 24-hour speed record of more than 47 mph

▲ The biggest and plushest Ford yet, the Model K touring car was also the heaviest, weighing in at more than 2000 pounds. With more than twice the horsepower and at almost twice the price, the Model K represented a clear step up from the entry-level Model N.

CHILDE HAROLD WILLS
Henry Ford's Alter Ego

Henry Ford generally is credited with having designed and developed the Model T. Actually, he was the catalyst of a small group that did so, and none in that group contributed more than Childe Harold Wills who, like racing driver Barney Oldfield, could have said, "Ford and I made each other, but I did the best job of it."

Wills has another minor, yet far-reaching, claim to fame: He furnished the lettering for the Ford company's time-honored script, lifted from a printing set he used as a teenager to make and sell calling cards.

Born in Ft. Wayne, Indiana, in 1878, Wills—tall, handsome, able, and original-minded—had a strong aptitude and passion for mechanical design. He preferred to learn by doing, and worked incessantly, although he had a penchant for lively society and liked to carry fine jewels in his pocket. He also shared something of Henry Ford's idealism and vision.

In 1902, a year before the formation of the Ford Motor Company, Wills spent part of his time helping Henry Ford build the famous racing car, 999. Working in an unheated shop, the two occasionally boxed to warm themselves. On a more personal level, Ford served as best man at Wills' wedding.

In making Wills his strong right arm, Ford did much to ensure the success of his company's designs and engineering. The two men were close collaborators on all of the firm's models through the Model T; indeed, their work is almost indistinguishable. Wills also helped plan factory layouts and routines, and became one of the country's best practical metallurgists.

"Mr. Wills and Mr. Ford got along about as well as any engineering couple I've ever run across," observed Fred W. Seeman, a veteran Ford employee. Ford valued his associate so highly that he allocated part of his own company dividends to him. Given Wills' talent and

◄ Henry Ford (at the wheel) wasn't especially fond of the elephantine Model K, preferring to produce lighter, more affordable cars. The car's excessive weight led to a number of mechanical problems including frequent transmission failures. The ensuing debate over the future of the Model K led to cofounder Alexander Malcomson's departure from the Ford Motor Company. The Model K proved to be less than popular and remained in the Ford lineup for only three model years.

drive, Ford also harbored an uneasy feeling that his subordinate might leave to make a car of his own, which he eventually did. He also came to feel that he had allowed Wills to get too close. "You know me too well," he once told him. "Hereafter I am going to see to it that no man comes to know me so intimately."

During World War I, Wills contributed importantly to tractor experimentation (the British needed Fordson tractors) and the design and manufacture of improved and cheaper Liberty aircraft engines. He and Henry Ford, along with Charles "Boss Ket" Kettering, the Wright brothers, and Elmer Sperry, also developed America's first missile, the Fordists supplying a four-cylinder engine for the 12-foot-long "flying torpedo." Developers were pledged to secrecy, and the secret was kept for many years. The idea was reactivated with Germany's World War II "buzz bombs."

Wills left the Ford company in the spring of 1919 to build his own vehicle. "It is my fault," Henry Ford said of the departure of his aide and another executive, John R. Lee, who joined Wills in his new venture. "They are very able men, and you have got to keep something in sight ahead of men of that type. I wasn't able to do it, and they can't be blamed for going into it [the automobile business] for themselves. On the day of his resignation Wills said, "I am anxious to do something worthwhile and this seems the opportune time to start." Upon resigning, Wills pocketed $1,600,000 of Henry Ford's dividends.

Determined to build the "perfect car," Wills and Lee built a factory and model employee community, Marysville, Michigan, named for Wills' wife, Mary. His luxury automobile, the Wills Sainte Claire, named for nearby Lake Saint Clair, utilized strong, lightweight, molybdenum steel and was the first car to have backup lights, according to a State of Michigan commemorative plaque at the plant site. The Gray Goose, as the vehicle was called, was launched in 1921. The company that manufactured it, never profitable, went into receivership in 1923 and was liquidated in 1926, after building some 14,000 cars. In 1935 the factory was bought by Chrysler, which razed the last of the Wills buildings in 2001.

A Chrysler metallurgical consultant the last seven years of his life, Wills died of a stroke on December 30, 1940, and is buried beneath a modest marker in Detroit's Woodlawn Cemetery. His legacy is preserved in the Wills-Sainte-Claire Museum, opened in 2002 on a Marysville street named for him. He also has been inducted into the Automotive Hall of Fame in Dearborn, Michigan.

Paradoxically, Wills, while carefully suppressing his first name in favor of the initial, "C," bestowed his full name on his second son.

1907

- Models R and S join the Model N as the final right-hand-drive Fords

- Production reaches nearly 15,000

- Market share explodes to 35 percent

- Legendary "Watch the Fords Go By," ad slogan is coined

- Ford dealerships open in Paris, France, and Hamburg, Germany

- Ford posts profits in excess of $1 million

- Ford departs from racing, to the chagrin of dealers

- U.S. automobile registration reaches 140,000

- Dealership opens in Denver, Colorado

▲ First seen in 1907, "Watch the Fords Go By" became one of the best-known auto slogans of the century. The phrase appeared on a huge electric sign atop Detroit's Temple Theater in 1908 and was seen all over the country on Ford-carrying trains.

▲ Anyone who could pay $2800 for a Model K roadster got a motorcar that was guaranteed to reach 60 mph, assuming that person was brave enough to attempt such a feat on the roads and tires of the day. Soon to be phased out, the Model K would soon cost as little as $1800, as Ford turned its attention to "cars for the multitudes."

▲ The new Model R was mechanically similar to the Model N but featured a larger body, wheels, full fenders, standard oil lamp, and a spare tire. The Model R cost $150 more than the $600 Model N. A close look at mud sprayed on the rear fender of the car pictured demonstrates some of the potential peril involved in early motoring.

▲ Plenty of elbow room was needed to maneuver around the Model K's massive inline six-cylinder engine, as revealed here without body panels. The big six displaced 405 cubic inches and drew fuel though a Holley carburetor. Meanwhile, the economical Model N continued to attract buyers with its $600 price tag.

- Early assembly line experimentation begins using ropes and pulleys

- Dealers received first Model T catalogs

- Existing car lines soldier on unchanged as Model T is prepared for October launch

- Roughly 800 "two pedal" cars are built before the Model T permanently switches to a three-pedal design

- Model K price is slashed by $1000 as car is phased out

- Ford sales drop to just over 10,000 cars

- Ford's market share slips to 16 percent

▲ Until the October arrival of the Model T, last year's cars continued on mostly unchanged. The two-passenger Model S roadster sold for $700, or as shown with the single "mother-in-law" seat for $750. Nineteen eight would prove to truly be the "calm before the storm," as demand for the Model T would soon wildly exceed supply. While 1908 would be the last year until 1932 with more than one model, the Model T and subsequent Model A would be produced in enough variations to cover the needs of an increasingly car-hungry country.

◄ The most popular of the early Model T bodies was the $850 touring car, shown here without the optional windshield. For $25 less, buyers could opt for the three-seat runabout. While Henry Ford was once quoted as saying "You can't build a reputation on what you are about to do," it is unlikely that anyone, automaker or buyer, realized the impact the Model T was about to have on the country. By the end of 1927, more than 15 million "Tin Lizzies" would be produced, most of them black. By this time, Ford had produced nine distinct models, all of which would soon be overshadowed by the success of the Model T.

CLARA FORD
The Believer

HENRY FORD and Clara Jane Bryant met at a dancing party in their rural Dearborn, Michigan, community in 1885. Clara Jane, a petite, attractive, lively 18-year-old with hazel eyes and dark hair, was intrigued by Henry's watch, which the 21-year-old had designed. It kept both "sun time" and standard railroad time, recently adopted by the government. On returning home that night, the practical Clara told her parents that she had met a quiet, pleasant, keen-minded young man. "He's a thinking, sensible person—serious-minded," she proclaimed.

A single letter from Henry's courtship of Clara survives. Dated Valentine's Day 1886, it provides a glimpse of the young swain's heart, as well as of his writing.

"Well i shall have to Close," the missive concludes, "wishing you all the Joys of the year and a kind Good night. May Floweretts of love around you bee twined And the Sunshine of peace Shed its joy's o'er your Minde from one that Dearly loves you H."

The two were married on April 11, 1888. Clara expressed such certainty that her mate would accomplish something notable that Henry called her "The Believer."

The couple's only child, Edsel, was born in 1893. Six weeks later, in the kitchen of their small home at 58 Bagley Avenue, Detroit, Clara fed gasoline into a metal cup that acted as a crude carburetor for Ford's first engine.

Clara's faith in Henry was tested in 1899, when her husband left a steady job as chief engineer at Edison Illuminating Company to fling himself into the uncertainties of the fledgling auto industry. After two false starts as an automaker, Ford in 1903 launched the firm that would make the couple's fortune.

The Fords lived in 16 homes before settling into their Dearborn estate, Fair Lane, in 1916. Clara ruled the domestic scene. Although Henry might disagree with some of her ideas—to paint over mahogany paneling, for example—he deferred in conformance with his philosophy, "Peace at any price." He did, however, occasionally maneuver around the mistress of the house. A cooking assistant once showed a live chicken to Clara, who, declaring that the fowl was too scrawny, ordered its exchange for a larger one. Leaving the mansion, the servant ran into Henry, who asked why he was removing the chicken. The servant explained. "Don't take it back," said Henry, "just wait a while and take the same chicken back to her." The servant did as he was told, and Clara, upon examining the bird, told him, "That's much better. This one will do fine."

Clara's passion was gardening. "One is nearer God's heart in a garden than anywhere else on earth," she wrote on a slip of paper. In 1926, she opened her prize rose garden. She also developed early rose, blue, peony, trail, and other gardens. In 1927, she was elected president of the Woman's National Farm and Garden Association. She also enjoyed boating and kept an electric boat, the Callie B., on the muddy Rouge River, which flowed in back of her home. Her husband called her Callie, as did her son and four grandchildren. A great, great, great-granddaughter is named Callie.

Although Fair Lane was less imposing and handsome than some visitors had imagined it, the Fords loved their home. Henry, upon returning from work, whistled a birdcall to inform his wife that he was back. If within earshot, she returned the call. Their evenings were quiet. She read to her husband, and they shared walks, birdwatching, and radio listening. She particularly enjoyed such programs as *Amos 'n' Andy*, *Jack Benny*, *The Quiz Kids*, *Beulah*, *Dr. Christian*, and the *Ford Sunday Evening Hour*. She and Henry entertained many important guests including Thomas A. Edison and Charles A. Lindbergh.

In 1921, Ford built for Clara an elegant 82-foot long, 100-ton railroad car, Fair Lane, at a cost of $159,000. Mrs. Ford and her friends often took the car to New York for shopping expeditions, and she and Henry traveled in it to their summer and winter homes. Edsel's family also used the Fair Lane to get to and from their summer home in Seal Harbor, Maine, and winter residence in Hobe Sound, Florida. In addition, the car was used to entertain Presidents Warren G. Harding and Calvin Coolidge, and such friends as Edison and botanist Luther Burbank. Because of wartime restrictions, the Fair Lane was sold by the Fords to the Southwestern Railway ("Cotton Belt Route") in 1942, and in 1972 was donated to the Cherokee Indian Nation in Tahlequah, Oklahoma. After being acquired and restored by Detroiter Dick Kughn in 1982, it was given to the Henry Ford Museum, where it is now displayed.

The Fords were considerable philanthropists, even though Henry disavowed organized charity. In 1915, they established Henry Ford Hospital, of which they were the primary benefactors for the rest of their lives. In the 1920s, they gave $3.2 million to the Berry Schools, now Berry College, Rome, Georgia, for a Ford Quadrangle

A doting Clara Ford bounces great-granddaughter Charlotte Ford on her lap as a smiling Henry Ford tries to get the tot's attention with a doll. Throughout her life, Clara proved to be a force in the Ford family. She was the patient partner and booster in Henry's early struggles to turn his automotive dreams into reality, and late in life, she played a crucial behind-the-scenes role in grandson Henry II's ascension to leadership of the company. Other family members pictured are, from left, Henry Ford II, Charlotte's father; Eleanor Ford; Eleanor's niece, Katrina Kanzler; Anne Ford, Henry II's wife; Josephine Ford; and Edsel Ford.

and other buildings. In 2001, the Ford company gave $9.4 million to the college to renovate the buildings, among them a dormitory, Clara Ford Hall. In 1947, 12 days before Henry's death, the institution awarded Mrs. Ford an honorary Doctor of Humanities degree.

Clara, while owning 3.1 percent of the Ford Company's stock, seldom intervened in company affairs. She did so on two important occasions, however. In 1941, when Henry vowed to shut down his company rather than sign a labor contract, she threatened to leave him if he did not immediately settle with his workers. He did. In 1945, she labored to convince her 82-year-old husband that the time had come to transfer the presidency to their grandson, Henry II. Henry again acquiesced.

Henry's sweetheart in springtime and his companion in all seasons, Clara nursed her husband through his autumnal years, culminating in Ford's death at 83 in 1947. A lonely widow, she wrote a friend that year, "I shall miss my companion this Christmas as we have spent so many of them together."

During widowhood, much of Mrs. Ford's time was devoted to charitable interests, receiving relatives and old friends at Fair Lane, and caring for her gardens. She also maintained an interest in Greenfield Village and

kept an eye on Henry II. "Young Henry" she wrote a friend in late 1947, "is doing a good job."

Clara gave to Dearborn's Christ Church the prayer book that Henry had given her on their wedding day. "I could not bear to think that it might be treated carelessly after my death," she told the rector. Suffering from a heart ailment, she entered Henry Ford Hospital a few days before her death on September 29, 1950.

Fair Lane, now called the Henry Ford Estate-Fair Lane, was deeded in 1951 to Ford Motor Company, which gave part of the property to the University of Michigan in 1958. The University of Michigan-Dearborn, which governs Fair Lane, and the Henry Ford Community College have campuses on the estate. In 1951, the Fords' home furnishings were auctioned in New York, to the everlasting regret of those restoring and maintaining the mansion. Designated a National Historic Landmark in 1967, the estate receives about 150,000 visitors annually.

The day of Clara's funeral, Ford's worldwide empire paused in tribute for three minutes. In Dearborn and Detroit, flags flew at half-mast as "The Believer" was laid to rest beside "a dreamer" who once said of his mate, "If I were to die and come back to another life, I would want the same wife."

1909

- First full year for Model T production
- All other models dropped
- Model T available in five different body types
- Sales reach almost 18,000
- Ford's market share tops 14 percent
- Orders halted for nine weeks as production lags behind demand
- First Texas dealership opens in Dallas
- Ford enters two cars in New York-to-Seattle race; one wins but is later disqualified

▲ Ford No. 2, "winner" of the New York-to-Seattle race, in an unidentified city somewhere along its 6000-mile return trek. The vehicle was heralded in Ford advertising and displayed at hundreds of dealerships before the victory drums were silenced. Accused of replacing the engine at some point along the route, the Ford team's victory decision was reversed by race officials.

▲ The high, enclosed passenger compartment on the formal Model T landaulet could look top heavy from the side. Similar to the $1000 wooden-roofed town car, the landaulet offered nearly identical passenger accommodations but had a fabric roof and cost $50 less. The roomy landaulet and town car were both designed to seat seven passengers comfortably.

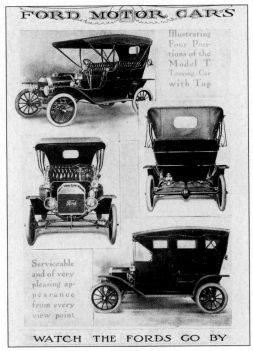

▲ Catalogs described the Model T as "Serviceable and of very pleasing appearance from every view point." Not everyone agreed, as the tall touring car looked ready to tip over. Ads described the T as "the one reliable car that does not require a $10,000 income to buy, a $5000 bank account to run, or a college course in engineering to keep in order."

▲ This Model T can be easily identified as one of the earliest produced, as only the first 800 were made with the shown two-pedal arrangement. Later cars would all use a three-pedal arrangement.

▲ Model Ts were loaded with innovations, including left-hand steering, transverse leaf springs, and an integral magneto. All-black didn't come in until '14. Earlier Ts came in colors.

▲ Thermo-syphon cooling replaced the water-pump-based system used on earlier Fords. Three-point engine mounting helped keep the engine in place on the rougher roads of the day.

▲ Oil-filled brass cowl and taillamps were standard equipment on the Model T touring car. Items such as windshields, headlamps, speedometers, and other accessories cost extra, however.

1910–1919

The World in Flux

IN A DECADE OF CONTRADICTIONS, the Boy Scouts of America was established in 1910, the same year white fans of boxing reviled the sport's first black champion, Jack Johnson. Shipbuilding produced the mighty liner *Titanic*, which sank in the frigid North Atlantic in April 1912. Factories became increasingly sophisticated, yet in 1911, 145 women who worked with their hands in a cramped room with inadequate exits died in a fire at the Triangle Shirtwaist Company in New York.

Woodrow Wilson won election as president in 1912, and was reelected four years later with a promise to keep the U.S. out of the European war that began in 1914. American troops were sent to France in 1917. The Allied Powers' severe postwar punishment of Germany stirred German resentment that would have awful consequences years later.

In Russia, civil war erupted between czarists and Bolsheviks, and in the Turkish-Italian war, an airplane was used for the first time as an offensive weapon.

Most Americans, though, were more alarmed over the Eighteenth Amendment, which ushered in Prohibition in 1919. Ford dealers could drink to the success of the car they were selling, but not with spirits—at least, not legally.

1910

- The Ford Motor Company moves into a spacious new factory in Highland Park, Michigan, on January 1; designed by architect Albert Kahn and built with reinforced concrete and 50,000 square feet of windows, it is dubbed the "Crystal Palace"

- All models adopt all-wood bodies for this one year only

- Coupes switch to front-hinged doors

- Fiscal-year production listed as 19,050; calendar-year output nearly doubles to 32,053

- Factory race driver Frank Kulick is a frequent winner in a specially prepared two-seater

▲ This Model T runabout was photographed along the route of the 1910 Munsey Tour, a reminder of when just about any kind of extended driving trip had about it the air of an adventure, given the primitive roads—and machinery—of the day. The runabout accounted for almost 1500 deliveries in the fiscal year that ran from October 1, 1909, to September 30, 1910.

▲ The popularity champ of the Model T line continued to be the five-passenger tourer, despite a $100 price increase to $950. The extra money did cover the addition of new standard equipment, such as the top, windshield, carbide headlamps, and a speedometer. For this year only, bodies were produced without external metal sheeting. Brewster Green was the paint color selected for 1910 Fords.

▶ All Ford models underwent considerable price cuts for 1911; for example, the starting price for this touring car was now $780, or $170 less than the year before. But buyers didn't get less car, they got more. The engine added a removable connecting-rod pan and bigger transmission access door, both in pursuit of easier serviceability. The front axle gained two-piece spindles with separate steering arms and the rear axle was beefed up. Steering-wheel diameter was increased to 15 inches.

■ Selden patent suit is settled in Ford's favor on January 9 when U.S. Court of Appeals rules he is not in violation of the patent, freeing him from having to pay royalties to the Association of Licensed Automobile Manufacturers

■ Ford buys Keim Mills, a supplier of pressed steel parts in Buffalo, New York, acquiring the manufacturing expertise of William S. Knudsen in the process

■ Price cuts and new models help hike sales

◀ While the touring car was winning over Model T customers left and right, demand for the coupe amounted to just 45 orders. Its $840 base price *didn't* include the carbide headlights seen here. All carried-over body styles adopted new fender designs.

▲ The growing demand for the Model T was met by further expansion of satellite assembly operations. A St. Louis, Missouri, assembly site opened in 1911. Factory output of touring cars jumped to 26,405 for the fiscal year.

▶ An open roadster, one of the year's two new body types, gamely presses on in the 1911 Glidden Tour. This car and the torpedo roadster, the latter identified by its use of doors, featured a lowered steering-wheel angle and distinctive fenders.

1912

- New touring car and torpedo roadster bodies are ushered in after the start of the new year

- The new tourers are known as "fore-door" models when ordered with front door panels; only the right-side door actually opens, however

- A panel-body Model T delivery truck is added to the product line; the $700 vehicle lasts just one season

- Satellite production sites are added at Kansas City, Missouri; Long Island City, New York; and Minneapolis, Minnesota

- Frank Kulick makes final factory-backed racing run on Lake St. Clair

▲ A smoother, more unified look graced the body of Model T touring cars built soon after the start of 1912 (though accounts differ as to whether the change was effected in January or April). Ford prices were cut again—the cost of a tourer retreating to $690—which was hardly an impediment to the cars' popularity. Of the 78,440 made for calendar-year 1912, the touring car accounted for 50,598 assemblies.

▲ None other than Henry Ford himself is shown at the wheel of a "fore-door" touring car. (The other people in the photo are unidentified.) Removable panels added to the front of the body now enclosed all passengers within the bodywork. Only the passenger side featured a functioning door, however. The driver-side panel was fixed and served only to balance out the looks of the car. Panel kits were made available to retrofit 1911 and early 1912 cars.

▼ The torpedo roadster was also bestowed with a new body during the year, but at the loss of some rakish distinctiveness. Taller bodysides, conventional front fenders, and a more-upright driving position diminished the car's sporty character. On the plus side, though, the price declined to $590. The runabout, newly renamed the commercial roadster, sold for the same fee. Production of all roadsters came to 13,376 units.

► Drivers shuttling a wintry caravan of Model Ts to a New York dealer pose for a group photo. The procession is led by a roadster with the new for 1913 "turtle deck" design. In the days before car-hauling trucks, it was common for dealers to recruit teams of drivers to fetch their allotment of new vehicles from assembly points in "drive-aways." Ford's network of regional assembly plants was growing.

■ Production at the Highland Park plant grows dramatically with the introduction of the moving assembly line system; starting with the manufacture of magnetos in April, the process includes whole cars by the summer

■ New domestic assembly branches start up at Chicago, Illinois, and Memphis, Tennessee

■ The thirst for Model Ts seems to go unabated; 168,220 are manufactured during the year

■ Touring car and roadster bodies are redesigned again; roadsters adopt a removable "turtle deck" with storage space and tourers add body bracing to keep doors from flying open

■ Use of brass parts begins to diminish

◄ Many of the far-flung Ford assembly operations got their start as local sales and service branches. This roadster was equipped with a specially built pickup box to help one of the Ford agents of the Model T era dispense that service. Though factory-built light trucks based on the T were still a few years away, after-market conversions were gaining popularity.

► Bird-lover Henry Ford so admired the writings of naturalist John Burroughs that in 1913, he made a gift of a new touring car like the one seen here to Burroughs. The 50-year-old industrialist and the 75-year-old author struck up a friendship, and later that year, during a visit with Burroughs in Massachusetts, Ford was exposed to the writings of 19th century thinker and poet Ralph Waldo Emerson. Many of Emerson's ideas struck a responsive chord in Henry Ford, who would quote him often in coming years.

JAMES COUZENS
Henry's Partner

HENRY FORD HAD his share of good luck. His entry into automaking and the Model T's introduction were perfectly timed. He also was partnered, quite by chance, with James Couzens, who contributed as much to the Ford Motor Company's early success as Ford himself.

One of the firm's 12 charter shareholders, Couzens owned 2.5 percent of the company when it was founded in 1903, and held 10.5 percent by 1907, making him the second largest shareholder. Ford originally owned 25.5 percent, and had acquired 58.5 percent by 1907. The only employees who owned shares, Couzens and Ford came to regard other stockholders as parasites.

Born in Chatham, Ontario, Canada, in 1872, Couzens was determined to succeed mightily, even reproaching his mother for giving birth to him in Canada. "I can never become King of England," he scolded, "but if I had been born in the United States, I could be president." Nonetheless, in 1890 he migrated to Detroit, where he eventually became director of the Michigan Central Railroad's freight office. In this capacity he favorably impressed shippers, among them a large coal dealer, Alex Malcomson, who hired him as his office manager and business advisor.

When Malcomson and Henry Ford became the Ford company's biggest shareholders in 1903, Couzens, by now a trusted Malcomson lieutenant, was delegated to watch over Ford's business affairs. As Ford focused on product development and production, Couzens came to manage the rest of the firm. If not crating cars for rail shipments, paying bills, collecting moneys due, and overseeing bookkeeping, he was supervising sales, advertising, and publicity, appointing dealers, setting up sales branches, and negotiating with suppliers.

Able, exacting, truculent, and all business from his bump-toed shoes to his derby hat, Couzens had a "don't tread on me" attitude reinforced by outspokenness and a terrible temper. On the job, wags said, ice on the Great Lakes broke up when he smiled his annual smile.

Paradoxically, Couzens was a loving family man with compassionate, even tender, feelings toward youngsters. Although he became a capitalist multimillionaire, he had profoundly democratic instincts, and earned an unparalleled reputation as a radical. A dragon at the cashbox, he gave away most of his fortune. Appreciative of publicity, he was tactless with the press, characteristically ordering the *Detroit News* to fire an offending reporter and forbidding the publication to "ever again mention the name of the Ford Motor Company."

Couzens deemed it good business to publicize Henry Ford. One of his advertisements, based on Henry's assertion, proclaimed, "Our Mr. Ford made the first Gasoline Automobile in Detroit and the third in the United States" (both claims untrue). Another ad declared that "Henry Ford has been the greatest factor in the development of the automobile industry . . . in the world." Tossed such bouquets, Henry kept the flowers.

Couzens initially credited Ford with having originated the company's famed five-dollar day in 1914. "It was quite natural that Mr. Ford should be credited with this project," he said later, "because he was the head of the company, a majority stockholder, and it was to the benefit of the Ford Motor Company . . . to keep the name Ford much before the public." After leaving the company, however, the junior partner said of the plan, "I will say that I, personally, am responsible for it." Over the decades, a spirited, futile discussion has ensued as to whether or not the larger credit belongs to Ford or Couzens. Suffice it to say, as noted by historian Allan Nevins, "The proposal would probably have been vetoed had Couzens violently opposed it, and could certainly never been approved without Ford's hearty support."

Couzens and Ford increasingly disliked each other, as indicated by a wide gap between them in formal photographs. By working in separate spheres, however, they avoided a major clash until 1915. That year, divergent views on America's World War I neutralism, war loans to the Allies, and national preparedness led to a showdown.

Also, in 1913, while a company executive, Couzens accepted the controversial chairmanship of the newly formed Detroit Street Railway Commission, and began devoting increasing attention to civic affairs. Ford was displeased. "If Jim is on the job, I'd rather have his judgment than anybody's. But his judgment off the job isn't as good as somebody else's on the job." During an argument over control of the company's house organ, the *Ford Times*, Couzens resigned, remaining a director. In 1919, he sold his stock to Henry Ford for $27 million (worth roughly $300 million in today's money), receiving a higher share price than any other stockholder at the time.

While serving as Detroit's police commissioner from

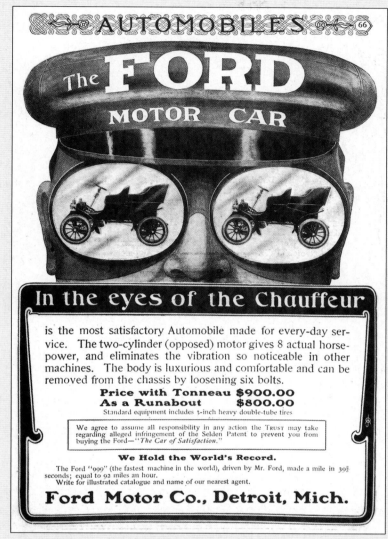

AUTOMOBILES

66

The FORD
MOTOR CAR

In the eyes of the Chauffeur

is the most satisfactory Automobile made for every-day service. The two-cylinder (opposed) motor gives 8 actual horsepower, and eliminates the vibration so noticeable in other machines. The body is luxurious and comfortable and can be removed from the chassis by loosening six bolts.

Price with Tonneau $900.00
As a Runabout $800.00
Standard equipment includes 3-inch heavy double-tube tires

We agree to assume all responsibility in any action the TRUST may take regarding alleged infringement of the Selden Patent to prevent you from buying the Ford—"The Car of Satisfaction."

We Hold the World's Record.

The Ford "999" (the fastest machine in the world), driven by Mr. Ford, made a mile in 39⅖ seconds; equal to 92 miles an hour.
Write for illustrated catalogue and name of our nearest agent.

Ford Motor Co., Detroit, Mich.

James Couzens found it worthwhile to keep Henry Ford's automotive exploits in the public eye; this 1904 ad reminded readers that Ford personally set a land-speed record with the 999.

1916 to 1918, Couzens convinced himself that he was needed and electable as Detroit's mayor. Others disagreed. John Dodge, with his brother, Horace, a Ford shareholder and owner of Dodge Brothers Manufacturing Company, did not think he could be elected "dog catcher or coroner." E. Roy Pelletier, ex-head of Ford advertising, refused to handle Couzens' publicity, saying it was impossible to "sell a man so lacking in good fellowship." Couzens nonetheless won handily, voters being persuaded by his promise to conduct himself "so that I have my own self-respect, regardless of whether people like me."

As mayor, the "maverick millionaire," as Couzens was dubbed, challenged accepted patterns of conduct and provided bold, energetic leadership. His temper remained untamed. If not denouncing Detroit Board of Commerce leaders as a "pack of curs," he was branding Detroit Edison Company's president as a "liar," the latter epithet earning an ejection from City Council chambers. In the opinion of his biographer, Harry Barnard, he was "one of the few outstanding mayors in American history."

Appointed to the U.S. Senate by Michigan's Republican governor in 1922, Couzens summed up his political views with the statement, "I am a Republican, but not like Harding, Coolidge, and Hoover! . . . If being a Republican means kowtowing to the president, I do not care to be a Republican." A newspaper headline accurately pegged him as "James Couzens—One-Man Bloc."

During 14 years in the Senate, Couzens clashed repeatedly with fellow Republicans on issues ranging from liberalizing national prohibition laws to demanding the first investigation of the Department of Internal Revenue. When Secretary of the Treasury Andrew Mellon counterattacked by investigating Couzens' tax returns, the senator proved in court that he had overpaid $900,000 in taxes when selling his Ford stock.

Couzens' freewheeling independence eventually led to his political demise. Anathema to party regulars, he had no political organization of his own. He also alienated many voters by opposing such proposals as an ex-soldiers' bonus and the Townsend Old Age Pension Plan. Finally, in 1936, he supported President Franklin D. Roosevelt's bid for reelection, heresy for a Republican. His defeat in that year's primary was a foregone conclusion. In the long run— even in the short run—it did not matter. He was ailing and had only two months to live. In late October, he underwent an operation from which he did not awaken from the anesthetic.

If Couzens is less well remembered than he should be, it was the way he wanted it, for he generally refused to permit buildings or institutions to be named for him. By contrast, more than 100 places, institutions, and other landmarks bear Henry Ford's name.

Couzens' greatest benefaction, the Children's Fund of Michigan, would have been named the Couzens Foundation, if Couzens' associates had prevailed. The philanthropist not only rejected the name, but also stipulated that the fund—established in 1929 with a gift of $10 million—spend itself out of existence within 25 years.

Largely ignored by old-car enthusiasts, Couzens also has been forgotten by the great company that he helped build; Henry Ford did it all. Couzens' memory deserves better.

1914

- Ford shakes up U.S. industry on January 5 by announcing a conditional $5-a-day wage and a cut in the work day to eight hours
- Detroit is overrun with job-seekers intent on Ford employment; many national business leaders decry the moves
- The high wage stems worker turnover and improves productivity
- Company establishes Sociological Department ostensibly to improve workers' standard of living; inspectors sent to visit employees' homes
- "Any color as long as it's black" policy adopted for Model T to speed up production
- Seven new assembly facilities open between Massachusetts and Colorado

▲ Versatility was a beloved Model T trait practically from its introduction. Among the uses to which "Tin Lizzies" were put was as firefighting vehicles. Though too small and light for pumper duty, they could be outfitted as chemical-hose units designed to provide quick and effective response to smaller fires.

▲ With the assembly line process in full operation and branch assembly operations popping up across the U.S., Ford turned out 308,162 cars in calendar-year 1914—accounting for more than half the year's new vehicles. The $500 runabout adopted a windshield with an inward-folding upper section and doors with rounded bottom corners.

▲ Other body manufacturers were turning the T into a utility vehicle. The wood-bodied "depot hack" often served resorts by helping to get visitors and their luggage to and from train stations. In time, the lightly protected depot hack would give rise to the more weathertight and comfortable station wagon.

▲ As incongruous as it may have seemed for a car for the common man, the Model T continued to list a town car among its factory-built body styles. The town car was substantially restyled for 1914 with smoother sides and flush-mounted doors. Also new was the two-piece windshield. Window panels on either side of the driver's seat afforded a bit of protection from the elements, but could be removed for more of an open-air feel. The primary market for the Model T town car continued to be taxi and livery services.

- Model T line expands with the addition of the centerdoor sedan and a fully enclosed convertible, the "Coupelet"

- Styling/feature changes for the year include hood louvers, a sloping cowl, electric "bullet" headlamps, and the restoration of upright windshields and rounded rear bumpers

- "Gentlemen, a million of anything is a great many," Henry Ford tells attendees at a banquet celebrating production of the one-millionth Ford

- Assembly of Model Ts begins in nine new facilities—10 if demonstration line set up at Panama-Pacific expo in San Francisco is counted

- Henry sails on ill-conceived "Peace Ship" to seek end to World War I

▲ Though the town car continued to be offered to regular retail customers, concessions were made to the taxi trade, where such a car had its greatest appeal. Taxi models featured leatherette upholstery for front and rear seats; other town cars had cloth on the rear seat. Regardless of type, town car prices started at $690, but were cut to $640.

▲ Henry Ford's program of gradual change for the Model T took another step in 1915 with the adoption of electric headlights. Housed in conical shells ringed in brass, the lights could be illuminated only when the engine was running—there was no battery to power them otherwise. This tourer also shows the new cowl and rear-fender styles.

▲ With a fixed windshield frame, retractable glass side windows, and a form-fitting fabric top, the new "Coupelet" was a precursor to the modern convertible coupe. Side windows were raised and lowered via adjustable straps. The introductory price of $750 was lowered as the year wore on.

▲ The other newcomer to the Model T roster was the five-passenger centerdoor sedan. Though closed bodies would come to be the dominant automotive style, that day was still long off in 1915; with just 989 made for the fiscal year, it was the rarest Ford. This prototype bears ornate coach lamps not seen on production cars.

- Model T's "brass era" ends with final use of the metal on radiators and hubcaps

- Prices continue to fall; a new touring car can be had for just $440

- Fiscal-year production of Ford cars tops 500,000 for the first time; calendar-year output is said to be more than 734,000

- New assembly sites open in Louisville, Kentucky; Milwaukee, Wisconsin; and Oklahoma City, Oklahoma

- Edsel Ford and Eleanor Clay wed on November 1

- Henry Ford sues the *Chicago Tribune* for libel, is sued by Dodge brothers over dividend payments

▲ Henry Ford busies himself at chopping firewood sometime in 1916. Tycoon or not, the former farmhand still enjoyed a turn of physical labor, as John Burroughs would note in a journal from a camping trip with Ford, Thomas Edison, and Harvey Firestone a few years hence. Closer to home, Henry, Clara, and Edsel Ford moved into their new Dearborn estate—Fair Lane—in January 1916. The house had its own power station that generated hydroelectric power—a favorite cause of Henry's—from the Rouge River that flowed nearby.

► Aside from the diminished use of brass parts, there was little apparent change to the 1916 Model Ts. The Coupelet did sport one of the few obvious changes to be seen: the addition of small oval "opera windows" in the sides of the folding top.

NORVAL A. HAWKINS
Salesman Extraordinaire

NUMEROUS EX-CONVICTS were given a second chance by Henry Ford, and none more justified this trust than Norval A. Hawkins, marketing head of the Ford Motor Company from 1907 to 1918.

In 1894, Hawkins, a Standard Oil cashier, was imprisoned after conviction for stealing company funds. Of his transgression, he confessed, "I put $3000 of the money into the oil business and, besides, I was always a pretty good liver."

Born in Ypsilanti, Michigan, in 1867, Hawkins, a tall, lean, fast-talker with sharp, gray eyes, studied accounting and became a CPA. In 1898, he cofounded Hawkins-Gies, an accounting firm. Six years later, he was appointed Ford's auditor, and in 1907 was made responsible for the firm's sales and advertising.

During Hawkins' reign, the number of Ford dealerships grew to 7000, more than the rest of the industry combined. Sales rose from 6398 cars in fiscal year 1907–08 to 730,041 units in 1916–17. Hawkins' leadership, including an accountant's attention to detail, contributed importantly to the company's success.

Dealerships, Hawkins insisted, were to provide clean, neat places of business, pleasing show windows, attractive cars for demonstrations, and top-notch service facilities. "Roadmen" routinely photographed agencies to make sure these conditions were being met, and also took snapshots of dealers, managers, and salesmen to ensure their businesslike appearance.

Dealers were instructed to separate repair garages and stockrooms from sales and display areas so that prospective customers would not see cars being repaired or hear the complaints of irate owners. Advertising for tow chains was banned for fear of suggesting the possibility of breakdowns. Strong efforts were made to persuade dealers to buy standardized Ford letterheads and outdoor and window signs. In company-owned sales branches, smoking, even by customers, was prohibited. Acceptance of a tip by a branch employee brought instant dismissal. In addition, Hawkins exhorted dealers to make good use of the company's advertising literature, which the company claimed was "the most elaborate and instructive series" ever prepared for automobile prospects.

Hawkins also coordinated factory and dealer advertising. Dealers were asked to copy sample ads in the *Ford Times* "so that everybody stands equally strong and on the same footing with no chance for disagreement or misunderstanding." Moreover, they were asked to coordinate their local schedules closely with the company's national advertising campaigns. Finally, they were expected to advertise with consistency. If brisk demand left them without automobiles to sell, they were told to buy space for "good will purposes."

Another of Hawkins' better ideas was the *Ford Times*, introduced in April 1908. Within two years the magazine was reprinted in French, Spanish, Portuguese, and Russian, and, on the basis of being sent to 2100 dealerships around the world, claimed the widest geographical circulation of any American publication. Initially an internal-external house organ, the magazine evolved by 1914 into a publication aimed at "The automobile public in general—and to Ford owners in particular." It reported on a wide variety of developments at the factory and in the field.

Hawkins also was one of the auto industry's earliest proponents of market research. He asked Model T owners as early as 1912 why they bought a Ford car and instructed branch managers to obtain specific market data in their territories.

Finally, Hawkins was the father of one of the most striking sales promotion events in business history—Ford's offer of July 31, 1914, to rebate between $40 and $60 to each purchaser of a Model T should sales exceed 300,000 units during the following year. Coupled with the offer was a price reduction of $60 for each Model T and a promise not to cut prices again until August 1, 1915.

The announcement appeared in virtually every newspaper in the country, deserving as much publicity as the company's five-dollar day, *The New York Times* reported. Many other newspapers were effusive in their praise of the offer. In many communities during the rebate year, the best Model T salesmen were persons who had bought Fords after August 1, 1914. On August 1, 1915, the company announced that it had sold 308,213 automobiles during the previous year, and set the amount to be refunded to each buyer at $50.

When America's entry into World War I scaled back civilian car production, Hawkins, his responsibilities diminished, took leave in 1918 to serve as a transportation consultant to the Army's Ordnance Department. Upon returning to the company later that year, he found a former assistant entrenched in his position. Although offered a job as a special sales representative for Europe and South America at his previous salary, Hawkins was offended, and resigned in January 1919.

From 1921 to 1924, Hawkins served as a GM sales and advertising consultant at a salary of $150,000 a year, after which his career declined. He filed for bankruptcy in 1935 and died of a heart attack in 1936.

1917

- The front of the Model T gets a major facelift

- Ford enters the truck market by offering a beefed-up one-ton Model T chassis

- First Fordson farm tractor produced in October

- Henry Ford II born to Edsel and Eleanor on September 4

- Several assembly plants close after U.S. enters World War I

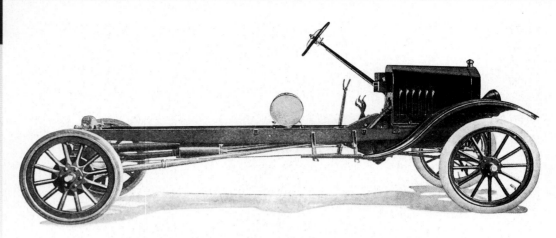

▲ After several hit-or-miss efforts with delivery cars based on the Model T passenger car, Ford entered the truck business in earnest on July 27 with the production of the first one-ton chassis. Selling for $600, it consisted of a lengthened and strengthened Model T frame, stouter rear springs, artillery-style rear wheels with solid-rubber tires, and a worm-drive rear axle. No complete bodies were cataloged.

WILLIAM S. KNUDSEN
"Too Big for His Britches"

JUST AS Henry Ford II's firing of Lee Iaccoca paved the way for Lee to become Chrysler's chairman in the Seventies, so Henry Ford's dismissal of William S. Knudsen in 1921 opened the door for "Big Bill" to become general manager of Chevrolet, president of General Motors, and America's top production official during World War II.

Knudsen was born in 1879 in Denmark, where he was a bicycle mechanic. In 1900, he emigrated to America with an accent that never completely left him. He liked to tell how, as he came down the gangplank of his ship, he paused to look at the New York skyline until a harsh voice yelled out, "Hurry up, you blankety-blank! Get a move on!" "I've been hurrying ever since," he would laugh. In time, Knudsen learned to shout "Hurry up!" to factory workers in 15 languages.

Six feet tall, physically powerful, tough-minded, and resourceful, Knudsen in 1902 joined John R. Keim Mills—which made pressed steel parts—in Buffalo, New York. By 1908, he was general superintendent of the Keim plant, by then a major Ford supplier. Impressed by Keim's management and products, Henry Ford asked the company to operate a Model T assembly plant, then bought the firm in 1911.

In 1912, most of Keim's workmen participated in a wildcat strike. "That suits me," Ford told Knudsen and other executives. "If the men don't want to work, get some flat cars and move the presses and machinery

to Michigan." The equipment was dismantled and dispatched to Ford's Highland Park Plant, along with Knudsen and more than 60 other loyalists. Within three days, the machinery was again producing parts. The strikers lost their jobs; the old Keim plant eventually resumed Model T production with new workers.

Knudsen, who had a strong independent streak, was hesitant to join Highland Park's workforce, headed by production bosses Ed Martin and Charlie Sorensen, with whom he had clashed at Keim. Fortuitously, he was assigned to expand and improve the company's assembly plant network, thus escaping Highland Park's tensions while fully utilizing his knowledge of factory layouts, machines, and processes. Fourteen U.S. assembly plants were planned and built under Knudsen's supervision, and later three more in Europe, including the Danish capital, Copenhagen.

Meantime, Knudsen, who confessed to having a violent temper, learned to control the weakness. He became quieter, more pleasant, and less aggressive than such hard drivers as Sorensen, and won rather than forced the cooperation of his subordinates. Said an associate who knew both men well: "Sorensen was a wild man, and Knudsen was a mild man."

In 1918, Knudsen was directed to supervise production of Ford's submarine chasers, the most ambitious of the company's World War I endeavors. The Eagle boats were built in an immense new Rouge Plant building in which Knudsen laid out three production lines, each capable of carrying seven boats, or a total of 21

◀ The Model T moved into a new phase in 1917. A taller, rounded hood was mated to a new black-enameled radiator. The cowl was also changed slightly to better accept the revised hood. Front fenders now curved over the tires they covered. Meanwhile, engine revisions were made to improve cooling. Even though some assembly sites were turned over to the military when the U.S. entered World War I in April, Ford still made 107,240 new roadsters.

vessels in the stocks at one time. Before the B (for boats) Building got into full production, however, the war ended, and the Eagle boat contract was greatly scaled back.

In 1919–20, the redoubtable Knudsen was sent to Europe by Henry and Edsel Ford to survey and draft a plan for foreign operations. In varying degrees, his plans were implemented after his departure from Ford on February 28, 1921.

Knudsen's break with his employer seems to have reflected dissatisfaction on both sides. Henry Ford, according to Ford biographer Allan Nevins, objected to some of Knudsen's unspecified personal habits. Knudsen, while admiring Ford for his foresight, originality, native shrewdness, and courage, resented Ford's countermanding of his orders or telling others to ignore them. Matters came to a head, opined Ford's executive secretary, Ernest G. Liebold, when Knudsen was directed by Edsel Ford to carry out his European plans. Sorensen, insisting that European affairs should be his responsibility, protested to Henry Ford, who spoke to Knudsen, precipitating the latter's departure.

Within months, General Motors' Alfred P. Sloan Jr. offered him a place on the corporation's general staff. Joining GM at $30,000 annually, he soon was made vice president of ailing Chevrolet at a salary of $50,000, matching what Ford was paying him when he left.

At Chevrolet, Knudsen overhauled and modernized factories, improved product, and lowered prices. The results were soon evident. Chevrolet sales dramatically increased, as Model T sales declined, hastening Henry Ford's decision to abandon the Tin Lizzie. Chevrolet continued to vie with Ford as the nation's top-selling car throughout Knudsen's 11-year reign at Chevrolet and, after 1933, as head of all of GM's American and

Canadian vehicle operations. In 1937, he was named GM's president and pictured on the cover of *Time*, a sure sign that he had "arrived."

In 1940, as America geared up for defense production, Knudsen was asked by President Franklin D. Roosevelt to serve as a dollar-a-year commissioner for industrial production on the National Defense Advisory Committee. As an immigrant from a country recently overrun by Nazi Germany, Knudsen accepted—over Sloan's objection. Again, he made the cover of *Time*.

Knudsen quickly became embroiled with Henry Ford, who initially agreed to produce Rolls-Royce airplane engines for the British government, then reneged when his isolationism reasserted itself. Knudsen was chagrined, as was Edsel Ford, who had acted as intermediary between government and company. Henry Ford, in turn, felt that "William" was mixed up with the wrong people in Washington (Roosevelt and his advisors) and had gotten "too big for his britches."

In 1942, Knudsen was commissioned a lieutenant general in the Army, and spent the remainder of the war directing production for the Department of War. After the war he planned to rejoin GM, not as president, that job having been filled by Charles E. "Engine Charlie" Wilson, but as an "inspector general" of its plants, an assignment for which he was superbly qualified. But when he took his suggestion to Sloan in 1945, he was rebuked for having left the corporation. The turndown broke Big Bill's spirit.

In October 1946, Knudsen became chairman of Hupp Corporation, a remnant of the former automaker, then making parts for Ford-Ferguson tractors. He died of a cerebral hemorrhage on April 27, 1948, and is buried in Detroit's Acacia Park Cemetery.

1918

- Henry Ford steps down as company president at end of year; is replaced by Edsel

- With the convertible Coupelet out of the lineup, a closed coupe makes its return

- More Ford assembly facilities converted to production of war materiel

- Model T ambulances serve Allied armies

- Plant to build sub-chasing "Eagle Boats" established on future site of Ford's Rouge complex

▲ Civilian automobile production faced substantial government-mandated cutbacks after the United States entered World War I in 1917. But output didn't stop altogether, and neither did efforts to promote cars that were made. Here, an array of 1918 Fords—headed by the reinstated coupe model—appear at an unidentified auto show. Some Ford assembly plants made military goods like helmets and aircraft engines.

▲ Ford's new coupe was the first such Model T since about 1912. Better proportioned than the ungainly, towering earlier model, it drew a healthy 14,771 orders. For this year only, with the windows down, the door posts could be removed for a "hardtop" look.

▲ Ford Motor Company put this Model T one-ton truck chassis to good use serving the company's needs. A stake bed and a fabric-top cab with minimal protection against the elements was added. Fiscal-year truck chassis production came to 41,105.

▶ There were all kinds of uses for the trucks made from the heavy-duty Model T chassis. This screen-side adaptation with parallel bench seating protected and served with an unidentified police department. Numerous body fabricators made special bodies to serve a variety of needs, such as panel-side and open-side deliveries, tankers, and pickup-style "expresses." Cab styles also varied, from little more than a suspended wood roof to fully enclosed.

- Electric starting and demountable wheel rims—both options—modernize the Model T

- Town car dropped

- The 3-millionth Model T is produced on April 2

- Ford factory wage rises to $6 a day

- Construction of Rouge plant begins in earnest

- Henry Ford loses suit brought by Dodge brothers over dividend payments; before the end of the year, he buys out all shareholders

- Henry wins libel suit against *Chicago Tribune,* gets six cents in damages

- A second son, Benson, is born to Edsel and Eleanor Ford on July 20

▲ Fiscal-year production of Model T passenger cars was off in 1919, due in part to a postwar economic slowdown. However, closed cars like the coupe and this centerdoor sedan seemed to suffer less erosion of sales than the open models. It couldn't have hurt any that the closed models were the first to offer the modern options of battery-driven electric starting and demountable rims that made tire changing easier.

▼ Though it looks quite finished with a form-fitting cargo box and shiny bed rails, this Model T pickup was made from a roadster with its turtle deck removed. A large toolbox was mounted to the running board. Ford often promoted the roadster as being a fine basis for light-duty commercial purposes, and it's not hard to imagine that this company-owned vehicle wasn't the only one of the year's 48,867 runabouts pressed into something other than passenger-car duty. A bare car chassis continued to be available, as well; it cost $475.

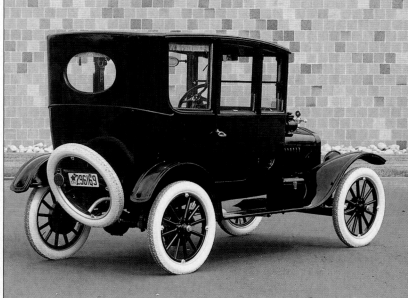

▲ Company records indicate that 24,980 centerdoor sedans were manufactured between August 1, 1918, and July 30, 1919, Ford's fiscal year. The sedan was the most expensive model in the line at $875, but that didn't count the charges for electric starting ($75) and demountable rims ($25). Among the centerdoor's features for interior privacy and comfort were roller shades the could be pulled down over the rear quarter windows and quaint oval backlight.

The Decade That Roared

WHILE MILLIONS of citizens enjoyed the first "talkie" films, got intimate in Fords and other automobiles, and drank themselves silly on bootleg booze, American women triumphed in their long struggle to vote; the Nineteenth Amendment made it official in 1920. Amusingly, many people credited the female vote with the ascension of handsome Warren Harding to the presidency. No matter who put him there, insider deals for lucrative naval oil leases made his administration a national scandal.

Meanwhile, Al Capone and other enterprising businessmen pursued their own brand of corruption, supplying liquor, loose women, gambling, and sundry other vices to a hedonistic nation.

King Tut's tomb was uncovered in 1922, and Charles "Lucky Lindy" Lindbergh flew the Atlantic solo in 1927. Benito Mussolini rose to power in Italy; in Germany, an agitator named Adolf Hitler began to make political headway.

On February 14, 1929, seven of Chicago's Bugs Moran gang were slaughtered in a North Side garage. Someone said, "Only Capone kills like that," but an even worse killing came eight months later, when the stock market crashed and plunged the U.S. into unprecedented economic depression.

1920

- Ford sales plunge to nearly half previous year's numbers

- Market share falls to just 22 percent

- Prices are slashed by an average of $150

- Huge inventory of cars prompts extension of Christmas shutdown until February 1921

- Widespread rumors forecast Ford's financial demise

- A new payment system that requires dealers to pay for cars upon receipt improves cash flow

- Winter ushers the country into a mild recession

▲ This runabout sold for $650 with an electric starter and demountable rims. While enclosed cars were slowly gaining favor with the buying public, open cars like the runabout still appealed to more-frugal motorists. Even greater economies could be realized by purchasing the base runabout. At $550 without an electric starter or demountable rims, the runabout was the cheapest entry in Ford's lineup of passenger cars.

▶ Getting into the upright Ford coupe required a high, unladylike step. The popular closed coupes commanded a hefty $200 premium over their open-bodied brethren. Despite a down year for Ford, coupe sales surged from around 11,000 in 1919 to more than 60,000. Truck chassis sales were also on the rise, reaching 135,000, nearly double the amount sold the prior year.

◀ By the Twenties, custom-bodied commercial Fords were a common sight. Second only to the touring car in sales, Ford's unfinished truck chassis were fitted for duty in countless ways. Priced at $640, the Model TT trucks typically left the factory as little more than cabs atop bare chassis. Trying not to be left behind, many former carriage builders found new life finishing Ford trucks for special duties.

■ Sales surge as price cuts take effect

■ Production reaches an all-time record 900,000

■ Market share triples to almost 62 percent, while rest of industry slumps

■ Model T body lowered slightly, otherwise unchanged

■ Legendary production guru William S. Knudsen defects for position at Chevrolet

■ Prices continue to drop to as low as $325 for a two-passenger runabout

■ Fordsons become the nation's best-selling tractors

▲ A whopping $180 cut dropped the price of a centerdoor sedan to $795. While similar in appearance to last year's model, the rear quarter panel was now an integral part of the body, not a separate piece. While optional on the runabout, demountable wheels were standard equipment on sedans.

▲ During the year the runabout's price dropped from $395 to $370, and then to $325. Once again, runabout sales lagged well behind the touring car, due in part to the lack of rear seating. So strong a turnaround year was 1921 that the touring car alone outsold all 1920 Ford models combined. While sedan and coupe sales were steadily increasing, the midpriced touring car continued to be Ford's best-selling model.

1922

- Ford Motor Company purchases Lincoln Motor Company for $8 million

- Edsel Ford named president of Lincoln

- Ford production soars to more than 1.2 million

- Exports account for more than eight percent of sales

- A modified Model T wins the Pikes Peak Hillclimb

- Seventy-three percent of Fords are now purchased on credit

- A term of endearment, "Tin Lizzie" takes hold as Model T's nickname

◄ Introduced a year earlier by Henry Leland, Lincoln became a Ford product in 1922. Ford purchased the ailing Lincoln Motor Company for $8 million on February 4. At $4600, the least-expensive Lincoln cost more than six times as much as the most-expensive Model T.

► While the Model T was designed to be a car "for the masses," the Lincoln was designed for the motoring elite. The Lincoln's 90-horsepower V-8 produced more than four times the power of the Model T's engine. At a time when Ford's heaviest car, the four-door sedan, still weighed less than a ton, fully equipped Lincolns tipped the scales at 4600 pounds.

▲ Ford trucks came with a seemingly endless variety of specialty-built bodies, including this "Fire Chief Runabout." Truck sales surged along with the rest of the line, with more than 150,000 units delivered.

▲ Henry Ford (left) and Henry M. Leland stand behind their sons, Edsel and Wilfred, as the senior Ford purchases the fledgling Lincoln Motor Company. Edsel Ford was named president of the new acquisition.

ERNEST G. LIEBOLD
Henry Ford's Watchdog

During the teens and Twenties, Ernest G. Liebold, as one of Henry Ford's most trusted aides, played a more important role in Ford history than generally realized.

Born in Detroit in 1884, Liebold, after attending a local business college, joined a Highland Park, Michigan, bank located near the Ford company's Piquette and Highland Park plants. Progressing from messenger to bookkeeper to teller, his abilities caught the eye of James Couzens, Ford's business manager. In 1912, Couzens asked him to organize a new Ford-financed bank, the Highland Park State Bank, then serve as its president. After successfully launching the institution, he was assigned by Henry Ford to reorganize and manage a Dearborn bank in which the magnate had a private account. At this point, he began handling Henry's personal finances and correspondence, and also was assigned to organize and supervise several of Ford's private projects, including Henry Ford Hospital, the Peace Ship, and tractor experimentation

From the outset, Ford was impressed by Liebold's devotion and efficiency. Once a course was set, the subordinate was rigid and unswerving. He refused to cultivate his associates, saying, "I make it a rule not to have any friends in the company. You are then in a position where you don't give a goddamn what happens to anybody." When an associate dropped by his office to wish him a Merry Christmas," Liebold looked up from his work, hesitated, and finally responded, "Well, all right."

Ford's press buffer until about 1920, Liebold antagonized newsmen with his brusque heavy-handedness. Journalists, in an effort to embarrass him, magnified his every real or imagined mistake. They succeeded, for in 1921 Liebold confided to a friend, "I have long ago learned that one cannot associate with newspapermen without being stung. It has happened so often with me that I find no further enjoyment in their company."

Liebold's treatment of the press met with Henry Ford's approval. "When you hire a watchdog," the auto king said, "you don't hire him to like everybody that comes to the gate." Indeed, Ford shared Liebold's opinion of reporters. "They're all a bunch of skunks," he told an aide, "and you know what happens to people who play with skunks."

In 1918, Henry and Clara Ford gave power of attorney to Liebold. This signal of trust was reinforced in 1923 when, upon completion of Dearborn Engineering Laboratory, Henry assigned his aide a "Mahogany Row" executive office near his own.

During the Twenties, Liebold efficiently managed numerous enterprises for Henry Ford and the company, ranging from the Detroit, Toledo & Ironton Railroad and *Dearborn Independent*, to the Dearborn Country Club and an employee housing development, to the purchase of mines, forests, and hydroelectric sites.

A vicious anti-Semite, Liebold perhaps more than anyone else implanted anti-Semitism in Henry Ford's mind.

"I am sure that if Mr. Ford were put on the witness stand, he could not tell to save his life just when and how he started against the Jews," said the *Independent*'s first editor, Edwin G. Pipp. "I am sure that Liebold could tell."

Pipp's view was echoed by another Liebold colleague, newspaperman Fred L. Black, who observed, "If I were to put the number-one blame on anyone it would be Liebold."

It was most likely Liebold's influence on Henry that led to pieces in the Ford-controlled *Dearborn Independent* with headlines such as "The International Jew, The World's Foremost Problem."

In 1938, Liebold, as if to publicly acknowledge his feelings, accepted Nazi Germany's Order of Merit of the German Eagle, First Class. Six weeks later, he was on hand when German counsels awarded Henry Ford the Grand Cross of the Supreme Order of the German Eagle.

Overwhelmed by stress brought on by the 1933 Detroit banking crisis, in which Henry and Edsel Ford were deeply involved, Liebold eventually broke down and fled to Northern Michigan for a respite.

Liebold's brief absence undermined his close relationship with Henry Ford, and enabled archrival and company strongman Harry Bennett and a crony, Frank Campsall, to usurp much of his authority. For years, Bennett had sought permission from Ford to fire Liebold, but was now in the best position to make a case against him.

The industrialist was hesitant to do so, Bennett reasoned, because Liebold knew too much and the boss "was afraid of him." Finally, in 1944, the 81-year-old Ford, his mental powers failing, tacitly approved of Liebold's dismissal.

Liebold's reminiscences, recorded by the Ford Archives in the early Fifties, are the longest—at more than 1400 pages—in the archives. At the time, the ex-Fordist was a plumbing company representative; wags said a "toilet-seat salesman." He died at age 72 in 1956.

- Model T receives first major restyling
- Lower, more-streamlined Model Ts an instant hit with buyers
- Production reaches 1.8 million vehicles
- Market share hovers around 50 percent
- "Tudor" and "Fordor" sedans debut
- Runabouts now priced as low as $269
- Doors on all Fords are now front hinged
- Ford resumes advertising after a six-year hiatus
- Touring-car sales alone top 900,000

▲ First to wear new styling was the touring car. The bodies sat lower on the chassis, and the once bolt-upright windshield panes now raked gently back. Priced as low as $298, the touring car was $142 less expensive than a year ago.

▲ The touring car's new "one man" top was purported to be less difficult to raise and lower, though its operation could still be cumbersome. Nineteen twenty-three proved to be a banner year for sales of the tourer; 929,092 were made during the calendar year.

▲ The foul-weather protection offered by side curtains was often less than complete. As the public's expectations of motoring comfort rose, demand for closed coupes and sedans increased. Combined coupe and sedan sales rose to more than 550,000 cars, 200,000 more than the previous year.

▲ Henry Ford, outfitted as a Western desperado, clowns with Thomas A. Edison on a camping trip. Ford, a great lover of the outdoors, enjoyed escaping back to nature whenever possible.

◄ Lincoln's newest car, the Model L, was reported to easily exceed 70 mph. Happy with their designs, Henry Ford made few changes to the cars after acquiring the company. Lincoln sales topped 7800 in 1923, up 2300 over the prior year. Though quoted as saying "I've no use for a car with more spark plugs than a cow has teats," Henry Ford seemed comfortable with the eight-cylinder Lincolns.

► Still Ford's most popular body style, the touring car received a taller radiator and a longer hood as part of the Model T freshening. Despite a new look, all Ford variants continued to soldier on with what was basically the same 20-horsepower, four-cylinder engine that had powered the first Model Ts in 1908.

◄ Aftermarket builders created stake-body trucks with open cabs as well as the closed cab shown here. Truck prices started at $380, down $65 from the prior year. Ford trucks enjoyed the same styling enhancements as the rest of the Model T line. Visible here are the higher fenders and wider running boards that distinguish the freshened trucks from previous models. While their fenders remained Model T black, a small number of cars and trucks left the factory sporting newly available colors. Black would remain the dominant Model T hue, but colors such as Phoenix Brown and Gun Metal Blue would become increasingly available in the next few years.

- The 10-millionth Model T rolls off the assembly line in June

- Henry Ford presents the Prince of Wales the 11-millionth Ford in October

- Prices drop to new lows, $265 for a runabout, $295 for a touring car

- After just two years, the 300,000th Ford is sold on weekly credit plan

- Ford hangs on to 50-percent market share though sales slide slightly

- Ford earns a record $100 million profit

- First factory-bodied trucks produced

▲ The marketing of the increasingly affordable Model T attempted to position the vehicle not as a luxury, but as part of a normal middle-class lifestyle. Note the careful placement of a woman behind the wheel in the ad above. With more than 10 million cars on the road, there was no segment of the population Ford could afford to ignore.

▲ This smartly attired, professionally employed woman was the perfect icon for Ford's broadening advertising reach. While most automotive advertising targeted wealthy males, Ford pitched its cars as empowering the common man, or woman. The coupe shown in the ad above cost $525, about a third of the average worker's annual income.

▲ The rugged Model T chassis was available with a body, just a cab, or stripped. Unfinished chassis were ready to be mounted with any of a variety of special bodies.

◄ During June, the 10-millionth Ford rolled off the assembly line. Special ads and a cross-country sprint by the landmark vehicle marked the occasion.

At $265, the question was no longer whether the average worker could afford an automobile, but why they might want one. Advertising like this struck at the heart of a population that would soon embrace automotive mobility as a national birthright. The runabout was close to being as inexpensive as any Ford would ever be. Five dollars would come off the price next year, but after that demountable wheels and electric starters would become standard equipment, driving the price over $300.

▲ This closed van with sliding-door entry and after-market "Bi-flex" bumper delivered flowers in Detroit. A growing accessory industry provided drivers with the opportunity to customize vehicles to fit their needs.

▲ Roll-down side curtains turned a canopied express truck into a $520 screenside delivery. Though Ford was now building cabs and bodies, outside coachbuilders still provided the bulk of Model T truck bodies.

▲ With the population of vehicles growing faster than roads were being built, Model Ts were often expected to traverse surfaces that would halt modern vehicles. Body designs would lower as roads improved.

▲ Wood construction was common on bodies fitted to Model T truck chassis. Though newly lowered bodies made entering and exiting such vehicles easier, protection from the elements was still lacking.

WILLIAM J. CAMERON
His Master's Voice

WILLIAM J. CAMERON, Henry Ford's leading spokesman from 1920 until the early Forties, did more to shape Ford's public image than anyone except the boss himself.

Born in Hamilton, Ontario, Canada, on December 29, 1878, Cameron at age nine moved with his family to Detroit. From 1904 to 1918, he was a reporter and editorialist for the *Detroit News*, where he gained a reputation as one of the best newspaper writers in America. His essay, "Don't Die on Third"—an exhortation to get to home plate on any undertaking—was one of the most reprinted editorials in American history.

In December 1918, Cameron joined Henry Ford's national newspaper, the *Dearborn Independent*, and in 1919 was temporarily assigned to a news agency set up by Ford to publicize his position in a libel suit he had filed against the *Chicago Tribune*.

Cameron became thoroughly familiar with Ford's views through authorship of "Henry Ford's Own Page" in the *Independent*. He also doubled as Ford's public relations advisor and chief press interpreter, arranging most of the manufacturer's interviews, sitting in on and steering most of them, and eliminating foolish or tactless statements from resultant drafts and manuscripts.

Cameron was more than a censor, for without his assistance, interviewers often found it difficult, if not impossible, to understand the meaning of much of what Ford said. The auto king often spoke in parables that were quite incomprehensible without an intimate knowledge of his mind.

Cameron all but divined Ford's thoughts. Often, as his master's voice, he broke into interviews with, "What Mr. Ford means is—" and then proceeded to expound on Ford's views. The industrialist, as he listened to the flawless presentation of his ideas, would nod pleasantly. Never, so far as his associates knew, did Ford repudiate his aide's comments.

In the Twenties and Thirties, Henry Ford all but made his personal headquarters in Cameron's Dearborn Engineering Laboratory office. The publicist also was a regular at Ford's daily executive luncheons.

When Ford launched an anti-Semitic crusade in the *Independent* in 1920, Cameron, who had become editor, was assigned to research the "Jewish Question." Disgustedly undertaking his assignment, he noted in his initial report "what a wonderful race they were and how little he had known of their history, and what a magnificent history it was."

Yet Cameron was either unable or did not try to dissuade Ford from attacking Jews. Rather, according to one observer, he bent to the demands of his employer "with the same pseudo-enthusiasm of an advertising man suddenly called upon to promote a toothpaste no different than a hundred others. It was an assignment."

In time, Cameron apparently came to believe much of the anti-Semitic material that he wrote or that crossed his desk.

As editor of the *Independent*, Cameron in 1927 was chief witness for the defense when Ford was sued for libel by a Jewish lawyer, Aaron Sapiro, accused of cheating his clients. Testifying for five days and maintaining perfect aplomb under severe cross-examination, Cameron declared that he had the sole responsibility for the *Independent*'s editorial content, and that he had never discussed with Ford any article on any Jew, or sent Ford an advance copy of the weekly, nor even seen Ford read a copy of the newspaper. The defense, in short, took the position that Ford had given Cameron and his staff a free hand in shaping policy and had simply been an innocent bystander.

It was unquestionably true that Ford had paid less and less attention to the *Independent* as the years passed. But it was obvious that he bore the ultimate and direct responsibility for the newspaper's anti-Semitic articles, 91 of which were reprinted in an uncopyrighted book, *The International Jew*, and circulated worldwide. Indeed, on any number of occasions, Ernest Liebold, Cameron, and the *Independent*'s promotional literature boasted that "The *Dearborn Independent* is Henry Ford's own paper and he authorizes every statement occurring therein," and that the paper has the "personal assistance of Mr. Ford's guidance and instruction and the benefit of his keen foresight and experience."

When Ford settled the Sapiro suit out of court, the industrialist removed Cameron from the *Independent*, while retaining him as a behind-the-scenes publicist. The newspaper itself, discredited and sagging in circulation, was permanently suspended in December 1927.

Cameron remained in the shadows until 1934, when he was assigned to prepare and read six-minute "intermission talks" on the Ford Motor Company's highly acclaimed *Ford Sunday Evening Hour,* a weekly radio concert featuring the Detroit Symphony Orchestra. If the orchestra was responsible for the program's critical acclaim, it was Cameron's talks that set the show

The Ford International Weekly

THE DEARBORN INDEPENDENT

By Year $1.50   Dearborn, Michigan, August 6, 1921   Single Copy Ten Cents

---

**And Now Leprosy
Is Yielding to Science**
Years of experimenting brings a remedy

**Fountain Lake, the
Home of John Muir**
A story of naturalist's wilderness abode

Fighting the Devil in Modern Babylon
First of a series of articles on New York by Rev. Dr. John Roach Straton

Jewish Jazz—Moron Music—Becomes

Our National Music
Story of "Popular Song" Control in the United States

The Chief Justices of the Supreme Court
Only ten men have held this post since the tribunal was first organized

**Teaching the Deaf to
Hear With Their Eyes**
How Chicago is educating afflicted children

**Many By-Products
From Sweet Potatoes**
Recent discoveries prove great possibilities

William Cameron became editor of the Ford-owned weekly *Dearborn Independent* in the Twenties, when it published a series of anti-Jewish articles.

apart from all others of its era and made it the company's most important public relations activity during 1934–42. Cameron himself conceived the program's "commercial" format—comments reflecting Henry Ford's views on such matters as morals, holidays, history, the lives of great Americans, economics, business practices, and politics. There was no direct effort to sell Ford products.

Cameron had a free hand in writing his talks. "I worked in a vacuum," he recalled later. "There was nobody to consult with, nobody to advise me." Twice he asked Henry Ford about the content of the messages. Ford waved him away with "You know what's best." Cameron complained that preparation of the hour was "killing . . . like having a baby every week."

At times a heavy drinker, Cameron sometimes delivered his remarks while drunk. Ford's advertising agency, N. W. Ayer, and Ford officials, concerned lest the commentator might not be sober enough to get from his home to the auditorium, assigned an escort to him the afternoon and evening of each broadcast, and also had Fred L. Black stand by to read the message if Cameron appeared too tipsy to go on the air. "My Sundays," Black moaned later, "were ruined for years." But Cameron was extraordinarily constant. He missed only one broadcast, because of an attack of influenza, during the eight years he was on the air. Moreover, he performed as well drunk as sober; only a huskiness in his voice betrayed his inebriation.

World War II forced cancellation of the "Sunday Evening Hour," and Cameron was further pushed toward the sidelines in 1942 when the Ford company set up a news bureau for which Henry Ford's henchman, Harry Bennett—who detested Cameron—assumed responsibility in 1943. The bureau, not Cameron, released many of Ford's most important wartime statements. Cameron, reporting as always to Henry Ford, continued to prepare lesser pronouncements and letters for the founder.

Cameron remained in Ford's good graces throughout his career, despite some habits that Ford abhorred and a streak of independence that the founder tolerated in no other executive. When the publicist ignored an edict requiring *Independent* employees to start work at 8:30 A.M. and, in fact, often delayed his arrival at the office until early afternoon, Ford merely remarked, "Well, he's all here when he gets here." When Cameron drank excessively, the manufacturer, for years an uncompromising prohibitionist, told associates, "This is due to sickness. We're going to cure him. We'll never give up." When Cameron spurned invitations to attend Ford's weekly old-fashioned dances (summonses that few other executives dared refuse), the founder did not censure him. Alone among company officials, Cameron was immune from Bennett's hatchet. For years, Bennett entreated Ford to say the word that would send the publicist packing. But Bennett himself was the first to go.

To the end of his company career, Cameron maintained that "other men dwindled in size when Ford entered a room." In April 1946, the publicist retired. "My services," he explained later, "were with Mr. Henry Ford, and he was no longer there." With pride, Cameron noted that he had remained with the company two-and-a-half years beyond the usual retirement age of 65. Few Ford officials of his generation could say the same.

One of the few Henry Ford-era executives to receive a pension, Cameron moved in 1952 to Oakland, California, where he died on August 1, 1955. He is buried in Dearborn's Northview Cemetery.

- Prices reach all-time lows: $260 for runabout, $290 for touring car
- Production slips to just over 1.6 million vehicles
- Market share slips to 44 percent
- New Ford advertising campaign touts safety and reliability
- Model Ts receive second facelift
- Factory opens in Mexico
- Dealership opens in Japan
- Ford truck production reaches almost 270,000
- Birth of William Clay, Edsel and Eleanor's third son, on March 14

▲ Edsel Ford (left) poses with William Stout (right) to commemorate the sale of the Stout Metal Airplane Company to the Ford Motor Company. Affectionately known as the "Tin Goose," Ford would produce a total of 199 Tri-Motor aircraft like the one in the background.

▲ Henry Ford often credited his success to "sticking with one model," referring to his wife, Clara Ford. Henry called Clara "The Believer" because she recognized his potential when no else did.

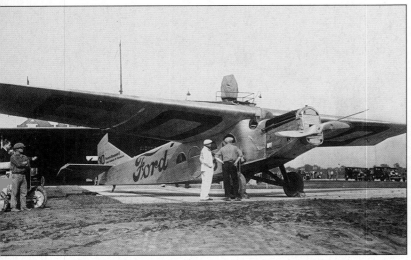

▲ Based at Ford Airport, this Stout Model 2-AT was the flagship of Ford's airline service. Dubbed the "Maiden Dearborn," the plane featured enclosed seating for passengers, but an open cockpit design left pilots exposed to the elements. Subsequent planes in the AT series would be of "Tri-Motor" design and make space for the pilot inside of the aircraft.

▲ As Chevrolet and other rivals grew stronger, demand for the Model T began to wane. Despite an ad campaign touting the affordability of Ford ownership, dealers began to lose faith. Edsel Ford argued with his father to begin development of a new model, but Henry would only agree to a redesign of the existing Model T.

► A Fordor sedan offered a cozy ride for the family, but at $660, it cost twice as much as a touring car. Ventilation continued to be provided via a two-piece windshield and a pop-up cowl ventilator. One-piece windshields would become the norm by the 1928 introduction of the Model A, as the two-piece systems sealed poorly at the higher speeds the new cars were capable of reaching.

▲ Unlike the upright windshields on their closed-cab brethren, the windshields on open-cab Model Ts raked slightly rearward. By the introduction of the Model A, wooden wheels like these would no longer be available on Ford vehicles.

▲ Pickup truck owners have always enjoyed customizing their vehicles. Optional extra-large rear tires must have aided traction when this truck left the beaten path. Getting into the driver's seat was made easier by the addition of a running board.

◄ Lincoln production this year reached a record 8380 cars. All 1925 Lincolns were equipped with "Electro-Fog" starting aides. The Electro-Fog device sprayed a vaporized mixture of gas and air into the carburetor to facilitate starting in cold weather. Owners reported the device not living up to expectations.

1926

- Sales drop 17 percent to just under 1.4 million

- Market share falls to 36 percent

- For the first time, used cars are recognized as competition for new cars

- Model Ts now available in several colors. Of course, black is still offered.

- Electric starters become standard on all Model Ts

- Though Model A is only two years away, Ford vehemently denies replacement of Model T

THE FORDOR
$660
F.O.B. DETROIT

BEAUTY. COMFORT. CONVENIENCE. UTILITY

▲ With the exception of this Fordor sedan, Model T bodies this year sat 1.5 inches lower, running boards were wider, and headlights moved to the fenders. Finally, closed cars came in a choice of colors.

▲ For the first time since 1911, touring cars got a functional driver's door. In addition to their sporty appeal, touring cars were much less costly than the coupes and sedans.

▲ The touring car was still the best-selling Model T, but the runabout was close behind. At about 365,000 produced, the touring car outsold the runabout by a narrow 20,000-car margin. Closed cars continued to gain ground on their open stablemates, with coupes and sedans combining for more than 650,000 sales.

TUDOR
$520
F.O.B. DETROIT

"The Torque Tube Drive"—An Original Ford Idea

▲ "Torque Tube Drive," as described in this *Saturday Evening Post* ad, was nothing new to Ford, but it sounded impressive. While Fordor sedans soldiered on with two-piece windshields, other closed cars were equipped with single-pane front glass.

▲ This Fordor sedan sported an optional front bumper but not the wire wheels that were growing in popularity. At $660, the Fordor sedan remained the most expensive car in the Ford lineup. Sedans were now available painted in Fawn Gray, Highland Green, Royal Maroon, and, of course, black. Nickel-plated radiator shells were now standard equipment on all sedans.

▲ Wire wheels, a nickel-plated radiator shell, a front bumper, and a running-board step plate are some of the options added to this well-trimmed runabout.

▲ The two-passenger coupe was the best-selling closed car in the Ford line. At $520, the coupe offered closed-car comfort for $60 less than the Tudor sedan.

▲ Although among the slower-selling Model T variants, 75,000 pickups still managed to find homes. This open-cab version has the optional nickel-plated radiator shell and wire wheels.

▲ Almost 230,000 truck chassis left the factory; some were outfitted like this. Though rolling on the standard wood-spoke wheels, the oak-finished passenger body gives this truck a touch of class.

- Model T production ends after 19 years and more than 15 million cars
- Last-year Model T production reaches nearly 520,000

- Under-$300 Ford a thing of the past; new standard equipment drives runabout to $360
- Wood-spoke wheels disappear as wire wheels are made standard

- Ford auto production halts completely in preparation for Model A
- Charles Lindbergh gives Henry Ford his first airplane ride in the *Spirit of St. Louis*

▲ ▼ Now standard across the line, wire wheels adorn this last-of-an-era Tudor sedan. By the end of the Model T's run, closed coupes and sedans were selling almost as well as the touring car and runabout. Due in part to a $50 lower price, the Tudor sedans outsold their Fordor brethren nearly four-to-one. The Tin Lizzie's life span exceeded that of any other car until the Sixties, and its production record stood until 1972, when surpassed by the Volkswagen Beetle.

▲ At a glance, this touring car didn't look much different from its 1909 predecessor, though much had changed. Neatly crowned fenders were now bolted to the body, and wire wheels eventually became standard. The bumpers on this car were a $15 option.

HENRY FORD
The Man with a Better Idea

HENRY FORD, born on a Michigan farm in 1863, was a complex, controversial man. Married in 1888 and Edsel's father by 1893, he built his first engine in 1893, his first car in 1896, and cofounded Ford Motor Company in 1903. His greatness and acclaim were built on seven major foundation stones, plus a remarkable variety of other activities and enterprises. They include:

• The Selden Patent Suit—During this 1903–11 suit, Ford successfully defended himself against the Association of Licensed Automobile Manufacturers, which had refused him and others a license to make cars. During the suit, Ford, highly publicized for the first time, was lauded as a giant-killer, as a symbol of revolt against monopoly, and as a magnificent individualist. He would be so regarded for the remainder of his life.

• The Model T—The log cabin of the motor age, the Model T was represented in its day as providing a service to the people greater than that of the telegraph, the telephone, rural free mail delivery, the phonograph, radio, and electric power. The vehicle's reputation has withstood the test of time. In 1993, *Time* named the "mass-produced Model T" as one of the century's "greatest technological breakthroughs." In 1998, *Life* named the car the 17th most-important happening of the millennium. That same year, the Tin Lizzie topped *Parade* magazine's list of cars that "stand out for their technical cultural or commercial significance," and a year later the flivver was named the "top" car of all time by Britain's *Autocar* magazine. As a capstone, the Model T in 2000 was named "Car of the Century" by the Global Automotive Elections Foundation, which supervised voting by 135 automotive journalists representing 32 countries. These rankings reflect as favorably on Henry Ford as on the Model T itself inasmuch as the car has always been affectionately regarded as a mechanical extension of Ford himself.

• Mass Production—The breakthrough of all manufacturing breakthroughs, mass production has contributed more to worldwide affluence than automation, robotics, and "lean production" combined. Like the Model T, it has been cited as one of the most important developments in world history. Named the 17th "top news story of the century" by journalists and historians surveyed in 1999 by the Freedom Forum's Newseum, mass production also was rated as the 17th "greatest achievement of the 20th century" by TV's The Learning Channel, based on advice from a dozen historians. Ford's association with mass production has contributed importantly to his reputation.

• The Five-Dollar Day—The $5 day, which in 1914 more than doubled factory wages while reducing the workday from nine to eight hours, was the most publicized event of Ford's career. The avalanche of publicity quickly made the automaker a world figure. He was, the press reported, shy, modest, sincere, and simple, a rich man with a poor man's tastes. He was a fighter, as witnessed in his role in the Selden Patent Suit, yet was a gentle man who loved birds and attributed his success to his wife's moral support. Above all, he was a friend of the working man. Combining fact and fancy, the reportage created public perceptions spanning Ford's lifetime and redounded immeasurably to his image and that of his company. In 1954, the London *Economist* referred to the $5 day as the most important event in the history of wages. It remains so to this day.

• The Peace Ship—A so-called "Peace Ship" was chartered by Ford in the naive hope of ending World War I through sponsorship of mediation among warring nations. The ship's 1915 Atlantic crossing, with Ford aboard, initially was ridiculed by the press. Although the mission failed, it increased Ford's popularity with the masses, which sympathized with its goals. Even the press eventually changed its tune, describing Ford as "God's fool," and observing that he had at least tried to end the war. Respect for Ford's idealism unquestionably contributed to his amazing strength as a senatorial candidate in 1918 and to the persistent "Ford-for-President" talk between 1916 and 1923.

• The Dodge Suit—The 1916 Dodge lawsuit greatly strengthened Ford's folk heroism. John and Horace Dodge, 10-percent owners of the Ford company, insisted that the firm distribute dividends to stockholders so that the brothers' profits could be invested in the new Dodge car. Ford preferred to reinvest dividends in his company, specifically, the Rouge Plant. The trial was highly publicized, and Ford, as a witness, delighted the public with his views. In opposing the Dodges' wish for maximum dividends, he declared that his primary business objective was to increase employment, raise wages, and cut prices, rather than make huge payments to himself and other shareholders. "Business is a service, not a bonanza," he insisted.

Although the Dodges won their suit, Ford's remarks reaffirmed public belief that Henry Ford was a champion of the little man. In 1959, Jesuit scholar Rev. R. I. Bruckberger spoke for many when he wrote, "Mr. Ford's remarkable dialogue is as important in econom-

HENRY FORD
Continued

ics as the Declaration of Independence is in politics. . . . Indeed, this fantastic dialogue should be looked upon as the businessman's Hippocratic oath."

• The *Chicago Tribune* Suit—Ford's 1916–19 libel suit against the *Chicago Tribune* both detracted from and added to his reputation. Ford sued the newspaper after it erroneously reported that the company refused financial assistance to employees mobilized for National Guard duty on the Mexican border, and also accused Ford of being an "ignorant idealist." To defend itself, the *Tribune* had to prove that Ford was every whit an ignorant idealist. This time as a witness, Ford revealed himself to be one of America's most poorly informed national figures. He did not know, for instance, when the American Revolution was fought, and ventured the year 1812. The *Cincinnati Times-Star* spoke for many in editorializing that "a little education along historical lines may be good even for an idealist."

Ford won the suit, but was mocked with a damage award of six cents. His ignorance disillusioned intellectuals. Among millions of common folks, however, his performance produced an opposite reaction. Many people could no more have dated the American Revolution than Ford. Many also would have admitted, as Ford had on the stand, that it was difficult for them to read. Also, his remark "History is more or less bunk" struck a responsive chord in the hearts of countless ex-schoolboys and girls who thought the same but lacked Ford's terseness of expression.

The range of Ford's activities set him apart from any other American industrialist. His company not only made cars, trucks, tractors, and airplanes, but also mined coal, iron ore, and lead, and owned timberlands, sawmills, rubber plantations, and a score of "village industries." It operated a railroad, blast furnaces, coke ovens, foundries, steel mills, lake and ocean fleets, and dozens of assembly plants around the world, and also produced glass, artificial leather, textiles, gauges, paper, and cement while farming 10,000 acres.

In addition to his industrial endeavors, Ford also built and operated Henry Ford Hospital, Henry Ford Museum and Greenfield Village, the Dearborn Inn, and schools ranging in size and scope from the Henry Ford Trade School to 15 one-room schools. He also published a national newspaper and operated a radio station. In addition, he restored Michigan's oldest inn, the Botsford Inn, and the nation's oldest hostelry, the Wayside Inn, and, with his son Edsel, established the Ford Foundation, whose assets came to dwarf those of any similar institution.

Ford's crusading also contributed to his reputation. He believed that he could be a force for constructive change, and unlike most visionaries and crusaders, had the drive and wealth to ride his dreams.

The auto king's crusades were remarkably diverse. If not saving birds; reducing waste; and reforming education, ex-convicts, and prostitutes, he was extolling the work ethic and just-in-time production; proclaiming that every criminal was "an inveterate cigarette-smoker"; exposing a fictitious character called "the International Jew"; providing jobs of equal pay to the physically handicapped and African Americans; insisting that soybeans and wheat were "divine foods"; or attempting to convince a jazz-mad generation that the Virginia Reel was more fun than the Charleston. Of his crusades, it could be said, as was said of Winston Churchill, "He was usually right, but when he wasn't—well, my God!"

Ford's multifarious activities were widely publicized and contributed importantly to the public belief that he had a daring and highly original mind, virtually unique technical skills, and a never-ceasing desire to serve humankind. "Only once or twice in a century," summed up *The New York Times* in 1992, "is the world blessed . . . with such a fount of industrial innovation and vigor [as Henry Ford]."

Ford, unlike many tycoons, also benefited from his common touch. Farm-reared, self-made, and with only eight grades of schooling, he mixed easily with those who worked with their hands. "He's just like me," some said, "except that he's got a billion dollars." He was shy, although not modest, and found it torturous to give a speech. He spoke to groups only 16 times, and then very briefly. One of his more memorable "speeches," delivered to prisoners in Sing-Sing, consisted of six words: "Glad to see you all here."

Ford's reputation has transcended the auto and business spheres since the Twenties. From that time onward, he has been regarded as one of the nation's, indeed one of the world's, most esteemed citizens. In 1924, University of Michigan President M. L. Burton ranked him as one of the four greatest men of the first quarter of the twentieth century. In 1926, the industrialist placed second in a worldwide YMCA poll to determine the greatest living men in the world. That same year, America's police chiefs voted him as the greatest person on Earth. In 1927, Belleville, New Jersey, schoolboys, when asked, "Who would you like to be if you were not yourself?" voted only Charles A. Lindbergh and President Calvin Coolidge ahead of Henry Ford.

Ford's legend and legacy remain durable, as evidenced by his rankings in the plethora of "greatest" surveys conducted during the Nineties and at the turn of the millennium. The following are representative:

In 1991, 60 historians and other authorities, asked by *Life* to select the twentieth century's 100 most influential figures, voted unanimously for only three persons—Ford and the Wright brothers. In 1993, *Time* rated Ford the century's second-greatest person, behind Sigmund Freud. In a 1996 book, *Great People of the 20th Century*, produced by the editors of *Time*, Ford was named one of the period's 73 "greatest people." "Ford," the book notes, "was damned as a communist, an anarchist, and an anti-Semite; he was also praised as the greatest living American, whose diverse interests made him seem a kind of machine age Leonardo." In 1997, more than 100 U.S. history professors surveyed by the Siena College Research Institute ranked Ford as the third "most significant" American of the twentieth century.

In 1998, the auto king was listed as the 12th wealthiest American of all time by *American Heritage*, which stated that the $1 billion with which he was credited in 1947 had the buying power of $36.1 billion 51 years later. Also in 1998, *Life* ranked Ford as the 15th most important person of the millennium, the selections being based on the number of people affected by the nominee and the extent to which he or she changed daily life. Given these criteria, Ford, among the billions of people who have inhabited the earth during the past 1000 years, is outranked only by Edison, Columbus, Luther, Galileo, da Vinci, Newton, Magellan, Pasteur, Darwin, Jefferson, Shakespeare, Napoleon, and Hitler.

Ford's greatness is not universally accepted, however. In 1992, *American Heritage* invited historians and politicians to nominate the single most-overrated figure in American history. Historian Bernard Weisberger nominated Ford. "Despite popular misconceptions," he observed, [Ford] "did not invent the automobile, the assembly line, vertical integration, or mass ownership of cars." Weisberger is essentially correct, but Ford's contribution to and identification with these phenomena is so great as to make it seem that he invented them, which perhaps explains his election to the National Inventors Hall of Fame, one of numerous halls of fame to which the industrialist has been named.

Ford was pictured on the cover of *Time* for the fifth time on December 7, 1998, on this occasion as one of the magazine's 100 "most influential business geniuses" of the century. In 2000, he was named *Fortune*'s "Businessman of the Century," ahead of GM's Alfred P. Sloan Jr.; IBM's Thomas J. Watson; and Microsoft's Bill Gates. The same year, Ford was named by the *Wall Street Journal* as one of 10 persons who most "changed the world" and did the most to "transform entrepreneurship" in the twentieth century. In 2002, the magnate was inducted into the European Automotive Hall of Fame at the Palexpo, home of the Geneva Auto Show.

Another measure of Ford's greatness are the continuous press references to industrial leaders and others as "the Henry Ford of" a country, a company, or a sphere of activity. Louis Renault, for example, has been referred to as the Henry Ford of France, Soichiro Honda as the Henry Ford of Japan, Henry J. Kaiser as the Henry Ford of shipbuilding, Milton Hershey as the Henry Ford of candy, William J. Levitt as the Henry Ford of suburban development, Ray Kroc as the Henry Ford of hamburgers, Steven Jobs as the Henry Ford of computers, and drug kingpin Carlos Riva as the Henry Ford of cocaine. The list goes on and on.

Ford, as the foregoing suggests, is a man for the ages. A 1930 assessment of the industrialist is equally valid today. "It could be," said author Nivin Busch Jr., that "if it were possible to preserve alive, for the interests of history, one man from each century and country—not, of course, the best or the wisest, but the one who represents more thoroughly the hopes, crudities, background, and achievements of his place—no one could better represent this time and the United States than Henry Ford." Perhaps Ford's importance is best summed up by General Motors' great inventor, Charles F. Kettering, in 1943. "A thousand years from now," he observed, "when the Churchills and the Roosevelts are but footnotes in history, Henry Ford will loom as the most significant figure of our age." Concurring in 1992, *The New York Times* described Ford as "the quintessential American."

Ford, in any event, will long be remembered for his great achievements. By preaching high-volume production, low prices, and universal consumption, he became the most important person in a far-reaching revolution. For better or worse, his vision actually did help remold the world.

Ford has many tangible monuments, chief among them the Ford Motor Company, the Ford Foundation, Henry Ford Museum and Greenfield Village, Henry Ford Hospital, Henry Ford Community College, and Henry Ford Centennial Library, plus inns, chapels, and statues in Dearborn, England, and Brazil. Of his monuments, perhaps the most poignant is a four-foot-high stone memorial to him in Dearborn's tiny Springwells Mall. Atop the stone is a metal strip with five words, "The Shadow Passes, Light Remains"—a gentle reminder that Henry Ford's legend and legacy live on.

Ford died by candlelight on a stormy April 7, 1947, the powerplant at his Fair Lane estate knocked out by the flooding Rouge River. Unseeking of glory in death, he is buried beneath a simple, horizontal slab in the tiny Ford family cemetery. Few people visit the grave site, located in Detroit several miles from Fair Lane and the Henry Ford Museum and Greenfield Village. Among them have been newly elected officers of the Dearborn Chapter of the Early Ford V-8 Club of America, who, standing over Ford's grave in 1974, took a formal oath "to have the best V-8 chapter in the country, so help us Henry!"

1928

- Model A finally arrives

- A reported 10 million people come to see the new Ford in its first 36 hours on the market

- Model A development costs Ford $250 million

- Ford assets estimated at almost $1 billion

- Model A gets safety glass, an industry first

▲ Identified as "Pioneers of America," at an event of the same name, a rare gathering of early 20th-century luminaries pose for a photograph. From left to right they are: tire magnate Harvey Firestone, Sears-Roebuck executive Julius Rosenwald, Thomas Edison, tea and spice importer Sir Thomas Lipton, Bethlehem Steel founder Charles Schwab, Henry Ford, autobuilder Walter P. Chrysler, Eastman-Kodak founder George Eastman, and Delco Remy president Charles Wilson.

FORD

▶ Roadsters could be had with or without a rumble seat for the same $480. This car has the optional trunk, stone guard, and spare-tire cover. Model A prices ranged from $460 for a phaeton to $585 for a Fordor sedan. A purpose-built, four-door taxi could be had for $600. Only 264 were produced.

▲ Cold weather probably made the snug rumble-seat arrangements more palatable. Step plates mounted on top of the rear fenders aided rear-seat ingress and egress, but the process could still be less than graceful.

▲ Shown here around the time their film *The Gaucho* was released, Douglas Fairbanks Jr. and Mary Pickford enjoy the view through the window of a business roadster with its optional rumble seat open.

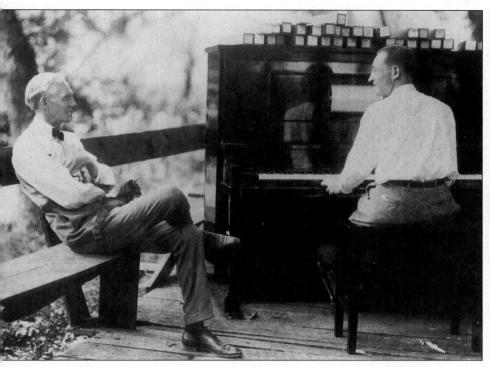

▲ Henry Ford listens as his son, Edsel, pumps away on a player piano. Both Fords enjoyed music, although Henry's tastes ran to old-fashioned fiddling and songs like "Turkey in the Straw," "Uncle Remus," and "Jeanie with the Light Brown Hair," while Edsel preferred more serious fare.

▲ Actually published in December 1927, ads like this one contributed to the reported 10-million-person swarm that hit showrooms to view the new Fords. The first "pictures" of the new Fords may have only been drawings, but they were enough to stir up substantial interest. Edsel Ford worked with designer Joe Galamb to pen the new designs.

▲ Most popular of the lower, prettier Ford bodies was the Tudor sedan, outselling the Fordor sedan by more than two-to-one. A Model A could reach 65 mph, a 20 mph improvement over the Model T.

▲ Some observers felt the new Fords looked like "little Lincolns," and this ad for the Fordor sedan seemed to support that impression. As the lady of the house confers with a member of her staff, the text reminds that Ford colors "are rich in tone, yet carefully chosen, with a quiet good taste that endures."

► Light trucks used the Model A passenger-car drivetrain, hood, and cowl, but with a painted body-color radiator shell. This truck, with an extra-tall cargo box, served the Wisconsin Telephone Company. As with cars, truck buyers enjoyed the Model A's new 200-cid, 40-horsepower four-cylinder engine.

◄ Two truck groups went on sale: a light duty 70-series derived from the passenger-car line, and the heavier-duty 80-series Model AA (shown). Payload capacity of the bigger trucks went up to 1½ tons. Truck drivers especially appreciated the move from the Model T's 20-horsepower engine to the Model A's 40-horse powerplant.

► One nifty commercial offering was the road-ster pickup, an update of a Model T offering. The trucks used Model A front ends and carryover Model T cargo boxes. Prices ranged from $395 for open-cab models to $445 for closed-cab ver-sions.

LINCOLN

◄ Color was still a relatively new part of the auto world, and Lincoln made the most of it in these high-style ads. While most Model A advertising focused on the technical aspects of the cars and the benefits of their ownership, the Lincoln "bird ads" spoke more conceptually about "the quest for perfection," and "the inherent fineness of Lincoln quality."

► Illustrated by Stark Davis, these ads represented a rare foray into commercial work for the artist. Preferring oil on canvas, Davis' work consisted mostly of wildlife, and most frequently birds. Prints of Davis' Lincoln ads remain popular with auto buffs today.

◄ Though Lincoln offered several body styles, customers had the option of having a coachbuilder finish their cars for them. This four-passenger sport sedan built by the Derham Body Company of Rosemont, Pennsylvania, features a leather roof covering and wicker inserts just below the windows.

1929

- Millionth and 2-millionth Model As built

- Car production doubles over previous year

- Market share reaches 32 percent

- Open cars finally get external door handles

- Color choices and availability expand

- Sales of the popular Tudor sedan exceed 500,000

FORD ▲ Fordor sedans were frequently identified by the manufacturers of their bodies. The most popular makers were Murray and Briggs; this sedan featured coachwork by the latter. While a $100 price advantage helped the Tudor sedans earn favor with the public, the $625 Fordors more than held their own, racking up sales of just under 150,000.

▲ The cabriolet brought style to the Model A line. The $670 two-seater was available in a number of colors, but the fenders were always black.

▲ Shown here with the top up, the phaeton continued in the Ford lineup in Model A guise.

► Created by Edsel Ford, the town car was aimed at those who favored formal style but didn't want to flaunt their wealth. At $1400, with open chauffeur's compartment and sliding divider window, it cost $775 more than a Fordor sedan.

◄ The $550 "five-window" sport coupe offered substantially better visibility than the $525 oval-windowed business coupe. With gas, oil, and water canisters; a grille guard; and step plate, this Model A was well-equipped with optional treats.

▲ Oval windows were a new feature on business coupes. Unlike other coupes, the business coupes did not have a hard top, but were finished with simulated leather stretched over a metal frame.

▲ Only $450 bought a Model A roadster, with either a trunk or rumble seat. The "flying quail" hood ornament adorned many a Ford of the day.

▲ Though the deluxe delivery car shared its body with the Tudor sedan, it could be identified by the single rear side glass that extended to the back of the cab. The $595 delivery car came without a rear seat.

▲ Though it was losing favor in its day, the open-cab pickup is prized by collectors today. While the body remained unchanged from the Model T era, the pickup rode on a somewhat modernized Model A chassis.

1929

LINCOLN

▶ The hot styling trend at Lincoln was the side-mounted spare tire as shown on this series 152 phaeton. At extra cost, buyers could choose to have the top, spare-tire cover, and trunk cover made of matching fabric. Spare tires could be mounted on either, or both, sides of the car.

▲ A handsome machine-turned instrument panel attempted to replicate the look of aircraft gauges. Large steering wheels were a necessity in the days before power steering.

▲ The greyhound radiator cap first appeared in 1926 as a $25 option. As customers balked at the price, Lincoln made the leaping dog standard equipment on most models for 1927.

▶ This well-equipped Model 173 sedan was outfitted with both the side-mounted spare tire and the folding rear trunk rack. Though advertised by Lincoln as five-passenger cars, standard jump seats raised seating capacity to seven. Real leather was used to finish the roof. Like this one, most Lincoln sedans were built with rear-opening "suicide" back doors.

► This convertible sedan featured a body by coachbuilder Dietrich. At $2400 more than the sport phaeton, sales of the special-order car were slow. By midyear, with only 60 orders on the books, production was finally halted. Despite Lincoln's reputation as a luxury-car builder, its chassis saw use in a number of commercial applications including hearses, ambulances, and panel vans.

◄ This one-off show car featured a body designed by LeBaron and was displayed at the year's salon shows held to display Lincoln's wares to well-heeled buyers. Though technically available on a special order basis, the $10,000 price tag assured that this aero phaeton would remain unique. Note the aircraft-style running lights atop the front fenders.

► Though the manufacturing process was never as refined as on the automobile side of the business, Ford continued to produce legendary Tri-Motor aircraft. Powered by three Pratt & Whitney "Wasp" engines, Tri-Motors were capable of reaching a top speed of 135 mph. An unloaded Tri-Motor weighed about 7500 pounds, or about three times as much as a Fordor sedan.

HENRY FORD AND JEWS

O F HENRY FORD'S MISTAKES, none has proved more far reaching and costly than his anti-Semitic crusading. For decades, the legacy of Ford's anti-Semitism haunted Henry Ford II and the Ford Motor Company. Finally, by the Eighties, thanks to unremitting correct behavior toward Jews, the problem lay dormant. In 1998, however, it was revived by accusations that Ford of Germany had collaborated with the Nazis and used slave labor during World War II.

Why was Henry Ford anti-Semitic? In answering the question, let it first be noted that anti-Semitism was rife in the America of Ford's day. His attitude toward Jews was further shaped by boyhood influences. In the rural area in which he grew up, the only Jews ever seen were roving peddlers. More directly, Ford was influenced by the *McGuffey Readers*, for which the magnate had a lifelong devotion. The *Readers* contained a number of stories about Jews and Christians, to the distinct disadvantage of the former. One is based on Shakespeare's *The Merchant of Venice*, in which Shylock demands his pound of flesh. Ford, notes Neil Baldwin, author of the 2001 book, *Henry Ford and the Jews: The Mass Production of Hate*, knew the *Readers* very well, indeed could quote spontaneously from them line-for-line.

Ford's anti-Jewishness had more of loutishness about it than of deep-seated bigotry or malice. Moreover, his limited education and ignorance of public affairs made it relatively easy for him to conclude, as he did, that an "international Jewish banking power" had started World War I and kept it going; that Jews were plotting "to destroy Christian civilization"; and that most Jews were "mere hucksters, traders who don't want to produce, but to make something out of what somebody else produces." While protesting that most Jews were not producers, the magnate employed thousands of Jewish laborers in his plants. "We see that they work, too, and that they don't get into the office," he told a reporter.

As to what prompted Ford to publicly attack Jews, there are a number of theories. His weekly newspaper, the *Dearborn Independent*, needed a circulation boost. "ONE SINGLE SERIES . . . OF FEARLESS, TRUTHFUL, INTERESTING, PLAIN-SPOKEN articles," declared staff member Joseph J. O'Neill in a 1919 report, "may make us known to millions. . . . LET'S HAVE SOME SENSATIONALISM." O'Neill did not suggest a subject, but Ernest G. Liebold, general manager of the *Independent* and Ford's executive secretary, may have done so. Liebold was viciously anti-Semitic, as attested by dozens of his letters in the Ford Archives.

Another powerful influence on Ford may have been exerted by his close friend, Thomas A. Edison. His letters to Ford and Liebold show an anti-Semitic bias and approval of the *Independent*'s anti-Jewish articles.

In making harsh accusations against Jews, as the *Independent* did for 91 straight weeks in 1920–22, Ford referred less to race or religion than to certain traits that he abhorred and for which the term "Jew" seemed convenient. He would conceivably have called J. P. Morgan an "international Jew." He did call some of Morgan's gentile associates "Jews." He also sincerely believed that in exposing "the international Jew's" attempt to disrupt gentile life by war and revolt—thus gaining control of politics, commerce, and finance—he was performing a great service to mankind. He felt that "good Jews" should rejoice in the exposé of the "international" element.

Ford's campaign was the first systematic anti-Semitic crusade in American history. For inventiveness and effrontery, it had few parallels in all of the literature of anti-Semitism. Jewish interests were held responsible for a decline in public and private morals, for intemperance, for high rents, short skirts, rolled stockings, cheap movies, vulgar Broadway shows, gambling, jazz, scarlet fiction, flashy jewelry, nightclubs, and so on. The *Independent* also revived a discredited forgery, *The Protocols of the Learned Elders of Zion*, which contended that Jews everywhere were conspiring to attain world domination.

Many Jews, including editors of Jewish newspapers, were baffled by the attacks, and some, while expressing admiration for Ford and the Model T, asked the manufacturer what they were all about. Some suggested that he must not be aware of the onslaught, or that if he was, he was misinformed; they volunteered to meet with Ford or his representatives to clear up the misunderstanding. Such proposals were slapped down by Liebold. Although no Jewish organizations or groups formally declared a boycott of the Model T, many Jewish firms and individuals ceased buying Fords. So did some gentile firms doing business with Jewish concerns and dependent on their goodwill. Ford branch managers and dealers, particularly those in cities with large Jewish populations, complained of sales declines and economic pressures that the *Independent*'s campaign had brought down upon them.

From 1922 to 1924, the *Independent*'s criticism of Jews was only sporadic, like its criticism of arms-makers, bankers, bootleggers, Wall Street, and Hollywood. Between 1920 and '22, however, Ford arranged for the publication of four brochures, each containing a score

German consuls to Detroit and Cleveland present Henry Ford with a Nazi government award in 1938. Offended American Jews boycotted Ford products.

or more of the *Independent*'s 91 articles, along with a comprehensive compilation of them, entitled *The International Jew*. More than 3000 of these uncopyrighted books were distributed by foreign anti-Semites.

The publications undoubtedly influenced many persons, all the more because they carried the imprint of one of the most famous and successful men in the world. "You have no idea of what a great influence this book had on the thinking of German youth," said Baldur von Schirach, leader of the Nazi youth movement. A prominent Jewish attorney, after a completing a world tour in the mid Twenties, stated that he had seen the brochures in the "most remote corners of the earth." "But for the authority of the Ford name," he maintained, "they would have never seen the light of day and would have been quite harmless if they had. With that magic name they spread like wildfire and became the Bible of every anti-Semite."

Ford's picture was said to be on display at the headquarters of the German National Socialist [Nazi] Party, and the auto king was reported to be financing Adolf Hitler's movement. Hitler denied receiving funds from Ford; in fact his agent reported that "if I had been trying to sell Mr. Ford a wooden nutmeg, he couldn't have shown less interest in [our] proposition." Still, Hitler's ravings and public speeches against Jews frequently were based on Ford's anti-Semitic literature. Ford, moreover, was the only American mentioned in the American edition of Hitler's *Mein Kampf*.

In 1924, the *Independent* launched a second series of anti-Semitic articles under the general title "Jewish Exploitation of Farmer Organizations." The articles dealt in large part with the activities of Aaron Sapiro, a prominent Chicago attorney who had written a standard contract for cooperative farms and had done much to promote this arrangement. When Sapiro was accused of cheating his clients, he filed a million-dollar lawsuit against Henry Ford for defamation of character.

A juror's blunder—an accusation by a woman on the panel that Ford's counsel showed excessive anxiety to keep the case from going to the jury—led to a mistrial. The case then was settled out of court, Sapiro receiving a personal apology from Ford, plus a monetary award. Simultaneously, Ford formally retracted all of his past attacks on Jews. He perhaps did so to spare himself the ordeal of going on the witness stand in front of 118 million Americans. He may also have been influenced by the fact that he was in the midst of the critical changeover from the Model T to the Model A, and could ill afford the hostility of Jews and those sympathetic to them. For good measure, Ford axed the *Independent* a few months after his apology.

For a half-dozen years after 1927, Ford enjoyed amiable relations with Jews. In the early Thirties, however, copies of *The International Jew* began turning up in large numbers throughout Europe and South America. Ford did not countenance the books, but he could not prevent their publication since they had not been copyrighted. Jews nonetheless suspected him of duplicity, and their fears were reinforced in 1938 when the auto king, on his 75th birthday, accepted the Grand Cross of the Supreme Order of the German Eagle, an award created by Hitler and the highest honor Germany could bestow on a foreigner. The award made a vivid impression on American Jewry, and prompted an effective boycott against Ford products. In the meantime, Ford continued to make public statements that gave credence to allegations made against him by Jews.

Shortly after America's entry into World War II, Ford, in a burst of patriotism, sought to close the wide gulf which separated him from the Jewish public. Following a meeting with Richard E. Gutstadt, national director of the Anti-Defamation League of B'nai B'rith, the industrialist issued a nationally publicized statement intended "in our present national and international emergency" to "clarify some general misconceptions concerning my attitude toward my fellow citizens of Jewish faith." Ford stated that he considered the "hate-mongering prevalent for some time in the country against the Jews of distinct disservice to our country, and to the peace and welfare of humanity." Regarding reprints of *The International Jew*, he insisted that he had sanctioned no one to use his name as the sponsor or author of such publications.

Ford's statement ended his generation-long effort to explain his attitude toward Jews. His prejudices were born of ignorance, but he came to believe in their validity. On various occasions he apologized to Jews or "clarified" his stand toward them. But his apologies were self-serving. His anti-Semitism remained with him to the end, and was the darkest blot on his career.

Depression!

AS PANICKED URBAN DWELLERS besieged banks across America, the nation's farmers suffered unimaginable drought that turned their precious topsoil into useless dust. As a result, thousands of farms were repossessed. President Herbert Hoover took the fall for these calamities, losing the 1932 election to Franklin D. Roosevelt, a patrician easterner with an uncommon understanding of the common man. He became a symbol of hope and recovery when he ramrodded his "New Deal" plans into law in 1933.

Japan illegally occupied Chinese Manchuria in 1931, setting in motion events that, eventually, Japan would not be able to control. In 1933, moderate politicians in Germany unwisely appointed Adolf Hitler chancellor, assuming they could control him. But by 1934, Hitler had declared himself *Führer*, and instigated repressive laws against Jews. He invaded Poland in 1939, igniting World War II. In an acknowledgment of strong isolationist sentiment, FDR did not immediately involve the U.S. in the conflict.

Charles Lindbergh's infant son was kidnapped and killed in 1932. Aviatrix Amelia Earhart vanished above the mid Pacific in '37, and a rogue's gallery of wild punks who robbed small-town banks became legends. Among them, John Dillinger and Clyde Barrow professed a fondness for the Ford V-8.

1930

- Model A is freshened up with a new grille, hood, and cowl

- New passenger-car models include a Victoria coupe and two-door phaeton

- Ford customers can now select several models with DeLuxe trim

- Production falls by nearly 400,000 cars

- New plants open in Edgewater, New Jersey, and Long Beach, California, to replace older facilities

- Extended-wheelbase chassis added to Model AA truck line

▶ The Model A lineup grew broader with the addition of some new styles. One of the new-comers was this two-door phaeton. It was a DeLuxe-trim alternative to the traditional four-door phaeton and sold for $645. Late in the year, a five-passenger Victoria coupe joined the roster.

◀ A taller, narrower grille tipped off passersby that the Model A Ford approaching them was a 1930 version. Of course, that change required a new hood design that flowed into a widened cowl. Reshaped fenders and headlamp buckets completed the package. One of the jauntiest bearers of the new look was the $645 cabriolet convertible, which drew 25,868 orders during the calendar year.

▲ Roadster buyers with a little extra cash to lavish on their motoring budget could opt for a DeLuxe rumble-seat version. For $495, they drove home a car equipped with cowl lights, a tan top, tan leather upholstery, and brown carpeting.

▶ Aside from the two-door phaeton and the Victoria, both of which came only with DeLuxe appointments, Ford also newly offered customers DeLuxe versions of the rumble-seat roadster, five-window coupe, and Fordor sedan. On sedans, the principal improvement was inside, where seats were upholstered in a choice of mohair or bedford cord, and a better grade of headlining was used. A DeLuxe sedan cost $650.

► As the Ford passenger-car lines were expanded, so were the truck offerings. Among the new models cataloged were several dump-bed styles that offered a choice of manual, mechanical, or hydraulic operation. All were built on the 131-inch-wheelbase Model AA chassis. Truck styling was carried over from 1929 until June, when updated styling—including a new cab design—and a companion 157-inch-chassis Model AA debuted.

◄ Little by little, flying was gaining acceptance from travelers by the start of the Thirties, thanks in large part to the Ford Tri-Motor. But government contracts to deliver airmail were still the most dependable source of revenue for many early airlines. The Tri-Motor's deep cross-section wings provided storage space for mail sacks. The Depression began to slow down Ford aircraft production in '30.

LINCOLN

► The Model L, direct descendant of the original Leland-built Lincolns, was in its final year in 1930. As such, little was done to change the cars. During the year, fenders painted to match the dominant body color became standard and a shift to five-lug wheels was made. Among the 3515 Lincolns made during calendar-year 1930 was this seven-passenger limousine with body by Willoughby with its odd Brewster windshield.

- Lincoln introduces Model K series with all-new styling and chassis, more-powerful engine

- Ford cars adopt new body-color sections in grille shells and one-piece running-board splash aprons; sedans later add slightly canted windshields

- 20-millionth Ford manufactured

- Henry Ford tries to stay optimistic amid Depression gloom; "These are really good times, but only a few know it," he says in a March interview

- Still, calendar-year output of the Model A falls by more than 550,000 cars; Ford slips back behind Chevrolet in sales

- More body types offered for Model AA

FORD ▲ The Model A moved into its final year on the market with minimal change. This town sedan shows the revised grille shell with body-color-matching sections, as well as the slightly sloped windshield adopted for four-doors in mid 1931.

▲ A new—and rare—addition to the Model A family was the convertible sedan, with a folding top that tracked up and down on fixed side rails. A DeLuxe-equipped $640 car that appeared at the end of May, it accounted for 4864 domestic-market sales.

▶ With the chance to be on the market for a full year, orders for the Victoria coupe shot up to 33,906. The car started the year offering shoppers a choice of an exposed metal roof or one covered in artificial leather. Beginning in April, though, only the former was offered. The Victoria came with a standard rear-mounted spare tire and offered some enclosed luggage space in the rear bustle; it was accessible by pulling forward the rear seatback. Owners could get added cargo space by ordering a side-mounted spare and a rear trunk rack.

◄ Henry Ford himself drove the 20-millionth Ford off the River Rouge assembly line on April 14, 1931. A town sedan with the new visorless slanted-windshield style, it was dispatched to Fair Lane to pose for pictures with the first Quadricycle before being sent off on a national promotional tour. Despite the attention the car brought to Ford in Depression-wracked America, U.S.-market production sank drastically to 488,059 cars.

▲ The Ford station wagon straddled the line between passenger car and commercial car. It featured the brightly trimmed frontal styling of the passenger models, but rode on the Model A commercial-car chassis. Murray and Baker-Raulang assembled the wood bodies.

▲ Another of Ford's part-car/part-truck vehicles was the DeLuxe delivery. Its Budd-built body featured a cargo area 57.6 inches long, 43.6 inches wide, and 45.8 inches tall. In the spring of 1931, a drop-floor version with added cargo space was offered.

▲ The interesting—and short-lived—DeLuxe pickup was new to the '31 Model A commercial line. Bowing on May 1, it was a good 25 years ahead of its time, featuring as it did a smooth-side bed that appeared to be integrated with the cab and chromed bed rails.

▲ The real workhorses of the Ford truck family continued to be the Model AA 1½-ton jobs. The array of commercial bodies that could be ordered from the factory was expanded, but that didn't prevent outside suppliers from building specialty bodies to meet specific needs.

LINCOLN

▶ Lincoln leapt into the modern mode with its 1931 models, the all-new K series. Riding a wheelbase stretched out to 145 inches on a redesigned frame, the new Lincolns were able to make good use of a more-substantial grille and hood. One thing that didn't change was Lincoln's reliance on top coachbuilders for many of its body styles. Dietrich created this four-passenger convertible.

◀ Among Lincoln's several factory-built body designs was a five-passenger phaeton distinguished by fan-shaped front quarter vent windows that could be retracted into the doors. As a dual-cowl model with a separate windshield for rear passengers, it neared the 5000-pound mark, sold for $4600, and reached 77 well-off customers. Model K starting prices ranged from $4400 for phaetons to $7400 for Brunn and Willoughby town cars.

▶ Perhaps the least-changed aspect of the new line of Lincolns was the engine, and even that was notably improved. The 60-degree design and displacement of 384.8 cubic inches were retained, but horsepower was boosted to 120. Compression was raised, valve timing was altered, and a new Stromberg dual-downdraft carburetor fed into a revised intake manifold. At 275 built, this LeBaron convertible was the marque's most popular open car.

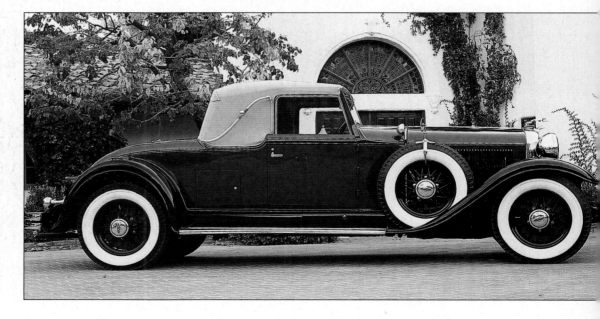

- Ford pulls off another publicity coup when it introduces a V-8 engine to the low-price field in late March

- Four-cylinder fans aren't forgotten; an improved version of the Model A engine is offered as well

- Perky new Lincoln-inspired styling graces '32 Fords; the car's look and the "flathead" V-8 will make the "Deuce" a darling of hot rodders for years to come

- Not to be upstaged, Lincoln brings out a V-12; Edsel Ford paces the Indianapolis 500 in one

- Model BB trucks feature new cabs and chassis revisions

- Production slumps again; 16 assembly sites close during the year, many never to reopen

▲ Henry Ford poses with the 90-degree L-head mono-bloc V-8 he put in his namesake car in early 1932. Finally convinced of the need for something more than four cylinders, but disdainful of sixes, he issued orders in 1929 to begin development of an eight.

FORD ▲ A three-inch stretch in wheelbase (to 106.5) and new styling touches like a vee'd body-color grille shell and ribbed single-bar bumpers bestowed a degree of elegance on '32 Fords. This DeLuxe roadster is one of 2283 built with a V-8 for the domestic market.

► The V-8 Ford debuted on March 31, 1932. Designated the Model 18, its 221-cubic-inch V-8 produced an advertised 65 horsepower at 3400 rpm. The compression ratio was 5.5:1. Engineers Emil Zoerlein, Carl Schultz, and Ray Laird secretly developed the engine on Henry Ford's orders. Featuring aluminum pistons and a single-barrel carburetor, its block was cast as a single unit, which was a key factor in keeping down the manufacturing cost. As a result, a V-8 Ford, like this DeLuxe phaeton, sold for just $50 more than a four-cylinder Ford.

► The '32 Ford featured a new frame design and 18-inch-diameter wheels in place of the 19-inchers used previously. This lowered the car's center of gravity and improved handling. The Fordor sedan was one of five body styles available in a choice of basic or DeLuxe trim. (Some other models were built only with one level of equipment or the other.) DeLuxes came with cowl lamps and a nicer grade of upholstery. V-8 DeLuxe sedans started at $645, or $55 more than a base Model 18.

▲ The five-passenger Victoria coupe was another of the Fords that made the jump from the Model A era into the V-8 generation. In Britain, *The Motor* published a road test in which it reported pushing a Model 18 "Vicky" from 0 to 60 mph in 16.8 seconds.

▲ Ford began the year with another four-cylinder car, the Model B. Its engine displaced 200.5 cubic inches, as in the Model A, but horsepower was hiked to 50. Of course, Model Bs, like this DeLuxe Tudor sedan, lacked V-8 badging on hubcaps and the headlamp tie bar.

▲ Coupe customers could choose between a Sport model (with the look of a cabriolet with its top up), a three-window version, or this five-window type. When ordered with a rumble seat, as is this V-8-powered example, $25 was tacked on to the tab.

▲ The most expensive car in the 1932 Ford line was the Model 18 convertible sedan. With the V-8 under-hood, it sold for at least $650. In that form, it garnered just 842 orders. Another 44 were built as Model Bs. All featured DeLuxe trim.

◄ Slightly facelifted styling details hid the fact that a new V-12 engine was under the hood of certain 1932 Lincolns. Dubbed the Model KB, they were powered by a 150-horsepower, 447.9-cid powerplant. The 65-degree L-head engine featured seven main bearings to support its meaty crankshaft. KBs, with prices in the $4300-$7200 range, continued to rest on the 145-inch wheelbase ushered in for the '31 Model K. This five-passenger sedan was one of 216 made.

▶ The duo that made up the vaudeville comedy team of Olsen and Johnson pose with a new KB four-door sedan. Aside from the five-seat version, there was a seven-passenger model that cost $4700 and accounted for 266 orders. All 1932 Lincolns featured a revised radiator style, a switch to hood vent doors, fender-top parking lights, and 18-inch-diameter wire wheels. Various coach-builders provided bodies.

◄ Brunn ran off just two of the Double-Entry Sport Sedan—both with different upper bodywork and paint schemes—for Lincoln's toney Salon shows. Built on the KB chassis, they featured long doors that could be opened from either end. Lincoln still made a V-8 line, now called the KA. Horsepower of the carry-over engine was nudged to 125; wheelbase reverted to 136 inches.

1933

- Fords are completely redesigned on a new, longer chassis

- V-8 engine sees numerous improvements

- Lincoln KA adopts new "small" V-12

- Ford production rises past 300,000 cars; Lincoln output falls by more than 50 percent

- Essentially stock Fords take first seven places at prestigious Elgin Road Races in Illinois

- Greenfield Village historical park formally opens on June 12

- Last of 199 Tri-Motor aircraft produced

FORD ▲ Ford unveiled an all-new car, the Model 40, on February 9, 1933. Built on a 112-inch-wheelbase chassis that featured a new frame with a central X-member, the Model 40 was 17.4 inches longer overall than the '32. Up-to-the-minute styling included a raked, slim-profile grille, an absence of running-board splash aprons, and skirted fenders.

◄ Prices of the 1933 Fords were about $15 higher than those of their immediate predecessors. They ranged from $425 for a four-cylinder two-seat roadster to $610 for a DeLuxe V-8 Fordor sedan. The most-wanted open car in the lineup was the DeLuxe V-8 cabriolet: The $585 rumble-seat-equipped convertible tempted 7852 buyers. (Another 24 customers ordered the same car with the four-cylinder engine.) Cowl lamps, twin chrome horns, and dual taillights were part of the DeLuxe equipment.

▲ Station wagons continued to roll on the commercial chassis but delivered a lot of DeLuxe passenger-car style. Snap-in curtains continued to stand in for glass windows in the doors, rear quarters, and tailgate.

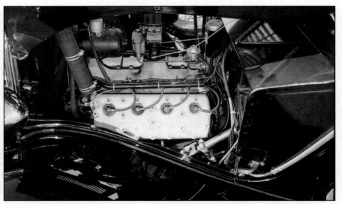

▲ The Ford V-8 got aluminum heads with a higher 6.3:1 compression that helped deliver a nominal 75 horsepower. Cooling and ignition were improved, too. The four-cylinder remained available, but unpopular.

▲ Early on, the V-8 labored under the suspicion that it would burn far more gas than a four. To counter, the company commissioned economy runs that showed results of 18.3 to 22.5 mpg in varied, rigorous drives.

▲ Miss America for 1933, Marion Bergeron, of Connecticut, waves from atop the hood of a DeLuxe V-8 Fordor sedan. Production came to 45,443, well more than twice the number of base-trim V-8 four-doors.

LINCOLN

▶ Lincoln's biggest news for 1933 had to do with the "lesser" KA series, which adopted a 381.7-cid L-head V-12 quite unlike any previous Lincoln engine. The real prestige, though, continued to reside in the more august KB range. One of the more intriguing members of the line was this Judkins-bodied sedan limousine, a seven-passenger vehicle with a divider window between the front and rear seats.

◀ Distinguishing external features of the new Lincolns were a return to hood louvers, skirted fenders, and the deletion of a full-width headlamp tie bar. What couldn't be seen were a stronger chassis, reworked transmission, new thermostatic shock absorbers, and brakes with driver-adjustable pressure settings. But the Great Depression still gripped America and Lincoln sales were substantially down. For example, the Model KB Judkins coupe found just 12 buyers.

EDSEL FORD
Unsung Hero

EDSEL FORD WAS A CHILD of the automotive age. As a six-week-old in 1893, he heard one of America's newest sounds—the sputter of his father's first gasoline engine. When less than three years old, he rode in Henry Ford's first car, also one of America's first motor vehicles. In adulthood, Edsel was one of the world's leading auto executives. Yet he is little known.

Edsel shunned publicity throughout his life. When asked by company publicists to pose for pictures at business functions, his usual reply was, "See if you can't get father to do that. He likes that sort of thing. I don't." Edsel's reputation for shunting newsmen to the elder Ford provoked the *Philadelphia Inquirer* to complain in 1942 that his longest statement to the press had been, "See father."

What kind of a man was Edsel? First and foremost, he was a gentle man and a gentleman. Almost every account of him mentions, if not emphasizes, this point. "He was a gentleman under all circumstances," observed W. C. Cowling, Ford's sales chief during the Twenties. "Edsel Ford was always a true gentleman," echoed H. C. Doss, a Cowling successor. "You always figured there was one gentleman here," remarked an engineer who worked on the Model A, "and that someday he was going to run the place, and that it would be a fine place to work when he was running it."

Although Edsel was devoid of character flaws or major faults, he was criticized on two counts. In 1918, his father's political opponents badgered him over Henry's decision to keep him on the job and out of World War I. Others complained at times that he should remonstrate more strongly against some of his father's actions.

Edsel's confidential secretary, A. J. Lepine, probably knew his boss better than anyone except Edsel's family. Interviewed by the Ford Archives in 1952, he described Edsel as follows:

"He had a keen mentality . . . and bright, observing, intelligent eyes. . . . He had a sense of humor, quick laugh, and a bright smile. He also had a very good memory . . . and was even-tempered and well-controlled. . . . He never said anything sarcastic or resentful about people. He expressed his disapproval with silence. . . . He never used profanity, well, hardly ever," the secretary corrected himself. "He might come out occasionally with some apt expression . . . but he didn't use just any cheap language."

An immaculate dresser, Edsel wore tailored suits and London- and New York-made shoes with thick soles (perhaps because he was five-feet-six inches in height, although he seemed taller because he was slender and stood straight). He smoked in his office lounge, ignoring his father's ban on smoking on company property. He also drank alcohol socially, despite paternal disapproval.

Beginning in his teens, Edsel daily visited Ford's Highland Park plant, where he made himself useful in the mail and experimental rooms. He was named company secretary at age 22, president at 26. As an indication of his father's faith in him, in 1920, he was given 41.6 percent of the company's stock, instantly making him one of America's wealthiest men.

During the Twenties, Edsel increasingly assumed responsibility for the business side of management. Working quietly and efficiently, he had a better grasp of the company's worldwide activities than anyone else. Also, far more than his father, he maintained organizational cohesiveness and kept the great ship on course.

While administering the company, Edsel devoted untiring attention to his great love—styling. It was he who brought to the automobile industry the realization that an automobile could be beautiful as well as functional. Working with the leading auto body designers/builders of the day, he literally transformed the Lincoln from one of the ugliest of cars into the world's most attractive mass-produced vehicle.

Edsel's devotion to styling led to the 1923–24 design improvements that enabled the Model T to dominate the U.S. auto market for several years longer than it otherwise would have. A few years later, his contribution to Model A styling prompted his father's remark, "We've got a good man in my son. He knows style—how a car ought to look."

Edsel also was the driving force behind the studied elegance of the company's 1936 Lincoln-Zephyr, the first successful streamlined car (although it cannibalized the larger Lincoln's sales). He also inspired the pre-World War II Lincoln Continental, Frank Lloyd Wright's choice as the most beautiful car of all time, and certainly one of the world's most admired cars.

Within the company, Edsel was responsible for sales, advertising, purchasing, and what is now called strategic planning, plus financial operations. His supervision could be close. For example, he personally approved every company advertisement. He was not given responsibility for engineering or manufacturing (his father's preserve) nor, unfortunately, for labor relations, which his father delegated to his tough aide, Harry Bennett.

In the best of times, the pillars of the Ford Motor Company were Henry Ford and his son, Edsel. They are seen here with Edsel's wife, Eleanor, and sons Benson (second from left) and Henry II (center).

Apart from design, Edsel's great love was aviation. Thanks mostly to Edsel, the prime motivator of Ford's aviation activities, the company was the world's leading civilian-aircraft manufacturer during the last half of the Twenties and early Thirties. During this period, it also pioneered guided flight by radio; started America's first all-metal, multiengine commercial airline fleet; and inaugurated the first regularly scheduled passenger airline in continuous domestic service. Ford also was the first firm to fly contract airmail in the U.S., and built one of the world's first airport hotels, the Dearborn Inn.

Edsel also had charge of the company's pavilions at the world's fairs and big regional expositions of the 1934–40 era. In 1935, he visited San Diego's California-Pacific Exposition 19 times without being recognized by newsmen or other visitors. He was delighted.

Edsel and his wife, Eleanor, were noted philanthropists and patrons of the arts. They were the leading benefactors of the Detroit Institute of Arts, and virtually adopted the institution during the depressed years of the Thirties.

One of their most important legacies is the institute's renowned Diego Rivera murals depicting industrial Detroit. Upset that the murals reflected Rivera's communist beliefs, the *Detroit News* and others urged that the artwork be "whitewashed and forgotten." Edsel, in the name of artistic freedom, allowed the work to remain.

As time progressed, Edsel's relationship with his father deteriorated and was painful. Henry, so proud of Edsel during his youth, failed to rejoice in and make constructive use of his son's admirable qualities. On the contrary, he restricted and nullified them in an unceasing effort to remold Edsel into a hard-nosed executive such as Harry Bennett. Edsel, however, remained true to himself.

Edsel's mother, Clara, watched fearfully as tensions mounted between father and son. For his part, Edsel, although often frustrated and sometimes heartsick over treatment received from his father, had too much filial loyalty to fight back. "Father built this business," he would say, "and if that's the way Father wants it, that's the way it's going to be." But years of persecution and the gulf between the two men took their toll. Some thought that the antagonism wore down Edsel's spirit and body.

Edsel's last two years were devoted mostly to company war work. To friends who expressed concern about his failing health and suggested he slow his pace, he merely shook his head and replied, "The war won't wait."

In January 1942, Edsel underwent an operation for stomach ulcers. Although able to resume his duties after a short rest, he fell ill again, of stomach cancer, later that year. Continuing to work until mid April 1943, he died on May 26 at the age of 49. His death dealt Henry and Clara Ford the severest blow of their lives, one from which Henry, particularly, never recovered.

Edsel is buried in Detroit's Woodlawn Cemetery. Not one of the Detroit newsmen who wrote his obituaries and/or attended his funeral service knew him. Some of the writers admitted that they had seen him only at public meetings, if at all.

Numerous efforts have been made to honor Edsel's memory. Aside from the ill-fated Edsel car, they include Detroit's Edsel Ford Expressway, now a part of I-94; the Henry Ford Hospital's Edsel B. Ford Institute for Medical Research; Dearborn's Edsel Ford High School; Detroit's Henry and Edsel Ford Auditorium; the Edsel Ford Library at Hotchkiss School, Lakeville, Connecticut; the Edsel Bryant Ford Professorship of Business Administration, Harvard University; and the Edsel and Eleanor Ford Wing of the Detroit Institute of Arts. In 1968, Edsel became one of the first 10 inductees into the Automotive Hall of Fame. He is mentioned in two State of Michigan historical markers. One stands before the Edison Avenue home in Detroit in which he lived with his parents from 1908 to 1915. The other marks the gracious Grosse Pointe Shores, Michigan, mansion in which he found more peace and quiet than anywhere else in the world. The estate is open to the public.

- Ford Motor Company comes out ahead by $3.7 million, its first profitable year since 1930
- Ford and Lincoln lines show more refinement than innovation in styling

- and engineering; both makes record production increases
- All Lincolns now powered by a single engine, an enlargement of the year-old KA powerplant

- Production of the Ford four-cylinder engine is discontinued in March
- Teetotaling Henry Ford allows alcohol to be served at new-model press preview

- Notorious bank robbers Clyde Barrow and John Dillinger write Henry in praise of the V-8
- Ford Rotunda exhibit building opens at World's Fair in Chicago

FORD

► Subtle variations to the '34 Ford included a flatter grille with a thicker surround, straight-edged hood louvers, twin hood latches, and shallower headlamp buckets. This DeLuxe V-8 Fordor is outfitted with an accessory trunk predictive of the sort of built-in cargo compartments that would soon have a big influence on sedan buyers.

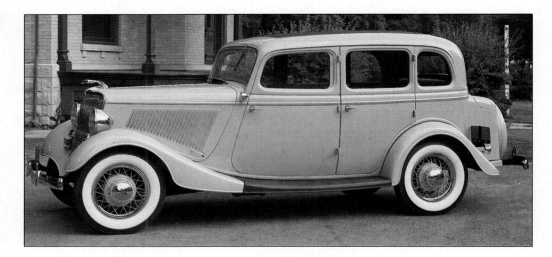

▲ Production of the Model 40A—as the '34s were known—came to more than 515,000 cars. The most popular of all was the base V-8 Tudor: 124,870 built.

▲ Closed cars, like this DeLuxe V-8 five-window coupe, adopted "clear vision" ventilation. Front-door glass was adjustable to provide an opening at the forward edge.

▲ Elliott Roosevelt, son of then-President Franklin D. Roosevelt, poses with his '33 Ford phaeton in May 1934. Henry Ford and FDR were often at loggerheads.

▲ Even with a $20 price increase to $660, sales of the V-8 station wagon nearly doubled to 2905 in 1934. Just 95 were built with the short-lived four-cylinder, though.

▲ The Model BB trucks that appeared for 1932 were only slightly changed in the succeeding two years. One change for '34 was a switch to a full-floating rear axle. V-8 installations in trucks grew as rapidly as in cars.

▲ Two wheelbase lengths were available for the 1½-ton BB chassis, 131.5 inches and 157 inches. Bus builders paid $510 for a long-wheelbase chassis like the one here, upon which a Wayne body has been added.

LINCOLN

▶ Lincoln's available roster of coachbuilders for its semicustom bodies was reduced by 1934—the Depression had seen to that. Just 159 cars with bodies by Brunn, LeBaron, Judkins, Dietrich, and Willoughby were turned out, including just 15 of this Brunn town brougham. The seven-passenger vehicle was built on the 145-inch KB chassis. It sold for $6800, which by then was the top starting price for a new Lincoln.

▲ Model KA Lincolns, such as this Victoria coupe, continued with the 136-inch wheelbase instituted for 1932, but they no longer had their own engine. The 1933-vintage KA V-12 was enlarged to 414 cubic inches and became the sole powerplant for all Lincolns. This unit made 150 horsepower, the same as the KB's old engine.

▲ A body-color grille shell, a return to hood vents, and more-thoroughly skirted fenders keyed '34 Lincoln styling. Factory output rose to 2433 cars, led by the KA four-door town sedan, which drew 450 orders.

1935

- Completely restyled Model 48 line vaults Ford past Chevrolet for the year's sales leadership

- Repositioned seating improves passenger comfort; Ford calls it "Center-Poise Ride"

- A four-door convertible and sedans with built-in trunks are new model offerings

- Lincoln also gets new styling and reconfigured seating

- Ford trucks completely redone; Model 51 replaces Model BB

- Test track opens in Dearborn; Edsel Ford forms first styling staff

- Fleet of Ford-powered racers runs at Indy 500

▶ Sensational new looks, improved ride, and important mechanical refinements made the Model 48 Ford the best-selling car in America in 1935. Nearly 820,000 were made. The roadster was arguably the sportiest of the year's styles and it was the least-expensive DeLuxe-trim car. Prices started at $550 for the two-seat job.

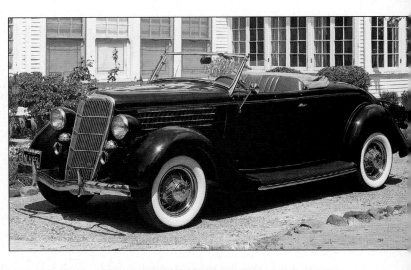

▲ Ford clung to transverse leaf springs at both ends of its cars, but for '35, the front spring was moved ahead of the front axle. This allowed the engine and seats to be moved forward for a better ride in models like the DeLuxe five-window coupe.

▲ Buyers of DeLuxe Tudor and Fordor sedans could, for the first time, choose between the traditional "flatback" model or this new "trunkback" style.

▲ The DeLuxe level also offered coupe shoppers a choice between the five-window or this three-window version. At $570, the three-window cost $10 more.

▶ Opting for a trunkless sedan saved a Ford customer $20, but that wasn't enough to prevent many buyers from springing for the added convenience, especially as "hard times" were beginning to ease. This DeLuxe Tudor sedan, with a $575 base price, attracted 84,692 orders; the companion touring sedan with trunk saw 87,326 copies. The gap was even greater among Fordor buyers. Regardless of trim or style, all '35 Fords came with improved mechanical brakes.

► Driver Ted Horn (right) prepares to settle into his Miller-Tucker-Ford racer for the 1935 Indianapolis 500. Preston Tucker got Ford backing for car builder Harry Miller to build a fleet of front-wheel-drive racers with modified Ford V-8 engines. Four of the cars qualified for the race, but all dropped out—three of them sidelined by the same unforeseen steering problem. Horn's 16th-place finish was the best for the Fords. A DeLuxe convertible sedan served as pace car for the event.

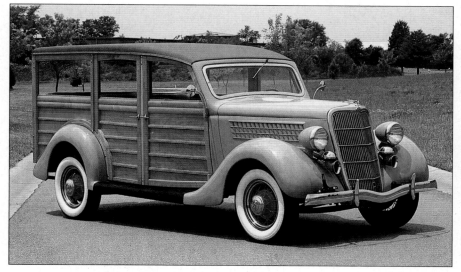

◄ Ford's station wagon featured a new body design. There was a changed pattern to the horizontal side ribs and a switch to front-hinged front doors, which now included roll-up glass windows. The spare tire moved from the right front fender to the tailgate. At $670, it was second only to the new convertible sedan in terms of price. Highlights of the new Ford look included a narrower, streamlined grille, sleek body-color "bullet" headlight shells, chrome-trimmed horizontal hood louvers, and enveloping fenders. External horns made their final appearance in '35.

LINCOLN

► Lincoln tried to advance by retreating in '35. It dropped all models selling for less than $4000 to concentrate on its costlier higher-profit cars. Among them was this leather-topped Judkins berline. The five-place vehicle cost $5500; just 34 were made. While two chassis lengths were still offered, all Lincolns were now listed as Model Ks again. A new grille, fenders, and headlamps updated the appearance.

1936

- Ford surges ahead of Chevrolet in model-year output

- Chevrolet catches Ford to claim calendar-year production victory

- Subtle styling revisions, including graceful vertical grille bars, result in collectible classic

- Ford builds 3-millionth V-8 engine

- Streamlined Lincoln-Zephyr debuts

- Henry Ford backs Kansas Governor Alfred E. Landon for president

FORD ▲ Edsel and Henry Ford pose with a group including aviation pioneer Orville Wright (third from left). In January, Henry wrote to Wright to ask that he "give back to America" the airplane with which he and his late brother, Wilbur, made history. The plane is now on display at the National Air and Space Museum.

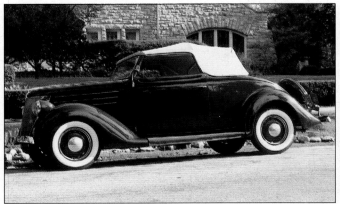

▲ A painted coupelike windshield frame and a more complete all-weather top are key items that distinguish this $675 club cabriolet from the $65 less-expensive roadster. Only 4616 were produced.

▲ Early '36 convertible sedans were "fastbacks." Because increasingly sophisticated buyers wanted more luggage space and a concealed spare tire, it became a "trunkback" by the middle of the year.

▲ This DeLuxe five-window coupe cost $580 including the $25 rumble seat. Without rear seats, Ford determined that roll-down rear windows were not needed.

▲ Fordor buyers could again choose between the fastback body shown here, or the increasingly popular trunkback. Trunkbacks added $25.

▲ Celebrities didn't always choose domestically built vehicles. Here, Clark Gable drives a strikingly stream-lined British Jensen-Ford custom cabriolet. Rakish suicide doors had been abandoned on U.S. Fords.

CUNNINGHAM BROUGHAM

▲ Rare even in its day, this specially bodied Brougham town car came from the Cunningham Motor Car Company. Though riding on Ford mechanicals, it was identified as a Cunningham.

▲ The rakish-looking DeLuxe cabriolet featured the same engine as the rest of the Ford lineup; a 221-cubic-inch, 85-horsepower, "flathead" V-8. Wire spokes were replaced across the line by new "artillery-style" wheels. Once a prominent front-end feature on all Ford cars, horns were moved under the hood and out of sight.

▲ Unlike standard panel trucks, this DeLuxe edition had twin chrome horns, body-colored wheels, white-wall tires, and additional body insulation.

▲ Trucks, such as this V-8 pickup, still had externally mounted horns. Ford's light-duty trucks were still based on what was essentially its car chassis.

LINCOLN

▶ An evolving Ford Motor Company is showcased by an old-era Lincoln K (right) and new Lincoln-Zephyr (left) flanking a contemporary Ford. While all three cars are 1936 models, the Lincoln's V-12 engine and custom coach-work represented an era fast coming to a close.

EUGENE T. "BOB" GREGORIE
Edsel's Collaborator

EUGENE T. GREGORIE WAS Edsel Ford's styling alter ego, and the pair had more creative synergy than any other Detroit designer and auto leader. Their most important collaboration was the Lincoln Continental, a design Gregorie sketched in less than an hour.

Born on New York's Long Island in 1908, Gregorie, the son of a prosperous importer, skipped college in favor of working for a New Jersey yacht builder and a New York naval architectural firm. Wishing to design cars, he moved to Detroit in 1929, working briefly for General Motors. Joining Ford as a body designer in 1931, he soon caught Edsel Ford's eye. As he gained rapport with Edsel, Gregorie found himself answering more and more to the company's president. The relationship rankled Gregorie's superiors, though.

The first memorable car associated with Gregorie was the '36 Lincoln-Zephyr, designed to fill a gap in the medium-price field. The Zephyr's basic design came from John Tjaarda, of Briggs Manufacturing Company, a Ford supplier. Edsel, dissatisfied with the front of Tjaarda's concept, directed Gregorie to work with the Briggs stylist in developing an improved one. In the process they fashioned the first successful streamlined car in America. "By refining and completing the styling done by Tjaarda," engineer Larry Sheldrick said later, Gregorie "made his reputation with Edsel," and paved the way for the 27-year-old to become chief of Ford's Design Department, established in 1935.

Edsel expressed interest in a "continental-type" car after returning from a 1932 trip to Europe. In 1933–34, Gregorie designed two "one-off" sports cars for his patron. The concept went on the back burner until 1938, when Gregorie envisioned a "continental" on a Zephyr chassis. The next morning, he sketched a long-hood, short-deck design for the car he had in mind, and in the afternoon showed it to Edsel, whose reaction was, "Oh, boy! That looks great! That's it! Don't change a line on it." During prototype construction, it was realized that the trunk was too small to hold a spare tire. The solution: mount the spare outside of the trunk; a Continental trademark was born.

An immediate hit with Edsel's friends in Florida, the Lincoln-Zephyr Continental was ordered into production. Owners included Babe Ruth, Pablo Picasso, and Clark Gable, who rushed out to buy one after seeing the model given to Mickey Rooney by Henry Ford. Acclaimed architect Frank Lloyd Wright declared it "the most beautiful car in the world."

Gregorie, like other Ford executives, was orphaned by Edsel's death in 1943. During an ensuing purge, he was fired. After spending a year as a Detroit design consultant, Gregorie was invited by Henry Ford II to rejoin the Ford organization. He sailed along until HFII brought in Ernest Breech as executive vice president in August 1946. In the ensuing scramble to design an all-new Ford for 1949, Breech's new engineering chief, Harold Youngren, hired an outside styling consultant, George Walker. When a design from the Walker team was selected for the '49 Ford, Gregorie had had enough (though his theme was adopted for the 1949 Mercury). Resigning on December 15, 1946, at age 38, Gregorie moved to Florida, where he designed and supervised construction of big trawler yachts.

For many years, he and his wife, Evelyn, lived aboard handsome cabin cruisers, then settled on St. Augustine's Anastasia Island. The designer died at age 94 in St. Augustine on December 1, 2002.

◄ ▼ The most popular of the all-new Lincoln-Zephyrs was the four-door sedan. An unusually low ride height allowed passengers to step directly from the car to the ground, allowing the marketing people to refer to the running boards as "narrow, rubber-covered side bumpers."

▲ ► The front and rear doors opened at opposite ends, creating an extra large space when opened simultaneously, but front passengers were still required to negotiate past a central pillar. The Lincoln-Zephyr sedan had a base price of $1320.

◄ A father proudly presents the cavernous rear-passenger compartment of this Lincoln seven-passenger limousine to his family. The limousine was Lincoln's best-selling model, and with a starting price of $4700, it was also the most expensive. The private rear compartment featured two forward-facing jump seats that folded out of the way when not in use.

► Lincoln convertible sedans were available in short- and long-wheelbase versions, the $5500 long-wheelbase LeBaron and the $5000 short-wheelbase phaeton pictured here. Combined sales of both models totaled just 45 cars, only 15 of which were phaetons. While the LeBaron was considered a "custom" vehicle and had to be special ordered through the coachbuilder, "semicustom" phaetons could be ordered from the factory.

◄ With a $4200 asking price, the five-passenger coupe was among the year's least-expensive Lincolns. Despite the price, the coupe was also one of the least popular; only 36 were sold.

► Though stylish even with the top up, the convertible Victoria afforded drivers little rearward visibility when protected from the elements. The $5500 car was expensive and rare; only 10 found homes.

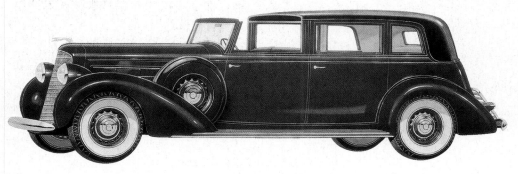

◄ A standard-equipment phone allowed chauffeurs to keep in contact with passengers of this $6700 Brougham. Only 10 of these stately limousines were sold during the model year.

► At the Dearborn test track, Henry and Edsel stand behind display models of Ford's V-8 offerings. A smaller-displacement version of Ford's existing 85-horse-power V-8, rated at 60 horsepower, was newly available. Ford advertising now boasted, "High mileage, low price and a choice of two engines."

- 25-millionth Ford built

- Ford offers car buyers a second engine choice, a new, smaller V-8

- Ford strongmen and union organizers clash at the "Battle of the Overpass"

- Newly streamlined Fords receive steel roofs

- Last year for slantback bodies

- Aging Lincoln K-series cars receive their last redesign

- A Ford V-8 wins the Monte Carlo rally

- President Franklin Roosevelt purchases a Ford convertible sedan for use at his personal retreat

◄ Tudor "trunkback" sedans came in both standard and DeLuxe trim levels. Though the trunkless "slantbacks" were also equipped with trunklids, actual storage space was nominal. Tudor trunkback prices: $638 in standard trim, $674 for DeLuxes.

▲ Standard Fords, like this two-seat coupe, had painted windshield surrounds and a single windshield wiper. Whitewall tires were added by the owner.

▲ A standard "woody" wagon could have roll-down front windows and sliding-glass rear panels, or be equipped with side curtains in back for $20 less.

▲ Aimed at small business, the sedan delivery was a passenger-car-based model. The spare could be mounted inside, or on the rear cargo door as shown here.

▲ This DeLuxe convertible sedan shows off Ford's swept-back vee grille, fuller fenders with faired-in headlamps, and two-piece vee windshield.

▲ Al Pearce, host of radio's popular *Al Pearce and His Gang*, stands proudly next to his Ford Deluxe sedan. Pearce's skit-based comedy show ran from 1933 until 1947 and help launch the careers of a number of young talents, including Mel Blanc.

LINCOLN

▲ ▼ New to the Zephyr line was the three-passenger coupe. Sporting the same rakish front end as other Zephyrs, and wearing one of the lowest price tags, the three-passenger coupe quickly became one of Lincoln's most popular cars. While K-series sales stagnated, the fresh-looking new Zephyrs helped boost Lincoln sales to just under 30,000, an all-time high.

▲ The Zephyr's redesigned instrument panel featured a stylish vertical column that housed major instruments, as well as the radio and speaker.

▲ Though low-priced for a Lincoln, the "easy to own" Zephyr coupe cost almost twice as much as a standard Ford five-window coupe. Whitewalls were extra.

- Sharp recession slows economy after mid-Thirties recovery
- Ford output tumbles by half, Chevrolet recovers number-one sales spot

- Industry production falls 40 percent
- Slantback bodies disappear from lineup
- Henry Ford II elected to board of directors

- Lincoln-Zephyrs receive first major restyling
- Ford pickups sport oval grille as part of extensive restyling

- Henry Ford turns 75 and suffers stroke; accepts Grand Cross of the Supreme Order of the German Eagle from representatives of Adolf Hitler's government

FORD

▶ Although the '38 Fords used '37 bodies, they were heavily revised up front. DeLuxe models like this one sported a more-sloping hood and a new grille. Standard models received a more modest freshening of the '37 front end. It cost $770 to drive home with a new convertible coupe, not including the amber fog lights.

▲ Still friendly, one-time Ford production guru Bill Knudsen talks with Henry at the latter's 75th birthday celebration. Knudsen was now president of GM.

▲ DeLuxe Fords like this two-seat, five-window coupe came with the 221-cid, 85-bhp V-8 engine as standard equipment. With 22,225 made, it was Ford's most popular coupe in 1938.

▲ Like other DeLuxe Fords, the fading-away convertible sedan got a longer sloping hood, a heart-shaped grille with rounded corners, and more-rounded fenders. Only 2743 were built.

▲ Though the chassis was unchanged, the redesigned Ford trucks looked all new. Styling changes included a new cab, heavily chromed oval-shaped grille, carlike fenders, and heavier-looking bumpers.

▲ Abundant space awaited Fordor sedan passengers. The owners of this DeLuxe model had a choice of two upholstery fabrics, both grey: mohair or flat wale cord. A driver-side armrest was standard.

▲ Ford contended that its layout of controls and gauges made for "easy driving." The "banjo" steering wheel was seen on many Thirties Fords. DeLuxe door panels were finished in the same material as the seats.

LINCOLN

► Lincoln offered both a three- and five-passenger version of its restyled convertible coupe for '38. All Zephyrs featured a new front-end design that incorporated flush-mounted headlamps and a more softly sculpted grille. Last year's center-hub covers were replaced by larger-diameter chrome discs.

▲ Only 2600 of these swoopy Zephyr coupes were built this year, half the previous year's total. Whitewall tires were not included in the $1295 price.

▲ This one-off Model K "Touring Coupe" with hardtop-like styling was built for the wife of the owner of coach-builder Judkins, a Lincoln body supplier.

The Ford Motor Company
now offers

FIVE QUALITY CARS

FORD   DE LUXE FORD   MERCURY   LINCOLN-ZEPHYR   LINCOLN

▲ With the addition of Mercury, Ford could now boast a lineup that catered to almost every need. The distinction between Ford and "DeLuxe Ford" models might seem dubious, but the price difference could be more than $100—a substantial figure then.

- New medium-priced Mercury line introduced

- Four-model Mercury line sports 95-horse-power V-8

- Ford trims model line; Phaeton, club coupe, and convertible club coupe disappear

- Two milestones reached: 6-millionth V-8 and 27-millionth vehicle

- Chevy wins sales race by nearly 90,000

- Ford last major builder to stick with floor shifters

- All Ford products adopt hydraulic brakes

FORD

◄ DeLuxe Fords, including this $702 five-window coupe, came only with the larger, 85-bhp V-8. Ford's "flathead" engines were treated to new downdraft carburetors. The engine upgrade resulted in improved torque, but horsepower numbers remained the same.

▲ There was nothing dowdy about Ford's DeLuxe Tudor, which looked ready to pounce. Headlamps were farther apart for '39, no longer alongside the grille. Bodyside trim strips enhanced the car's graceful profile.

▲ Extra-cost fender skirts added pizzazz, while flip-out rear-quarter windows allowed plenty of air to breeze through this sedan. The DeLuxe Fordor cost exactly as much as the convertible coupe, $788.

▶ Who wouldn't covet a 1939 convertible coupe—with plenty of accessories to boot! Teardrop headlamps sat deep in the fenders. Hoods were also deeper and lacked last year's louvers. The new styling paid off, as DeLuxe convertible coupe sales doubled over the previous year, to 10,422. Then, too, the U.S. economy was stronger than it had been the year before.

◀ This magazine ad assured readers that the man pictured "is not an Eskimo, parked outside his igloo. He's a Ford engineer, busy at his job of making better cars." Perhaps putting some of the swagger into Ford's boasts of improving design was a decision to move all body manufacturing back under one roof. Prior to 1939, Ford contracted body stamping and assembly to outside companies. Ford's decision resulted in an immediate reduction in the number of bodies available.

▶ Priced at $916, the DeLuxe woody wagon was one of the costliest '39s. Though wagons would become more popular after World War II, at the time they were something of a novelty, and still sold in fairly modest numbers. Only 6155 DeLuxe wagons were built, plus another 3277 standards. Still, Ford wagon sales led the market. The new DeLuxe front-end design featured a vertical-bar grille and increased space between the headlamps. A deep, enveloping "alligator" hood finally did away with separate side panels and made access easier.

▲ Assembly line workers lower one of the first 6 million Ford V-8s onto a waiting chassis. V-8s would remain Ford cars' only power source until 1941, when a six-cylinder engine would be added.

▲ Henry visits with young Shirley Bulson, who's astride the revolutionary new Ford 9N. The tractor featured a patented Ferguson-System hitch, enabling quick attachment to virtually any farm implement.

▶ Separately mounted headlamps and a tall barrel-style grille gave Ford trucks little kinship with passenger cars, but both finally had hydraulic brakes. Henry Ford's work on hydraulic brakes had actually begun several years prior, but development was slowed when the aging magnate had suffered a stroke. Slowing down with time, the senior Ford became increasingly less willing to embrace new technology or fresh styling.

◀ This restored '39 chassis-and-cowl unit once provided fire protection to its maker's mammoth River Rouge manufacturing complex. Built on a 134-inch wheelbase—one of the standard chassis lengths then offered—it is powered by a 239-cube V-8. This 95-bhp engine, which also found its way into the new Mercury car line, was an option for many Ford truck models. Outfitted with General-Detroit firefighting gear, the pumper also features a four-speed gearbox.

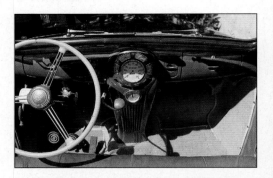

LINCOLN

▲ ▶ The elegant Lincoln-Zephyr center console featured lesser gauges positioned around a large, easy-to-read speedometer. Although other carmakers had moved shifters to the steering column, Lincoln-Zephyr and the rest of Ford's makes stubbornly clung to floor-mounted units.

◀ Eager to demonstrate the depth and breadth of its product offering, Ford Motor Company advertising periodically cataloged its entire lineup. Previously without offerings in the $1000 price range, Mercury added a much-needed rung to the Ford price ladder. Ford products now ranged in price from the economical $599 Ford five-window coupe to the extravagant $6900 Lincoln Model K Brougham for seven passengers.

MERCURY

▶ Mercury's debut helped fill a market gap between the high-line DeLuxe Fords and the Lincoln-Zephyrs in terms of size and price. The new line's 116-inch wheelbase also slotted nicely between the Ford's 112- and Lincoln-Zephyr's 125-inch chassis. A slightly larger engine boasted 95-horsepower, 10 more than Ford's best.

Even better than the winged feet you've always longed for in this well-going world is the Mercury 8. In its fleet forward movement is as smooth as a bird's . . . and as graceful as your own self in motion.

The Mercury 8 is between the Ford V-8 and the Lincoln-Zephyr in price range and combines many of the virtues of each. But its lines are sleeker . . . and impressively long . . . sixteen feet, four inches over all.

The spare inside is lavish too. And with its richness of appointments, and scientific soundproofing, the Mercury 8 is most aptly described by that classic fashion-phrase—Quiet Elegance.

But you must see it . . . drive it . . . sense the security of the new hydraulic brakes and feel the fleet power of the V-8 engine. Mercury 8 is the new mode in motor cars—the most talked about car in America.

The Ford Motor Company now offers you the Ford, Mercury, Lincoln-Zephyr and Lincoln motor cars.

FEATURES *116-inch wheelbase • 95-horsepower V-type 8-cylinder engine • hydraulic brakes • new soft seat construction • through scientific soundproofing • balanced weight distribution and center-poise design • large luggage compartment.*

This advertisement will appear in the March, 1939, issue of Harper's Bazaar and February 15, 1939, issue of Vogue.

▲ The four-door town sedan was the best-selling model of Mercury's freshman year. The sleek four-door accounted for nearly half of the 71,000 Mercury cars sold. With starting prices that hovered right around $1000, the new line was priced around $150-$200 more than comparable Ford DeLuxe models. Despite the styling similarities across all Ford product lines, the Ford DeLuxe and Mercury cars shared not a single body panel.

► The 1939 Mercury could be ordered in four body styles: a $916 two-door sedan, a $957 club coupe, a $957 four-door town sedan, and the $1018 sport convertible coupe shown. Original plans had called for the new cars to be called "Ford-Mercury," and for them to be sold by Ford dealerships. Designer E. T. Gregorie convinced Edsel Ford that the two makes should be distinct in the minds of buyers.

▲ Mercury dashboards sported a rainbow-shaped speedometer and placed the clock far to the right, quite unlike Ford's more-conventional two-dial arrangement.

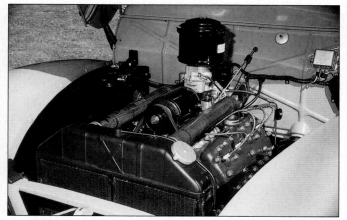

▲ Bigger than Ford's 221-cubic-inch engine, and smaller than the Zephyr V-12, Mercury's new 239-incher was well-suited for duty in the new midpriced cars.

1940–1949

War and Recovery

WHAT WOULD PROVE to be a decade of momentous, world-shaking events started out badly, as France and much of the rest of Europe fell before the Nazi juggernaut. Great Britain stood alone until the United States entered World War II following the Japanese attack on Pearl Harbor, Hawaii, at the end of 1941.

Less than four years later, Hitler was dead, and Germany prostrate. Japan, too, met defeat in 1945, in a manner that made the world keenly aware of all things "atomic."

America's wartime ally, the Soviet Union, became a belligerent postwar force. Then, in 1949, China fell to Mao Tse-tung's Communist revolution. President Harry Truman and a new alliance called NATO took a hard line against the creeping ideology.

The G. I. Bill of Rights provided a generation of young men with unprecedented access to higher education, prosperity, and homes of their own; a New York development called Levittown became the template for the new American suburbia. New cars, including Ford's impressive 1949 models, sold briskly.

In 1947, pilot Chuck Yeager broke the sound barrier, and Jackie Robinson defined "heroism" when he integrated big-league baseball.

1940

- War buildup begins
- New Rouge plant to build aircraft engines
- Ford builds 28-millionth vehicle
- Lincoln Continental debuts in showrooms
- Chevrolet's sales lead widens to 220,000 cars and trucks
- Headlamps are now sealed beam
- Ford of Germany falls under Nazi control

► Edsel and Henry Ford examine newly available sealed-beam headlamps. Though 77 years old, Henry was still actively piloting the auto giant. As a result of his early death, and Henry's reluctance to hand over the reins, Edsel never got a free hand to run the Ford Motor Company.

FORD

▲ Though ready to shift over to war production, Ford assembly lines produced cars and trucks at a normal pace in 1940. Here, alignment of headlamps is checked after body-color bezels are fitted to a Standard Tudor sedan.

◄ Only a model year after the 27-millionth Ford trekked from San Francisco to the New York World's Fair, this 28-millionth Ford appeared at the fair as part of the "International Goodwill Tour." Look closely at these specially made tires to find the Ford logo embossed on the whitewalls.

▲ The DeLuxe convertible coupe gained a hydraulically powered top, but lost the rumble seat. With the convertible sedan out of the lineup, the coupe was the sole ragtop. Even with only one model, convertible sales remained fairly strong, with almost 24,000 finding homes. At $849, the DeLuxe convertible cost $61 more than it did in 1939.

▲ Wagons were available in Standard and DeLuxe versions. Precious few, however, were equipped with aftermarket Marmon-Herrington four-wheel-drive conversions, as is this Standard model.

▲ E. T. Gregorie's redesign of the 1939 car line was finally applied to trucks. This handsomely finished ½-ton model saw duty as a Bell Telephone installer's truck in Michigan.

LINCOLN

◄ The reaction to Edsel Ford's personal "continental" convertible was strong enough to see the car placed into series production for 1940. A modification of the Zephyr, it appeared first as a convertible with an enveloping cabriolet-style top. Later in the model year, it was joined by this coupe. Of 404 first-year Zephyr Continentals, just 54 were closed cars.

▲ Though he described the Continental as "the most beautiful car ever built," architect Frank Lloyd Wright chose to customize his own car. Note the half-circle rear windows and the exaggerated arc of the roof.

▲ The Zephyr sedan was again Lincoln's best-selling car. Lincoln sold almost 16,000 of the $1400 sedans, down slightly from 1939. A hot-water windshield defroster was a new option this year.

MERCURY

▶ With a larger-than-expected rear-passenger area and roll-down rear windows, these two-doors were known as "sedan coupes." Like all 1940 Mercury Models, this one wears the "Mercury 8" badge just below the chrome strip on the side of the hood.

▲ Touting the all-weather benefits of the convertible's new hydraulic top, this ad for the Mercury club convertible promised adventure for the "young at heart."

▲ Chromework was cleaned up for 1940, but some fussy detailing remained. Note the red horizontal stripes on the rear bumper guards.

1941

- War buildup signals end of Great Depression

- Ford ads boast of roominess; cars get bigger, heavier

- L-head six-cylinder engine joins Ford lineup

- Now three Ford price levels: Special, DeLuxe, and Super DeLuxe

- Detroit-area Ford plants become unionized after April strike

- Henry Ford II becomes ensign in Naval Reserves

- Mercury adds a station wagon to its roster

- Lincoln fields long-wheelbase Custom series

FORD ▲ Ford's sportiest offering may have been this Super DeLuxe convertible. The optional rear skirts on this car raised the $950 base price by $12.50. Plagued by breakdowns, the vacuum-operated top mechanism was replaced by a simpler electrical system.

▲ This DeLuxe Tudor was pressed into the service of the Connecticut State Police. It cost $772 without police equipment.

▲ The DeLuxe Fordor sedan cost $46 more than the DeLuxe Tudor; consequently it sold about half as well. Lower bodywork flared to cover the running boards.

▲ Half-ton trucks used front-end styling inspired by the standard 1940 cars. V-8 pickups started at $605.

▲ Three-quarter- and one-ton pickups had different chassis and styling than the ½-ton trucks. The hubcaps here bear a V-8 logo, but four- and six-cylinder trucks made do with the Ford insignia.

► An ax-wielding Henry Ford strikes an experimental trunklid made of soybean-derived plastic to demonstrate its resiliency. Later, an all-plastic-bodied "soybean car" toured public events. While popular with the press, the plastic body panels proved difficult to bond to metal parts, and never made it into production.

CHARLES E. SORENSEN
Cast-Iron Charlie

CHARLES E. SORENSEN ranks as one of America's greatest industrial-production managers. Born in Copenhagen, Denmark, in 1881, he emigrated with his parents to the U.S. in 1885, then to Detroit by 1900. A patternmaker, he joined Ford in 1905. During World War I, Sorensen was assigned by Henry Ford to organize tractor production in Dearborn. Within three years, his superb industrial knowledge and force of personality thrust him into the leadership of the Rouge Plant; by 1926 he was presiding over Ford's branch and assembly operations. By the late Twenties, he was directing the company's worldwide operations. One of the few executives whose advice was valued by Henry Ford, Sorensen was, in turn, completely loyal to the auto king.

Before moving to the Rouge, Sorensen played an important role in the development of mass production at the Highland Park Plant in 1912–13. His foundry expertise and his brusque manner earned him the sobriquet "Cast-Iron Charlie."

After Ford's acquisition of the failing Lincoln Motor Company in 1922, Sorensen was sent to inspect Lincoln's manufacturing facilities, and found them wanting. The company's founders, 78-year-old Henry M. Leland, and his son, Wilfred, had been assured by Henry Ford that they would be permitted to manage the business. Sorensen, with Ford's tacit approval, brushed the notion aside. As Ford men took charge, the dismayed, embittered Lelands were driven out.

For decades, Sorensen, like almost all Ford employees, was titleless. Finally, in 1941, he was awarded a vice presidency and directorship.

During the pre-World War II defense buildup, Sorensen played a key role in negotiating the contracts that were to make Ford the country's largest producer of aircraft engines and the first firm to mass-produce bombers. During wartime, his work was discussed in highly flattering terms, and he became, as much as Henry Ford, a symbol of the company's production prowess. In 1942, *Fortune* headlined an article on the Ford company's war work "Sorensen of the Rouge," with the subtitle, "Besides Making Engines, Tanks, and Guns, He Is Running the Biggest Bomber Factory in the World." The article included a full-page color photo of Sorensen, and described him as "the creator of Willow Run." That same year, an Associated Press story lauded him as the "manufacturing genius of the Ford Motor Company," and gave him major credit for developing the moving assembly line.

As Sorensen's public profile increased, Henry Ford, who long had considered himself the company's only production genius, became more abrupt toward his lieutenant, and less attentive to his recommendations. In 1944, the jealous Ford forced Sorensen's resignation, dealing the company a crippling blow in the process.

Serving as president of Willys-Overland from 1944 to 1946 and vice-chairman until 1950, Sorensen found it difficult to put aside his years of Ford service. Asked how he felt about leaving Ford, he tapped his chest and said, "It hurts here." Sorensen died in Bethesda, Maryland, in 1968. He was inducted into the Automotive Hall of Fame in 2001.

◄ The Zephyr club coupe sported a new fold-down rear-seat center armrest. Buyers could select from a number of new colors, including Volanta Coach Maroon, Rockingham Tan, Plymton Gray Metallic, and Spode Green. With 3750 sales, the club coupe was second in sales only to the Zephyr sedan.

▲ With its moniker officially simplified to "Continental," Lincoln's newest line rode into its second model year with only minor changes.

▲ Visibility was sacrificed for beauty when this Continental cabriolet had its top up. Limited running changes included replacing the rectangular gauges with round instrumentation.

MERCURY ▲ Spiffy club convertibles enjoyed a switch to
electrically powered tops, replacing troublesome hydraulic systems. Slightly fewer than 8600 found their way into buyers' garages.

▲ This town sedan features the bright drip rails that were added to the Mercury line as a midyear change.

1942

- Customers clamor for cars, fearing wartime shortage

- New Ford products arrive three months before start of war

- Lincoln introduces semiautomatic "Liquamatic Drive"

- Civilian car production ends February 10

- Civilian truck production ends March 3

FORD ▲ Station wagons used mahogany paneling with maple or birch framing. All wagons featured faux-leather roofs and the distinction of being the longest and heaviest cars in the Ford line. At $1125, the Super DeLuxe Wagon was also the most expensive.

▲ A reduced-height frame gave this DeLuxe Fordor sedan a lower, sportier stance, while softer springs improved the ride. Both the six-cylinder and V-8 engines produced 90 horsepower. The price of a DeLuxe Fordor increased $62 this year, to $875. An optional heater added $23. Because of the war-shortened model year, sales were limited to slightly more than 5100 cars, down from almost 26,000 of the '41s.

▲ The Super DeLuxe Fordor in this publicity photo was too nicely equipped for military service. A dechromed Special Fordor proved to be the War Department Ford of choice for use at U.S. bases.

▲ As war rationing escalated, automakers' use of the strategic metals used in producing chrome was eventually halted. Automakers with chrome parts left were required to "black out" their cars (often by painting trim) to avoid having an unfair competitive advantage. Blacking out the grille of this toothy Super DeLuxe convertible would have proven challenging. Only 2900 convertibles were built before automobile production was halted.

▲ Half-ton pickups received a new flat-front look with squarer fenders and vertical-bar grille—far removed from Ford's passenger cars. Price: $675 with V-8.

▲ A longer rear roofline on the still popular $825 sedan delivery body allowed a 92.5-cubic-foot cargo area. Access to cargo was through the rear door only.

LINCOLN

► A new top design that permitted roll-down rear windows was the most significant upgrade to the Zephyr convertible coupe. The rarest of all Lincolns this year, a mere 191 were built. This car's whitewall tires, chrome wheel trim rings, and yellow fog lights, were optional equipment.

▲ Full-size running boards and chrome handles were among the numerous custom features of Franklin D. Roosevelt's Lincoln "Sunshine Special." The car had 1942 styling, but was based on the retired K chassis.

▲ Sporting new 15-inch wheels and tires and a slightly lowered body, the Zephyr Coupe was Lincoln's sportiest offering. Though the least-costly Lincoln at $1748, only 273 found buyers.

► Partly in response to Cadillac's move to bolder front-end design, Continental's softly contoured grille was given a heavier-looking, more-upright treatment shared with other Lincolns. Power windows and front-seat adjusters become standard. The previously standard-equipment wheel trim rings were now optional.

▲ The Custom series consisted of two nine-passenger cars mounted on a long 138-inch wheelbase: a sedan and a divider-window limousine. Both shared the same notchback roofline. Total production of the sedan seen here came to just 47.

► The final Lincoln of the war-shortened model year rolls off the assembly line on January 31. This Zephyr sedan might have been equipped with such accessories as an Adjust-O-Matic radio with Touch Bar Tuning, an auxiliary under-seat heater, and a vanity mirror. This car was built without the optional white-wall tires.

MERCURY

▶ Mercury station wagons shared Ford's wooden side panels and imitation-leather roof, but boasted Lincolnesque frontal styling and a larger, stronger 100-horsepower V-8. A scant 857 of the $1336 wagons were built.

◀ Roll-up rear windows were new for the club convertible, which listed for $1215. Like other Mercury models, the convertible sat on a slightly lowered chassis. This angle offers a clear view of how running boards were being disguised. The "A" ration stamp on the windshield was a familiar sight to wartime drivers, most of whom faced severe restrictions on the amount of fuel they could buy per week.

▲ This driver has an excellent view of Mercury's redesigned dashboard. The center grille covered the radio speaker, and was flanked by the speedometer on the left and a clock on the right.

▲ The previously fixed-in-place rear windows on this business coupe now could be opened. After reaching almost 100,000 in 1941, Mercury sales totaled just less than 23,000 for the war-shortened model year.

HARRY BENNETT
Ford's Hatchet Man

A FICTION WRITER would be hard-pressed to devise a more picaresque or colorful character than Harry Bennett, Henry Ford's chief aide during the Thirties and Forties. Bennett also was characterized as a hatchet man, spy, sleuth, gangster, thug, satrap, captain of the palace guard, Henry Ford's personal man, Henry Ford's commander-in-chief, and Ford's Rasputin.

Bennett knew where he stood. After two ingratiating newsmen drafted a flattering biography of him, they submitted it to him for his approval. Bennett expressed disappointment, saying that no one would recognize him from what had been written.

"In what way, Harry?" asked one of the authors.

"Well," he responded, "you don't say I'm a son of a bitch." The manuscript was handed back; it never appeared in print.

An ex-sailor and amateur pugilist, the five-foot-six-inch Bennett was stocky with reddish hair, sharp blue eyes, and handsome features. Alternately charming and ruthless, he joined Ford Motor Company in 1916. His rise began in earnest in 1921 when he was given charge of the Rouge's Service Department, then responsible only for plant security. During the next half-dozen years, the department gradually assumed control over all personnel matters, including spying on workers. By 1927, the service chief was one of the company's half-dozen most powerful men, and his star was in the ascent.

Bennett's power and influence were tied to his special relationship with Henry Ford. Although the reasons for that relationship are complex, several were of special importance. One was Bennett's willingness to do anything Ford told him to do, including his "dirty work." "What I like about Harry," Ford said, "is that if I want something done, he will do it, and in a hurry." In time, people questioned whether "Mr. Ford says" represented Henry's or Harry's thinking. "Just how powerful is Harry Bennett?" one Ford man asked another. "Too powerful to risk finding out," was the sensible reply. With a few exceptions, employees came to fear Bennett, knowing that he could send them packing at his whim.

Also, beginning in the early Twenties, Bennett had an open tie with Detroit's underworld. This connection presumably enabled him to shield the Ford family from kidnapping, then a prevalent threat.

Another factor was the spread of discontent in the nation's factories during the early Thirties. Bennett's private army thwarted disturbances, sabotage, and union organizing drives. Many of Bennett's "servicemen" were former boxers, wrestlers, and football players; ex-policemen discharged by trial boards; and ex-convicts and parolees. "They're a lot of tough bastards," Bennett acknowledged, "but every goddamn one of them's a gentleman."

During the Thirties and early Forties, Bennett's top priority, aside from pleasing his boss, was keeping unionists at bay. In 1937, his servicemen severely mauled union organizers, including Walter Reuther, as they attempted to distribute pamphlets to Ford workers crossing a street overpass adjacent to the Rouge Plant. After the "Battle of the Overpass," the National Labor Relations Board filed a complaint accusing Ford of violating almost every labor practice defined by the Wagner Act. Nonetheless, the Service Department—aptly described as "a standing army unique in America," "the 'O.P.G.U.' [Russian secret service] of the Ford organization," and the "largest privately owned secret service force in existence"— constantly harassed and sometimes beat up employees suspected of union sympathies.

When unionists, principally UAW-CIO organizers, pressed for NLRB-monitored representation in Ford's Detroit-area plants, Bennett's reply was characteristically blunt: "If the NLRB orders an election, we will of course hold one, because Mr. Ford will observe the law. CIO will win it, of course, because it always wins these farcical elections, and we will bargain with it because the law says so. We will bargain until hell freezes over, but they won't get anything." After a strike in April 1941, the UAW won recognition at the Rouge and Lincoln plants. "It's a great victory for the Communist Party, [Michigan] Governor Murray Van Wagoner, and the National Labor Relations Board," Bennett declared. To the surprise of Bennett and everyone else, Henry Ford awarded the UAW its most generous contract ever.

Ford also admired Harry's guts. The service chief did not know the meaning of fear. During the Communist-led "Hunger March" on the Rouge Plant in 1932, Harry was the sole Ford man to confront the marchers. Trying to quell the disorder, he identified himself, and was felled by a shower of slag. As he fell, he instinctively seized and pulled down one of the marchers' leaders. At that moment, Dearborn and Detroit policemen opened fire, instantly killing the unionist. Displaying more energy than discretion, Bennett clambered to his feet only to be knocked unconscious by the mob. Rescued by police, he was rushed to Henry Ford Hospital. "If I had to enumerate his outstanding qualities," said archrival manufacturing boss Charles E. Sorensen, "I'd put fearless personal courage first."

A psychological element also was important in the Ford-Bennett relationship. Ford had failed to mold his son, Edsel, in his own image. In Bennett, he found many of the hard-nosed traits and beliefs he had vainly tried to implant in his son, and in time gave the cocky, brash Bennett a scope he had denied the sensitive, urbane Edsel. By the early Forties, when Bennett and Henry Ford met almost daily, the subordinate had become something of a substitute son.

Bennett's power lay with Henry Ford, who on two occasions told newsmen that his bow-tie-wearing aide was the "most remarkable" and the "greatest" person he had ever met. "Hitler need not be a problem," Ford assured an Englishman. "Harry and six of his men could get rid of him for you in no time." While dancing with Bennett's wife, the industrialist declared that Harry "should be president of the United States." In turn, Bennett late in life described Ford as "the greatest man who ever lived."

From the Thirties to 1945, Bennett spent more time with Henry Ford than anyone except for Mrs. Ford, and had more influence with the magnate than any other business associate. He increased his power sharply in the early Forties by taking advantage of Ford's waning mentality. In 1943, after Edsel's death, he was named to the company's Board of Directors. For the next two years, Bennett, in Henry's name, controlled or strongly influenced every part of the firm.

Bennett's luck ran out in September 1945 when Henry transferred the presidency to his 28-year-old grandson, Henry Ford II, whose first act was to fire his late father's nemesis. Bennett hoped that Henry Ford would save him, but the failing magnate, by then disinterested in company affairs, did not react. After sacking Bennett, Henry II cleared the decks of the ex-sailor's chief mates.

Of Bennett, Henry II said in 1980, "Harry Bennett was the dirtiest, lousiest son of a bitch I ever met in my life, save one." "Who was the other one?" he was asked. "Iacocca," he replied. Henry II added that Bennett "stole the place blind. . . . I don't know how he did it, but he did it."

In 1973, Bennett offered his opinion of Henry II. "I didn't trust Henry," he said. "We got along face-to-face, but he was two-faced. He couldn't tell the same story twice. The older he got, the more stuck he got on himself. You couldn't tell him anything. He also went to Mommy with everything. . . . Henry did everything under the sun against me. Sometimes I felt like hitting him in the nose."

For many years, Bennett had no personal salary. But he received $10,000 checks from Henry Ford, plus farms which he sold for more than $1 million. In 1943, he was put on an annual salary of $65,000. In the meantime, he availed himself of Ford materials and workmen whenever it suited him. The construction and maintenance of his several homes probably cost him nothing.

Bennett's main residence was a castle overlooking his favorite boyhood swimming hole in the Huron River near Ann Arbor, Michigan. Surrounded by a huge tract of land, including an island in the river, the castle, built in 1926–27, was supplemented by a large steam-heated swimming pool, horse stables and a riding ring, a boat well and dock, and a house built for Bennett's mother. After Mrs. Bennett's death, the dwelling was converted into a 50-seat theater.

Bennett and Henry Ford planned the castle with the enthusiasm of small boys fashioning a robbers' lair or a pirates' nest. Given Ford's personal interest, no expense was spared. The castle had tunnels, towers, spiral staircases, gunports, searchlights, mismatched steps, hidden rooms, secret doors, sliding panels, a "Roman bath," a lion/tiger den, and all of the electronic and mechanical security equipment that could be dreamed up in the Twenties. One tunnel terminated in a cave that was decorated with artificial stalactites and stalagmites molded by Bennett. The house acquired a reputation as one of the most mysterious and bizarre residences in Michigan, if not the nation. Dr. Frankenstein and Alfred Hitchcock would have loved it, visitors said.

After his discharge from Ford, the 52-year-old Bennett retired to a ranch near Desert Hot Springs, California. Devoting himself to puttering and oil painting, he never worked for pay again. In 1951, still smarting from his dismissal and wishing to expose Henry Ford II's foibles, he and a collaborator, Paul Marcos, authored a book, *We Never Called Him Henry*, which Bennett later regretted having done.

In 1969, Bennett and his wife, Esther, moved to a modest home in Las Vegas, Nevada, a concession to Mrs. Bennett's medical needs. Bennett himself, after a 1974 stroke, was mostly confined to a wheelchair. He suffered a heart attack in 1977 and died in a Los Gatos, California, nursing home on January 4, 1979.

Bennett is remembered as one of Michigan's most controversial persons. "Legend and fact about him will be discussed for years to come," the *Detroit Free Press* correctly predicted as early as 1958, "for he was a 'little giant' in the massive auto industry." In 1983, Bennett was described by the *Detroit News* as one of the Motor City's three "most manly men," the others being city founder Antoine de la Mothe Cadillac and Teamsters boss Jimmy Hoffa.

1943-45

- Among the most prolific of wartime producers, Ford Motor Company builds planes, jeeps, tanks, trucks, and cars

- Gasoline rationing goes nationwide by December 1942

- Edsel Ford dies on May 26, 1943

- Eighty-year-old Henry Ford reelected company president on June 1, 1943

- Henry Ford II released from naval duty, and on July 26, 1943, is elected vice president

- At his wife's insistence, Henry Ford finally retires on September 21, 1945, leaving Henry II in charge

- Civilian car production resumes at Ford in July 1945

► Wearing the uniform of a Naval Reserve ensign, Henry Ford II poses with his grandparents, Henry and Clara Ford. Concerned about the aging, elder Ford's ability to honor Ford Motor Company's wartime contracts, the U.S. government released HF II from military service to return to his corporate post.

▲ Though the "jeep" was designed largely by American Bantam, the small company was unable meet demand for the nimble little off-road truck. Willys-Overland became the prime contractor, but Ford influenced the final design and built many wartime jeeps.

► Among Ford's defense products were four-engine B-24 Liberator bombers, one of which is inspected here by Harry Truman (right). By the time of the massive Willow Run plant's closing, Ford had produced almost 9000 B-24s.

▲ Though unable to sell cars, automakers were determined to remain in the public's eye. Ford's "A Report to America" highlighted its wartime activity.

▲ Typical Ford wartime advertisements included images of the company's combat-ready products and reminders to purchase war bonds.

▲ Benson Ford, Henry II's younger brother, did his wartime duty as an Army lieutenant.

▲ As hundreds watch, a flower-bedecked Clara Ford speaks at a ceremony honoring Henry's birthday. The 79-year-old Ford would remain actively involved in the company throughout the war.

◄ Admiral Chester Nimitz (second from left) enjoys the view from the back seat of a Ford-built jeep. Though Willys' improvement on the American Bantam design was selected by the War Department, several elements of a Ford proposal were incorporated into it. The flat hood recommended by Ford proved useful as a table for maps and meals. Another Ford design element to make it onto the final Jeep was the integration of the headlamps into the grille, as opposed to on top of the fenders, where they were more exposed to harm. In all, Ford produced 281,000 GPW ("General Purpose Willys") jeeps.

HENRY FORD II
His Father's Son

THERE WAS NOT MUCH in Henry Ford II's youth to suggest that he could—and would—successfully lead one of the world's largest firms. Born into affluence in 1917, he had an idyllic boyhood, riding horses, sailing, and playing golf and tennis at family residences in Grosse Pointe Shores, Michigan; Seal Harbor, Maine; and Hobe Sound, Florida. At Hotchkiss, a Connecticut prep school, he was a so-so student.

A pleasant, blue-eyed, apple-cheeked, six-foot, 190-pounder, Henry II at 21 was named a Ford company director while in his third year at Yale University. The appointment meant little inasmuch as grandfather Henry Ford ignored the board. A fun-loving, but mediocre, student at Yale, young Henry was caught submitting a ghostwritten paper, and was not allowed to graduate. "I didn't write this one either," he jovially remarked in 1969, before giving a speech to the Yale Political Union.

After college, the Ford scion might have become another John Duval Dodge, whose excesses led to disinheritance by his father, John; or a Horace E. Dodge Jr., whose chief distinction was his ability to stay aboard a polo pony; or a Walter P. Chrysler Jr., an art collector purely and simply. Instead, he shaped up.

In 1941, Henry II was given an ensign's commission, and assigned to desk work at the Great Lakes Naval Training Station near Chicago. Two years later, after the death of his father, Edsel, he was released from the Navy "to assist in managing the company's business." The government hoped that he might soon rise to a position of importance with the firm, put a stop to its incessant infighting, and help it to realize its full war-production potential. Actually, once on the job, Henry II devoted most of his attention to preparing the company for the postwar market.

In 1945, upon succeeding his 80-year-old grandfather as president, Henry II displayed the grittiness that would characterize his long administration. First he fired old Henry's corrupt henchman, Harry Bennett, then dislodged a thousand of his cronies. Next, he hired a mentor, Ernest R. Breech, and began to get the firm back on track.

Initially, Henry II deferred to the more-mature Breech. But within a dozen years, he was capable of running the company, and Breech, made aware of the fact, departed. A risk-taker, Henry gathered facts, listened, and made decisions. "I am almost never sure that I am right," he once said, "but I often go ahead anyhow." When he made mistakes—and he made some doozies—he was big enough to admit them.

Henry II was a generalist, not a specialist, in finance, design, marketing, labor relations, or anything else. But he had an abiding interest in overseas operations, long neglected by fellow executives preoccupied with the big home market. Channeling some of the company's best brains abroad, he promoted Stateside those who produced, and saw to it that international operations were encouraged and adequately funded.

"The Deuce," as some called him, also was a good judge of managerial personnel. His choices of Breech to help him reorganize the company and of Philip Caldwell to succeed him were superb. So would have been his selection of Robert S. McNamara as president had not the ex-Whiz Kid resigned to become Secretary of Defense. He bet on some presidents who wouldn't do, notably Arjay Miller, an excellent staff, but not operations, executive; Semon E. "Bunkie" Knudsen ("It just didn't work out"); and Lee Iacocca ("I just don't like you"). All the while, he nurtured many able administrators, bequeathing a rich legacy of talent upon retirement in 1979.

Henry II did not suffer fools lightly, nor those who shortchanged their homework or tried to hoodwink him. Conversely, he valued and rewarded professionalism whenever he found it, and often treated executives and others better than they deserved.

He mended fences with Jews alienated by his grandfather, and built bridges for blacks. In the late Sixties, he led efforts in riot-torn Detroit to provide work for hardcore-unemployed African Americans. Dispensing with written job tests, he hired thousands of blacks and provided special buses to take them to plant locations. He then recommended his inner-city hiring program to President Lyndon B. Johnson, who pushed for the formation of the National Alliance of Businessmen, set up to operate the JOBS program—an acronym for Job Opportunities in the Business Sector. Henry II served as the alliance's chairman.

Avoiding the rough-and-tumble of direct labor negotiations, Henry II was comfortable with union leaders and rank-and-filers. He once returned from a European vacation expressly to attend a retirement banquet for the head of the UAW's Ford Department. When he visited Ford plants during his own retirement, he was roundly cheered by employees. A statue of him shak-

The two Henry Fords look pleased as they study a scale model of their company's sprawling Rouge plant.

ing hands with UAW President Walter Reuther stands in the UAW-Ford National Program Center in downtown Detroit.

Henry's pet peeve was lawyers. "They think they know everything," he grumbled. "They waste time, and they cost a lot of money." To the annoyance of the company's general counsels, he refused to appoint them to the board. "They can sit in on the meetings if they want," he explained, "so why put them on the board?"

Henry II's favorite Ford car was the '49, if only because its success proved that his self-styled "New Company" could produce a winner. He enjoyed his work until the mid Sixties, after which government regulations, Japanese competition, oil crises, and Lee Iacocca began taking the fun out it. Ralph Nader's safety crusading enraged him.

Another source of frustration was the Ford Foundation, which the Ford family controlled lock, stock, and barrel until 1956, when the company went public and the foundation began selling off its Ford stock so as to diversify its portfolio. At that point, Henry became just another trustee, with no more voting power over the institution than any other trustee.

"I gave the foundation away," he moaned later. "I had it in my hands. . . . [W]ith a pen in four seconds, I could have given the shares to . . . the Edison Institute, Henry Ford Hospital, the [Henry Ford estate] Fair Lane, any nonprofit organization. . . . I was young, inexperi-

enced, and stupid, and I made a horrible mistake. I'll never live it down, and I regret it sincerely. But what in the hell can I do about it? I can't do anything about it."

Fed up with the Ford Foundation's liberal policies, and disinterest in business and Ford family sponsored causes, Henry II resigned his trusteeship in 1977. His initial letter of resignation was a strongly worded blast at the foundation, but he was persuaded by a trusted advisor to tone it down. That he did, complaining only that the foundation, although a "creature of capitalism," did not in the slightest recognize this fact in anything it did.

Henry II also had second thoughts about having spearheaded the drive to build Detroit's Renaissance Center, which he hoped would pave the way to Motor City revitalization. The RenCen concept surfaced after HFII was told that his company employed only a handful of people in Detroit—adjacent Dearborn didn't count. Wishing to make a big splash, Henry arranged for construction of a 77-story hotel surrounded by four 39-story office towers. Investing $100 million, the Ford Motor Company took a third interest in the project; thanks to HFII's arm twisting, 51 other auto firms also bought in.

Alas, the Renaissance Center, opened in 1977, was not a success. The hotel was too big, and office rentals reached a respectable level only after large numbers of Ford employees were transferred from Dearborn. Upscale retailers, to the extent they were enticed, quickly bailed out. At considerable loss, Ford scaled back its stake in the enterprise in 1983, and gave up its management the following year. In 1996, General Motors bought the complex for $72 million to serve as its world headquarters.

First as crown prince, then as metro Detroit's "king," Henry II was treated like royalty. A newspaper cartoon caricature aptly depicted him with a crowned head, scepter in hand, lording over such lesser nobles as the mayor and the presidents of GM, Chrysler, and the UAW. As the *Detroit Free Press* observed, "there is no other magnifico of comparable radiance to Henry Ford II. . . . An Iacocca [then Chrysler chairman] is nothing without a product to peddle. . . . [UAW President Douglas] Fraser, however flavorful his description of corporate chieftains as 'horses asses,' evokes little interest. [GM Chairman Thomas] Murphy heads a corporation larger and more powerful than Henry's, but stripped of his title or even in full regalia, is a mere cipher. The Fords are our Medici [and] Henry Ford serves as a Caesar for our times."

Ford's hometown popularity was put to the test at a large Society of Automotive Engineers banquet in 1975. The previous day, Henry II had been detained for drunken driving in Santa Barbara, California. A married man, he shared the car with an attractive blonde,

HENRY FORD II
Continued

Kathleen Duross, later his third wife. When questioned by the press, Ford remarked, "Never complain, never explain." Banquet participants, aware of the arrest, wondered whether he would show. He did. As the master of ceremonies began to introduce head-table guests, he asked the audience to hold applause until all introductions had been made. The fourth person presented was HFII. Spontaneously, every man in the audience stood and gave him a thunderous ovation.

On the national scene, Henry II was once named one of America's 10 best-dressed men. Asked by the press for a response, he quipped, "That's in the low-price field, I presume." In addition, he was selected by *Harper's Bazaar* as one of the world's 10 leading candidates for the title, "Prince Charming," along with Britain's Prince Charles, Canadian Prime Minister Pierre Trudeau, dancer Mikhail Baryshnikov, and screen star Warren Beatty.

Henry II had three marriages, three children, and two divorces. He married Anne McDonnell in 1940, Cristina Vettore Austin in 1965, and Kathleen Duross in 1980. He was divorced from his first two wives in 1964 and 1977, respectively. Anne died at age 76 in 1996. Cristina, once a flamboyant jet-setter, has faded from public view. Kathy resides in North Palm Beach, Florida.

Socially, Ford had several sides. Drunkenness brought out boisterousness and boorishness. At a Business Council cocktail party in San Francisco, he requested the band to swing into a lively tune, to which he danced between the tables, arms overhead, fingers snapping to the rhythm.

Henry II generally preferred life's best. But he also enjoyed the simple life. At a fair in Johannesburg, South Africa, he canceled a luncheon reservation made for him at the "very swishy" Chamber of Mines pavilion in favor of a hot dog, Coke, and ice cream procured by himself from a sidewalk stand. Eating on a nearby bench with his wife and guide, he exclaimed to his companions. "God, this is a wonderful experience." He graciously served tea to office guests, and, thanks to a secretarial file, knew whether or not they preferred lemon, milk, or sugar. He also habitually opened office and car doors for others.

First experiencing chest pains in 1975, Henry II was forced to cancel a visit to China the following year because of angina. Reduced vigor played an important role in his decision to retire in 1979. Upon stepping down, he apologized to his successor, Philip Caldwell, for leaving the company during a business downturn. As the Ford company suffered through record losses in the early Eighties, he was asked by newsmen about a possible return to active management. "You couldn't pay me enough money, or give me enough things to get me back," he replied. "I am out." Henry II did, however, serve as chairman of the company board's Finance Committee, which enabled him to weigh in on all important decisions. He set up an office first in the Renaissance Center, then in a building near Ford's World Headquarters, while maintaining a lesser, seldom-used office at the headquarters.

Two years before Henry II's retirement, Gianni Agnelli, head of the family that founded and controlled Fiat, aptly summed up Henry. Speaking before the Foreign Policy Association in New York, Agnelli said, "Henry Ford has surely been the most significant motorcar man in the world since the war—the most significant and the most successful, the most outspoken."

Henry II remained no less candid in retirement. After giving a speech at the University of Pennsylvania, he was queried by reporters about changes in marketing practices. "Let me tell you," he replied, "that I don't think that, speaking for Ford Motor Company, we've made any progress in the sales and marketing end of our business in the last 50 years. We haven't done anything really new. It's the same old monkey business." Ford's marketers cringed.

In Henry II's fifth year of retirement, 1985, Iacocca authored his best-selling autobiography, which appeared to have two primary objectives: stroke Lee's vanity and vilify Henry II. Henry did not read the book, and refused to comment on it. Indeed, after Iacocca left Ford, HFII, in the words of a confidant, paid no more attention to Lee "than to a fly." As for Iacocca, if he wrote his book "to get even," he succeeded, because his book, appearing at the height of his popularity, certainly harmed his former boss's reputation.

Henry II died of Legionnaires' disease in Henry Ford Hospital on September 29, 1987. His ashes, the press reported, allegedly were scattered by Kathy Ford and his son, Edsel II, over the Detroit River near the Renaissance Center. A funeral service was conducted at Christ Church, Grosse Pointe, and memorial services were held in Detroit's St. Paul's Cathedral and in St. George's Church in London. In a letter written to Kathy and Edsel II, Henry expressed the hope that his services would be in a celebratory spirit. As family and friends filed out of St. Paul's and St. George's, jazz bands played his favorite song, "When the Saints Come Marching In."

In 1996, Ford renamed its World Headquarters complex the Henry Ford II World Center, and installed a bronze statue of HFII in the lobby. "He looks so much alive," Edsel II said of the blue-eyed, life-size sculpture, "it gives me goose bumps." Henry's nose was in danger of becoming shiny, as visitors fondly rubbed their fingers over it.

- Civilian automobile production resumes in full; public clamors to buy warmed-over 1942s

- Car prices leap an average of $400

- Ford builds 70,000 more cars than Chevrolet

- Despite huge demand, Ford racks up losses of more than $8 million

- Ford and Lincoln pare down number of available models

FORD ▲ While steel remained in short supply, wood for the Sportsman convertible was abundant in Ford's forests near Iron Mountain, Michigan. To build the car, solid wood blocks were hand cut, fitted, and varnished. No two cars were exactly alike, but all carried a V-8 newly grown to 239 cubic inches and 100 horsepower.

▲ The six-passenger sedan coupe came only in top-rung Super DeLuxe trim, priced at $1307 with V-8 power. Fewer shoppers were interested in front-seat-only business coupes after the war.

▲ Super DeLuxe models enjoyed upgraded cloth upholstery. Three could squeeze into the front seat of a '46 Ford without pain. Note the pull-out handbrake, a common sight on postwar cars. Low-line Specials were cut.

► Frisky even in stock form, Fords gained easy popularity in police fleets. They also attracted a growing pack of hot rodders, who took advantage of the countless hop-up possibilities of the newly enlarged flathead V-8. Parts suppliers began offering an array of performance parts such as dual-exhaust headers and high-compression cylinder heads.

LINCOLN

► As the war went, so did the Zephyr name. With heavier-looking front bumpers, Lincoln's least-expensive offering was now known simply as the club coupe. Lincoln's V-12 engine began the year rated at 130 horsepower, but manufacturing problems quickly led to a small reduction in cylinder bore as well as a drop in power to 120.

▲ Driven by Henry Ford II, this Continental would be only the second Lincoln to pace the Indianapolis 500. Edsel Ford piloted the make's first Indy pace car in '32.

▲ An eggcrate grille style replaced prewar horizontal bars on 1946 Lincolns like this four-door sedan. Very early '46 Lincolns lacked standard road lights.

MERCURY
▲ The Mercury Sportsman shared its body and woodwork with Ford's similar, but less-expensive, Sportsman.

▲ Previously gum wood, body panels for the station wagon were now of birch and mahogany. It sold for $1788—without a Marmon-Herrington 4×4 conversion.

- Corporate patriarch Henry Ford dies April 7, at the age of 83

- With development of a completely redesigned '49 Ford under way, current line stagnates

- Ford and Mercury sales dip, while Lincoln sales soar 75 percent

- Surging Chevrolet outsells Ford by almost a quarter of a million cars and trucks

- Despite slumping sales, Ford turns a $65-million profit

- Ground is broken for a new research and development center at Dearborn

FORD ▲ It would be hard to mistake a wood-paneled Sportsman for an ordinary convertible. Only produced in Super DeLuxe trim, 2250 were made, up slightly from the prior year. Price: $2282 including the V-8.

◄ Smaller than the Tudor, but with more rear-seat room than the coupe, sedan coupes nestled nicely in the Ford lineup. Though the least-expensive sedan coupe cost almost $200 more, it outsold the coupe nearly seven-to-one. Available only in Super DeLuxe trim, the sedan coupe stickered at $1409 with the V-8 engine.

► Woody wagons remained part of the Ford lineup, all wearing Super DeLuxe trim. Priced at $1972 with a V-8 ($1893 with the six-cylinder engine), the four-door wagon held eight passengers. Middle- and third-row seats could be removed for added cargo space. A total 16,104 were built, slightly fewer than in 1946. Today, all Ford "woodies" are especially prized by collectors of vintage cars.

▲ Mourners line up to pay their last respects to a legend: Henry Ford became a permanent part of the history he once referred to as "more or less bunk" when he died at home on April 7.

LINCOLN

▼ ► Lincoln's best-selling car, the sedan, returned this year with a few trim changes. This well-equipped sedan sported extra-cost whitewall tires and chrome wheel trim rings. Sedans started at $2554, but an optional interior upgrade package added $168 to the tab.

▲ Priced about $2000 less than a Continental coupe, the $2533 Lincoln club coupe soldiered on as the make's price leader. Unlike the four-door sedan, it had external trunk hinges.

◄ Almost unchanged, the Continental returned with an asking price of $4662. The last vestiges of the Continental's rear-mounted tire would appear as late as the Nineties in the form of the rounded rear decks on certain Lincoln products. To this day, decorative rear-mounted spare-tire racks are commonly known as "Continental Kits."

▲ In a costume from her motion picture, *The Loves of Carmen*, Rita Hayworth poses with a Continental cabriolet.

▲ Another Continental, another celebrity: A cabriolet proves to be a worthy conveyance for baseball legend Babe Ruth, perched on the top boot (center) at an unidentified parade a year before his death.

▶ Club convertible buyers had a choice of red or tan leather upholstery. The little-changed ragtop rolled on with an asking price of $2002. The "waterfall" grille design, first seen on the '46 models, would be a Mercury styling point for years.

ERNEST R. BREECH
Henry Ford II's Mentor

Henry Ford II is generally credited with having resurrected the Ford Company after World War II, but Ernest R. Breech was the chief architect of the firm's rebirth.

Born in 1897 as the son of a Lebanon, Missouri, blacksmith, Breech worked his way through two years at Drury College in Springfield, Missouri, then studied accounting and business at Chicago's Walton School of Commerce. Becoming a CPA in 1921, he joined the Yellow Cab Manufacturing Company in 1923, and became a General Motors employee when Yellow was absorbed by GM in 1925. By 1939, he was a GM vice president and group executive. During 1942–46, he served as president of Bendix Aviation Corporation, which was partly owned by GM. Over the years, he gained a reputation as hard-driving and resourceful.

In 1945, Henry Ford II, having replaced his grandfather as company president, was by his own admission "green and looking for answers." A mentor was needed. Two men headed Henry II's candidate list—Ralph Cordiner, chairman of General Electric Company, and Breech, the latter strongly recommended by Henry II's uncle, Ernest R. Kanzler, an astute, broad-based businessman.

Invited to become Ford's number-two man, Breech initially was reluctant to switch jobs, partly because he regarded the disorganized Dearborn organization with "contempt and pity." He relented, after telling his wife, "Well, here is a young man who is only one year older than our oldest son. He needs help. I hate to take on

this job, but if I do not do it I will always regret that I did not accept the challenge." After negotiating a lucrative contract, he became Ford's executive vice president in August 1946.

As an admirer of General Motors, Henry II wished for his company to be revamped in the mold of the world's most profitable industrial organization. Breech was made to order for the task. He and Henry II immediately assigned Ford executives to read Peter Drucker's 1946 book, *The Concept of the Corporation*, which focused on GM's organizational structure and policies. They also copied GM policy statements and manuals, merely substituting the word "Ford" for "General Motors" in many of the documents.

In addition, Breech imported a cadre of GM-trained executives, notably Lewis D. Crusoe, whom he made his executive assistant and the "Whiz Kids'" boss; Del Harder, given charge of manufacturing; and Harold T. Youngren, hired to direct engineering. These executives and others helped Breech decentralize the company and set up line and staff organizations worthy of challenging General Motors and Chrysler, then the industry's top two producers. One man displeased with the changes was Charles B. "Tex" Thornton, leader of the Whiz Kids, who had been reporting directly to Henry II. He departed the company in 1948.

In 1955, Breech's efforts were rewarded with the company chairmanship. Henry II remained CEO. Breech's annual salary and supplemental awards reached as high as $500,000 in the Fifties, and he also became a substantial shareholder through the exercise of stock options.

◄ A midyear freshening would change the body-color grille surround on this Mercury coupe to chrome. Updates were minor as the wait for all-new '49s was on. This two-door sedan was one of just 34 built before the style was canceled during 1947.

To Henry II, Breech was worth his pay. Summing up his former mentor in 1982, HFII observed, "He was an outstanding executive, and did an absolutely superior job. He was broad-gauged, not narrow-minded, or petty. He was a great motivator of people, and knew finance systems and other business procedures as well as anybody could. He had been in general management long enough to have a very definite feel of general management, and did a very good job at it. . . . I was very lucky to get him and couldn't have asked for anybody better."

This opinion was corroborated by William T. Gossett, Ford's general counsel from 1947 to 1962, who placed Breech on his list of the company's 10 all-time ablest executives. "He was a man of spectacular intellectual brilliance, Gossett said. "He took the CPA exam with 1500 people in Chicago . . . and not only was he number one, but he got a gold medal for his achievement . . . . [Also], he could mimic anybody and tell great stories. He could stand up before a group without a note and present a speech worthy of a standing ovation. He was, as *The New York Times* said of him, 'whip smart.' As an example, we were in Wall Street . . . going over papers, and came across a position expressed in an algebraic equation. The bankers said to him, 'We've got a mathematician. . . . Let's show it to him, and he'll work it out.' Breech said, 'I'll work it out.' He then went through that algebraic equation just like a hot knife through butter. . . . Everyone was immensely impressed."

As HFII matured, his dependence on Breech lessened. After informing his mentor that he had "graduated," Breech, in agreement, resigned the chairmanship in 1960, retaining Board membership until 1967. In recognition of his services, the company in 1962 named one of its lake boats the *Ernest R. Breech*. In 1961, Breech became chairman of troubled Trans-World Airlines (TWA), controlled by eccentric billionaire Howard Hughes. Within three years, he had made TWA the world's second-most profitable airline. He retired in 1969.

During his Ford years and beyond, Breech was bedeviled by the accusation that he had muffed a chance for Ford to buy Volkswagen in 1948 and by criticism of his role in the Edsel car disaster, which occurred on his watch. In Mel Hickerson's 1968 book, *Ernie Breech: The Story of His Remarkable Career at General Motors, Ford, and TWA*, Breech acknowledged that he was interested in merging Ford of Germany and Volkswagen in 1948, while correctly noting that ownership of the German firm was in such dispute that no foreign company could reasonably hope to acquire it at the time. He made no response to press imputations that he had said of the Beetle, "The car is not worth a damn."

In defense of his Edsel involvement, Breech wrote a full chapter for the Hickerson book. Recalling a 1954 meeting of Ford executives to consider whether or not to build the Edsel, he wrote, "I was the only person who disagreed with the fine men in that room. Finally I yielded and said, 'Well, I am going to go along with this only because you fellows are so "heady" on it.'" He added that the Edsel debacle was not the "financial tragedy to the Ford Motor Company that has been pictured," noting that stamping, engine, and other plants built or enlarged to handle expected Edsel production speeded the launch of the company's compact Falcon.

Breech's most important monument is Drury College's Breech School of Business Administration, which he financed in 1960. The Ernest and Thelma Breech Pavilion at Henry Ford Hospital's Fairlane Center in Dearborn was named for him and his wife in 1981. He died at age 81 in 1978, and was inducted into the Automotive Hall of Fame the following year.

1948

- Production of aging lineup curtailed early to make way for all-new Ford, Lincoln, and Mercury lines

- Chrysler, as well as General Motors, outsells Ford

- Redesigned trucks are launched as the new F-Series

- Truck production reaches record highs

- Last old-style woody produced—later wagons to have steel body shells

- Continentals, V-12 make their last stands

FORD ▲ The lines of the sedan coupe were gradually being perceived as dated by car shoppers, especially as some other manufacturers had already introduced all-new postwar designs. Only 45,000 found buyers this year, half that of '47.

◄ The Sportsman convertible and its hand-finished wooden flanks would disappear from the lineup before the redesigned '49s arrived. Only 28 of them would roll off the lines, all with V-8 engines.

▲ Never again would a Ford station wagon feature as much wood in its construction as it did in 1948. Production ended early to make way for all-new '49s.

▲ Ford interiors had changed little since 1942. Redesigned door panels and new upholstery were the extent of updates.

▲ San Diego law breakers faced a tight squeeze into the back of this black-and-white coupe sedan. Civilian versions cost $1330 with a six, or $1490 with a V-8.

▲ A bright spot in an otherwise dismal year, the fully redesigned F-Series trucks—like the F-1 pickup—were an instant success. One-piece windshields were new.

LINCOLN

▶ The Zephyr era at Lincoln came to a close with the springtime end of the '48 model year. Neither the antiquated transverse-spring chassis nor the long-lived V-12 engine would carry over to 1949. Just 6470 base-series Lincolns were run off for the year. Model availability and prices were the same as in '47, meaning this convertible cost $3142 to start.

▲ One of the last of the Edsel Ford-era cars, the Continental, faced its final model year unchanged. Costing up to $2000 more than lesser Lincolns, the Continentals never sold in great volume, but their presence in the line helped to underscore the make's luxury credentials.

► Aware, perhaps, that owners might want to preserve these last-of-the-breed Continentals, Lincoln treated them to a paint-finishing process it called "Porcelainization." Visible through the window of this car is the standard body-colored dashboard. Despite the short model year, a "healthy" 452 cabriolets and 847 coupes rolled off the assembly line.

◄ Through the years, Mercury has wavered between being a "senior Ford" and a "junior Lincoln." It certainly was the former when the brand was introduced for 1939, and that philosophy carried through to 1948, when this sedan coupe was built. A three-position locking ignition switch was one of the few telltale innovations for the '48 model year.

► As expected, the four-door sedan was the most-ordered Mercury of 1948. But, considering that all-new '49s hit showrooms in late April, it's not surprising that production of the last prewar-style sedan came to just 24,283 units, or about 19,000 fewer than the year before. The Lincoln-Mercury Division—which had been formed in late 1945 to manufacture and market those marques—got a new boss this year: Benson Ford.

- All FoMoCo makes dramatically restyled, discard transverse "buggy springs" in favor of independent front suspension and rear leaf springs

- Ford model-year production beats Chevrolet by more than 100,000

- High development and tooling costs drive prices $200-$300 higher

- DeLuxe and Super DeLuxe trim levels replaced by Standard and Custom

- Lincoln offered in base and Cosmopolitan series, each with its own wheelbase length

FORD ▲ A revolving turntable at the Waldorf-Astoria Hotel highlighted five Custom models: Fordor, station wagon, Tudor, convertible, and club coupe. Preview visitors could gape at Ford's flush-fender body and inspect the underside. Except on convertibles, the X-member chassis was gone, replaced by a ladder-type frame. The new model was lighter and livelier, scampering to 60 mph in as little as 15 seconds.

▲ Ford's "lifeguard body" is seen here in the early stages of assembly. Build quality suffered initially as lines were hurried to meet demand.

▲ Ford brothers Benson and Henry II chat with corporate management whiz Ernest Breech at the New York introduction of the new Ford lineup.

▶ Print advertising proclaimed it "A dream wagon, with its heart of steel and the new Ford feel." Real wood continued to be used on the wagon, but was now fitted to a steel body. The two-door "wide-door" body was advertised as "a blessing to parents of small children." Seating for eight was still provided. Wagons were available only in Custom trim. Price, when equipped with a V-8, was $2119.

▲ An interior view reveals a speedometer that has finally been centered over the steering wheel. The vertical chrome strakes of past Ford dashboards gave way to a sleeker horizontal design.

▲ Far more customers chose a Custom Tudor sedan at $1511 over the standard edition, which cost $86 less. More than 433,000 Custom Tudors went to dealers, versus 126,270 of its cheaper siblings.

▲ Naturally, an invigorated Ford needed a fresh convertible. The sportiest of the lot, this Custom ragtop attracted more than 51,000 customers with its $1886 price tag. The all-new Chevys arrived several months later, giving the new Fords plenty of time in the limelight.

◄ Slab-sided in profile, three inches lower, slightly shorter and narrower, the '49 Ford marked a dramatic change from prior models. Ads boasted of "Mid Ship" ride, "Picture Window" visibility, and "Hydra-Coil" front springs.

► F-1 trucks could now be had with a heavy-duty three-speed transmission instead of just the standard four-speed. Grille bars lost their earlier red striping, and wheels were painted the same color as the body. Like passenger cars, the small trucks were now available with "Magic Air" heating, drawing fresh air through a cowl vent.

◄ The "Bonus Built" trucks were claimed to offer "living room" comfort, and strong sales suggest some buyers agreed. Car and truck buyers who opted for the V-8 engine were treated to a host of technical updates including new valve guides, which helped reduce oil consumption.

► A longtime staple of the Good Humor fleet, Ford's F-1 trucks capably served as mobile ice cream parlors. The ringing of the bells mounted above the windshield were enough to send every kid in earshot scrounging for loose change. In later years, the bells would be replaced a loudspeaker, and the ringing by circus music.

LINCOLN

▶ The '49 Lincoln lineup was substantially revised. The Continental was gone, replaced to an extent by the Cosmopolitan, essentially a longer-wheelbase version of the standard Lincoln with exclusive bodywork. The standard Lincoln shrank slightly, riding a new 121-inch wheelbase. All Lincolns used a refined version of Ford's 337-cid truck V-8.

The Biggest News in the Fine Car Field!

TWO COMPLETELY NEW 1949 *Lincolns*

IN A CHOICE OF MAGNIFICENT BODY STYLES AND TWO SEPARATE PRICE RANGES

The *Lincoln*

The *Lincoln Cosmopolitan*

Nothing could be Finer — or Newer!

◀ Considered the rarest of all '49 Lincolns, the "junior" convertible rode the shorter chassis of the standard Lincoln. Though actual build numbers are unavailable, demand was understood to be so low that the production was halted midway through the model year. The small "non-Cosmopolitan" convertible did not return for 1950.

▲ A roofline that sloped gently into the trunk distinguished the Cosmopolitan Town Sedan from its notchback Sport Sedan companion. Both sold for $3238.

▲ Out in Hollywood, a pleased-looking Ronald Reagan admires the new Cosmopolitan coupe. Meanwhile, Jane Wyman seems less impressed.

GEORGE W. WALKER

"Cellini of Chrome"

IN AN INDUSTRY that has had a full measure of colorful styling executives, none was more flamboyant than George W. Walker. "His favorite TV shows must have been Westerns," said his publicist, George A. Haviland, "because that's the way he lived life."

Born in 1896 in Chicago and reared in Cleveland, Walker studied art in Los Angeles and Cleveland. Launching his career in Cleveland in 1923, he initially specialized in fashion illustration. In 1929, he moved to Detroit and started an industrial design firm that would style more than 3000 products ranging from baby bottles, clocks, and radios to lawn mowers, truck tires, and tractors.

In 1935, Walker spent nearly $3000 in staff time and materials to prepare a portfolio of futuristic automotive designs to show to Henry Ford. Glancing at the sketches, Walker recalled, Ford "didn't say a word. He just walked out of the room. Ford hated unfunctional things, and my designs were sure unfunctional."

Eleven years later, Walker was invited by Ford Executive Vice President Ernest R. Breech to evaluate in-house design chief Eugene T. Gregorie's ideas for the first new postwar Ford. After deprecating Gregorie's design, Walker submitted an alternate proposal (apparently provided by Dick Caleal, a former Studebaker designer Walker brought in on the project). It was selected over Gregorie's concept and became the 1949 Ford. Walker served as a company consultant until 1955, when he was named vice president and director of styling.

Among Ford executives, Walker's lifestyle was unique. A cigar-smoking, five-foot-ten, 220-pounder who resembled an aging movie star, he owned 70 custom-made suits and 40 pairs of shoes, and splashed on Faberge cologne. "A stylist," he explained, "must show style." He spent $30,000 to refurnish his spacious office, which featured white furniture, including a large kidney-shaped desk, complemented by black mouton fur carpeting. His "finest moment," he said, "was driving along Miami's Biscayne Boulevard in my white Continental. I was wearing a pure-silk, pure-white embroidered cowboy shirt and black gabardine trousers. Beside me in the car was my jet-black Great Dane. . . . You just can't do any better than that. . . . I was terrific." To his delight, he was pictured on *Time*'s cover in 1957 and described as the "Cellini of Chrome." Also shown on the cover was the Edsel's horsecollar grille. Walker, observed Haviland, was "totally uninhibited. He loved feminine flesh." His eccentricities included eavesdropping on William Clay Ford Sr., whose office was next door. He did so, in the presence of visitors, by putting his ear or a glass to the wall.

Walker often is given full credit for having designed the cars with which he is associated. Actually, he relied very heavily on talented associates—Elwood Engel, Joe Oros, Gene Bordinat, Don DeLaRossa, and others. In addition to the 1949 Ford, Walker supervised or had a hand in the styling of most of Ford's cars of the Fifties. An exception was the Continental Mark II, Walker's stylists having lost out to a design team put together by William Clay Ford Sr.

Walker's talents were downsized by other Ford designers, who referred to him as a promoter, publicity seeker, and politician. "George Walker was all front . . . all surface," R. F. Hintermeister recalled. "I don't know how he got the job because I don't think he had an original bone in his body."

Reinforcing Hintermeister's views, Dave Ash remarked, "George had a fantastic personality, but was not very knowledgeable. He was extremely shrewd. He knew how to get the right people around him to give him the appearance of being knowledgeable. He was a fashion illustrator, not a car designer."

Echoed John Najjar, "I never saw George design. I saw George talk design and draw females and other things on a pad while talking to higher-ups. . . . He was an industrial designer. He had a successful place [consultancy], and he knew how to hire people capable of interpreting his oral designs. In that sense, he was a designer."

Others praised Walker, or gave him mixed reviews. James Wright, who headed Ford Division and the Car and Truck Group, viewed him as an "excellent designer." William Clay Ford Sr. described him as "a terrible executive, an atrocious executive. But he had great design flair." George Haviland was more generous. "He made an immeasurable contribution to the company because he had two things, both very necessary: He was creative, he knew design. Secondly, he knew how to make people appreciate a design."

Mandatorily retired at age 65 in 1961, Walker plumped for Engel, then Oros as his successor. Both were passed over in favor of Bordinat. Walker moved to Gulfstream, Florida, and was elected its mayor in 1972. In 1989, he moved into a self-designed home in Tucson, Arizona, where he died at age 96 in 1993.

► The Cosmopolitan convertible was Lincoln's most-expensive model. Priced at $3948, it cost $763 more than the coupe, but $798 less than last year's Continental cabriolet. Calabash Yellow and Calcutta Green were colors exclusive to the Cosmopolitan ragtop.

MERCURY ▲ Mercury's best-selling model was the four-door sedan, pictured here with an optional sunshade. By racking up sales of nearly 156,000 cars, it alone easily trumped production of all 1948 Mercury models combined. Starting prices now ranged from $1979 for a coupe to $2716 for a station wagon.

▲ Mercury's new cars helped sales increase sixfold over 1948. Mercury made an interesting decision to stay with front-opening rear doors, a design element that was growing less common in the market.

▲ Though it shared its two-door body with Ford, the Mercury station wagon still rode a four-inch-longer wheelbase. Compared with the rest of the line, the wagon was a slow seller, with only 8044 finding homes.

HENRY FORD AND AFRICAN AMERICANS

When Henry Ford died in 1947, African American publications were effusive in their praise of the auto king. Much of their editorial opinion was summed up by the *Journal of Negro History*, published by the National Association for the Advancement of Colored People. Ford, the *Journal* declared, "endeavored to help humanity by offering men work at living wages and making it comfortable for them in his employment. In this respect he was a great benefactor of the Negro race, probably the greatest that ever lived."

Why was Ford so helpful to African Americans? An important clue points to William Perry, a black man employed by Ford in 1888–89. Born near Windsor, Ontario, Canada, where his descendants still live, Perry was hired by Ford to help him clear timberland in the Dearborn area. The pair, both 25 years old, spent many days manning a crosscut saw, a long, limber blade with handles at both ends requiring two persons to operate. Their work forged a bond of friendship that endured more than 50 years.

The significance of the friendship was revealed years later in one of the jotbooks in which Ford wrote many of his inner thoughts. The notation observed that blacks and whites should work together with "the colored man [sawing] at one end of the log, the white man at the other."

Ford began working in Detroit 1891. Perry became a bricklayer about the same time, but was forced out of his trade by a heart ailment in 1913. He arranged to see Henry Ford on February 9, 1914, by which time Ford was world famous, and his company was the world's largest and most-profitable auto producer.

After chatting in Ford's Highland Park, Michigan, office, the industrialist and his friend spent more than an hour inspecting machinery in the powerhouse. At the end of the tour, Ford signaled the powerhouse superintendent and told him to put Perry to work. Mindful of Perry's heart condition, Ford told the superintendent to see that Perry was comfortable in his job. William Perry thus became the Ford company's first black employee, the forerunner of hundreds of thousands to come, among them heavyweight boxing champion Joe Louis, Olympic star Jesse Owens, and Detroit's first African American mayor, Coleman Young.

In time, Perry became as much of a Ford fixture as the powerhouse whistle. Despite poor health and advancing age, and in the face of mass layoffs during the Twenties and Thirties, Perry remained on the Ford payroll until his death at age 87 on October 9, 1940. He remains the oldest employee ever to be on the company's active-service payroll.

At the time Perry joined Ford, almost all U.S. manufacturing firms turned their backs on skilled and semi-skilled African Americans. The elevation of a black to a foremanship or white-collar position was almost unthinkable. Generally, the only industrial jobs open to blacks were those that whites disdained. Consequently, blacks increasingly toiled as sweat laborers in the metal industries, where the work was dirty, hot, and arduous. Moreover, African Americans usually were paid less than whites, even if they held the same job classification. Then came Henry Ford.

He placed African Americans in virtually all of his company's hourly rated job classifications, including tool-and-die making—the most skilled and prestigious of plant work. In the process, Ford saw to it that blacks and whites worked side by side and were paid the same wages for the same jobs. Eventually, Ford began promoting African Americans to foremanships and other positions in which they supervised both blacks and whites. African American supervisors were authorized to challenge plant managers and superintendents, and to fire white foremen and managers accused of racial discrimination.

In 1919, Ford began hiring African Americans for white-collar positions. The first such employee was Eugene J. Collins, a young Coe College graduate, who, within 30 minutes of having presented himself at the employment office, was running carbon and silicon tests on cast iron in the company's control-analysis lab. Collins' employment was consistent with Henry Ford's general employment philosophy, expressed in a 1919 policy statement: "We have learned to appreciate men as men, and to forget the discrimination of color, race, country, religion, fraternal orders, and everything else outside of human qualities and energy."

Ford's labor policies were shaped by his personal motto, "Help the Other Fellow," which was widely publicized by the Ford organization during the half-dozen years after the introduction of the $5 day in 1914. The way to help men, Ford believed with fervor, was to provide an opportunity for them to help themselves. In 1916, the company employed people representing 62 nationalities. Aside from reaching out to blacks, the company embraced other often underrepresented segments of the labor force. For instance, by 1919, the firm had found places for 9563 persons with some kind of physical handicap—19.8 percent of all employees. The Ford Motor Company had a remarkably diverse workforce more than a half-century before such employment became more commonplace.

HENRY FORD AND AFRICAN AMERICANS
Continued

Ford's lifelong concern for African Americans was expressed in a variety of ways. He strongly felt, for example, that blacks should have greater educational opportunities. He built schools and churches for African Americans in Georgia and Michigan, and spent more than $500,000—a large sum for the day—to sustain and rehabilitate the largely black community of Inkster, Michigan. Starting in 1929, Ford and his wife annually attended services at St. Matthew's Episcopal Church, a black church in Detroit, a gesture that meant much to the city's African American community.

Ford also maintained a warm friendship with George Washington Carver, the widely respected African American botanist/chemist, and supported his research. On several occasions, the magnate visited the scientist's laboratory at Tuskegee Institute in Alabama. Carver, in turn, journeyed to Michigan to assist Ford in his research into nutritional uses for roadside vegetation—weeds. The pair professed to enjoy what one Ford employee called "grass sandwiches."

Also, at a time when few national radio programs featured African American performers, Henry Ford insisted that his company's national symphonic radio broadcast—the *Ford Sunday Evening Hour*—present such black artists as Dorothy Maynor and Marian Anderson, the latter one of the most celebrated singers of her time.

In addition to treating African American workers more equitably than any other large employer, the Ford company hired blacks in much larger absolute numbers and percentages than any other U.S. industrial firm. During the Twenties and Thirties, the percentage of African Americans employed at Ford exceeded the ratio of blacks in the total Detroit population. In 1929, for example, when 7.7 percent of Detroit's population was black, eight percent of Ford's Detroit-area employment was black. In 1940, when African Americans comprised nine percent of Detroit's population, 11.5 percent of Ford's Detroit-area work force was African American.

The company also had a unique hiring system for African Americans. Most Detroit firms hired blacks through the Detroit Chapter of the Urban League, the Employers Association of Detroit, or the Michigan Employment Association. Ford's first African American employees were simply hired at the employment gate or by Henry Ford and like-minded executives.

Blacks hired by Ford officials had certain advantages. They usually were spared dismissal and plantwide pay cuts during general layoffs and recessions. Moreover, African Americans with executive backing often were given favored treatment. James Price provides an example.

Two generations of African American Ford employees are pictured here in 1953. Clement Johnson Sr. (left) and his son, Clement Jr., were both draftsmen.

Price worked in a tailor shop patronized by Ford executives, including production boss Charles E. Sorensen. After Ford doubled wages to $5 a day in 1914, Price asked Sorensen for a job. The next day, the pair met at the Highland Park plant. "Jim," Sorensen said, "you're going to be the first colored man here to get a job that means something. I'm going to put you in charge of a toolroom. If anybody abuses, insults, or humiliates you, I want you to come to me."

Starting work at the handsome wage of $6.15 per day, Price's stock went up in 1917, when Sorensen called a meeting in his toolroom and ordered every other tool attendant to model his room "after Jim's system." In 1924, when the company's buyer of abrasives was fired for graft, Sorensen asked Price to clean up the mess. After doing so, Price became Ford's abrasives buyer and the company's first African American "star man," a designation enabling him to wear a star-shaped badge awarded only to well-placed salaried employees. In 1934, Price acquired the additional responsibility of purchasing the company's industrial diamonds. Until his retirement in 1947, he was generally regarded as one of the industry's outstanding buyers of abrasives and industrial diamonds.

Henry Ford introduced a new supplemental employment system in 1918, when discipline problems arose between the company's black and white workers. Over lunch, Ford discussed the problem with the Rev. R. L. Bradby, pastor of Second Baptist Church, Detroit's largest African American church. Impressed by Ford's concern over his workers, including problem employees, Bradby asked the magnate, "How long do you keep a man before you wash your hands of him?" Ford replied, "We're here to save the devil."

Following the luncheon, Bradby was asked to recommend high-caliber black workers to Ford's employment office. He also was given a pass to all of the company's buildings and invited to help settle racial disputes. For the next two decades, he was an inseparable part of Ford's African American relations.

In 1923, when 5000 African Americans were working in the Rouge Plant, another African American minister, Rev. Everard W. Daniel, was asked to supplement Bradby's work. As pastor of St. Matthew's Episcopal Church, whose membership included a large percentage of Detroit's African American intelligentsia and business leaders, Daniel was influential far beyond his congregation. He was, in fact, regarded by many Detroiters as the city's leading African American spokesperson. Daniel also received a pass to Ford property, and, by 1925, he and Henry Ford had developed a warm personal relationship. Ford, a nominal Episcopalian, donated funds for St. Matthew's parish house. Over the years, Daniel introduced numerous visiting African American leaders to Ford officials, and was asked by Henry Ford to represent him and the company at formal ceremonies, including the installation of black college presidents.

In time, other African Americans, including clergymen, physicians, businessmen, politicians, and personal friends of Ford executives acquired the privilege of recommending workers for employment at Ford. For a time the system worked well: Top-notch people were recommended. During the Thirties, however, as Henry Ford paid less attention to the factory, his devious aide, Harry Bennett, gained control over the work force. As more people were empowered to make recommendations, corruption crept in, culminating in job selling during the Great Depression.

Job selling took many forms, most of them involving the exchange of money. Pay someone so much, and a recommendation could be had. The sale of jobs to both African Americans and whites became and remained an unsavory aspect of Ford employment until the UAW-CIO organized Ford's plants in 1941.

As a result of Henry Ford's high employment of African Americans, the company had great influence in Detroit's black community. From 1920 on, the company was the city's largest employer of African Americans. It's little wonder that locally they developed a great loyalty toward Henry Ford and his company.

This loyalty was put to the test when the UAW-CIO attempted to organize the Ford company between 1937-41, at which time the firm's 10,000 black workers were assiduously courted by both the union and the firm. Among Ford employees, blacks, handicapped employees, and Henry Ford Trade School graduates were the least-receptive to the union's blandishments. Hundreds of black employees, in fact, participated on the company's side in the Battle of the Overpass, a 1937 skirmish in which Ford security men roughed up Walter Reuther and other union leaders. Detroit's African American community applauded its members' role, a black newspaper referring to one African American worker, who had knocked down four unionists, as the "uncrowned hero" of the pitched battle.

As part of its organizational effort, the UAW promised "to unite . . . occupations, without regard to race, creed, or color." The union was immediately rebuffed by leading members of the black Detroit Interdenominational Ministers' Alliance, who wrote Henry Ford to affirm their belief that blacks were best served by his labor policies and to offer assurance that he could "count on our group almost one hundred percent." Parishioners, accordingly, were exhorted not to "bite the hand which had fed them."

The reference to Ford's labor policies was a telling blow, for the union obviously could not convince black workers that it would be able to increase their numbers at Ford as long as the company employed almost twice as many blacks as General Motors, Chrysler, and Briggs Manufacturing Company combined, all of which had contracts with the UAW-CIO. Ford, moreover, offered its black employees opportunities for skilled employment and advancement that were unavailable in the already-unionized segment of the auto industry.

When the Rouge Plant was struck in 1941, several thousand African Americans—some estimates run as high as 5000—remained inside out of loyalty to Ford. All but 200 to 300 of them remained loyal to the company throughout the strike. The UAW-CIO finally organized Ford, but no thanks to the company's black workers, who overwhelmingly voted for no union, or a rival union, the UAW-AFL, as instructed by Ford.

Henry Ford and his company maintained an enlightened employment policy toward African Americans for as long as the magnate lived and beyond. Measured by today's standards, one can argue that Ford should have done what he did for African Americans as a matter of course; indeed, should have done more. But Ford, like everyone else, must be judged within the context of his time, and in that sense he stands apart from all other major employers. To this day he remains one of the greatest benefactors of African Americans. Surprisingly, the company has done little to publicize as much. In the light of Henry Ford's anti-Semitism when weighed against his favorable treatment of African Americans, one can only speculate if he would have developed a better opinion of Jews if the sawing partner of his youth had been Jewish, rather than black.

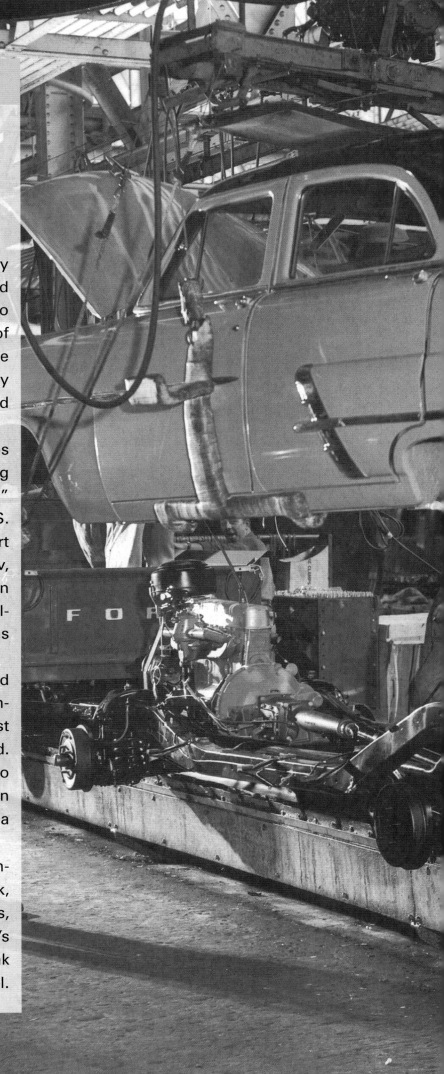

1950–1959

Big Challenges

ALTHOUGH SELF-ASSURED and immensely powerful, the United States spawned Wisconsin Senator Joe McCarthy, who claimed to have ferreted out scores of "card-carrying Communists" in the State Department and elsewhere. He finally shot himself in the foot when he claimed similar infestation of the U.S. Army.

Communist North Korean troops poured into South Korea in 1950, kicking off a bloody, three-year UN "police action."

Dwight Eisenhower became U.S. president in 1953; his Soviet counterpart was stout, hotheaded Nikita Khrushchev, who reveled in America's dismay when the USSR launched its *Sputnik* satellite in 1957. Meanwhile, American teens rocked 'n' rolled.

France abandoned a place called Vietnam in 1954. Two years later, Hungarian patriots who revolted against Communist rule were brutally crushed. In Cuba, revolutionary leader Fidel Castro booted out President Fulgencio Batista in 1959. Castro eventually looked to Russia for sponsorship.

Atomic spies Julius and Ethel Rosenberg were executed. In Little Rock, Montgomery, and other Southern cities, blacks demanded a place at America's table. Recession came in 1958, and sank a not-bad Ford-built car called the Edsel.

1950

- Ford launches vinyl-top Crestliner sports sedan; Lincoln Lido and Capri, Mercury Monterey also wear padded tops

- Lincolns may be ordered with Hydra-Matic, bought from GM

- Ford's market share reaches 24 percent, highest since the mid Thirties

- Ford slips to second place in car volume at 1.2 million; Chevrolet builds nearly 300,000 more

- Clara B. Ford, wife of Henry, dies in September

▶ Fords received subtle exterior trim changes for 1950. Custom club coupes like this one started at $1511 and accounted for 85,111 sales. Whitewalls, wheel trim rings, and fender skirts were extra-cost options.

FORD ▲ The gussied-up Crestliner was introduced midyear as a stopgap answer to General Motors' pillarless hardtop coupes until Ford could field a true hardtop. Available only as a two-door sedan, exclusive features included distinctive two-tone side trim, special hubcaps, basketweave-pattern vinyl top, and upscale interior trim.

▲ With the midyear addition of a "stow-away" fold-flat middle seat, the two-door wood-sided wagon was newly advertised as the Country Squire. Ford wagons found 22,929 customers. "Woodies" featured laminated wood panels inset in steel bodies. Price: $2028.

▲ Interior upgrades included new seat springs and cushioning, new fabrics, and wider sun visors. The "Magic Air" heater, a $57.95 option, had a higher-s motor for a claimed 25 percent increase in air flow

▲ Custom convertible coupes started out at $1948, but plentiful accessories like spotlights, gravel guards, fuel-door trim, full wheel covers, fender skirts, and back-up lights could quickly add to the base price.

▲ F-1 pickups were virtually unchanged save for slight engine modifications and a late model-year switch to a column-mounted gearshift lever for three-speed trucks. This example wears original Ford accessory fog lights.

LINCOLN

▶ The costlier of the two four-doors in the Lincoln lineup was this Cosmopolitan sport sedan, with a price of $3240. Lincoln's most popular model was the $2576 standard sport sedan. While sedan exteriors were largely carried over from the '49s, freshened dashboards topped the list of interior updates. Racking up 11,741 sales, the standard sedan outsold the four-door Cosmopolitan by exactly 3400 cars.

▲ Lincoln's biggest news of the year came in the form of a relatively small sale, to the White House. The order was for nine seven-passenger limousines and one open-air parade car, the latter to replace President Truman's "Sunshine Special" convertible, a throwback to the Roosevelt era. Though similar to Lincoln's standard limousine, the "White House specials" included a number of security features, including hidden side steps for Secret Service use.

▲ New door-trim panels headed the list of Cosmopolitan interior changes. New color-keyed steering wheels were now matched to interior colors.

▲ Passengers may have noticed a quieter ride, as all '50 Lincolns now featured fiberglass sound insulation. The Cosmopolitan's chrome front-wheel-arch "eyebrows," unique among Lincolns, would disappear for 1951.

► Priced at $2576, the standard Lincoln sport sedan cost $664 less than the four-door Cosmopolitan. Like all Lincolns, motivation came from Ford's largest V-8, a 337-cid unit good for 152 bhp, eight fewer than archrival Cadillac's 331-cube overhead-valve V-8. Straighter new grille styling did away with the perceptible "frown" that was seen on the face of 1949 Lincolns.

◄ Thanks to having been James Dean's ride of choice in the Fifties film classic *Rebel Without a Cause*, Mercury coupes circa 1950 went on to become automotive icons. This well-equipped club coupe cost $1980, not including the visor, spotlights, and two-tone paint. Responding to the coupe's soft, rounded shape, auto buffs dubbed them the "bathtub Mercs."

▲ In a peculiar bit of copywriting, Mercury advertising referred to the convertible coupe as "smart, sleek-looking and massive." A full-leather interior replaced the previously standard-equipment leather-with-whipcord-accent upholstery. Price: $2412. Linewide changes included restyled instrument panels, the adoption of Econ-O-Miser carburetors, and quieter cooling fans.

▲ The Mercury sport sedan cost about $500 more than a Ford Custom Fordor, but was better equipped. It was also Mercury's best-selling model, finding more than 132,000 buyers.

▲ Without a direct competitor ready for 1950, Mercury responded to the pillarless-hardtop craze with the Monterey. A midyear introduction, the Monterey sported fender skirts and a choice of vinyl or canvas top.

▲ Lincoln-Mercury General Manager Benson Ford (in driver's seat) and Indianapolis Motor Speedway President Wilbur Shaw pose in the Mercury that served as the pace car for the 1950 Indianapolis 500.

▲ As with Ford's woody wagon, structural wood panels were fitted to the Mercury's steel body framing. At $2561, the wagon was Mercury's most expensive model, and its slowest seller. Only 1746 were sold.

1951

- Korean War intensifies; production cutbacks ordered by Washington
- Government limits civilian use of zinc, tin, and nickel
- Ford joins hardtop frenzy with pillarless Victoria coupe
- Ford-O-Matic automatic transmission added to options list
- Mercury adds own Merc-O-Matic self shifter to lineup
- Both Ford and Chevrolet production numbers slip
- Ford recovers from cash crunch thanks to popular 1949–51 restyle
- Lincoln output rises to 32,574— but ranking drops to 18th

FORD

▶ A new "dual-spinner" grille was the most visible of the year's trim changes, and Ford's first automatic transmission, the three-speed Ford-O-Matic, debuted as a $164 option. The wood-sided Country Squire remained the sole station wagon and was also the priciest Ford at $2029. Its sales rose to 29,017 for the model year.

◀ The hastily engineered Custom Victoria debuted on January 28, 1951, as Ford's first production hardtop. Despite the late introduction, its 110,286-car production run outpaced Chevrolet's Bel Air by nearly 7000 units. Victoria prices started at $1925, only $24 less than a convertible. It was available only with a V-8. All '51 Fords but the wagon got a new dash.

▶ Lost in the Victoria hardtop's shadow, the cheeky Crestliner returned for its final season. The Victoria cost $330 more, but it outsold the $1595 Crestliner by a more than 12-to-1 ratio. Despite its lame-duck status, the Crestliner received a number of updates, including a revised two-tone color break. Only 8703 were built.

◄ Accompanying 1951's revised grille were restyled hubcaps, fresh headlight bezels, and a new hood ornament. Chrome "wind splits" merged into larger twin-point taillights, and side trim on Custom models now wrapped around the rear. Overall output sank 200,000 units in a slow year for the industry. Convertible production decreased more than 9000 units to 40,934 as the post-World War II "seller's market" evaporated. Convertibles came standard with V-8 power and listed for $1949. Minor improvements to the 239-cid V-8 included a waterproof ignition system and a larger-capacity fuel pump, but output was unchanged at 100 bhp.

▲ Participating in the 1951 Mobilgas Economy Run proved to be a test of endurance as well as frugality, as contestants trekked through the desert southwest. Even with Ford-O-Matic, a V-8 could manage 18 mpg.

▲ A triple-tooth grille highlighted styling changes to light-duty trucks. Dual wipers were now standard, and a larger rear window and wider cargo box were among the functional upgrades.

LINCOLN ▲ A wide, chrome rocker-panel strip was added to the Cosmopolitan profile as part of the '51 freshening. Gone was the front-wheel chrome "eyebrow" that previously differentiated Cosmopolitans from lesser Lincolns. Buyers of the updated "Cosmo" sport sedan evidently liked what they saw, as sales leapt to 12,229, almost 4000 cars more than the prior year.

▲ The Cosmopolitan's clean lines were well-suited for soft top duty. This already-rare convertible coupe came equipped with the optional Hydra-Matic automatic transmission. Not having an automatic of its own, Lincoln was put in the precarious position of buying Hydra-Matic transmissions from General Motors. Lincoln advertising was careful to avoid mentioning that its cars could be equipped with the same transmission as rival Cadillac.

◄ This standard sport sedan features an optional chrome rocker-panel trim piece borrowed from a Mercury. The sport sedan was once again Lincoln's best-selling model, but by the narrowest of margins. A total of 12,279 cars found homes, only 50 more than did Cosmopolitan four-doors. Price: $2553.

▲ The special-edition Lido coupe returned for its second and final year priced at $2702, or $197 more than the standard Lincoln coupe. The "master-crafted" Lidos featured a "vinyl-leather-covered steel safety roof."

▲ A padded roof gave the Cosmopolitan Capri some flair, but the fancy coupes failed to attract much attention. Vertical taillights were new to all Lincolns even though the two series had different rear styling.

MERCURY

▶ Mercury's station wagon was once again its least-popular model. At $2530 before options, the eight-passenger wood-trimmed wagon was the most-expensive car in the line. Though racking up only 3800 sales, the big Merc managed to out-sell such woody-wagon competitors as the Buick Super Estate Wagon. This wagon features a number of extra-cost options, including a windshield visor, driver's-side spot-light, and fender skirts. Construction of Ford and Mercury station wagons was farmed out this year.

▲ Mercury was facing the final year in its current "bathtub" form. A bolder grille and extended rear fenders helped create a longer and lower silhouette.

▲ Only slightly less rare than the Mercury wagon, the Monterey coupe returned for a second and final year. Price: $2116 with canvas top, $2127 with vinyl top.

◀ Mercury's four-door sport sedan was its most popular car. Critics felt that this year's extra brightwork and added heft detracted from the car's originally clean design that debuted for '49. Almost 160,000 buyers thought otherwise however, plunking down an even $2000 to drive one home.

1952

- Fords get second full restyle in three years

- Overhead-valve 215-cid "Mileage Maker" six cylinder debuts

- New Crestline series includes Victoria hardtop, Sunliner convertible, Country Squire wagon

- High-end Capri series now caps redesigned Lincoln lineup

- Lincoln introduces ohv V-8 with 160 horsepower

- Mercury branches into two model lines

- Only 671,733 cars built, down from 1,013,381; but Chevrolet suffers similar drop

- Ford production landmarks include 39-millionth car and 1.5-millionth tractor

▲ Portraits of Edsel and Henry Ford overlook a meeting of top Ford Motor Company decision makers. They are, from left, John R. Davis, Theodore Yntema, Benson Ford, John Bugas, Ernest R. Breech, Henry Ford II, Delmar Harder, Lewis Crusoe, and William Gossett.

▶ Ford had come a long way since Henry the elder created his Quadricycle (pictured here with grandson William Clay Ford) in 1896. Even more changes were in the offing. The two-decade-old flathead V-8 was about to expire, replaced by a cut-down version of the ohv V-8 that went into '52 Lincolns.

FORD ▲ All-new styling and some tempting engineering innovations helped give Ford a leg up on the competition. Offered only with V-8 power, this Victoria exhibits an intriguing selection of accessories, including dual spotlights, fender skirts, and full disc hubcaps. The chrome strip atop the rear side sculpture could be dealer or owner installed. Inside was a redesigned interior with "Flight-Style Control Panel" and new suspended pedals.

▲ Station wagon volume jumped sharply, to 49,919 units, with new all-steel bodies and wider model availability. Pictured here is the midlevel, six-passenger Customline Country Sedan, priced from $2060.

▲ Police fleets had long been partial to Fords. This '52 Tudor (V-8 powered, naturally) served the Houston, Texas, police. Law enforcement vehicles were usually base models, but this one is a midrange Customline.

◄ Appearance changes on pickups were limited to revised hood trim and slightly different color choices. Underhood, an all-new ohv six-cylinder engine could be had. The 215-cid powerplant produced 101 bhp at 3500 rpm with a compression ratio of 7:1. Ford bumped up the compression ratio of the V-8, boosting its horsepower rating from 100 to 106; it wouldn't do to have a six produce more horsepower than the venerable flathead V-8.

LINCOLN

► Only 1191 Lincoln Capri convertibles were built, versus 5681 hardtops. Lincoln's one-piece grille/bumper design launched a styling trend, as did the gas-filler cap hidden behind the license plate. Price: $3665 for the convertible. In the marketplace, Lincoln was now aiming less at Cadillac customers and more toward buyers of Oldsmobile Ninety-Eights.

▶ Now the entry-level Lincoln, Cosmopolitans sported the same redesigned chassis—with ball-joint front suspension—as the new Capri. A new 160-bhp overhead-valve V-8 was standard on all Lincolns, as was Hydra-Matic drive. The new engine would be Lincoln's first volley in a horsepower war that would be waged for the rest of the decade.

▲ With the Cosmopolitan name demoted to the standard series, Capris now sat atop the Lincoln line. Available as a four-door sedan, hardtop coupe, or convertible coupe, Capri rode the same 123-inch wheelbase as the Cosmopolitan, but came with a fancier interior and added exterior trim.

MERCURY

◀ Sleek is the word for the top-down Mercury Monterey convertible. Sporting a longer, lower profile, the topless Monterey was far different from its rounded "bathtub" 1949–51 predecessors. Note the wide, nonfunctioning hood "jet scoop." The round "grille guards" on this Monterey were an extra-cost option. Despite the svelte redesign, Mercury sales were well off the previous year's numbers, but no more than the rest of the industry. For the first time, Mercury offered two lines of cars, with Monterey the top series.

▲ New Mercurys like this Custom four-door sedan featured several advertising-worthy features such as "sealeg" rear shock absorbers and "Centri-Flo" carburetors. Engine refinements resulted in a 13 bhp jump to 125.

◄ Mercury's station wagon was now a woody in name only. The all-steel wagons now featured the look of wood over the door skins and rear quarter panels, but only the light frame pieces actually started life as trees. Now available with six- or eight-passenger seating, and only as a four-door, Merc wagon sales slumped to less than 2500, down 1300 from the year before. Prices rose slightly; an eight-passenger wagon cost $2570, a $40 increase.

▲ Wagon interiors were truer to their wood-body heritage. Furniture-quality door and dashboard trim gave the car a parlorlike feel. This car was equipped with the optional Merc-O-Matic automatic transmission.

► Less ornately finished than its Monterey cousin, the Custom hardtop coupe could look rather plain. Customers didn't seem to mind though, buying 6100 more Custom coupes than Monterey hardtops. A Custom two-door hardtop without "Sea-Tint" windows cost $2100. Mercury heavily promoted the virtues of its new "mono-pane" curved windshield and wraparound back window. A new "interceptor" aircraft-style instrument pod was a hit with customers.

- Ford celebrates 50th anniversary with Ed Sullivan TV special
- Ford joins Lincoln and Mercury in offering power brakes, steering
- Korean truce signed; government eases auto-production allocations
- Ford builds 1.25 million cars, only 100,000 less than Chevrolet
- Lincoln engine tweaks result in a 45-horsepower boost to 205
- Ford six wins class in Mobilgas Economy Run at 27 mpg
- Totally redesigned trucks available with automatic transmissions
- Legendary flathead V-8 engine enters its last model year

▲ Edsel Ford's sons pose with the Mercury XL-500 and Continental "Nineteen Fifty X" dream cars. From left are Benson, William Clay, and Henry II.

▲ Seated in the front row of this 1953 gathering of Ford executives are William Clay Ford, Ernest R. Breech, Henry Ford II, and Benson Ford. Henry II had brought former GM executive Breech on board as an executive vice president in July 1946.

▲ Demand for hardtops was rising fast, fueled partly by the stylish lines of cars like this Crestline Victoria in Flamingo Red and Sungate Ivory. Fender skirts and full wheel covers were popular options.

FORD ▲ Most glamorous of the '53 offerings was the Crestline Sunliner convertible, which cost $2043 with standard V-8. Styling revisions included a new grille with a "bullet" hub and ribbed crossbar, rectangular parking lights, and twin-section taillights.

▲ The budget-minded Mainline series consisted of the business coupe, Tudor sedan, Fordor sedan, and two-door Ranch Wagon. This business coupe is unusually accessorized with skirts, spotlights, and continental kit.

◀ With 305,433 units produced, the $1582 Customline Tudor sedan was second only to the Customline Fordor sedan in sales. Advertising literature for '53 pushed resale value and boasted 41 "Worth More" features like "Magic Action" double-sealed brakes, "Presto-Lift" counterbalanced hood, and "Power Cushion" semicentrifugal clutch. All steering wheels got a special 50th anniversary commemorative medallion.

▲ A Zanesville, Ohio, police officer stands next to his six-cylinder-powered Mainline Tudor sedan. Ford also offered a special 125-bhp "Interceptor" flathead V-8 as a police-exclusive extra-cost option.

▲ Costliest (and heaviest) of the '53s was this Country Squire wagon with its woody-look panels, which sold for $2203. Ford claimed 8.5 feet of load space with the tailgate and center seat down, and rear seat out.

▲ In its Golden Anniversary year, Ford was chosen to pace the Indianapolis 500 race. William Clay Ford drove a specially trimmed Sunliner pace car. A limited number of pace-car-replica convertibles were offered for sale. This one sports two popular add-ons: rear fender skirts and a "Coronado" dummy continental kit.

► Fully redesigned—and renumbered—F-series trucks debuted in March 1953 as the one major new product in Ford's Golden Anniversary year. The line included the F-100 ½-ton pickup, starting at $1330. A set-back front axle trimmed the wheelbase by four inches, to 110. Buyers could choose a 101-bhp ohv six or, for the last time, the venerable flathead V-8. Clean, well-proportioned styling helped lift sales by 34,900 units to 116,437.

LINCOLN

► A Lincoln Capri two-door hardtop not only felt luxurious but it looked rakish, especially when viewed from the side. Despite its good looks, Lincoln sales continued to drag behind those of luxury leader Cadillac. A 205-bhp V-8, which represented a gain of 45 from '52, powered all Lincolns. The top-selling Capri hardtop cost $3549 including Hydra-Matic transmission.

◄ Not wanting to exclude any potential buyers, Lincoln unflinchingly promoted the virtues of its vehicles to women, noting that the "smallest lady can easily fit," and that "power brakes respond to the touch of a ballet slipper." It is unlikely that any automaker today would promise to give "feminine hands control they have never known before." This is the $3226 Cosmopolitan sedan.

► The $2133 Monterey four-door sedan was the second most popular Mercury of '53. Its 64,038 orders were about 12,000 shy of the number placed for Monterey two-door hardtops, but almost 4300 ahead of the Custom four-door total. Though frequently added to restored cars today, sun visors like the one pictured here were falling out of vogue.

◄ Shown here in cheery Yosemite Yellow, the head-turning Mercury convertible coupe was available only in Monterey trim. Convertibles featured a new, faster-opening top mechanism. Front-fender "Monterey" badges were new this year, as were smaller fender skirts. The new skirts were standard on all Montereys except the wagon, and optional elsewhere.

▲ Ford's 40-millionth U.S.-built vehicle was this Mercury Monterey convertible coupe. Posing with the car are, from left, Henry Ford II; Benson Ford, then head of the Lincoln-Mercury Division; and William Clay Ford.

1954

- New "Y-block" V-8 replaces Ford and Mercury flatheads
- Larger six-cylinder engine is now standard across Ford line
- Lincoln engine gets internal improvements; brakes are bigger
- Ford Skyliner, Mercury Sun Valley debut with Plexiglas roof panels
- Ford cars now available with power windows and seats
- Ford edges Chevrolet in model-year sales race by a scant 22,000 cars
- Lincolns continue their success in *Carrera Panamericana* road race
- Ford and Mercury get ball-joint front suspension, replacing kingpins

FORD

◄ Ford ads praised the Skyliner immodestly, promising "freshness of view" and "vast new areas of visibility." Though green-tinted, its roof brought complaints of excess interior heat on sunny days. A snap-in sunshade helped. The see-through sold for $2164, with 13,344 built.

► The no-frills Mainline four-door sedan accounted for 55,371 sales. A small badge on the fender indicates that this one is powered by the all-new-for-'54 ohv V-8. Dubbed "Y-block" because of its cross-sectional shape, it stemmed from a project that mandated a single basic design for all corporate engines. Displacing 239.4 cubic inches, the new engine was the same size as its L-head predecessor, but produced 20 more horsepower—130 to the old flat-head's 110. The "Y-block" was standard in the convertible and optional in all other models for about $80.

◄ This Sunliner convertible displays some of the upgrades granted to the top-ranked Crestline series, namely new badges on the rear quarters and triple hashmarks ahead of the rear wheels. Output slipped a bit to 36,685, but stood ahead of the similarly priced Skyliner hardtop. Chrome exhaust tips, fancy mud-flaps, fuzzy dice, and visor-mounted tissue holder were common aftermarket accessories.

► The real-wood framing of the 1952–53 Country Squires was replaced by fiberglass pieces with a maple-grain look in 1954. The use of this new material saved time in manufacturing and installation, and cut replacement costs. New options included power brakes ($41) and a four-way power front seat ($64). The Country Squire was still the priciest Ford car at $2339.

◄ The F-100's standard ohv six was enlarged to 223 cid, and horsepower increased to 115. The new Y-block V-8 came in two commercial versions: the light-duty "Power King" in displacements of 239 or 256 cubic inches, and the heavy-duty "Cargo King" in displacements of 279 or 317 cubic inches. Six-cylinder trucks like this one carried a four-pointed star badge on the new-for-'54 grille; V-8-equipped models wore a V-8 emblem in its place.

LINCOLN ▲ Raising the price of a Lincoln Capri convertible by $332 doubtless didn't help sales. Only 1951 were built this year. Sheetmetal did not change, but the grille looked bolder, new full-length upper-bodyside chrome spears sat higher, and integrated tail-/back-up lights brought up the rear.

▲ A total of 13,598 Capri sedans rolled off the line, making it the best-selling Lincoln sedan of the 1952–55 era. Price: $3711. Advertising heralded a "trend towards Lincoln," though sales figures didn't support the claim.

SIDNEY WEINBERG
The Director Who Had It

OF ALL THE FORD MOTOR COMPANY directors during Henry Ford II's regime, none was so influential or interesting as Sidney Weinberg.

As he was Jewish and a Wall Street investment banker, Weinberg never would have been a confidant of the first Henry Ford. To Ford's grandson, however, he was "a trusted adviser . . . in a company way, in a personal way, in every way, more so than anybody I have ever been associated with."

Born in 1891, Weinberg's formal education was limited to Brooklyn's Public School No. 13 and Browne's Business College. For the fun of it, he wore a Phi Beta Kappa key that he bought at a pawnshop. Yet, several universities—including Harvard—awarded him honorary doctor's degrees.

Joining Goldman, Sachs & Company in 1907, Weinberg became a partner in 1927, and subsequently a director of such blue-chip companies as General Foods, General Electric, B. F. Goodrich, and McKesson & Robbins. During World War II, he also was vice-chairman of the War Production Board. Weinberg was well connected, to put it mildly.

A cofounder of the Business Council in 1933, Weinberg and Henry Ford II became acquainted when the latter joined the council in 1947. At the time of the Ford Motor Company's first public stock offering in 1956, both Henry Ford II and the Ford Foundation wanted Weinberg to represent their interests. "I told the Foundation I wanted him," Ford recalled, "and it should find somebody else." Simultaneously, Weinberg was invited to join the Ford Board of Directors.

In 1982, Henry Ford II was asked to evaluate each of the 27 outside board members with whom he had been associated. For the first and only time, he discussed each of them, and one in particular at length: Weinberg.

"The outstanding director among all these guys without any question was Sidney Weinberg," Ford said. "Nobody . . . could possibly touch him. He just had it. Some people have it and some people don't. Very few people have it as much as he did.

"He not only was a good director because of his extensive experience; he also was a personable fellow you could go to talk to one on one. I used to talk to him *ad infinitum*. I'd go to New York and just sit with him, and he'd call me if he didn't like something. When he was out here for board meetings, we'd talk about many things. He really shaped our board, picking as directors Cabot, Kellstadt, Mortimer, Boeschenstein, Burgess, Murphy, and Gadsden. . . .

▲ This replica celebrates the Lincoln that placed second in the stock-car class at the 1954 *Carrera Panamericana*, driven for the factory-backed team by Walt Faulkner. A privately run Lincoln won the road race through Mexico.

"You could go 100 percent with Weinberg. You've got to be a little bit careful with other directors, but not with him. And that wasn't just true with me. That was true of a multitude of other chief executives he had associations with. . . . He was terrific guy. He also had a great sense of humor and was great fun. . . . Oh, Christ, they broke the mold when they made that guy."

Weinberg, not Ford, set the tone for the dinners attended by outside directors and top inside directors the evening before each monthly board meeting.

"We'd have a free-for-all discussion," Henry II recalled, "but no decisions were made. Weinberg had a fetish about that. I remember one time we were having a board meeting on a train in Europe. . . . [W]e met in a car that had a bar in it. Champagne was available, so I said I'm going to have a glass of champagne, and asked if anybody wanted a glass of champagne before we started. Weinberg said, 'No, you're not going to have a glass of champagne.' I said, 'Why not?' He said 'Because you're going to have a meeting, and you're not going to have champagne.' So I said, 'Okay.'

"Weinberg then described . . . a company that decided on some very important expansion program at a dinner meeting where drinks had been served. He said the group had made a very dumb decision. Anyway, that was the last time that Weinberg would have anything to do with mixing drinks and decisions. So we never decide anything during our preboard dinners. . . . After a couple of drinks we get things off our chest that we probably wouldn't say in a formal meeting, but that's all."

Did Weinberg advise Ford on Jewish-related affairs? "No, never," HFII said. "His friends were mostly non-Jewish. He never paid any attention to Jewish charity . . . . I don't know why, but he just wasn't part of it."

As Weinberg approached 70, the mandatory retirement age for directors, Henry Ford II decided to waive the requirement in his instance. "I want to keep Sidney Weinberg on the board after 70," he informed General Counsel William T. Gossett. "Well, Henry," Gossett replied, "I'm certainly not going to oppose that, but have you thought it through? If he's given preferential treatment, you'll never get him off the board. You'll extend it one year, *ad infinitum*. If you do that for Sidney Weinberg, what about Don David, who preceded Sidney on the board. What about Paul Cabot?"

"I don't give a damn," Ford replied. "I'm going to change the rule to the extent necessary to keep Sidney on the board. I'll tell these other guys that it doesn't apply to them." "I didn't think he'd do it," Gossett recalled, "but he did."

Weinberg remained on the board until his death on July 23, 1969. At the time, Henry II was yachting off the Greek Islands. Visibly upset by the news, he cut short his vacation to attend the funeral of his mentor and friend.

In his letter to stockholders in the company's 1969 Annual Report, Henry II noted that Weinberg had "contributed brilliantly to the Company's progress during his 13 years as a director. His death was a loss to the nation, to the financial community, and to your Company." And Henry meant every word.

MERCURY

▶ Finding almost 80,000 buyers, no Mercury was nearly as popular as the $2452 Monterey two-door hardtop. At 256 cid, Mercury's new ohv V-8 was little larger than the old flathead, but generated 161 bhp, 36 more than before. While Ford was now making six-cylinder engines available on all its cars, the Mercury line remained exclusively V-8 powered.

◀ Like Ford's Skyliner, the Monterey Sun Valley had a transparent, green-tinted roof section made of quarter-inch Plexiglas. Just 9761 were built, selling for $2582 ($130 more than a plain hardtop). Show cars had transparent roofs before, but the Sun Valley and Skyliner were the first to offer this feature to the public. In addition to making scenery more viewable, the transparent roof was good for seeing overhead traffic lights—and provided better weather protection than a droptop.

▶ Mercury's value leader was the two-door sedan, offered only as a Custom at $2194. This example has a stick shift, but shoppers turned eagerly to Merc-O-Matic. A modest facelift included neatly faired-in wraparound taillights, a more aggressive grille, and a revised dummy hood scoop. Mercury moved up from eighth to seventh place in industry standings for 1954, passing up Dodge, but still trailing Pontiac.

■ Two-seat Thunderbird debuts—sells 16,155 copies to Corvette's 700

■ Lincolns drop Hydra-Matic; gain new three-speed Turbo-Drive

■ Fairlane replaces Crestline as poshest Ford

■ Crown Victoria adopts "basket-handle" roofline

■ Ford model-year car output is highest since 1923, yet quarter-million behind Chevy

■ Robert S. McNamara becomes Ford Division general manager

■ Company earns record $437 million profit

FORD ▲ Peaked headlight bezels, an all-new grille design, and bold, two-tone "checkmark" bodyside trim highlighted 1955's major facelift. Fairlane usurped the Crestline as top-dog series—and became the hottest seller, with 626,250 built. Of those, 49,966 were Sunliner convertibles like this one.

▲ With a host of vibrant pastel colors available, the new Fairlanes were the flashiest Fords yet—as this Sea Sprite Green and Neptune Green Victoria hardtop attests. Note the roofline, which was rounder and higher than that of the Crown Victoria's. With 113,372 units produced, Victoria hardtops handily outsold their Crown Vic sisters.

▶ A Fairlane Club Sedan cost $113 more than a comparable Customline two-door, and sold considerably fewer copies. Ford's standard six-cylinder engine added five horsepower (to 120). Optional Ford-O-Matic added a "speed-trigger" kickdown into low gear, which cut three seconds from 0-to-60 times. Ford had planned to increase displacement of the Y-block V-8 to 254 cubic inches, but bumped it to 272 cid upon learning that Chevrolet's new V-8 would have 265 cubes. The base 272 developed 162 bhp, which matched the Chevy V-8's output.

► Under general manager Robert S. McNamara, Ford engineers made vehicle-safety research a priority. Here, a Fairlane Town Sedan collides with a Fairlane Club Sedan in a factory crash test. "Lifeguard Design" features like seatbelts, deep-dish steering wheel, and padded dashboard would appear in 1956.

▲ The chrome "basket handle" across the new Crown Victoria's roof concealed its origin as a two-door hardtop. Crown Vics had a flatter roof, longer sloped pillars, and less rear-window curvature than regular Victorias. Price was $2202 plain, or $70 more with a Plexiglas roof insert. Only 1999 Crown Vics got the see-through top.

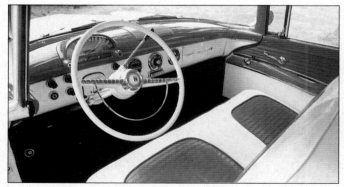

▲ Interiors were just about as colorful as Ford bodies. On the "Astra-Dial" instrument panel, a semicircular speedometer sat up high, with a window "for daylight illumination." A MagicAire heater was optional.

▲ Station wagons now made up a separate series. This Country Sedan came with either six- or eight-passenger seating, priced at $2156 and $2287, respectively. Ford bested Chevrolet in wagon production volume.

◄ The 1955 F-Series enjoyed a prosperous year, setting a truck-production record with 30 percent of the industry total. A new vee-styled two-bar grille headed up the styling tweaks, and a new Custom Cab package debuted. Selecting the option netted "luxury" accessories like armrests, headliner, upgraded seat cushioning, dual horns, chrome grille trim, and exterior "Custom Cab" nameplates beneath the windows. Workhorse pickups were gradually getting passenger-car pizzazz; the Goldenrod Yellow paint on this truck was a midyear addition to the 1954 models, and flashy Sea Sprite Green was added for '55.

► Henry Ford II appears happy with the Thunderbird he needed to match Chevrolet in the two-seater market segment. A mock-up appeared at the Detroit auto show early in 1954, and production began in September. Base price was $2944, $10 more than a Corvette.

▲ Ford never referred to the Thunderbird as a sports car, categorizing it as a "personal car" instead. Unlike Corvette, with its drafty side curtains, this two-seater included roll-up windows and a selection of power extras, all aimed at luxury-minded buyers.

▲ Exhaust outlets exiting from the rear bumper "bombs" originated at a standard 292-cid V-8 from the Mercury line that produced up to 198 horsepower.

LINCOLN

▶ Lincolns measured nearly a foot longer overall in their most extensive restyling since '52. The change failed to help sales, which trailed even Packard's. The extended rear fenders held reverse-slant taillights. Dual exhausts were standard, exiting via bumper cutouts. The Lincoln V-8's displacement was upped to 341 cid, and horsepower was up 20 to 225. Only 27,222 Lincolns were made for the model year; 1487 of those were Capri convertibles. This example wears accessory dual spotlights and door-handle trim.

◀ Lack of a wraparound windshield might have limited Lincoln sales, since even low-priced cars had one this year. This Capri hardtop, in popular Palomino Buff and white, has the optional "Multi-Luber," which delivered grease to the chassis with the touch of a button. Peaked headlight bezels and fine horizontal grille bars freshened the front end.

MERCURY

▲ Mercury styling now ran closer to Lincoln than to Ford. Only 1787 Montclair Sun Valleys were produced in their final season. The chrome rear-fender vents and package-shelf-mounted clear tubes indicate that this fully optioned example is equipped with the rare factory air-conditioning unit. Less than one percent of '55 Mercury production was equipped with the $594 comfort option. The Montclair was Mercury's new top series.

▲ Apart from station wagons, the 3685-pound Montclair ragtop was the heaviest model for '55. Montclair models got a standard 198-bhp, 292-cid V-8 with four-barrel carburetion.

▲ With 71,588 units made, the $2631 Montclair hardtop was the most popular model. Montclair hardtops and convertibles carried additional chrome trim under the side windows, which allowed for extra two-toning.

▲ The $2218 Custom two-door sedan was the price leader for '55. With a production run of 31,295, it was the best-seller of the lowest-priced Mercurys. Customs and Montereys came standard with a 188-bhp 292, but could get the hotter 198-horsepower version with dual exhausts as an option. Merc-O-Matic was also available for $190.

► Simulated wood trim adorned the sides of the $2844 Monterey wagon. A $2686 plain-sided Custom wagon was also available. Both rode a 118-inch wheelbase, one inch shorter than all other Mercury models. The Ford origins of the station wagon bodies were cleverly disguised by bodyside trim and unique "Mercurized" taillight assemblies that fit into the Ford body openings. Deeply hooded headlight bezels fostered the illusion that the '55 Mercs were longer than they actually were.

1956

- Ford stock goes on sale, starting with 10.2 million shares from the Ford Foundation

- Ford joins Automobile Manufacturers Association; Henry II elected president

- Ford builds 1.4 million cars, but trails Chevrolet's 1.56 million

- *Motor Trend* names entire Ford line "Car of the Year"

- New Lincoln aims at heart of luxury field again

- Continental idea reborn in Mark II hardtop

FORD ▲ A smart, subtle facelift included a wide-grate grille and horizontal parking lights in wraparound chrome pods. Keeping up with the rest of the industry, Ford switched to a 12-volt electrical system to handle the stronger starter motors needed for high-compression engines and increased loads from power accessories.

◄ Crown Victoria output sank to 9812 in its second and final season as Ford's glitter king. Only 603 of these got the tinted Plexiglas top; its significant extra cost and palpable interior-heat buildup on sunny days spelled the option's demise after this year. This liberally accessorized Meadowmist Green and Snowshoe White example wears the upscale wire wheel covers, a $35 option.

► Ford couldn't let GM market a four-door hardtop alone. The Town Victoria arrived at midyear, yet an impressive 32,111 found buyers. Redesigned instrument panels now featured round gauges clustered under an arched hood. Options included front and rear power windows at $100, power steering at $51, power brakes at $32, and a power front seat for $60.

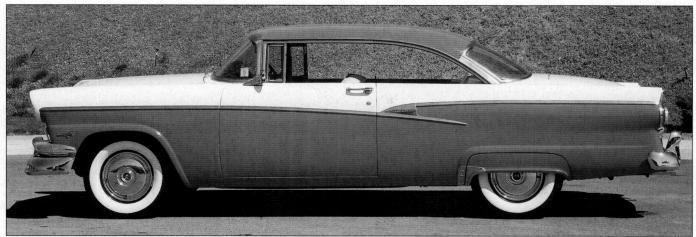

▲ Even the midrange Customline series got into the Victoria hardtop act as a response to Chevy's Two-Ten hardtop coupe. Sales lagged far behind the fancier Fairlane Victoria. All two-door hardtops got the more graceful Crown Vic roofline. The 223-cid six was standard in all full-size Fords, but 272-, 292-, and 312-cid V-8s were optional.

▲ Flip-open vents on the front fenders helped cool '56 T-Bird cockpits. Sun visors, glass wind wings, dashboard padding, and a deep-dish steering wheel were also added. Steering was slower and rear springs softer as Ford refined the T-Bird for personal luxury and not sports-car handling.

▲ Zany television personality Soupy Sales mugs in a new Thunderbird. The T-Bird's instant popularity made it a natural choice for PR exposure.

▶ Addressing complaints of poor over-the-shoulder visibility, porthole windows were now available on the optional hardtop; buyers chose them four-to-one over the blind-quarter version. The standard continental spare tire improved trunk space and weight distribution. Exhaust outlets moved to the outer edges of T-Bird's bumper. Weight and price crept up to 3038 pounds and $3151, and sales dropped to 15,631 units. A 312-cid V-8 with up to 225 bhp was optional.

▲ Station wagon output was up by about 5000 units and represented more than 15 percent of Ford's business. The Country Squire's base price rose to $2533, but Ford still sold 23,221, or 4210 more than in '55.

▲ The $2428 Parklane was essentially a Ranch Wagon with Fairlane side trim and interior. Nearly twice as many were sold as Chevy's rival Nomad. Eight-passenger Country Sedans also gained Fairlane trim.

◄ A new wraparound windshield and revised grille were the foremost changes for the F-100 pickup, which started at $1577 with a 6.5-foot bed. Buyers could again order a Custom Cab (now with the first chrome grille face in the postwar era), right-side taillight, and side-mounted spare. Newly available was a fashionable wraparound rear window, a $16 option that is highly coveted among collectors today. A record 289 truck models were offered, powered by a 133-bhp "Cost Cutter" six or a selection of V-8s, ranging up to 332-cid in "Big Job" models. Trucks also gained "Lifeguard Design" features like a standard energy-absorbing steering wheel and double-grip door latches. Light-truck production dropped slightly from the previous year's high, to 126,070.

LINCOLN

► Not only did Lincoln finally have a wraparound windshield, it was the biggest in the industry—part of a massive redesign. A near doubling of sales was typified by the 19,619 Premiere two-door hardtops built. The new chassis had box-section rails, and the V-8 grew to 368 cid and 285 horsepower. Advertising boasted that the all-new Premiere was "the longest, lowest, most powerful, most wanted Lincoln of all time."

▲ Production of Lincoln Premiere sedans almost matched that of the two-door hardtop—the only body styles, apart from the Premiere convertible. Note the distinctive rear quarter-window treatment. Wheelbase grew three inches, overall length seven inches, and width three inches compared with the '55 models.

▲ A four-door sedan and two-door hardtop were available in the lesser Capri trim level, but the convertible was exclusive the to the Premiere line. Note the rear-bumper exhaust tips.

▲ Luxury features like full leather trim, power windows, and four-way power seats abounded inside the convertible. The eye-grabbing lavender color is a factory shade called Wisteria.

▲ Ford attempted to revive the Continental name as a stand-alone, premium luxury division in 1956 with the Mark II hardtop coupe. Meticulous hand assembly and exhaustive testing resulted in impeccable quality.

▲ Despite its timelessly elegant styling and superior craftsmanship, the Mark II's $9695 sticker was out of reach for most buyers. Even at that price, Ford lost about $1000 on each one due to high production costs.

MERCURY

▶ Except for the Monterey station wagon, the $2900 Montclair convertible was the costliest Mercury. A $2712 convertible was also offered in the lower-line Custom series, but its sales paled in comparison. All Mercs got a large "M" hood medallion and slightly updated grille as part of the '56 facelift. Side trim was altered as well, and lent itself to "Flo-Tone" two-tone paint schemes.

◀ The best-selling Mercury was the $2765 Montclair hardtop coupe. Engines grew to 312-cid and produced 210 horsepower with the three-speed manual transmission, 225 with Merc-O-Matic. A 235-bhp version with a higher-lift cam became standard on Montclairs and Montereys at midseason. Suspension components were carried over from '55 with few changes. Road testers of the day praised the Mercury's handling characteristics.

▶ Mercury dubbed its new Montclair four-door hardtop a "Phaeton," borrowing a name from motoring's-pioneering days. The bodystyle was available in all four Mercury trim levels, but the top-line version Montclair was the most popular. Like their Ford counterparts, '56 Mercurys got new safety features like an impact-absorbing steering wheel, safety door locks, optional seat belts, and optional padded dashboard.

▲ Monterey stood just below Montclair in Mercury's hierarchy. This $2555 Monterey four-door sedan, the best-selling four-door model, shared its roofline with the lower-priced Custom and Medalist models. The pricier Monterey Sport Sedan and Montclair Sport Sedan had a lower, sleeker roofline profile.

► The Medalist name was initially applied only to a decontented two-door sedan. It became a series of its own at midyear, when four-door sedan, Phaeton four-door hardtop, and two-door hardtop body styles were added. The Medalist name was dropped for '57, but would reappear for a one-year stand in recession-plagued '58, when Mercury badly needed a cheaper entry-level series. The hardtop coupe shown here started at $2398.

◄ Custom wagons were available in a six-passenger version for $2722, or an eight-passenger version for $97 more. The simulated wood-sided Monterey could only be had as an eight-passenger model. Rear seats folded down for extra storage space. Mercury wagons still made do with Ford body panels camouflaged by trim, but new Mercury-exclusive wagons were in the wings.

- "Big" '57 sports massive restyle—most extensive overhaul in a generation
- Skyliner retractable hardtop debuts; so does Ranchero car/pickup

- Supercharged 312-cid V-8 thunders out 300 horsepower
- Ford outsells Chevrolet for model year, with record 1.67 million cars built

- "Classic" Thunderbird earns handsome facelift in final two-seat season
- Mercury gets its own body structure with distinctive concave rear panels

- Output drops to 41,123, but Lincoln clings to 14th place in industry
- William Clay Ford named vice president for product planning and styling

FORD ▲ The original two-seat Thunderbird entered its final year wearing fresh styling with cues that echoed full-size Fords. Moving the spare tire back into the trunk demanded a longer rear deck, but overall size shrunk. A continental kit remained optional, with few takers. Stylists wisely resisted tacking on doodads or tampering with the basic shape. Top power option was a new McCulloch-supercharged "F-code" 312 producing 300 advertised bhp—though some estimates put it closer to as much as 340. The engine carried a hefty $500 price tag and only 208 'Birds were so equipped. Without the typical fender skirts, whitewalls, and wheel covers, this F-code T-Bird takes on an aggressive look.

◄ Trim levels were shuffled, with the Fairlane 500 line topping the Fairlane, Custom 300, and Custom series. Fairlane and Fairlane 500 sedans had a hardtop look thanks to their thin, chrome-plated door pillars. Base Fairlanes, like this $2286 four-door sedan, carried unique rear bodyside trim. Sales of Fairlane sedans and hardtops lagged behind the fancier Fairlane 500s.

▲ No less alluring in its newly enlarged form, the Sunliner convertible sold for $2505, but options could add another $1000. Checkmark side trim in the Fairlane 500 series contained a gold-anodized insert.

▲ For a $437 premium over a regular droptop, buyers could choose the new Skyliner retractable hardtop; 20,766 did. The top mechanism used 600 feet of wiring spread among 10 power relays and three drive motors.

▲ In its second season, the airy Victoria hardtop sedan came in Fairlane or Fairlane 500 trim, with a $47 price difference between them. The top seller by more than 5-to-1 was the $2404 Fairlane 500, seen here.

▲ For a two-door sedan, the Fairlane 500 Club Sedan exhibited a lot of flash for its $2281 price. Enlarged round taillights for '57 went beneath modest, angled fins. A canted "dogleg" A-pillar was another feature of the redesign.

► Side trim on the Custom 300 sedans was similar to that used on the Fairlane 500, but sat lower on the body. Door pillars were thicker, too. Custom/Custom 300s and station wagons rode a 116-inch wheelbase, two inches shorter than the Fairlane/Fairlane 500 models. Rear bumpers were less bulky and tailfins more subdued than the higher-priced Fairlanes, as well.

◄ In this record production year, the lowest-priced Ford Customs sold slower than step-up Custom 300s. Ford's "Mileage Maker" six grew to 144 bhp, but shoppers liked the choice of V-8s with at least 190 bhp. Even the budget Custom models, like this two-door sedan, could be equipped with the 300-bhp supercharged 312.

▲ A record 321,170 station wagons were produced, comprising a substantial 19.4 percent of total '57 Ford production. Country Squires made up 27,690 of those wagons, a total that would not be bested until 1965.

◀ In addition to a basic Ranch Wagon, Ford offered a Del Rio—essentially the same two-door with flashier trim *à la* Country Sedan, and a replacement for the '56 Parklane. Front-hinged hoods and 14-inch wheels were new across the board. Safety continued as a sales stimulus. Inside, '57s got a "Safety-Curve" instrument panel with recessed controls (padding optional), smaller Lifeguard steering wheel, and safety-swivel mirror—plus available seatbelts.

▶ The Ranchero car/pickup debuted alongside the Skyliner retractable hardtop on December 8, 1956, at the New York Auto Show. It was a clever spin-off of the Ranch Wagon, and many components interchanged. Plain-sided base models and flashier Customs were offered. This example wears gold-anodized trim spears that were standard on Custom 300s, a common dealer add-on to Custom Rancheros.

◀ Trucks were completely restyled, with ribbed wrapover hoods, integral running boards, and flush-sided "Styleside" all-steel pickup beds. Separate-fender pickup beds, now designated "Flaresides," were still available. Other makes had already introduced smooth-sided cargo beds for costly custom models. But Ford's Styleside pickups cost no more than its fender-side jobs. Their popularity ushered in the modern pickup truck.

LINCOLN ▲ Only 444 model-year '57 Continental Mark II hardtops were built before production halted in May. Bodies showed little change, but the fuel filler sat in the left taillight. The humped decklid actually did house the spare tire, which was positioned at an upright angle in the trunk. Retractable hardtop, convertible, and hardtop sedan companions were considered, but abandoned with the rest of the Mark II project.

▲ A Landau four-door hardtop in both the Capri and Premiere series joined the four-door sedans for '57. Bolder, slightly canted fins, similar to those on the 1955 Lincoln Futura dream car, highlighted this year's facelift. A higher compression ratio helped bump the 368-cid V-8's horsepower rating up 15 to 300.

▲ Priced at $5149, Lincoln's Premiere two-door hard-top accounted for one-third of total production. The "Quadra-Lite" front ensemble held regular headlamps and smaller road lamps activated by a separate switch.

▲ The convertible was still exclusive to the Premiere line, but output increased 50 percent to 3676 units. All Lincolns got a padded dash, and power brakes were now standard in Premieres.

MERCURY

▶ Mercury raced into 1957 with all-new styling and more power, plus a longer wheelbase and many new engineering features. For the first time in its 18-year existence, Mercury could claim a bodyshell all its own. Glitzy, gadget-packed Turnpike Cruisers like this $3849 four-door hardtop arrived late in the season starting at prices $520 to $670 more than Montclairs.

▲ Racing legend Bill Stroppe built the experimental "Mermaid" racer from a '57 Monterey convertible. It attained an impressive 159.91 mph on the sand at the Daytona Speed Weeks trials.

▲ "Cruiser" skirts help give this loaded Turnpike Cruiser two-door hardtop a sassy stance. The standard 368-cid V-8 cranked out 290 horsepower. Cruiser rear windows retracted for "Breezeway Ventilation."

▲ The Turnpike Cruiser convertible (or Convertible Cruiser) was selected to pace the Indianapolis 500. Pace-car replicas carried small front fender-medallions denoting the "Turnpike Cruiser Engine," bright lower-rear-quarter trim, fender-top ornaments, and an external spare-tire carrier. Just 1265 of the $4103 Cruiser ragtops were made.

▲ Although eclipsed by the Turnpike Cruiser in price, the Montclair was more popular. With 30,111 buyers, the $3236 Montclair Phaeton hardtop coupe outsold the entire Turnpike Cruiser line. A continental kit and fender skirts made this one look even more massive. A lower floorpan gave Mercs more room inside. Montclairs came standard with Merc-O-Matic; its "Keyboard Control" pushbuttons can barely be seen at the lower left of the dash.

▲ Buyers could choose from six hardtop wagons. The Commuter two-door was the cheapest at $2903. Quad headlights, not yet legal in all 48 states, were standard on Turnpike Cruisers, optional on others.

▲ A large, wraparound rear window gave convertibles a hardtop look when the top was up. This Montclair convertible shows off its flashy two-tone top, which was not available on lesser Montereys.

▲ Colony Park was the new name for Mercury's flagship four-door wagon with woody-look trim. The $3677 nine-seater was the second best-selling wagon, outdone only by the six-passenger Commuter four-door.

▲ The Commuter four-door wagon, available in both six- and nine-passenger guise, sold for $2973 and $3070, respectively. Step-up Voyager models were also available in two- and four-door configurations.

■ America suffers worst recession in postwar era; car sales drop sharply

■ Edsel debuts; legendary flop eventually loses $250 million

■ Thunderbird reintroduced as four-seat hardtop and convertible

■ Only 987,945 Fords built compared to nearly 1.2 million Chevys

■ Lincoln adopts unibody construction, but weight goes up instead of down

■ Lincoln's 430-cid V-8 is biggest U.S. engine; also available in Mercury

EDSEL ▲ After three years of costly planning and market research, the Edsel debuted on September 4, 1957, amid glowing predictions and unprecedented hype. Poor timing, unconventional styling, gimmicky "advancements," and changing buyer tastes helped make it one of the biggest marketing flops in automotive history. Ford planned to sell at least 100,000 of the debut models, but moved only a little more than 63,000. From there it was all downhill, and the Edsel would vanish after a brief run of 1960 models. Interior gadgetry included a "cyclops-eye" rotating-drum speedometer and a "Teletouch Drive" automatic transmission controlled by pushbuttons in the steering-wheel hub.

◄ The inaugural Edsel line comprised the entry-level Ranger and step-up Pacer series on the 118-inch Ford platform (116-inch for wagons), and the highline Corsair and Citation on an exclusive 124-inch chassis. All shared the controversial "horse collar" vertical grille. The two lower series and all station wagons carried a 303-bhp, 361-cid V-8. Highline models, like this Citation two-door hardtop, got a massive 345-horse, 410-cube V-8.

▶ Wanting an additional medium-price car line to compete with General Motors and Chrysler, Ford management positioned the Edsel between Ford and Mercury. After considering thousands of potential monikers, the car was named for Henry Ford's only son—over the initial objections of the Ford family. Pacer convertibles like this one went for $3028; Citation ragtops were the costliest Edsels at $3801.

▲ The roofline profile betrays the Mercury origins of the bodyshell of this Edsel Corsair two-door hardtop, an indicator that the Edsel was not the revolutionary car Ford claimed it to be. The Edsel hit the marketplace at a very inopportune time—a sharp economic recession crippled all new-car sales in 1958.

▲ Offered in 1958 only, the $2876 two-door Roundup was the entry-level Edsel wagon. Only 963 were made. Comparable four-door Edsel wagons were named Villager, and came in six- and nine-passenger versions.

▲ Bermuda wagons sported faux wood trim and the slightly plusher Pacer interior. This Coral Pink and white example is one of only 1456 six-passenger models made. Another 779 came with seats for nine.

◄ Chrome headlight bezels, fender skirts, and a continental kit dress up this Skyliner. Though the retractable top mechanism was complex, the system was surprisingly reliable. The Skyliner was the heaviest and most expensive 1958 Ford. It tipped the scales at just over two tons and was the only regular Ford costing more than $3000.

▲ The Skyliner's hardtop had a formal, heavy C-pillar look that would soon be adopted by other Ford products. Output dropped to 14,713.

▲ All Fairlane 500s, including the Victoria hardtop coupe, wore new side trim and bulky quad taillights. Victoria sales volume slipped by more than 100,000.

▲ Group Vice President Robert McNamara, Ford Division General Manager James Wright, and Assistant General Manager Charles Beacham pose with a Fairlane, T-Bird, F-100, and heavy-duty F-Series truck.

▲ Realizing that the glamorous two-seater wasn't likely to turn a profit, McNamara wanted the next T-Bird to be a real moneymaker. That meant seating for four. His choice proved correct, and sales shot up to 37,892.

▲ The Country Sedan wagon's 37 square feet of floor space came in handy for outdoor excursions. Priced at $2557 and $2664 for six- and nine-passenger versions, respectively, 89,474 took to the road.

▲ Most of the passenger-car styling changes also appeared on the Ranchero car/pickup, but it kept the round '57 taillights. A deluxe Custom 300 cost $2236, and Ranchero output slipped to 9950.

◄ Custom sedans were popular police cars; this Texas State Patrol two-door sedan is fitted with spotlights, Motorola radio, and the 300-bhp Thunderbird Special "Interceptor" 352, one of a new family of engines. The blocky, Thunderbird-esque styling looked very natural in police livery, but some civilian buyers were turned off by the facelift. A dummy hood scoop and elliptical deck-lid indentation improved panel strength in addition to updating the styling.

► Other than a new quad headlight grille, little was changed externally on the F-100 truck for '58. Any of the standard truck colors could be combined with Colonial White for a two-tone effect. Ford's budget-priced Styleside pickup beds were popular with buyers, so Chevrolet introduced its similar Fleetside line at midseason. Ford still offered a separate-fender Flareside pickup bed, but the Styleside handily out-sold it. Both bed configu-rations were available in 6.5- or eight-foot lengths.

▶ Bearing no resemblance to the graceful Mark II, the heavily sculpted Continental Mark III came in four body styles. The convertible was the costliest at $6283; 3048 were sold. Though released and promoted as a separate make, Continental Mark IIIs were basically fancier Lincolns. With a 131-inch wheelbase, 229-inch overall length, and 80.1-inch width, the ragtop tipped the scales at more than 5000 pounds.

▲ Continental interiors wore fine fabrics or Bridge of Weir leather from Scotland. Naturally, interior room was extra spacious. Luxury features included air conditioning and an automatic headlight dimmer.

▲ To cope with the substantial weight, Lincoln enlarged its V-8 to 430 cubic inches, the biggest in America at the time. Shown is an ultrarare, nonregular-production version with triple two-barrel carbs and 400 bhp.

◀ Rarest of all '58 Lincolns was the base Capri four-door sedan; only 1184 were made. Lincolns and Continentals adopted unitized body construction and were built in a special new plant in Wixom, Michigan. Despite their proportions and heft, Lincolns were capable of nine second 0-60 times. They were also surprisingly nimble; test drivers universally praised their handling qualities.

▲ The new Continental's top-stowage system borrowed ideas from Ford's retractable hardtop. A metal panel raised out of the way, allowing the top to be raised or lowered. Lack of a protruding boot accentuated the long lines. A reverse-slanting rear window and eggcrate grille were exclusive to Continentals. Lincoln's goal was to "out-Cadillac" Cadillac for 1958 by producing bigger, plusher, and more powerful cars than its GM rival. The resulting "land yachts" were still trounced by Cadillac in sales; Lincoln moved only 29,684 cars to Cadillac's 121,778.

MERCURY

▶ Massive Marauder 383- and 430-cid V-8s were new for '58, but recession-wracked buyers were more interested in economy this year. Only 844 Mercury Montclair Phaeton convertibles were built, starting at $3536. The Turnpike Cruiser convertible was dropped, and its coupe and sedan sisters were now part of the Montclair line.

▲ The best-seller of the Montclair line was the Phaeton hardtop coupe with 5012 made. It priced from $3284 without options. All Merc-O-Matic-equipped cars got a "Keyboard Control" pushbutton gear selector.

▲ Like other Mercurys, the Colony Park wagon got surface changes for '58. The facelift included new quad headlights and restyled bumpers. Brochures claimed a "sports-car spirit and limousine ride."

■ Ford Galaxie luxury series debuts, takes 27 percent of volume

■ Skyliner retractable enters its final season

■ Ford output rises 47 percent—almost ties Chevrolet for number one in sales

■ Edsel line scaled back to Ranger, Corsair, and Villager wagon; drops to 14th in industry

■ Continental no longer marketed as separate from Lincoln

■ Mercury is longer and more sculpted; Turnpike Cruiser gone

▲ Billed as "the world's most beautifully proportioned cars," the '59 Ford line consisted of 23 models. Contrary to the radically finned Chevrolet and Plymouth, Ford's squared-up look echoed that of the restyled Thunderbird. The new design netted Ford the gold medal for exceptional styling at the Brussels World's Fair.

EDSEL

◄ Edsel's sole convertible came in the Corsair series. Only 1343 were produced. Corsairs got a new 225-horsepower, 332-cid V-8,-but $58 more bought a 303-horsepower, 361-cid V-8. Essentially reskinned Fords, all Edsels now rode a 120-inch wheelbase. Styling was toned down from '58 but, surprisingly, the unpopular vertical grille remained.

▲ At $2629, the Ranger two-door sedan was the cheapest '59 Edsel. Standard engine was a 200-bhp, 292-cid Ford V-8, but a 145-bhp, 223-cid inline six, also borrowed from Ford, was a no-cost option.

▲ The profile of a Corsair four-door hardtop shows Ford-like styling. Total Edsel production was a mere 44,891 units, a significant drop from 1958's already dismal sales. The Edsel's days were numbered.

FORD

► Ford's outer body panels were new, and much of the inner structure revised, on a 118-inch wheelbase. Hooded quad headlamps sat above a full-width grille with four rows of floating "stars." The Galaxie line debuted at midyear, bumping the Fairlane 500 from its perch as the poshest Ford. Galaxies started at $2528 for this two-door Club Sedan.

◄ With recession fears waning, the Sunliner convertible found plenty of takers; output leaped by more than 10,000 units to 45,868. Indian Turquoise and Colonial White was a popular two-tone mix, adding a dash of daring to the conservative bodies. Flashy ribbed rear-quarter-panel trim was exclusive to Fairlane 500s and Galaxies. The Skyliner retractable hardtop would be dropped after a 1959 run of 12,915.

► All closed Galaxies had roofs with a Thunderbird-style C-pillar. Galaxie advertising focused heavily on the line's similarities to the popular T-Bird, boasting of "Thunderbird Elegance." Solid colors, conventional two-tone paint (shown at right), or "Style Tone" color combinations (shown on the Sunliner above) were available. Galaxie Town Sedans like this one listed for $2582. Back-up lights were standard on Fairlane 500s and Galaxies, optional on other models. Optional fender skirts could be body color or bright stainless steel.

► Ford produced its 50-millionth vehicle in June 1959, and celebrated the milestone appropriately. This Galaxie Town Sedan toured the country with the 1909 "No. 2" Model T racer that competed in the New York-to-Seattle race. With 183,108 units produced, the four-door Town Sedan was the best-selling Galaxie by far.

▲ Ranchero car/pickups were based on big Fords for the last time. The six-cylinder engine was standard, but all V-8s were optional. In spite of new competition from Chevrolet's El Camino, sales rebounded to 14,169.

▲ The $3696 hardtop coupe accounted for the bulk of '59 Thunderbird sales. Convertible models gained a fully automatic retractable top late in the model year to replace the manual top initially offered.

► Thunderbird production nearly doubled in this full model year, to 67,456. As part of the minor facelift, pointed chrome moldings on lower-bodyside "bullets" replaced the former five hashmarks. Horizontal grille bars were matched in the taillight trim. A reworked rear suspension switched from coil to leaf springs. With a new optional Lincoln 430-cid V-8 good for 350 bhp, this year's 'Bird could fly to 60 mph in a snappy nine seconds or so. A total of 10,261 customers chose to spend $283 extra to secure the services of a convertible.

▲ Ford police cars were usually based on low-line Custom 300s rather than Fairlanes like the Town Sedan shown here. Cop cars could have any of the standard engines and got heavy-duty chassis components.

▲ Ford stressed utility in its station wagon advertising, referring to "bowling alley loadspace." Wheelbase was extended two inches to 118. Out of 269,378 wagons produced, 24,336 were Country Squires.

LINCOLN

▶ A base Lincoln Landau four-door hardtop cost $5090, as did the slower-selling pillared sedan. A two-door hardtop sold for $4902. Premieres came in the same body styles. Lincoln had its own grille, but shared sheet-metal with Continental. Ads pushed beauty, craftsmanship, prestige, and "sheer elegance."

◀ Hess & Eisenhardt, an Ohio specialty coach-builder, turned the Continental Mark IV into a padded-vinyl-topped Town Car sedan with a $9208 sticker. The company also issued a $10,230 limousine with a divider window and rear-seat radio/air-conditioning controls. Finished only in Presidential Black, these formal machines were built in small numbers: 78 sedans and 49 limos.

▲ Lincoln's Continental Mark IV series included this $6845 four-door hardtop, plus a hardtop coupe, four-door sedan, and convertible. Defying recent trends, Lincoln's 430-cid V-8 dropped to 350 bhp. Billed as the "world's most admired car," Continentals featured a reverse-angled, retractable rear window.

MERCURY ▲ The Park Lane series, introduced in 1958, again contained three body styles: Cruiser hardtop sedan and coupe, and convertible. All Mercurys were longer and roomier this year; Montereys, Montclairs, and station wagons rode a 126-inch wheelbase, while a 128-inch wheelbase was exclusive to Park Lanes.

▶ Wrapover "Panoramic Skylight" windshields gave Mercury 60 percent more glass area. Each model displayed a fresh grille and restyled trim. Mercury issued 6713 Montclair four-door hardtops, starting at $3437 with a 322-horsepower, 383-cid V-8 engine. Unlike the cheaper Monterey, Montclairs had bright rocker panels and wheel-lip trim. The Turnpike Cruiser name wasn't continued for '59.

◀ At $4206, top dog in the '59 Mercury lineup was the Park Lane convertible. A mere 1257 were built. Park Lanes came standard with the 430-cid V-8 engine, but horsepower dropped to 345. With slightly detuned engines, Mercs weren't quite as lively as before, but managed to exude luxury for a moderate entry fee. Total production was up slightly from the dismal '58 season, but still failed to top 150,000 units.

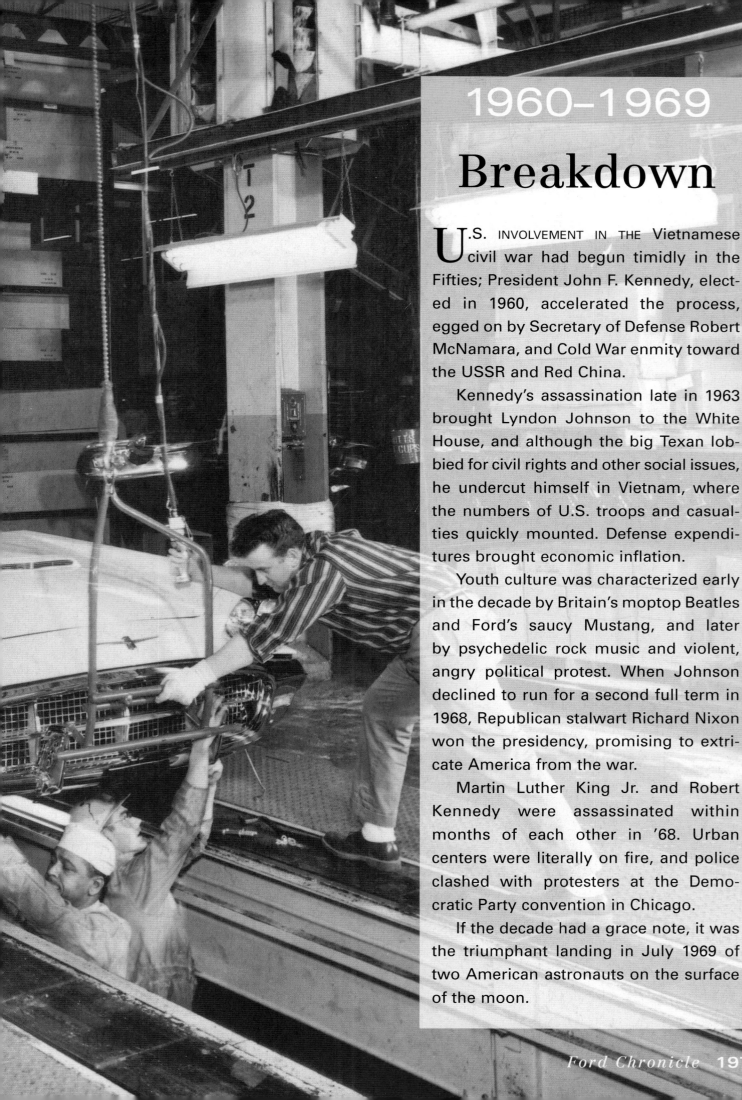

Breakdown

U.S. INVOLVEMENT IN THE Vietnamese civil war had begun timidly in the Fifties; President John F. Kennedy, elected in 1960, accelerated the process, egged on by Secretary of Defense Robert McNamara, and Cold War enmity toward the USSR and Red China.

Kennedy's assassination late in 1963 brought Lyndon Johnson to the White House, and although the big Texan lobbied for civil rights and other social issues, he undercut himself in Vietnam, where the numbers of U.S. troops and casualties quickly mounted. Defense expenditures brought economic inflation.

Youth culture was characterized early in the decade by Britain's moptop Beatles and Ford's saucy Mustang, and later by psychedelic rock music and violent, angry political protest. When Johnson declined to run for a second full term in 1968, Republican stalwart Richard Nixon won the presidency, promising to extricate America from the war.

Martin Luther King Jr. and Robert Kennedy were assassinated within months of each other in '68. Urban centers were literally on fire, and police clashed with protesters at the Democratic Party convention in Chicago.

If the decade had a grace note, it was the triumphant landing in July 1969 of two American astronauts on the surface of the moon.

1960

- Robert S. McNamara takes over as company president, then leaves to be Secretary of Defense

- Lee Iacocca promoted to Ford Division chief

- New Ford Falcon becomes America's most popular compact

- Mid-price compact Comet bows at midyear

- Edsel disappears after abbreviated season

- Thunderbird offers sliding metal sunroof

► Edsel finished with just two series: "Station Wagon" and Ranger. This ragtop was the rarest of the five Ranger models with just 76 built, versus a series total of 2571. All 1960 Edsels were basically retrimmed versions of this year's all-new standard Fords, with unique taillights—and no "horse-collar" grille.

EDSEL ▲ Edsel ended a token 1960 model run in November 1959 as Ford belatedly pulled the plug on its ill-fated medium-price make. This Villager wagon was one of just 275 built, of which only 59 were the nine-passenger version. Base prices ran around $3000. Design kinship with standard Fords was stronger than ever.

FORD ▲ Ford's largest cars were fully redesigned for 1960, becoming longer-lower-wider on an inch-longer wheelbase (now at 119). Styling was cleaner than ever. Glassier, too, with a compound-curve windshield replacing the previous wraparound style and its awkward "dogleg" pillars. Galaxie returned from '59 as the top-line non-wagon series. Among its five models was this Town Victoria four-door hardtop, priced from $2675.

▶ Slow sales precluded a new Skyliner retractable for 1960, but the ragtop Sunliner looked great in this year's new big-Ford clothes. The chrome hood windsplit seen here was a rarely ordered dealer accessory. Again part of the top-line Galaxie group, but not badged as such, the Sunliner drew 44,762 sales this season, slightly down on its 1959 showing despite a little-changed $2860 base price. The entire big-Ford line also recorded slightly lower year-to-year sales.

▲ The four-seat "Squarebird" was three years old in 1960, yet sales improved to nearly 91,000, a mark that wouldn't be bettered for several years. Rear-fender hashmarks and three-element taillamps were part of mild facelift. This convertible is one of 11,860 built. Base price was $4222 with 352 V-8. Lincoln's big 430 V-8 remained optional.

▲ A wide grille bar with three vertical teeth identified 1960 T-Birds, as did a revised nose emblem. A sliding metal sunroof, just visible here, was newly available for the hardtop, but found relatively few takers.

▲ Ford scored big with Falcon, one of 1960's new Big Three compacts. Simple, affordable, and easy on gas, Falcon rang up nearly 436,000 sales to trump Chevy's rear-engine Corvair and Chrysler's odd-looking Valiant.

▲ Ford's 1960 light-duty trucks got a new face with the headlights set in a chrome "dumbbell." This F-100 wears optional whitewall tires and two-tone paint, both increasingly popular options among pickup buyers.

▲ The Ranchero car/pickup was reborn for 1960 on the new Falcon compact platform. Starting at just $1862, this early example of "downsizing" outpolled the previous big Ranchero by drawing 21,027 sales.

LINCOLN ▲ Dearborn's flagships changed only in detail for 1960, but sales sank to just under 25,000 for Lincoln and Continental combined, the lowest total since 1948. Continentals, now called Mark V, remained the *crème de la crème*, with this convertible the most expensive standard model at a lofty $7056. Only 2044 were built, but this year's hardtop coupe, four-door sedan, formal sedan, and limousine saw even lower production.

◀ The Continental Landau hardtop sedan retained its reverse-slant roofline and power-down rear window, but 1960 was the finale for the big unibody Lincolns introduced for '58. This year's Mark Vs again shared a burly 430 V-8 with Lincoln standard and Premiere models, but recession-prompted detuning cut horsepower by 35 to 315.

MERCURY

▶ Mercury sales jumped past 271,000 units for 1960, helped greatly by the midseason debut of the compact Comet, an upscale spinoff of Ford's new Falcon originally planned for Edsel. The traditional big Mercs kept their new-for-'59 bodies, but gained fresh sheet-metal below the beltline. This $3794 Cruiser hardtop coupe from the topline Park Lane series saw just 2974 deliveries.

▲ Big 1960 Mercurys retained their 1959 rooflines and huge compound-curve windshield. A wrapped backlight continued on sedans like this mainstay Monterey, the year's top-selling standard Mercury at 49,594 units.

▲ Mercury reprised two ragtops for 1960: a premium Park Lane and this stylish Monterey. Respective sales were 1525 and 6062, reflecting the Monterey's huge price advantage of nearly $1000.

◀ Scarce then and even rarer now is this 1960 Monterey two-door sedan, still the only such car in the big-Merc line. Though starting price was attractive at $2631—lowest in the line—the model drew a modest 21,557 sales. Rear fender skirts were rare on period big Detroit sedans, but were factory-available for these Mercs. The 312- and 430-cid V-8s, standard depending on series, were slightly detuned from '59.

▶ Mercury wagons thinned from four to two for 1960. The Colony Park returned with woody-look side trim and luxury appointments, plus seating for nine instead of six. Its pillarless four-door hardtop styling was again shared with a more affordable Commuter, which also offered a six-passenger version. The Colony Park priced from $3837, big money in 1960, which helps explain why it drew a modest 7411 sales.

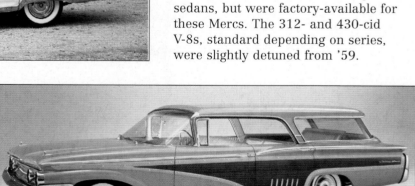

- Ford Division pips Chevrolet in model-year car output by fewer than 22,000 units
- Third-generation Thunderbird arrives, paces Indianapolis 500

- Dramatic new Lincoln Continental debuts; revives four-door convertible body style
- Ford introduces Falcon-based Econoline trucks

- F-Series trucks come in for a redesign
- Falcon adds sporty bucket-seat Futura two-door, a "mini T-Bird"
- Full-size Fords and Mercurys restyled

- Reorganized Big-M line picks up slack after demise of Edsel, includes two new low-priced Meteor series
- New big-block 390 V-8 option for full-size cars

FORD

▶ A lone '57 Pontiac (left) looks decidedly out of place in this view of Flora, Illinois, which was briefly known in 1961 as "Ford Town, U.S.A." In a promotional stunt worthy of P. T. Barnum—and maybe the Pied Piper— Ford Division sent in a fleet of new cars and trucks for each of the town's 1500 vehicle owners to drive for a week. This particular scene was likely staged, but shows that Ford held nothing back. It appears that those lucky enough to snag a Thunderbird had to "make do" with 1960 versions, however. Though we can't be sure, the promotion likely engendered much goodwill in Flora and perhaps even a few extra sales, but also some understandable disappointment when it came time to hand in the keys.

◀ A deft lower-body reskin gave full-size '61 Fords a simple, pleasing new look. Large, round taillamps returned after a year's absence, topped by tiny fins recalling 1957 styling. A T-Bird-style squared-off roofline again capped line-topping Galaxie models like this $2664 Town Victoria four-door hardtop. Expanding big-Ford engine options was a new 390-cid V-8 offering 300 bhp standard, with 330, 375, and a mighty 401 bhp available.

▶ A pair of no-frills Fairlane sedans again anchored the big-Ford line for '61. This four-door, which had a $2317 starting price, lacks the hood letters used on all this year's full-sizers, but is otherwise correct. Also back were Fairlane 500 versions with nicer trim and front-fender name script. With a new "horse-power war" starting in Detroit, drag racers preferred the lightest Fairlanes as starting points for fire-breathing quarter-mile specials.

◀ Accessory rear fender skirts adorn this '61 Sunliner. Ford's big rag-top drew slightly fewer sales this year despite little-changed prices, which started at $2849 with the standard 135-bhp 223 six; the base 175-bhp 292 V-8 added $114. A clean new concave grille used a horizontal bar ahead of a "polka-dot" background whose texture was simply stamped in rather than composed of multiple buttons.

▲ Adding dash to the '61 Falcon line was the midyear Futura two-door with vinyl bucket-type front seats and a Thunderbird-style center console, plus unique wheel covers and rear-fender trim. It was priced from $2162, $248 above the regular two-door.

▲ Ford's big-car instrument panel remained simple and slim for '61, contributing to bountiful passenger room. All-vinyl trim was standard on Sunliners, as shown here.

▲ The '61 Thunderbird was new from road to roof and striking from any angle. Wheelbase and overall size didn't change much, but everything else did. This hardtop priced from $4172, a sizable $417 above the 1960 version.

▲ Though some said it looked rocketlike, the '61 T-Bird was less fussy and more coherent than the jazzy 1958–60. The convertible top again hid away beneath the rear deck. Note the newly curved "cove" rear-seat area.

▲ Ford's new 300-bhp 390 V-8 was the sole engine for '61 Thunderbirds, and was well up to the cars' two-ton heft. T-Bird sales were well down from record 1960, but still healthy at 73,051, including 62,535 hardtops.

▲ A gold T-Bird convertible paced the field for the 50th-anniversary running of the Indianapolis 500, a first for Ford's personal-luxury car. It was an apt choice, as the '61s boasted greater rigidity, improved handling, and larger brakes. As ever, though, Thunderbird was meant for quiet, comfortable touring, not carving up back-country roads.

▶ Expanding Ford's truck fleet for 1961 was the Falcon-based Econoline, offered as a cargo van, passenger van, and this neat pickup. A trim 90-inch-wheelbase chassis tucked the engine and transmission up inside the cab beneath a sound-deadening cover. Despite having just an 85-bhp 144-cid Falcon six, the lightweight Econolines were useful haulers, stingy with gas, and easy and cheap to run. The tall-profile body design provided commanding "big-rig" visibility.

LINCOLN

◄ A complete break with the past, the all-new 1961 Lincoln Continental was much smaller and lighter than the out-sized 1958–60s—and arguably much more handsome. Indeed, its styling—directed by Elwood Engel—won several coveted awards for design excellence. There were just two models, a nostalgic four-door convertible (upper left) and a four-door sedan with frameless door glass (lower left). Both had rear-hinged "suicide" doors, a 300-bhp, 430-cid V-8, much improved workmanship, and classically "correct" styling.

MERCURY

► Responding to a shrunken medium-price market, full-size Mercurys were reorganized into low-priced Meteor 600 and 800 models, a premium Monterey series that included this $3128 convertible, and a parallel station wagon line. Styling retained vestiges of 1960, but the unique platform was retired after just two years, the Big-Ms becoming upscale Fords once more. These smaller, lighter, more-rational Mercurys seemed just right for the times, but model-year sales actually fell, skidding below 121,000, the worst showing since 1948. The ragtop Monterey drew 7053 orders.

▲ Meteor 800 was Mercury's midline '61 full size, offering sedans and hardtops with two and four doors in the $2715-$2840 range. Sales were not impressive at 35,005. The cheaper 600 sedans drew 18,117 sales.

▲ Comet returned for its first full model year with a new grille and a sporty bucket-seat S-22 version of the regular two-door shown here. Comet saved Mercury's hide for '61 by drawing more than 197,000 sales.

1962

- Fairlane bows as the first midsize Ford

- Mercury transfers the Meteor name to its own new intermediate

- Thunderbird adds a spiffy Sports Roadster and posh Landau hardtop

- Burly new 406 V-8 becomes the top full-size power option

- "Blue Oval" logo returns on all Ford cars and trucks

- Lincoln Continental refined, attracts higher sales

FORD ▲ Another lower-body reskin gave a fuller, "more important" look to Ford's full-size cars for '62. Galaxie now denoted the most affordable sedans; a new upscale Galaxie 500 line also listed hardtops and this Sunliner convertible. A bucket-seat hardtop and Sunliner arrived at midseason under "The Lively Ones" banner.

▲ The Galaxie 500 hardtop coupe was the second most popular full-size '62 Ford, attracting 87,562 sales. A midyear bucket-seat XL version drew 28,412 more. Respective starting prices were $2674 and $3268.

▲ Buyers didn't take to the 1960–61 Starliner hardtop coupe, but stock-car racers loved what it did for speed. To stay track-competitive, Ford tried to substitute this removable "Starlift" roof as an option for '62 soft tops.

▲ Answering pleas for another two-seat T-Bird was 1962's new Sports Roadster, basically the regular ragtop with a removable fiberglass tonneau hiding the rear seat. The forward end of the integral headrests mated with the tops of the front seats. Genuine wire wheels were included in the $5439 price, but not the rear fender skirts seen here.

◄ Ford unearthed more marketing gold by stretching its compact into a new Fairlane sized between Falcon and full-size Fords. It bowed with two- and four-door sedans in plain and fancy 500 trim, plus a bucket-seat 500 Sports Coupe. Falcon's larger six was standard, but two new Challenger V-8s were available: a 145-bhp 221 and a lively 164-bhp 260. Fairlane got off to a strong start with more than 297,000 sales.

► The Falcon Futura became even more "mini T-Bird" at mid 1962, when its roofline went from rounded to angular. All Falcons wore a fresh "electric shaver" grille. New, too, were Deluxe-trim sedans and wagons, plus a woody-look four-door Falcon Squire wagon. Ford's compact lost some sales to the new mid-size Fairlane, but was still quite popular with over 396,000 orders.

◄ Falcon's 1962 Deluxe models had more bright exterior trim than base versions, including a broad swath of ribbed aluminum on the lower rear fenders. Basic styling, though, was still much like debut 1960. So were the chassis and powertrains. Despite somewhat lower model-year volume, Falcon remained America's top-selling compact car, appealing as ever for low price, high mileage, and easy repair.

► Falcon was so popular that it passed the one-million mark in sales within three short years. Ford was proud to proclaim this feat by turning on the appropriate lights at its "Glass House" world headquarters and parking a '62 Deluxe two-door in front of the building-turned-billboard. We don't know how long it took to stage this publicity photo, but we're pretty sure the lights were turned off soon after it was snapped. By the way, the model here listed for $2071, not including the whitewalls.

► With buyers fast flocking to bucket-seat cars, Ford whetted their appetite for something truly sporty with the experimental Mustang I. Unveiled in 1962, the low-slung two-seater had a sleek fiberglass body over a trim 90-inch-wheelbase chassis with all-independent suspension. Just as advanced was the racing-style powertrain layout, with a 2.0-liter German Ford V-4 engine behind the cockpit and ahead of the rear-wheel centerline. A production version was briefly considered, but rejected as too costly to build and not likely to make money. Happily, the car itself is still in Ford's hands.

LINCOLN

◄ Lincoln promised that its "New Frontier"-era Continental would not be changed willy-nilly. Sure enough, the follow-up '62s were but subtly refined. The most obvious differences were repositioned headlamps and a new pattern for the grille and back panel. Buyers seemed to approve, as model-year sales bested 31,000.

▲ Despite a relatively large interior, slim center door posts, and no fixed top, the Lincoln Continental convertible sedan was surprisingly solid and quiet. Then again, Lincoln engineers had worked hard to make it so. This beauty is one of only 3212 built for '62, though that bettered the previous year's convertible output of 2857.

▶ Like counterpart Fords, full-size '62 Mercurys gained a slightly bulkier look via fresh lower-body sheetmetal, though weight and dimensions didn't change significantly. Vertical front-fender hash-marks brand this Monterey convertible as the bucket-seat S-55 version introduced at midyear with a companion hardtop coupe. Both offered new 406-cid "Marauder" V-8 options packing 385 or a mighty 405 bhp.

▲ Here's another look at the '62 Monterey S-55 ragtop. The license correctly points up the kinship between these Mercs and Ford's new Galaxie 500/XLs. This model is quite rare, as only 1315 were originally built.

▲ All nonwagon big Mercurys were Montereys for '62, but there were now standard and uplevel Custom series, each with a selection of sedans and hardtops. This Custom hardtop coupe was priced from $2972.

▲ Mercury finally put its name on the Comet for the first time in 1962, the same year that stubby fins and round taillights replaced the canted lamps seen on the 1960–61 models. This base two-door sold for $2084.

▲ Mercury's Meteor was the kissin' cousin of Ford's new intermediate Fairlane for '62, but was far less popular. This Custom two-door sedan was one of five models offered. Prices were in the $2340-$2500 range.

▲ Mercury wagons reverted to pillared styling for '61. The Commuter and faux-woody Colony Park returned for '62, each in six- and nine-passenger versions. Seen here is the nine-seater Colony Park, priced from $3289.

- Ford Motor Company turns 60, produces its 60-millionth vehicle

- Sporty midyear models add more youth appeal to Ford and Mercury car lines

- Ford truck volume hits new postwar high

- Major restyle brings "Breezeway" styling to full-size Mercurys

- Ford Falcon and Mercury Comet add convertibles and hardtops

- Big-block V-8 swells to 427 cid; hot 289 small-block V-8 introduced

- Ford is season champ in NASCAR racing; Mercurys win four races

- Parnelli Jones sets record with a new Mercury Marauder in winning Pikes Peak Hill Climb

- "Whiz Kid" Arjay Miller replaces John Dykstra as company president

FORD

▶ The bucket-seat Fairlane 500 Sports Coupe became a hardtop for 1963, one of several new youth-oriented Fords. A bench-seat 500 version was also offered. All '63 Fairlanes wore a new "face" that looked much like that of the restyled full-size Fords. This lovingly maintained Sports Coupe had a starting price of $2504—$180 more than a 500 hardtop.

▲ Though still 1960 underneath, this year's "Super Torque" full-size Fords offered more available power and handsome new lines. This bucket-seat Galaxie 500/XL hardtop coupe priced from $2674.

▲ Ragtop Galaxie 500 Sunliners returned for '63 in bucket-seat XL and bench-seat regular models. A small front-fender badge here signals the new 427-cid big-block V-8 option available for most big-Ford models.

▶ Semifastback Galaxie 500 hardtop coupes bowed at midyear to replace the Thunderbird-like roof. The new roofline's slicker aerodynamics were a big plus in long-distance stock-car races, combining with competition-tuned big-block V-8s to make Ford the season champ in NASCAR. (Tiny Lund drove one to victory in the 1963 Daytona 500.) This "slantback" XL packs the hot 406 mill, good for up to 405 bhp.

► Falcon's big news for 1963 was the addition of a Futura convertible and hardtop coupe, a first for Ford's compact. Each was also offered in a top-line Sprint version with a lively 164-bhp, 260-cube V-8 and available "four on the floor" manual transmission. The V-8 was optional for other Falcons. This Sprint ragtop priced from $2837. Just 4602 were built.

◄ Thunderbird was spruced up for '63 with a new grille pattern and a prominent bodyside creaseline that flattened the tops of the front wheel arches. The mainstay hardtop again came in this base model or as a more luxurious Landau with standard vinyl roof covering and dummy "S" bars on the rear roof panels. An even ritzier Limited Edition Landau bowed in January under the auspices of Monaco's Princess Grace; sales were purposely held to just 2000.

► The Thunderbird Sports Roadster returned for 1963, again at a whopping $700 premium over the standard convertible. That was evidently too much even for this well-heeled market, and a sales drop of more than two-thirds, to just 455, assured the Sports Roadster would not be back. Included in that small number are just 37 examples equipped with a 340-bhp "M" version of the 390 V-8, a rare 1962–63 option unique to the T-Bird. Total T-Bird sales this model year fell to 63,313, in part due to fresh competition, chiefly from Buick's swanky new Riviera.

◄ Big Fords were still much favored by "John Law," be it in real life—as evidenced by this restored Columbus, Georgia, patrol car—or on television, where Sheriff Taylor and Deputy Fife served the good folk of Mayberry. Police-package Fords for 1963 were typically low-line "300" four-doors outfitted with heavy-duty suspension, high-power V-8s, and officer-required equipment. Again this year, Ford offered a 330-bhp "Police Special" 390, basically the T-Bird "M" engine with a single four-barrel carburetor instead of three two-barrels.

▶ Ford still liked to call itself "America's Wagonmaster," and its '63 caravan was the broadest ever. The woody-look Country Squire remained the biggest and brightest of the bunch, again offered with two or three rows of seats. At midyear, Galaxie 500/XL front bucket seats, console, and other interior trim became a first-time option for Country Squires, which priced from $3018.

▲ Falcon wagons were grouped into their own series for '63, but with the same five model choices: standard and Deluxe two- and four-doors, and a woody-look four-door Squire. Here, the $2384 two-door Deluxe.

▲ Besides a pair of hardtops, the midsize Fairlane line added a trio of wagons for '63, including this $2781 four-door Squire with woodlike side paneling. Regular and Custom Ranch Wagons had plain sides.

◀ Ford's popular F-Series pickups had been fully redesigned for '61 with roomier cabs that eliminated the old wrapped windshield. Changes were modest for '62 and '63. The combination of one-ton F-350 with optional four-wheel drive and flush-fender Styleside box seen here was a real rarity; just 1470 F-350 Stylesides of all kinds were made. Ford also offered ½-ton F-100s and ¾-ton F-250s with two- or four-wheel drive and Styleside or flared-fender Flareside boxes. This was the last year pickups could be had with a Styleside bed integrated with the cab.

▶ Ford's compact Econolines were again little changed for '63, and still not as popular as the big F-Series models despite lower prices, better fuel thrift, and new options intended to make the little trucks seem more like cars. This pickup, for example, carries an option package that included nicer interior trim and five-leaf rear springs for a smoother ride than the standard four-leaf units could provide. Two-tone paint was available separately. Econoline pickup sales this year totaled 11,394 versus 48,620 for the passenger wagons and cargo vans.

LINCOLN ▲ Another new grille texture and an increase of 20 horsepower—to 320—were the significant changes made to the 1963 Lincolns. Sales of convertibles declined minutely, but demand for the sedan was nudged forward, just past the 28,000 mark. Base prices for both Continental models were increased by $196 for the year.

MERCURY ▲ Like sister Fords, full-size '63 Mercurys were handsomely restyled below the beltline and offered more model variations. This sporty S-55 convertible again topped the line at $3900, which included a brawny 300-bhp Marauder Super 390 V-8.

▲ Two "slantback" Marauder hardtop coupes joined the line at midyear, a bench-seat Monterey Custom and this bucket-seat S-55. Respective starting prices were $3083 and $3650. The S-55 saw just 2319 copies.

▲ Recalling the 1957–58 Turnpike Cruiser was a bevy of new 1963 "Breezeway" hardtops and sedans. All featured a rear window that dropped down at the touch of a button to assist interior ventilation. Models comprised entry-level Montereys and upscale Monterey Customs, plus this two-door hardtop and a four-door companion in S-55 trim. Nobody, not even Ford, offered anything like them. Styling returned to subtle fins and triple taillight clusters.

► If you wanted a big Mercury station wagon in 1963, it had to be a woody-look Colony Park, though you still had a choice of six- and nine-passenger models. A roll-down tailgate window replaced a separate liftgate on all full-size Mercury and Ford wagons starting with 1961. This Colony Park is one 13,976 built for '63. Prices started at $3295.

▲ Like Falcon, Mercury's compact line added convertibles and hardtop coupes for '63. Sporty bucket-seaters were S-22s; bench-seat models came as Customs. This Comet Custom ragtop drew a modest 7354 sales.

▲ Comet again listed two- and four-door wagons for '63. This four-door Custom was the most popular offering, yet sales came to just 5151. A larger 170-cid six became standard for Comet wagons at mid-model year.

► The midsize Mercury Meteors were facelifted for 1963, and sprouted wagon models and a pair of hardtop coupes: this Custom and a sportier bucket-seat S-33 version. All models benefited from a number of underskin changes, but somehow Meteor never found the sales success of sister Ford Fairlane, leading Mercury to try a new approach for '64. This $2448 Custom hardtop is one of 7565 originally built, versus 4865 for the $2628 S-33 version.

◄ Meteor's new station wagons comprised plain-sided base and Custom models, plus this woody-look Country Cruiser. Each came in six- and eight-passenger versions. Being intermediates, the eight-seaters ended up a bit tight in the third row, which was best left to children. This publicity photo faintly implies as much. Engines included two sixes and two small V-8s, but Meteor sales remained disappointing, declining to just under 51,000 for the model year.

EUGENE BORDINAT JR.
Art and Commerce

A FITTING EPITAPH FOR Eugene Bordinat Jr. could have been his own remark tying design to sales. "Beauty is a good 10-day sales report," he once said.

Bordinat, who served as vice president for styling from 1961 to 1980, was Ford's most versatile stylist ever. "He made great contributions as an engineer. He knew a lot about automobiles, body engineering, and the configuring of cars," said engineering executive H. L. Misch. "He was as much of a product planner as he was a designer," noted sales executive William P. Benton. "He could read and understand a balance sheet," said Bordinat's boss, William Clay Ford Sr.

The son of Willys-Overland's plant manager, Bordinat was born in Toledo, Ohio, on February 10, 1920. After attending Cranbrook Academy of Art in Bloomfield Hills, Michigan, he spent a year at the University of Michigan. In 1939, he joined General Motors as a summer design trainee. During World War II, he became a supervisor in Fisher Body's tank-building program, then served in the Army Air Forces. He returned to GM as a senior stylist in 1946, but within a year was supervising Ford's advanced styling studio, focusing on Lincoln-Mercury products.

A surprise successor to George Walker as head of Ford Styling, Bordinat combined an informal operating style with a hardheaded business approach, and built a solid reputation as a good manager. To Bill Ford he "was a good administrator. . . . He could organize the workload, and knew how to take care of and get the most out of a couple of thousand employees." To product developer Harold Sperlich, he "was able to manage a creative organization and keep the juices flowing." Bordinat was much admired for his presentation skills. "He could have been an actor," said design colleague John Najjar. "He knew language, knew how to throw his voice into a deeper register when presenting, and knew how to change the speed of his delivery." "Gene Bordinat was Styling's best spokesman," summed up Chairman Donald E. Petersen, who worked closely with the company's top designers when he was vice president for car planning and research.

Ford contemporaries enjoyed Bordinat's company. One associate described him as "a wonderful guy, a charming man, fun to be around. He had a great sense of humor, very sarcastic, like your gruff uncle. But you knew there was a heart of gold underneath." Said Sperlich, "He was an arty type, egotistical, and a classic stylist—flashy. But he was fun, and inventive, and a great partner in projects." Novelist Arthur Hailey wrote a Bordinat-like character into his book *Wheels* after meeting him.

Sartorially, Bordinat went to extremes. On the job he was a snappy dresser, favoring Italian-made suits. Dining in 1985 with *Detroit Free Press* columnist James C. Jones, he wore "a gold pendant swinging over a scarlet ascot and gold wrist ornaments weighing in at about one pound each." He tooled around in pearlescent cars; his stable included a costly Clenet roadster and a Mangusta sports car.

Bordinat was well-tuned to the market for most of his career. "He created some cars with tremendous longevity," observed design executive Fred C. Mayhew. Bordinat's favorite design project was the Lincoln Continental Mark III, which he called a "banker's hot rod." Toward the end of his career, he also was very fond of the Mark V. Ironically, the controversial Pinto was another favorite. But the styling boss may have lost some of his touch toward the end of his career. "I had a sense that . . . in the late Seventies, he wasn't willing to change with the times," Mayhew said. "He would, for example, make fun of cars being done in Europe."

"If I had anything critical to say about Gene," said Henry Ford II, "it would be that, rather than doing what he thought was the right thing, he was more apt to do what someone else thought was right. . . . He was influenced by a lot of people. He was certainly influenced by [Lee] Iacocca during the seven years that he was president and the previous years when he ran North American operations."

The fact that Bordinat swayed with the wind enabled him to head the company's design staff for 19 years, longer than anyone else before or since. "He read the bosses pretty well, and knew what they wanted," said product planner William R. Burmeister.

In retirement, Bordinat drafted an irreverent autobiography entitled *My Days at the Court of Henry II*. A New York publisher, after reviewing the content, suggested that it be "fleshed out" and given a more "anti-Iacocca slant." That would have been easy for Bordinat, who resented Iacocca's eagerness to take bows as the "father of the Mustang" and reluctance to share credit with others. But before the manuscript could be completed, Bordinat died on August 11, 1987, of an aggressive, undiagnosed lung ailment. His widow, Teresa, promised Bordinat associate L. David Ash that she would revise and resubmit the work for publication. She never did.

- Ford unleashes Mustang; buyers stampede to the "ponycar"

- Thunderbird fully redesigned

- Major facelifts for Falcon, Fairlane, Comet, and full-size Fords and Mercurys

- "Total Performance" Ford line is *Motor Trend's* "Car of the Year"

- Lincoln Continental grows slightly larger, keeps classic looks

- Mercury celebrates its 25th anniversary

- Falcon wins class in Monte Carlo Rally

FORD ▲ A lower-body restyle gave Ford Falcons a more "grown up" look for '64. The $2436 Futura Sprint hardtop drew 13,831 orders, and overall Sprint sales rose past 18,000. An eight-car Falcon team entered Europe's famed Monte Carlo Rally and came home with an impressive second overall and a first in the GT class.

▲ The 1964 Futura convertible priced from $2481 with the front bench seat shown here or from $2597 with the available buckets-and-console "sports interior." This year's makeover upped Falcon's width by one inch and overall length by half an inch. It also brought a slightly more imposing dashboard. In spite of Falcon's-fresh, new look, overall sales declined to 300,770 cars, plus another 18,190 related sedan deliveries and Ranchero pickups.

◄ Falcon was always about low-cost simplicity, and a model like this '64 Deluxe four-door station wagon still appeals as practical daily transportation. An 85-bhp 144-cid six remained standard for most models, but wagons and the Futura convertible substituted the 101-bhp, 170-cid engine that likely powered the bulk of this year's production. All body styles retained their previous rooflines for '64, but the cars looked almost completely new, thanks to another adept lower-body "reskinning" by Ford stylists.

► Unveiled at the New York World's Fair in April 1964, the Falcon-based Mustang uncovered a vast new market for high-style "sporty compacts" that sent rival automakers scurrying to their drawing boards. Technically a 1965 model, Ford sold almost 681,000 through August '65, including 101,945 ragtops. Prices as low as $2372 for the hardtop coupe and a plethora of "personal" options made Mustang an instant hit.

◄ Ford publicists scored a coup in getting the new Mustang on the covers of both *Time* and *Newsweek* simultaneously, just as the car was hitting showrooms. A month later, a Mustang convertible driven by Benson Ford, brother of company president Henry Ford II, paced the field at the Indianapolis 500. It was all part of a more aggressive "Total Performance" marketing campaign.

► When the Mustang pace car rolled from the starting line on Memorial Day 1964, it was followed by three Ford-powered racers that had been qualified for the front row of that year's Indy 500. The cars (from left) were driven by Rodger Ward, Bobby Marshman, and pole-sitter Jim Clark. Ward finished second. Power came from a 255-cid adaptation of the 221-cube small-block V-8. Mounted at the rear of a Lotus chassis, Clark set Indy fans abuzz with it when it debuted in 1963.

► Dominating all forms of motorsports was a major thrust of Ford's "Total Performance" campaign. For quarter-mile action, Ford unleashed the '64 Thunderbolt, a stripped two-door Fairlane packing a "high-riser" 427 V-8 with close to 500 bhp, plus exotic engineering. Though nominally priced at around $3900, the Thunderbolt was a virtual ready-made drag racer that terrorized the strips. A mere 100 were built.

▲ The midsize Fairlane entered its third season with another facelift, but maintained visual kinship with big Fords. Here, the "think young" bucket-seat 500 Sports Coupe hardtop, which priced from $2502.

▲ Though not the most glamorous '64 Fairlane, the 500 four-door sedan remained Ford's best-selling intermediate offering, drawing close to 87,000 model-year sales. Base price was $2317.

◄ Thunderbird was again all-new for '64, with somewhat more conventional looks and a jazzy interior with a dashboard fit for an airplane. The basic powertrain was much the same, as were dimensions, but new features abounded, such as a reclining front-passenger seat, automatic parking-brake release, and extended lube and oil-change intervals. The car's newness provided a shot in the arm to convertible sales, which jumped this year to 9198. This beauty originally priced from $4953.

► Thunderbird again offered two hardtops for '64: a base $4486 version and this $4589 Landau with the customary dummy S-bars on the rear quarters of a vinyl-covered roof. Respective model-year sales were 60,552 and 22,715. There was no Limited Edition Landau this year. Nor was there a Sports Roadster, though a similar rear-seat tonneau was available from dealers and is still seen on some '64 convertibles. Thunderbird enjoyed record model-year sales of 92,465 units, thus eclipsing the 1960 mark at last.

▲ Many critics felt the full-size Fords hit a new peak with the '64 models. Indeed, they were a big factor in winning *Motor Trend*'s "Car of the Year" honor for the year's entire Ford line. It was hard to believe the big Fords were still much like the 1960 models underneath, though there had been many engineering advances, and styling had been completely transformed. Here, the $3233 Galaxie 500/XL hardtop coupe, which drew 58,306 sales.

▲ Ford designers went all-out to make their '64 full-sizers look fresh and new, resulting in the most thorough and dramatic year-to-year styling change since 1960. Here, the popular Galaxie 500 four-door sedan.

▲ Space-saving "thin-shell" front bucket seats were a new feature seen on Galaxie 500/XLs and redesigned T-Birds. The big-Ford dash was slightly modified from '63, but XL interior trim was as brightly lavish as ever.

◄ The popularity of "slantback" hardtops prompted a "faster" roofline for '64 big-Ford sedans, ousting the more formal Thunderbird-type style. Pictured here is another Galaxie 500 four-door, which priced from $2678 and drew 198,805 sales. Unusually, it wasn't the line's most popular model this year; the 500 hardtop coupe claimed that distinction with nearly 207,000 orders.

LINCOLN

► Though it seemed little changed at first glance, the Lincoln Continental rode a three-inch longer wheelbase for '64. It also exchanged curved side windows for flat glass. The four-door sedan gained a wider rear window, as seen here. Lincoln sales improved 16 percent to 36,297.

▲ Lincoln Continental kept its classic looks for '64, but the slight upsizing made for a roomier back seat and longer rear doors for accessing it. Trunks were more spacious, too. Designers kept changing grille treatments, opting this year for a convex vertical-bar affair. Convertible sedan prices started at $6938. Sales of 3328 units were recorded.

MERCURY

◄ Mercury celebrated its 25th birthday while recalling the past with a reorganized big-car line reviving the Montclair and Park Lane names. Montclair was the middle series, above Monterey, and included this $3116 "Breezeway" sedan, plus a similar hardtop coupe and two Marauder slant-back hardtops. Unhappily for Mercury, total big-car sales eased to 110,300.

◄ All full-size Mercs got an "electric shaver" grille for '64. Montclairs like this Marauder hardtop coupe had unique lower-body trim. Engines were basically carryover, which meant that the burly 427 was still around. Parnelli Jones drove a big-block '64 to a second straight victory at Pikes Peak. Mercurys also won five NASCAR stock-car races.

► After emphasizing lower-priced "mediums" for three years, Mercury moved back upmarket with its 1964 Park Lanes, which were priced against top-line Buicks and Chryslers. The six-model group included this stylish Marauder hardtop sedan, which drew only 4505 sales.

◄ The compact Comet was heavily restyled for double duty as the "midsize" Mercury, replacing the Fairlane-based Meteor. Front-fender "ports" were a curious crib from Buick, but Comet sales improved to nearly 190,000, the highest since '61. This "202" two-door sedan was the most affordable model, priced from $2126.

► Like sister Falcons, the '64 Comets gained squarish new lower-body sheet-metal imparting a more "mature" look, but the grille and other design elements provided visual links with full-size Mercurys. The "big car" appearance was important, given the compact's new mandate of representing Mercury in the midsize field. The most interesting '64 Comets were a flashy new Caliente convertible and hardtop, joined at midyear by an even hotter Cyclone hardtop. But for an elegant little hauler, this Villager wagon was mighty appealing at $2734 to start, though just 1980 were built.

- Full-size Fords are totally redesigned
- New LTD models top big-car line, take Ford into luxury territory
- Mustang adds jaunty "2+2" fastback coupe
- Thunderbird gets sequential turn signals
- Ford dominates the NASCAR season, winning 48 of 55 events, including 32 in a row
- High-performance Mustang-based Shelby GT 350 introduced
- Jim Clark wins Indianapolis 500 in a Ford-powered mid-engine Lotus
- All-new full-size Mercurys bow "in the Lincoln Continental tradition"
- Lincoln Continental sees further refinements

FORD

▶ Full-size Fords were virtually clean-sheet new for '65, with taut, chiseled styling and a new-design frame with wider tracks, revised suspension, and side-rail "torque boxes" that damped out noise and harshness. This is the popular Galaxie 500/XL hardtop coupe, priced this year from $3233. A little more than 28,000 were built.

▲ Ford's low-line big cars were still popular with the fleet market and value-conscious retail buyers. This year's offerings comprised two- and four-door sedans in Custom and slightly nicer Custom 500 versions. This Custom two-door was the most affordable big Ford, with a starting price of $2313.

▶ The Sunliner name had faded away by '65, but Ford's full-size convertibles were as appealing as ever. This bench-seat Galaxie 500 priced from $2950. The buckets-and-console 500/XL started at $3498, but boasted a 200-bhp 289 V-8 as standard instead of a six.

◄ The wildly popular Mustang was an early 1965 debut, though many enthusiasts—and sometimes Ford itself—use "1964½" to describe early build models. For the "formal" '65 season, Mustang got several changes, including a larger base six and three optional 289 V-8s instead of a single 260. This hardtop coupe carries the optional GT package, which delivered such goodies as fog lamps, lower-bodyside stripes, firmer suspension, and extra gauges. Power front-disc brakes arrived as a separate late-season extra priced at just $58.

► Ford had one of Detroit's most popular period ragtops in the Mustang convertible, which tallied nearly 102,000 sales in the ponycar's extra-long debut model year. Even so, the Mustang hardtop outsold it by some 5-to-1, and convertible demand was starting to wane throughout the industry. This beauty is another GT-equipped model, signaled by a small identifying crest on the lower front fenders and "GT" letters on the gas cap. Some GT features were also available as separate options.

◄ A jaunty fastback coupe arrived for the formal '65 season to give Mustang buyers a third body choice. It was aptly called "2+2," as its tighter back seat was intended only for "occasional" adult use. The fastback naturally listed the same standard and optional features as the hardtop and convertible, but also boasted functional "flo-thru" ventilation via air-extractor grilles in the roof behind the door windows. An available fold-down rear seat allowed carrying longer items inside with the trunklid closed. Prices started at $2589.

► Having just been restyled, Falcon returned for 1965 with minor visual updates and the same model lineup. An early running change replaced the 170-cid six with the 200-cid engine as standard across the board. Sportier Falcons offered 289 V-8 options like Mustang's, but the more stylish ponycars were fast stealing sales from Ford's uplevel compacts. Thus, production of this Sprint ragtop plunged to a mere 300 units and calls for the Futura version fell by more than 50 percent to 6315. Base prices were $2671 and $2481, respectively.

▶ Thunderbird's big news for 1965 was adoption of standard power front-disc brakes, which resisted fade and water much better than drum brakes, important in a two-ton luxury cruiser. This convertible, which priced from $4953, wears the dealer-installed "Sport Tonneau" rear-seat cover inspired by the late Sports Roadster model, though fewer buyers ordered it this year.

▲ T-Bird sales dropped 19 percent for model-year '65 to just under 75,000—disappointing but not unexpected for the followup version of an all-new car. At midyear, the base and Landau hardtops were joined by this ritzy $4639 Limited Edition Special Landau, which was purposely limited to just 4500 copies.

◀ The T-Bird Limited Edition Special Landau came with "Ember-Glo" metallic paint, as shown here, or white, as above. Both complemented a parchment-color vinyl roof and matching upholstery. Carpeting and dashboard finish were common to both versions.

► Fairlanes got a somewhat busier look for '65, with knife-edge fenderlines and prominent bodyside creases à la this year's redesigned full-size Fords. Wheelbase added a nominal half-inch to 116 even, but the basic design was still 1962 and had plenty of newer competition. These and other factors combined to push Fairlane model-year sales below 224,000, a new low for Ford's midsize line. This 500 hardtop coupe was the second most popular '65 Fairlane with 41,405 sales versus 77,000-plus for the 500 four-door sedan.

◄ "Bigger is better" had long been gospel in Detroit, so it's no surprise that Sixties compacts and then intermediates quickly bulked up in appearance if not actual size. Fairlane was no exception, and Ford designers used every trick to give the '65 models a "big car" look—even this base-series $2230 two-door sedan. Note here the prominent lower-bodyside creaselines, squarish fenders, and raised rear deck above larger, rectangular taillamps. This car is mildly dressed up with optional whitewall tires and rear bumper guards.

► Station wagons in Ford's family of intermediates again came in base form and as a ritzier Fairlane 500, shown here. Respective prices started at $2567 and $2648. As usual, 500s came with extra exterior brightwork and nicer interior trim, including carpeting in place of a rubber floor covering. This one is further spruced up with optional two-tone paint, whitewalls, wire-look wheel covers, and a roof rack. A formerly optional 200-cid six was the new standard engine. V-8 choices ran to 289s in 200-, 225-, and 271-bhp ratings.

◄ Ford's ever-popular F-Series pickups now wore front-fender badges proclaiming "Twin I-Beam" front suspension. A clever cross between a traditional solid axle and fully independent suspension, Twin I-Beam consisted of two lateral members, one for each wheel, that mounted so that they crisscrossed each other. The idea was to combine greater wheel travel for ride comfort with solid-axle ruggedness, especially off the beaten path. This well-maintained F-100 is a short-bed Styleside with two-tone paint and an exterior chrome package.

LINCOLN

► Lincoln Continental maintained its classic styling for '65, with a horizontal-theme grille the most obvious visual change. Despite strong competition from a fully redesigned Cadillac, Lincoln sales improved once again, topping 40,000 for the model year. This convertible sedan carried a $6938 original base price.

MERCURY
▲ Like full-size Fords, the big '65 Mercurys were virtually all-new. Basic engineering was shared, but the Mercs had their own, longer wheelbase and clean, restrained styling "in the Lincoln Continental tradition," as ads emphasized. Model choices thinned a bit, but still included a Monterey convertible and this premium Park Lane ragtop, the year's costliest Mercury at $3599 to start. A modest 3006 were built.

▲ Mercury still pushed "Breezeway" styling in '65, but only with four-door sedans. Hardtops were now strictly "slantbacks" with fixed rear windows. This $2904 Monterey was the most popular Breezeway with 19,569 sales versus not quite 19,000 for the midline Montclair and only 8335 for the top-line Park Lane. Detroit enjoyed record sales for '65, and the big Mercurys shared in the wealth by attracting 181,699 orders, including wagons.

▲ Ford Motor Company sanctioned semifactory-extended-length executive limousines as Ford LTDs and Lincoln Continentals in the Sixties; here's how the same concept looked as a Mercury Park Lane. A new feature of the big Mercs for '65 was the adoption of coil springs for the rear suspension.

► Hardtops were no longer called Marauders for '65, but engines were, so the name continued to appear on rear roof pillars. Montereys like this hardtop coupe remained the most-affordable full-size Mercs, thus they had the least exterior chrome—all the better for showing off the crisp new lines. All models came with updated standard 390 V-8s packing up to 300 bhp. A 330-bhp version was available, as was a 425-bhp 427.

▲ Again Mercury's hottest compact, the Comet Cyclone hardtop coupe offered up to 225 bhp and a $2683 starting price. Exactly 12,347 of the '65s were built.

▲ All Comets got a fresh look for '65, with vertical quad headlights and somewhat busy side sculpturing. This swanky Caliente hardtop coupe started at $2403.

◄ Again bearing "test tube" faux wood trim, the Villager remained Comet's top-line wagon for '65, priced from $2762. Though equipped much like top-line Caliente models, it remained part of the midlevel "404" series that also included a plain-side Custom wagon starting at $2578. Also continued was a few-frills four-door in the bottom-rung "202" group, priced from $2491. The Villager was by far the rarest of this trio, as just 1592 were produced for the model year.

1966

- All-new Ford Falcon and Fairlane debut

- Jeep-fighting Ford Bronco off-roader debuts

- Full-size Ford lineup adds posh, big-inch Galaxie 7-Litre models

- Lincoln Continental fully redesigned, adds hardtop coupe body style

- All-new Mercury Comet bows; Cyclone is Indy 500 pace car

- Ford Division builds a record 2.2 million cars to beat Chevrolet output

- Ford GT-40 racer scores historic 1-2-3 sweep at 24 Hours of LeMans

► Returning from 1965 as the finest full-size Ford, the posh Galaxie 500 LTD continued as a hardtop coupe and this hardtop sedan. Ford ads exaggerated but slightly in claiming LTDs were "quieter than a Rolls-Royce." Buyers fast responded to Ford's push into the luxury league, snapping up 101,096 of the '66-model LTDs.

FORD ▲ Ford's midsize Fairlane was overhauled for '66 with smooth new styling on wider bodies that left room for big-block V-8s. Among those bodies was a first-time convertible, offered along with hardtop coupes in 500/XL trim (shown) and in new XL GT guise. GTs were quick, thanks to a standard 335-bhp 390 V-8.

◄ Though you weren't likely to see one at your local Ford dealer, this LTD-based "stretch" limousine was briefly available by special order in 1966. A contract coachbuilder carried out the conversion, but Ford's normal new-car warranty applied. It's unusual for a limo in having hardtop sedan styling instead of the customary fixed middle roof posts. The chassis was strengthened as well as lengthened.

▶ Mustang got only detail updates for '66, plus base prices hiked slightly, but sales kept galloping: a hearty 607,568 for the normal 12-month selling season. This 2+2 fastback, which started at $2607, is equipped with the popular GT package and styled steel wheels. The 2+2 remained the least-popular Mustang, drawing 35,698 sales versus nearly 500,000 hardtops.

▲ Thunderbirds were gilded a bit for '66, gaining a new face and full-width taillights. The Landau (shown) also got a wide-quarter roofline, as did a new lower-cost Town Hardtop that did without a vinyl roof.

▲ The fourth-generation T-Bird bowed out after '66. So did the ragtop after just 5049 sales. A torquey 345-bhp 428-cid V-8 was now optional for all T-Birds, but total sales fell again, this time to 69,176.

▶ The '66 Falcon was a much-changed compact, becoming a shorter version of the new midsize Fairlane. Models were pared to base and Futura sedans and four-door wagons. This Futura Sports Coupe was the most interesting, with its bucket-seat interior and top-line trim, but sales were modest at 20,289. Total Falcon sales dropped below 183,000.

◀ Being all-new the previous year, full-size Fords got mainly minor refinements for '66. Among them was a new feature for this top-line Country Squire and all other Ford wagons: the "Magic Doorgate." This referred to a tailgate with special two-way hinges that allowed it to be dropped down in the usual way or swung open like a door, a convenience that many buyers appreciated.

▶ Ford still offered a Falcon-based car/pickup in '66, but the compact's redesign made for a nicer-looking Ranchero with more people and cargo space. Buyers could choose from this $2330 standard model or a better-equipped $2411 Deluxe. Ranchero sales had never been high, but this year's total was respectable at 21,760.

◀ Responding to growing public interest in "off-roading"—and growing sales of the Jeep CJ—was the pert new 1966 Ford Bronco with four-wheel drive, a standard 170-cid six, and optional 289 V-8. There were three variations, all two-doors: this $2625 four-passenger wagon with removable steel top; a two-passenger pickup-style "sports utility," priced from $2480; and a bare-bones $2404 roadster without roof or doors, though those were available. Respective model-year sales were 12,756, 6930, and 4090.

▶ Grille treatments were an almost annual event for Ford's F-Series pickups, and 1966 was no exception. Here we have a mainstay ½-ton F-100 with two-wheel drive, the short Styleside box, "Custom Cab" trim, and exterior chrome package. Pickups were still generally work vehicles in the mid Sixties, but Ford and rival truckmakers were starting to notice a small but definite trend toward "duded-up" models like this. Nowadays, of course, a great many people buy well-equipped pickups instead of cars for personal transport—very many of them F-Series Fords.

LINCOLN

▶ Lincoln Continental was restyled for 1966, but kept its "classic" character. A projected hood and central grille section implied more power, and a new 462-cid V-8 delivered 20 ponies more than the previous 430—340 in all. Convertibles gained a glass rear window, but declined in popularity, with just 3180 made.

◀ Curved side glass returned to Lincoln Continental after a three-year absence and helped open up a little extra shoulder room. The '66 makeover did not change wheelbase, but increased overall length by almost five inches to 220.9. Base prices swelled, too—ever so slightly—with the top-selling four-door sedan up to $5750. Lincoln sales jumped a satisfying 36 percent to 54,755.

▲ A big factor in Lincoln's '66 sales upsurge was the return of a hardtop coupe model after six years. Priced $265 below the four-door at $5485, it drew respectable sales of 15,766. This advertising photo highlights the still-dignified but more flowing look applied to all Continentals, including *de rigueur* "hopped up" rear fenderlines.

MERCURY

► Full-size '66 Mercurys received several refinements to their year-old basic design, including a new 330-bhp 410-cid V-8 as standard for top-line Park Lanes like this $3387 hardtop coupe. Sales were down throughout Detroit after record '65, and the senior Mercury line shared in the retreat, dropping to just under 173,000.

◄ The Park Lane convertible again topped Mercury's prestige line for '66, starting at $3608. Sales remained modest, with only 2546 being called for. It no longer was the costliest Merc, however: A revived S-55 ragtop started at $3614. Just 669 were made. Monterey convertibles priced from $3237 and saw 3279 sales. A new "Stereo-Sonic Tape System," more commonly known as an eight-track cartridge tape player, was available for all big Mercurys.

▲ After two years as Mercury's "midsize," Comet literally grew into the role for '66 by becoming a twin to Ford's Fairlane. Convertible offerings were headed by this racy new $3152 Cyclone GT. Just 2158 were built.

▲ A Cyclone GT ragtop did pace-car duty at the '66 Indy 500. A number of others, like the one shown, served as parade cars. The GT boasted a standard 265-bhp 390 V-8, with 335 bhp available at extra cost.

◄ What Ford called a "Magic Doorgate" was a "Dual-Action Tailgate" at Mercury, where it was featured on all '66 wagons, including this $2790 Comet Villager. Comet's stem-to-stern redesign from senior compact to true intermediate was a definite sales asset, as orders improved by some 5400 units to nearly 170,500. A wider range of sporty high-power Cyclones helped, too.

- All-new Thunderbird bows with two hard-tops—and a sedan

- Ford Mustang restyled, offers big-block V-8s

- Full-size Fords get major design overhaul

- Mercury introduces Mustang-based Cougar, the first luxury ponycar

- Big Mercurys get fresh styling, add posh Marquis and Park Lane Brougham models

- Ford Ranchero car/pickup graduates to mid-size Fairlane platform

- F-Series trucks see first redesign in six years

- Shelby-Mustang adds big-block GT 500 models

- Racing Ford GT claims a second straight win in the famed 24 Hours of LeMans

- Henry Ford elected to Automotive Hall of Fame

FORD

◄ Thunderbird was clean-sheet fresh for '67, becoming larger and more luxurious than ever. The convertible was gone, but base and Landau hardtops returned, the latter shown here. But the biggest news was a lush $4825 Landau four-door sedan on a 2.5-inch longer wheelbase (117.2 inches). Total T-Bird sales improved to near 78,000.

▲ T-Bird's '67 styling was more massive and combined familiar cues with new elements like hidden headlamps. This standard hardtop priced from $4603. Its upscale Landau sister started $101 higher.

▲ Ford's midsize Fairlanes saw little change for '67, but a racing version of this 500/XL hardtop coupe claimed victory in NASCAR's Daytona 500. Big-block 427-cube V-8s with 410 or 425 bhp were still available.

► As in '66, Fairlane GTs with automatic transmission were badged "GT/A." Ragtops were rare either way, with only 2117 built for '67. Hardtop coupes totaled 18,670. This year, Fairlane GTs formed a separate series with the slightly less sporty 500/XL hardtop and convertible. XLs saw respective sales of 14,871 and just 1943. In another change, GTs were demoted to a 200-bhp 289 V-8. Big-block 390s now cost extra and delivered 270 or 320 bhp. GTs priced from $2839 for the hardtop, $3064 for the soft top.

▶ Full-size '67 Fords kept their existing wheelbases, but adopted more flowing lines that added three inches to overall length. Hardtop coupes gained a smoother roofline, too. This Galaxie 500 version, which priced from $2755, repeated as the line's most popular single model by drawing 197,388 sales. In other big-Ford news, LTD became a separate series and added a four-door sedan, while the big-block 7-Litre models became a package option for XLs.

◀ Big Ford wagons showed less rear-end change than other '67s, but designers still managed to give them "coke bottle" fenderlines per a general industry trend. As ever, the woody-look Country Squire was the best on offer from "America's Wagonmaster." This year, it priced from $3234 in six-passenger trim and from $3359 as a nine-seater. Ford Division recorded generally lower sales this year, in part because of a protracted 57-day auto workers strike.

▶ Falcon sales plunged nearly 65 percent for model-year '67 to an all-time low of 64,335, a big comedown for what had been one of America's most popular cars a few years earlier. Several factors were at work, but the main one was a market still shifting away from sensible compacts. Even so, the Futura Sports Coupe shown here was an appealing "think young" car in its own right—not as flashy as a Mustang perhaps, but a solid value with a $2437 starting price. Despite that, it sold only 7053 copies.

▲ U.S. Shelby Cobra sales ended in '67 due to forthcoming federal regulations. By this point, Carroll Shelby was building updated "427" roadsters with big-block Ford V-8s that could be tweaked up to 480 bhp.

▲ Cobra 427s were built in 1965–67 with more muscular "wide-body" styling than the small-block cars first made in '62. All Cobras had too much power for their chassis, but 427s were truly scary—and unforgettable.

◀ Dearborn marked another milestone in May 1967 with production of the 70-millionth Ford car since the company's founding in 1903. Though a happy event, it was small consolation in a year when Ford car sales dropped by nearly half-a-million units. Fittingly, the milestone car was a Galaxie 500 hardtop coupe, the best-seller in the full-size line and indeed the entire '67 Ford fleet except for the Mustang hardtop. Ford Division had lately resurrected the historic "blue oval" logo for a variety of corporate purposes, including signage, but still limited its use on vehicles to minor spots like door sill step plates.

◀ The '67 Mustangs got a full outer-body reskin that made for a huskier look and added two inches to overall length. Cars with automatic and the GT option, like this hardtop, were now badged "GT/A."

▲ Mustang finally faced direct competition for '67 in a much-revised Plymouth Barracuda and Chevy's new Camaro. With that and the auto workers strike, sales dropped 23 percent to 472,121. But that was hardly bad, and the original ponycar was still number one by far. Convertibles like this accounted for 44,808 orders.

LINCOLN

▶ Lincoln Continental returned from its '66 redesign with minimal exterior change. Inside, though, all models boasted a new "Fresh Flow" ventilation system that forced air from dashboard vents through extractors concealed in a low-pressure area at the rear. America's only convertible sedan now started at $6449, versus $5795 for the four-door sedan and $5553 for the hardtop coupe.

◀ Lincoln sales retreated to 45,667 for '67. Demand for the unique four-door open Continental, which had been waning from its high point in 1965, slipped to 2276 units. With that, Dearborn accountants decided they could no longer afford continuing the model, so this was its last year. But with yearly production always so modest, all Lincoln convertibles of the Sixties have since become prized collector cars. They're also sought-after for their clean, classic styling.

MERCURY

▶ Mercury joined in the ponycar craze with the '67 Cougar, a nicely restyled Mustang hardtop with a three-inch longer wheelbase and a greater luxury emphasis. Hidden headlamps and a 289 V-8 were standard for this $2851 base model and the upscale XR-7, whose $3081 starting price included leather seat surfaces, woodgrain dash appliqué, and full instrumentation. A sporty $3175 GT boasted a 390 V-8 and handling-oriented suspension.

◀ Cougars and Mustangs for '67 roll off the same assembly line. Though confined to a single body style, the Cougar attracted 150,893 customers in its debut year. The base version alone accounted for 116,260 deliveries, making it the single-most purchased Mercury of the season. The popular car's crouching mountain lion logo soon became so synonymous with Mercury that all of its vehicles were advertised as being for sale at "the sign of the cat."

▲ With America's youth flocking to ponycars and high-power intermediates, demand for big bucket-seat cars was down to a trickle. Mercury's S-55 was no exception, and would not return after '67. Reduced to a Monterey option in its final year, the S-55 saw production of only 145 convertibles and 570 hardtop coupes.

◄ Full-size '67 Mercurys sported a Lincoln-like bulged nose, but weren't greatly changed. Joining the top-shelf Park Lane group were a lush Brougham hardtop sedan and a formal-roof hardtop coupe called Marquis. Breezeway sedans were still listed, but no longer had reverse-slant rear windows. The S-55 sport package seen on this two-door hardtop added about $525 to the cost of a comparable Monterey.

▲ Priced from $2284 for '67, the Comet 202 two-door sedan was still the most affordable Mercury. This one, however, is a stealth "muscle car," packing an optional 425-bhp 427-cid V-8, signaled by small front-fender emblems.

- Ford Motor Company cars change to reflect new federal safety and emissions requirements
- Midsize Fords redesigned in Fairlane and new Torino models

- Lincoln responds to Cadillac's Eldorado with new personal-luxury Mark III hardtop coupe
- Mercury redesigns midsize Comet, adds upscale Montego models

- A new generation of Econoline vans debuts, but the pickup is dropped
- Mustang sales slide to some 300,000 units
- Semon E. "Bunkie" Knudsen shocks Detroit

by leaving GM to become new president of Ford Motor Company

- Racing Ford GT becomes the first U.S. car to win international sports-car championship

FORD

▶ Clean-sheet bodies with more flowing lines highlighted 1968's midsize Fords. Fairlane was downplayed in favor of related but flashier new Torinos, which formed a separate series. Fairlane offered base and 500 sedans, wagons, and "notchback" two-door hardtops, plus a new 500 fastback hardtop and this 500 convertible. The $2822 ragtop drew a modest 3761 sales.

◀ Replacing Fairlane GTs for '68 was a trio of new Torino GTs: convertible, hardtop coupe, and this racy new fastback patterned on the Mustang. At introduction, all came with bodyside stripes, styled wheels, all-vinyl upholstery, and a new emissions-friendly 302 small-block V-8. Available power options ranged up to a still-potent 427 V-8 with a mighty 390 bhp.

▶ Non-GT Torinos comprised a luxury-oriented sedan, hardtop coupe, and this natty Torino Squire wagon with the expected pseudo-wood body trim. At $3032 to start, the Squire was the costliest model in Ford's new upmarket midsize line. Torino was a fair commercial success and helped boost total Ford car sales to slightly above their '67 level.

▲ Torino was chosen pace car for the 1968 Indianapolis 500. This GT ragtop did the honors. The slick new Torino fastbacks were Ford's stock-car racing warriors this year, and they gave Dearborn another season trophy in NASCAR by winning 20 major events. Ford also won the '68 driver's championship in NASCAR, USAC, and ARCA.

► Falcon was mostly a rerun for '68, but sales mysteriously shot up, more than doubling to 131,000 units. Like other Ford Motor Company cars, Falcon mainly focused on added equipment and engine revisions for meeting the raft of new federal safety and emissions standards mandated for all '68 cars sold in the U.S. Shown here is the top-line Futura Sports Coupe. Priced from $2541, it drew 10,077 sales.

◄ Side-marker lights were one of Washington's many new requirements for '68 cars, and they're visible on this Falcon Futura sedan. Rectangular tail-lights and a revised dash design were other new features for the year. Unlike some other compacts, Falcon returned to its roots after '65, emphasizing high value and sensible economy with plain and fancy four-door sedans, two-door sedans (sometimes called club coupes), and four-door wagons.

► Fastbacks made a comeback in late-Sixties Detroit. The full-size Ford joined in for '68 with a rakish hardtop coupe in two trim levels. This sports-minded XL shared a new hidden-headlamp face with the year's XL ragtop, all LTDs, and the Country Squire wagon. A Galaxie 500 fastback was also available. All big Fords again wore new lower-body sheetmetal and reverted from vertical to horizontal headlamps.

► Mustang cantered into '68 with no basic design changes, but sales dipped 32 percent. This well-kept GT is one of 249,447 hardtops built for the model year, which was nearly 107,000 down on the '67 run. Fastbacks numbered 42,581 this season, convertibles 25,376. This car's distinctive "C-stripes" were a new appearance item separate from the GT option, and proved fairly popular. Mustang still offered plenty of other performance and dress-up options.

◄ Carroll Shelby's Mustangs returned for '68 with a fastback and convertible in small-block GT 350 guise and in big-inch GT 500 trim. At midyear, the 500s added the initials KR—for "King of the Road"—and gained a new "Cobra Jet" version of the Ford 428. Both engines were advertised at 335 bhp, but the CJ produced more like 400 actual horsepower. Though Shelby Mustangs still looked wilder than Ford's ponies, they were fast becoming less special. This $4117 GT 350 fastback was the year's popularity champ with 1253 sold.

▼ First offered in T-Birds, Ford's big-block 428 was muscled up into 1968's "Cobra Jet" with a four-barrel carburetor fed by "ram-air" induction.

▲ Replacing the 427 as a special-order Mustang option, the muscular ram-air Cobra Jet arrived in time for winter 1967–68 pro drag races. This modified fastback won a class trophy for owner/driver Al Joniec at the NHRA Winternationals in Pomona, California, after a quarter-mile run of 12.5 seconds at 97.93 mph.

► The race-winning mid-engine Ford GT drew its share of admirers, some of whom dreamed of having one to use on public roads. This one was converted for that role, and the British car development firm that entered Le Mans-winning GTs in 1968 and '69 built a few road-going Mark IIIs.

▲ The full-size LTD was one of Ford Division's best "better ideas" of the Sixties. While most Fords lost sales ground in '68, the top-liners actually bettered their '67 performance. The hardtop sedan shown here remained the most popular model, drawing 61,755 orders. Total LTD sales for the model year came to 138,752.

▲ Thunderbirds showed an eggcrate grille pattern and other cosmetic tweaks for '68. A new 429 V-8, engineered for this year's government emissions standards, was initially an option, but soon replaced the venerable 390 as standard. Total T-Bird sales fell below 65,000, of which 21,925 were the Landau sedan, shown here.

◄▲ Compact trucks had never sold that well, so Ford bowed a bigger, huskier new Econoline during '68 as an early 1969 offering. The pickup was dropped, but vans were now roomier and configured for easier servicing. Panel and wagon models came with short and long bodies. Passenger versions like the 12-seat Chateau Club Wagon offered camper packages (left) that proved popular with families.

LINCOLN

► Lincoln Continentals lost their stand-up hood ornament for '68 due to new federal safety rules, but it would be back. Meantime, the "star" logo moved down to the nose above a new thin-bar grille. A 365-bhp 460-cid V-8 replaced the 462 V-8 as a running change. A four-door sedan like this marked production of the 1-millionth Lincoln on March 25, 1968.

◄ The 1968 Lincoln Continental hardtop coupe received a revised roofline with wider, more "formal" rear quarters. The model priced from $5736. Its four-door sister was $234 more. Sales for these Lincolns slipped to 39,134, the lowest level since 1964. Relative year-to-year sameness didn't help, but the main factor was the late-1967 auto workers strike that cut into '68 production of most Ford Motor Company products.

► A better Lincoln idea bowed in April 1968 with the Continental Mark III, a $6585 hardtop coupe built on the four-door T-Bird chassis. Chairman Henry Ford II saw it picking up from the 1956 to 1957 Mark II, so the new car also had a humped decklid and long-hood/short-deck proportions. Though hardly cheap, the Mark III offered power everything, a *grand luxe* interior with extra noise insulation, numerous color choices, and a 460 V-8. Initial sales were encouraging at 7770 units.

◄ A new face moved full-size '68 Mercurys even closer to Lincoln appearance, but not too close. This Park Lane convertible sports wagonlike "Yacht Paneling" bodyside trim, which arrived in January as an option for this model and a new Park Lane fastback. The one-year option eventually was extended to lower-line cars, too.

▲ The Mercury Marquis returned for '68 solely as a hardtop coupe with its own formal roofline. Making some standard features optional cut price by $304 to $3685, but sales nevertheless dropped 39 percent to 3965 units.

▲ Cougar added a GT-E package with a 427 V-8 for '68, followed at midseason by a 428 Cobra Jet option and a high-winding 230-bhp 302 small-block. This XR-7 shows styling was little changed.

► Midsize Mercs for '68 comprised sporty Cyclones and new luxury-minded Montegos, plus one Comet hardtop coupe. All shared a basic design with this year's revised Ford Fairlanes. The line's only convertible was not a Cyclone, as might be expected, but a Montego in upscale MX trim. Priced from $2935, it saw 3248 copies, of which a mere 962 had optional front bucket seats.

◄ Cyclone was Mercury's performance line for '68, listing notchback and new fastback hardtop coupes in two flavors. Standard equipment for Cyclones was the new 302-cubic-inch corporate small-block V-8 and a fairly modest 210 bhp. All Cyclones could be ordered with a big 325-bhp 390, the mighty 427, or new 428 Cobra Jet. Of the 13,638 Cyclones built this model year, just 334 were GT notchbacks like the one seen here.

BUNKIE KNUDSEN
It Just Didn't Work Out

ON FEBRUARY 6, 1968, the day before Bunkie Knudsen was named president of the Ford Motor Company, *Wall Street Journal* reporter Laurence G. O'Donnell called a former General Motors employee. O'Donnell knew the recipient of the call had written speeches for Knudsen, and asked for his comment on the appointment.

"It won't work out," the source said. "Bunkie is a car guy and a nice guy, but he isn't strong or crafty enough to run Ford Motor Company. He won't fit in; he'll be like a rejected organ transplant." Nineteen months later, on the day of Bunkie's dismissal, O'Donnell phoned his contact again. His first remark was, "Before you say 'I told you so,' let me say you told me so."

Born in Buffalo, New York, on October 2, 1912, Semon E. "Bunkie" Knudsen had a distinguished pedigree. His father was William S. Knudsen, who, after expanding Ford's assembly plant network in the Model T days, was general manager of Chevrolet, president of GM, and the top production man for the War Department during World War II. When announcing Bunkie's move to Ford, Henry Ford II aptly observed, "Today the flow of history is reversed."

Joining GM in 1939, Bunkie rose steadily through the ranks, and by age 44 in 1956, headed Pontiac Motor Division, which was then producing well-engineered "grandma" cars. In the next few years, Bunkie improved Pontiac's image by removing the "silver streak" chrome trim that had decorated the center of the hood and trunk since 1935, and by touting the car's "wide track" stance. Within three years, Pontiac moved from sixth to third place in U.S. sales.

Successful at Pontiac, Knudsen was named general manager of Chevrolet in 1961. There, he introduced the Corvette Sting Ray, brought out powerful Super Sport versions of various Chevy offerings, and—for a time—plunged into NASCAR stock-car racing. In 1965, he was named group vice president for Canadian and overseas operations; the following year, he became an executive vice president.

Passed over for GM's presidency in November 1967, Knudsen resigned three months later. His availability seemed the answer to Henry Ford II's prayer. HFII was dissatisfied with the operational skills of Arjay Miller, Ford's president since 1963. Knudsen, with his presumed ingrained knowledge of General Motors managerial techniques, was thought to be just the man to remold Ford along the lines of much-admired GM. Also, it was hoped that Bunkie's GM background would enable him to meld the fractious Ford organization into a cohesive unit.

In his eagerness to land Knudsen, Ford did not require Bunkie to sell his 412,507 shares of GM stock (mostly inherited from his father), worth $3.3 million. Henry II also increased the $147,500 salary Knudsen had made at GM to $200,000, matching his own. In addition, he gave Bunkie 15,000 shares of Ford stock worth $870,000 as compensation for the $700,000 in accumulated bonuses he forfeited by leaving GM.

The job switch, *The New York Times* reported, "is one of the most dramatic turnabouts in Detroit's history." Among those affected was Lee Iacocca, executive vice president and director of North American Automotive Operations, who regarded himself as Miller's heir-apparent. "Lee has chewed his way through 10 layers of management to get where he is," a highly placed Ford executive observed, "and he will be determined to chew his way through anyone placed above him."

After joining Ford, Knudsen roamed the Ford empire, touring plants and other facilities in the U.S., Canada, England, and Australia. Wherever he went, his principal interest was product styling. Three days a week he visited Dearborn's Design Center as early as 6:30 A.M. Styling executives felt compelled to tag along on his "dawn patrols," as they came to be called, and resentment flared. Decisive when it came to styling, Knudsen's snap judgments rankled not only styling vice president Eugene Bordinat Jr. and his subordinates, but Iacocca and Henry II as well. One of Bunkie's first major moves was to restyle the 1970 Thunderbird's front end to resemble that of a Pontiac, a change that came to be called the "Knudsen nose." Bordinat, a caustic Iacocca ally, did not conceal his feelings. "Knudsen expresses a great interest in our vineyard," he told a newsman, "and he helps me toil-it. I mean that in both senses." Theodore H. Mecke Jr., Ford vice president for public affairs, went to the heart of the matter: "Bunkie was [brought in as] a car man. But there were other car men already on duty."

By his own admission, Knudsen made a mistake by not bringing with him a strong group of General Motors men, as had Ernest R. Breech in the immediate post-World War II era. Instead, he imported only three, installing them at Philco-Ford, Styling, and Lincoln-Mercury. "I was a loner in the Ford organization," he later lamented. In addition, he was pounced upon by Iacocca and his coterie from day one. In 1989, Bunkie gave another explanation for the briefness of his Ford career.

Bunkie Knudsen (left) shares the dais with his new boss, Ford Chairman Henry Ford II, and departing President Arjay Miller in 1968. The smiles would not last long.

Henry Ford II, he recalled, was on very good terms with President Lyndon B. Johnson, and hoped to be named ambassador to Great Britain after Johnson's anticipated reelection in 1968. In that event, Knudsen reasoned, he would be needed to run the company in Henry II's absence. When LBJ decided not to run for reelection, Ford's ambassadorial hopes were dashed. At that juncture Knudsen felt that he was expendable.

Henry II had a different explanation, as expressed in previously unpublished comments made in 1983:

"[Bunkie] alienated top people," Ford said. "He put what I'll call spies in various locations. I don't know how they reported back to him. They were at Lincoln-Mercury, Styling, and other places. . . . Bunkie obviously went a long way in General Motors, but didn't get the top job he wanted. . . . He wasn't here long enough to show his capabilities too well. He had some good ideas, I thought, but he alienated . . . the organization. When you do that, people start pulling tricks on you . . . they make you look like a jerk. . . . But he was a very nice guy, a very pleasant individual."

Asked whether or not it was difficult to fire Knudsen, Henry II replied, "Not once I made up my mind he wasn't working out."

In 1989, Knudsen recalled his dismissal as follows:

"Mr. Ford came to my office and told me he was sorry to tell me that I would no longer be with the Ford Motor Company. I said, 'It's your decision, but can you tell me why?' He said, 'It just didn't work out.' That's all he said. I said, 'Thank you,' and he walked out.

"That was the end of it until the Board meeting on Thursday, which I had been told to attend. At the Board meeting I was asked to leave while they discussed the situation. When I returned to the meeting, they asked me if I had anything to say. . . . The only thing I said was, 'I'm sorry it didn't work out. I thought I had spent my time doing everything I possibly could to build the Ford Motor Company.'

"Before I left," Knudsen added, "Mr. Ford told me I could have whatever I wanted—cars, etc. 'Mr. Ford,'" the independently wealthy Knudsen replied, "'I don't want anything. I don't need anything.' So I left." Bunkie continued to receive $200,000 annually for the remainder of his five-year contract.

Iacocca, when asked if saddened to see Knudsen leave, paused, contemplated his cigar, and barely repressing a grin, said, "I have never said 'no comment' to the press before, but I'll say 'no comment' now."

Cracked an observer, "The toughest job in the world is for an undertaker to keep from smiling at a $10,000 funeral." Another wag noted that HFII had reversed his grandfather's statement that "history is bunk."

After leaving Ford, Knudsen became majority owner of a new manufacturer of luxury motor homes, Rectrans, Incorporated, of Farmington Hills, Michigan, where he worked until his retirement in 1980. Bunkie Knudsen died of congestive heart failure in Royal Oak, Michigan, on July 6, 1998.

1969

- Redone Ford Mustang adds hot Mach 1 and Boss models, and luxury Grandé

- Even hotter muscle models join midsize Ford and Mercury lineups

- Ford Division wins second straight NASCAR championship

- Full-size Fords and Mecurys fully redesigned

- Mercury Cougar is all new, adds convertibles, rapid Eliminator hardtop

- Bunkie Knudsen steps down as Ford president in sudden corporate shake-up

FORD ▲ A stem-to-stern redesign made '69 Mustangs longer, lower, wider, a bit heavier, and much swoopier. Fastbacks were now dubbed "SportsRoof" models. This base version is optioned up with a hood-mounted tachometer beside a functioning air scoop, plus a racy air dam below the front bumper.

▲ Reflecting a snowballing market trend, Mustang convertible sales dropped for '69 despite the ponycar's redesign and a base price hiked just $35 to $2849. Model-year volume plunged 42 percent to 14,746.

▲ Mustang hardtops moved uptown for '69 with addition of the Grandé, which offered a standard vinyl roof, nicer interior, and a little extra outside brightwork from $2866, versus $2635 for the standard article.

◄ Even with aggressive new styling, Mustangs retained signature ponycar cues and proportions for '69. A jutting nose with quad headlamps, two within the grille, is evident in this view of a base SportsRoof fastback, which also bore a more-sweeping roofline and simulated air scoops high on the rear fenders. It, too, had a base price of $2635. The fastback was the basis for some new big-muscle Mustangs.

▲ Nineteen sixty-nine Thunderbirds displayed minor trim changes and a revived sliding-metal sunroof option. To Ford's dismay, sales plummeted to 49,272, the lowest model-year tally since 1958.

▲ Little-changed outside, Ford's midsizers offered a new 351 V-8 option, a bigger small-block shared with other models in the Dearborn stable. Torino GTs like this SportsRoof upgraded to a standard 220-bhp 302.

▲ The big '69 Fords were rebodied on a new 121-inch-wheelbase chassis, up two inches from 1960 to '68. Length grew two to three inches, and width and weight increased. The XL convertible and hardtop coupe remained the sportiest models. XL ragtops were rare; this is one of a handful packing a big 429 V-8 with "ram-air" hood scoop.

◄ Ford's '69 big-car redesign brought a racy "tunnelback" roofline to the Galaxie 500 hardtop coupe (shown) and its XL sister. The rear window sat between "flying buttress" pillars that gave a fastback profile. The LTD hardtop coupe got a more-formal design consistent with the topline series' luxury image. Sales of '69-model big Fords were strong, topping the 1-million mark.

▲ Ford's ultimate '69 racing engine, this new "semi-hemi" 429 V-8, was also sold in slightly tamer street tune in this year's new Boss 429 Mustang.

▲ Answering Plymouth's "budget muscle" Road Runner, the '69 Torino Cobra notchback hardtop and fastback SportsRoof delivered a 335-bhp 428 Cobra Jet V-8—and 0-60 mph in just six seconds—for less than $3200.

▶ Shelby Mustangs were redesigned like Ford's own ponycars, but again looked rather different. GT 500s like this ragtop kept a brawny 428 V-8; GT 350s adopted a new 290-bhp 351. But this year's new high-performance Mustangs hurt Shelby sales, and production was halted after a final 3786 cars—636 of them reserialed as '70s.

LINCOLN ▲ Lincoln Continentals received another round of considered refinements for '69, plus exterior changes including a grille that looked cribbed from snooty Mercedes-Benz—perhaps not unintended. Chicago's Lehmann-Peterson works was still building some 50 to 60 stretched "Executive Sedan" limousines like this a year.

◄ Lincoln Continental sales had another setback for '69, slipping to about 38,300. As ever, the sedan (shown) took the lion's share. This year it priced from $6063 versus $5830 for the hardtop coupe, which found 9032 buyers. Exclusive to the sedan was a new "Town Car" interior option with "super puff" leather/vinyl upholstery and "extra plush" carpeting. All '69 Lincolns continued to use the 460-cid V-8 engine that provided 365 bhp.

▲ The personal-luxury Continental Mark III started its first full model year virtually unchanged. At midseason, though, Lincoln added an optional "Sure-Track Braking System," an early form of antilock brakes. Despite so few changes, and a base price hiked $173 to $6758, the Mark III drew a healthy 23,088 sales for the model year. That was just 245 shy of the total posted by its nearest direct rival, the Cadillac Eldorado.

▲ The Mark III didn't skimp on luxury for rear-seat passengers, though room was a bit tight for larger folks. Hermann Brunn, scion of the great coachbuilding family, was a consultant on the interior design.

▲ Mark III's front cabin was definitely first-class, thanks to a "Twin Comfort Lounge" bench seat with dual center armrests, power adjustments, and lots of cushy padding. Carpeting was plush deep-pile.

MERCURY

▶ After just two years on the market, the Mercury Cougar was revamped along the same lines as the '69 Mustang. Styling was reinterpreted, with sweeping Buick-like creaselines on the bodysides. Convertibles joined hardtops in base and XR-7 guises, all with a standard 250-bhp version of Dearborn's new 351 V-8. This XR-7 hardtop, one of 23,918 built, priced from $3315.

◀ The performance Cougar for 1969 was the Eliminator, officially a separate model but available only by ordering a hardtop with two option packages. One included a hood air scoop and rear spoiler, the other a variety of minor trim items. Eliminator came with a 290-bhp 351. Options included big-block 428s with and without "Ram Air" induction, joined at midyear by a high-winding 302, also rated at 290, doubtless to placate nervous insurance companies.

▶ Mercury didn't separate Eliminator sales from those of other '69 Cougar hardtops, but the muscular cat was not a big commercial success. Cougar sales as a whole were well down this year, falling to the 100,000 level—and destined to go much lower still. But Eliminators are now prized among performance fans, as much for rarity as flash and go-power. This lovingly cared-for beauty is finished in Competition Orange, one of four colors available.

▲ Newly opened Michigan International Speedway used this new Cougar convertible as its official pace car for the 1969 racing season. It's a $3382 base-trim model with a few options. The upmarket XR-7 version started at $3595. Both were modest sellers, with orders totaling 5796 and 4024, respectively.

▲ Mercury redesigned its full-size '69s, with a new 124-inch wheelbase for all models save wagons and a sporty hardtop coupe on the 121-inch Ford chassis. Reviving the Marauder name, it came in base and uplevel X-100 form. The latter, shown here, included a standard 360-bhp 429-cube V-8 and styled aluminum wheels for $4091.

▲ The '69 Marauders shared a "tunnelback" roofline with Ford's big XL hardtop, but rear fender skirts and a matte-black decklid were unique to the X-100 Merc. This model drew 5635 sales, the base Marauder 9031.

▲ A unique "droop snoot" shaped for stock-car racing marked the limited-edition Cyclone Spoiler II fastback. Blue/white Dan Gurney and red/white Cale Yarborough editions honored Mercury's ace NASCAR pilots.

▲ Mercury matched Ford's new Torino Cobra with its own "budget muscle" midsize, the Cyclone CJ. The initials, of course, stood for Cobra Jet, as in a standard 335-bhp 428 V-8. The CJ came only in fastback form and, as expected of a Mercury, cost a bit more than the Ford: $3224 to start. With just 3261 built, the Cyclone CJ is scarce today.

Malaise

PRICE INFLATION and political corruption contributed to a decade of diminished expectations in which many aspects of American life and culture seemed shoddy and second-rate.

President Richard Nixon resigned from office in 1974 because of his role in obstruction of justice related to a 1972 burglary of Democratic headquarters at the Watergate office complex in Washington, D.C. He was succeeded by Vice President Gerald Ford, who had been appointed to that office following Spiro Agnew's 1973 resignation in the face of income-tax evasion and bribery charges.

Nixon's departure was in ironic contrast to his triumphal 1972 rapprochement with China, a major achievement in foreign policy that brought China into the family of nations.

An energy crisis in 1973 darkened America's spirits, and led to long lines at gas stations. Automobile horsepower, even on the Mustang, withered in favor of improved fuel mileage.

America's 1976 bicentennial coincided with the election of Jimmy Carter, whose bumpy presidency was highlighted by an Egyptian-Israeli peace accord in 1978.

Four hundred American cultists in Guyana drank cyanide-laced Flavor Aid in '78. In 1979, a nuclear reactor at Three Mile Island, Pennsylvania, leaked deadly radiation.

1970

- Lee Iacocca is named president of Ford Motor Company

- Ford gains control of Italian coachbuilders Ghia and Vignale

- Redesigned Torino earns *Motor Trend* "Car of the Year" honors

- New Thunderbird front-end features exposed headlamps

- Lincoln Continental gets totally new styling, longer wheelbase

FORD ▲ A freshened Thunderbird traded its trademark hidden headlamps for a more pronounced "beak." Despite a down year, the T-Bird's new look helped contribute to a modest sales gain over '69. Price of the vinyl-topped Landau: $5104.

▲ Speed lovers sought the performance of the "Boss" Mustangs. Despite the allure of 375 horsepower, only 498 Boss 429-equipped Mustangs were sold in '70.

▲ Ribbed lower-body trim and a special logo mark this Mustang fastback as a Mach 1. All Mach 1s featured a special grille with driving lights and a striped hood.

◄ The Mach 1 fastback coupe remained the hottest "volume" Mustang for 1970. Engine choices included the standard 250-bhp, 351-cid V-8; a four-barrel 300-horse 351; or the potent 335-horsepower 428 "Cobra Jet" with or without a ram-air setup. Base price was $3271. Mustang sales fell 50 percent for 1970, when minor styling changes brought a return to single headlamps. Insurance rates for high-performance cars were mounting, helping to depress ponycar sales.

▲ Only one convertible was included in the full-size lineup: this XL, complete with high front seatbacks, and a $3501 price tag. Production dropped by more than 1000 from 1969, with only 6348 going to dealers. More than four times as many XL hardtops were built. A 250-horsepower, 351-cube V-8 was standard equipment.

▲ A freshening of the full-size Fords included revised grille inserts and new rear bumpers with horizontal tail-lamps. Slumping sales meant that 1970 would be the last year for the XL series, which included this $3293 hard-top coupe. Only the Custom, Galaxie 500, and LTD lines would carry Ford's full-size flag into the next model year.

▲ With the demise of the Fairlane 500 convertible, Torino GT became Ford's lone roofless midsize offering. Fewer than 4000 of these rakish ragtops were built. Price: $3212. Reacting to the same slumping demand for convertibles as the rest of the industry, Ford Division would remove midsize convertibles from the lineup by 1972.

► Economy-minded gear heads purchased almost 8000 Torino Cobra hard-top coupes. Available only as a fastback, the $3270 Cobra boasted a standard 429-cid, 360-bhp engine and blackout hood treatment. Optional factory equipment included a "shaker" hood scoop, "Magnum 500" rally wheels, and a 375-horse upgrade of the 429.

▲ Ford needed an alternative to the sales-stealing imports, and found it in the compact Maverick. A whopping 578,914 went to buyers its first year out.

▲ Heralded in ads as the "first car of the '70s at 1960 prices," Mavericks were nothing special in engineering, but the $1995 base price tag caught people's attention.

► The popular F-Series light-duty pickups soldiered on into the Seventies largely unchanged. A modern rectangular grille replaced last year's rounded-bar arrangement. Trim levels included the base Custom, mid-level Sport Custom and Ranger, and new high-end Ranger XLT. This F-100 sports the XLT trim. With the addition of new colors, F-Series trucks now came in a staggering array of 48 two-tone combinations.

► Despite its $1305 premium over the just-redesigned standard Continental coupe, most buyers of two-door Lincolns opted for the Continental Mark III. The personal-luxury coupe was little changed from the 1968 to 1969 models, but a power sunroof, six-way "Comfort Lounge" Seats, and new metallic colors were added to the options list. Base price: $7281.

MERCURY ▲ The Montego-based Cyclone family included sporty base, flashy GT, and thundering Spoiler hardtop coupes. *Road Test* magazine reported a quarter-mile trap speed of 14.61 seconds for an automatic-transmission-equipped Spoiler with optional Traction-Lok rear axle. This Spoiler is painted Grabber Orange.

◄ For 1970, the Cougar prowled with a new vertical central grille and revised taillamps. Just $3114 would put a driver behind the wheel of a new two-door hardtop, and almost 50,000 leapt at the chance. Cougar fans looking for a little more flair could opt for the high-line XR-7. Decked out with an upgraded interior, unique black and chrome grille, and custom badges, the Cougar XR-7 cost $3413.

► Having just enjoyed a thorough redesign for 1969, a freshened grille topped the short list of changes to the Monterey lineup. Full-size Mercurys were now available in basic Monterey, midlevel Monterey Custom, and high-end Marquis and Marquis Brougham trim levels. Combined sales for the entire full-size Mercury lineup reached almost 100,000. This $3520 Monterey Custom four-door sedan contributed 4823 cars to that total.

◄ At the top of the big-Mercury mountain was the Marquis series, including the Brougham models. The Marquis Brougham four-door hardtop wore a sticker price of $4500 sans options, and racked up almost 12,000 sales.

► Never a consistent player in the sporty big-car field, Mercury tried one last time in 1970 with the Marauder and Marauder X-100. The X-100 took on a more purposeful look with optional styled wheels and matte decklid paint treatment.

▼ The more powerful X-100 shown here came with standard high-back vinyl bucket seats and a potent 429-cubic-inch engine. Base Marauders cost $3503, X-100s $4136. Sales of both totaled just over 6000 cars.

► The Monterey hardtop coupe was available for value-conscious shoppers who wanted something a little tamer than the Marauder. Available in base and Custom trim, two-door hardtop sales topped 10,000. Price for this Custom: $3329.

◄ As with its Ford Torino cousin, the Montego was redone for 1970. Mercury's midsize cars were now about four inches longer and slightly heavier than their predecessors. Power came from a 250-cid six or a choice of 302-, 351-, or 429-cid V-8s. The Montego MX Brougham shown here came with concealed headlamps, but its vinyl top cost extra.

◄ First seen in Europe in 1969, the Anglo-German Ford Capri found its way into U.S. Lincoln-Mercury dealerships the following year. Though introduced in June 1970, the first Capris were actually considered 1971 models in the States.

▲ At $2295, the Capri offered the feel of a sporty Euro GT for slightly more than the price of a Maverick. At introduction, its only engine was a 71-bhp four.

▲ First-year Capris came only with bucket seats and four-speed manual transmissions. Air conditioning and an AM radio were available as optional equipment.

1971

- Ford responds to Chevrolet's Vega with subcompact Pinto

- Maverick line grows to include new, larger four-door model; related Mercury Comet debuts

- Next-generation Mustangs larger, heavier, and more boldly styled

- Redesigned Cougar gets a new formal look, deemphasizes sport

- Some Mercury dealers opt to sell "exoticar" DeTomaso Pantera

- Lincoln celebrates its 50th year with Golden Anniversary Town Car

- Full-size Fords and Mercurys restyled

FORD ▲ Full-size Fords featured a new front end. A redesigned fascia with a heavy bumper and prominent center grille defined a styling theme that Ford's big cars would wear for years to come. The new look led to stronger sales, as Ford found buyers for nearly 1 million of its full-size cars. Total Ford sales broke 2 million.

◄ Buyers continued to balk at the Thunderbird's formal restyling. A handful more than 36,000 were sold, down from close to 50,000 in 1970. Accounting for more than 20,000 sales, the $5438 Landau coupe was the line's best-selling model, outselling the Landau sedan and standard hardtop coupe combined.

► Ford's restyled full-size lineup ran the gamut from practical to posh. Low-end Customs anchored the price range at $3288, while the luxury-oriented LTD Brougham checked in at $4140. LTD and Brougham four-door sedans featured frameless door glass, but a fixed center pillar. This $3931 LTD sedan was one of 92,260 made.

▲ Filling a gap created by the demise of the XL series, the LTD line now carried Ford's sole full-size convertible. Waning demand for roofless cars had sealed the fate of many large ragtops, and the open-air LTD was living on borrowed time; 1972 would be its final year. Just 5750 found homes this year. Suggested starting price was $4094.

▲ The LTD Brougham hardtop coupe was Ford's most expensive full-size two-door. For their $4097, customers received standard wheel covers, upgraded upholstery, a deluxe steering wheel, and high-back front seats. Sales were modest compared to the midline Galaxie 500 coupe, which accounted for more than twice as many orders.

▲ A new Mustang Boss 351 replaced both prior Boss models for 1971. Only 1800 copies of the new Boss rolled off the assembly line, all packing a potent 330-horsepower, 351-cubic-inch V-8 engine. Slow Boss sales could be blamed on the car's $4142 price tag. A six-cylinder Mustang hardtop coupe could still be had for less than $3000.

▶ Ford joined the sub-compact revolution with the Pinto. Challenging both the imports and Chevrolet's new Vega, Pinto offered a low price and fuel economy that was better than anything else in the Ford lineup. This specially turned-out Runabout was used by company chairman Henry Ford II. All Runabouts had an importlike rear hatch and a base price of $2062.

▲ First-year Pinto sales soared to almost 350,000 cars, immediately making it one of Ford's best-selling models. The basic two-door sedan started at just $1919.

▲ Though eclipsed by the success of the Pinto, Maverick sales remained strong. The youthful new Grabber model was available with a 210-bhp V-8.

▲ While the Maverick Grabber was getting all the attention, a new four-door sedan was ringing up sales. Priced at $2234, the new sedan cost only $159 more than the fastback, but sat four in relative comfort on a longer wheelbase. The standard engine was a 170-cid, 100-bhp six. Options were 200- and 250-cid sixes, and the 302-cube V-8.

▲ Subtle grille and trim refinements were the only evident Torino changes for 1971. The line's luxury leader was the Brougham shown here. Base price: $3248.

▲ Slightly more than 4400 Torino Brougham four-door hardtops were sold, as well as almost 8600 two-door hardtops. Wheelbase was 117 inches.

▲ An homage to years gone by, simulated wood adorned the bodysides of the Torino Squire station wagon. The comprehensive Torino line now included 14 models, ranging in price from the $2672 base four-door sedan to the $3560 Squire. The most popular '71 Torino was the 500 formal hardtop coupe; almost 90,000 found buyers.

◄ Ford trucks were always ready to get dirty, but the new LTS line was designed with muck in mind. Created specifically for construction and off-road use, the LTS models boasted the same payload ratings as Ford's road-going trucks, but were far better suited for traversing unpaved work sites. The angled-back front bumpers were designed to consume less space when tight corners were being negotiated. Likewise, fiberglass bodywork protected the recessed headlamps from potentially damaging worksite debris.

LINCOLN

▶ The Ford Motor Company issued this Lincoln "family reunion" portrait featuring significant cars from the brand's history. In the foreground is the 1971 Continental four-door sedan, Lincoln's best-selling model. Lincoln's 50th anniversary year proved a good one for sales, as almost 63,000 cars were sold, 3500 more than the prior year.

▲ Riding a 9.8-inch shorter wheelbase, the Mark III was considerably smaller than the standard Continental coupe, but it was much more expensive. The $8813 Mark III cost $1641 more than the "regular" two-door Continental.

MERCURY
▲ This top-of-the-line Marquis Brougham four-door hardtop sold only half as well as the base Brougham sedan. Prices were up a whopping $533 this year, to $5033.

► A Cyclone Spoiler in name only, few buyers fell for the paint-and-stripe package that surrounded a smaller engine for '71. The defanged Cyclone Spoiler's only available engine produced just 285 horsepower, down 75 from last year. Only 353 of the $3801 coupes were produced. Fading buyer interest made this the Cyclone's last year.

◄ Mercury's top-of-the-line wagon was the Colony Park. The previously optional roof rack was now standard equipment. Production totaled 20,004 for 1971. Available in six- and nine-passenger styles, base prices were $4806 and $4933, respectively.

► Mercury revived the old Comet name for a new compact that looked suspiciously like the Ford Maverick on which it was based. The four-door sedan cost $2446. Despite its longer wheelbase and four-door convenience, it sold only about half as well as the $2387 two-door model.

► Substantially bigger than before, the redesigned Cougar adopted a bulkier, more formal appearance. Initial customer response to the new look was weak; 62,864 rolled off showroom floors, almost 10,000 fewer than in '70. Cougar was one of the few Fords still available as a convertible, but by '74, the body style would be killed. Base price for the XR-7 hardtop: $3289.

1972

- Three-door wagon added to Pinto lineup in base and Squire trim

- New-look Thunderbird line loses sedan variant

- All-new Mercury Montego loses Cyclones; similarly revised Ford Torino drops convertibles

- Mercury Capri now sprightlier with new V-6 engine option

- Lincoln's high-end Mark III replaced by all-new Mark IV

- New-model barrage pushes Ford market share to near 29 percent

FORD ▲ Though not the sexiest horse in the Mustang stable, the affordable hardtop coupe was easily the most popular. More than 57,000 shoppers bought base models, nearly half of all Mustangs sold. Price with six-cylinder engine: $2729.

▲ The patriotic "Sprint" treatment on this Mustang was nothing more than a paint, trim, and decal package—not a separate model. Though Sprint hardtops and fastbacks were readily available, only 50 convertibles were made, all for a Washington, D.C., festival. With the 429 gone, the top engine choice was down to a 275-bhp 351 V-8.

◄ Torino was all-new for 1972. The two-door model shown here rode a 114-inch wheelbase; sedans and wagons shared a 118-inch version of the chassis. While a 250-cid six-cylinder engine was standard, buyers overwhelmingly opted for one of the five available V-8 options. Customers responded favorably to the redesign, snapping up nearly half a million new Torinos, almost 175,000 more than the prior year. Prices ranged from $2641 for the standard sedan, to $3486 for the Gran Torino Squire wagon. Base and Gran Torino hardtop coupes featured a notchback roof style.

◄ Adorned here with optional bodyside striping, the Gran Torino Sport featured a unique sloping roofline and V-8 power. A 302-cid engine was standard, but performance seekers could upgrade to any of several larger powerplants. Buyers grabbed up almost 61,000 Grand Torino Sports, all with nonfunctioning hood scoops. Sport prices started at $3094.

► Full-size Fords featured cleaner grille treatments reminiscent of the new Thunderbird. Among the 19 models that comprised the big Ford lineup, only taxi and fleet vehicles were still available with six-cylinder engines. All retail buyers now enjoyed V-8 power, thanks to the standard 302-inch mill. Exclusive to two-door models was a new power sliding sunroof option. The Galaxie 500 hardtop sedan shown had a base price of $3604 and drew 28,939 customers.

▲ Just one of seven full-size Ford wagons, the woody-look LTD Country Squire was billed as the "best selling wagon in the country." The Country Squire boasted almost 100 cubic feet of cargo room and six- or eight-passenger seating. A 351-cid V-8 engine was standard, but the power hungry could opt for the big 429 and 208 net horsepower.

▶ This promotional photo heralded the arrival of a new cross-line option package that promised to "Put a little Sprint in your life." The Sprint "A" package available on Pinto, Maverick, and Mustang was little more than a patriotically themed paint, trim, and decal package. The more substantial Mustang-only Sprint "B" package added a sports suspension, larger tires, and Magnum 500 wheels. A maple leaf decal replaced the rear-fender American flag on Canadian-market cars.

▶ Though its basic design traced back to 1967, Ford's F-Series trucks continued to win over shoppers. A record 819,933 left dealership lots.

▲ The all-new Thunderbird now shared its basic structure with the Continental Mark IV, and was a much larger 'Bird as a result. Only one hardtop was available, down from three the previous year. The standard engine was a 429-cid V-8, but buyers could opt for a 460-cube unit that generated 224 bhp under the newly accepted net power ratings. Sales rose 60 percent, reaching 57,814. Price: $5293.

LINCOLN

► While this is indeed a 1972 Continental Mark IV, it was produced late in 1971, hence the seemingly erroneous banner. The new-look Mark IV was an immediate hit with buyers, chalking up nearly 50,000 sales—an impressive bump of 21,500 over the previous model-year's Mark III numbers. As before, a hardtop coupe was the sole model available. The new Mark was clearly a boulevard cruiser, without any pretense of sporting character remaining.

▲ Sales of full-size Continentals rose for '72. More than 10,000 hardtop coupes were sold. Riding a 127-inch wheelbase, they carried a 460 V-8 good for 224 bhp.

▲ The $8640 Mark IV rode a 3.2-inch-longer wheelbase than its predecessor. It was less agile, less roomy, and thirstier, but that didn't deter potential customers.

▲ More than 36,000 Continental four-door sedans were produced for 1972, making it Lincoln's most popular "standard" model. Base price: $7302.

MERCURY

▶ The Cougar line again consisted of base and XR-7 hardtop coupes and convertibles. Cougar found a total of 53,702 buyers. Horsepower numbers were dropping in response to new emissions regulations. Cougar's standard 351-cid engine was now making 164 net horsepower, down 76 from the gross rating of the year prior.

▲ The poshest of Monterey two-door hardtops was the Custom. Never as popular as the tonier Marquis coupes, fewer than 6000 found homes. Base price: $4035.

▲ The zippy Capri was finally hitting its stride, as more than 90,000 Americans drove home in one of these imported coupes. A new V-6 engine raised the horsepower total to 107. The base price with the V-6 was $2821. Capri tipped the scales at just over 2100 pounds, or about 3000 less than the Lincolns with which it shared a showroom.

▲ The midsized Montego was wearing all-new skins, though still looked much like its mechanical twin, the Torino. This top-of-the-line MX Villager cost $3438.

▲ Most buyers preferred the Marquis to the similar but less-poshly attired Monterey. Marquis hardtop sedans outsold their Monterey cousins by almost 12,000 cars.

► Shoppers could opt to spice up their two-door Comets by selecting the GT package. The $173 upgrade included bucket seats, bodyside decals, white-stripe tires, and a nonfunctional hood scoop. With a nod toward sportiness, Mercury made bucket seats a stand-alone option on all Comets. Overall sales were virtually identical to 1971, but with more than 53,000 purchased, the two-door Comet earned the title of best-selling single Lincoln-Mercury model. The two-door's starting price was $2342.

◄ With an average price almost $500 more than Ford's similarly sized sedans, it is unlikely many big Mercs saw law-enforcement service like this Monterey Custom Missouri Highway Patrol cruiser. The availability of the 460-cid V-8 might have helped make a compelling argument, though. The Custom four-door sedan accounted for 16,879 sales. Monterey's emissions-challenged top V-8 was now good for only 224 horsepower.

1973

- Horsepower figures continue to fall as a result of federal emissions regulations

- Buying public snaps up ragtop Mustangs on word that Ford is ending all convertible production

- Continental Mark IV finds 70,000 buyers, a new series record

- Richard Nixon presents Soviet leader Leonid Brezhnev with a new Lincoln Continental

- F-Series trucks get all-new cab designs

FORD ▲ Thunderbird's optional rear-pillar "opera windows" were trendy, but did little to enhance visibility. Bigger front bumpers were a response to federal safety regulations. Sales skyrocketed as 87,269 of the $6437 coupes were snapped up.

◄ The ever-growing Mustang would shrink before the next model year. "We started out with a secretary's car," said Ford design chief Eugene Bordinat, "and all of a sudden we had a behemoth." Buyers didn't seem to mind the size very much, as 135,000 bought one. This well-optioned hardtop is quite a bit over the $2760 base price. As with the rest of the Ford lineup, the Mustang's power numbers were down again.

► The fastback coupe had a slow year compared to the more conservative hardtop. Fewer than 11,000 were sold. Mustang buyers were required to spend time studying the options list. For '73, there were five models, two vinyl roofs, and three engine choices. One variation would soon disappear, however, as a convertible model would not return for 1974.

► Although government regulations and waning buyer interest had all but killed the muscle-car era, the Gran Torino Sport still looked the part with its raised-white-letter tires and racing mirrors. The racy trim and "SportsRoof" body helped sell 51,853 Sports, ranking it among the most popular Torino models. Motivation came from 302-cubic-inch V-8, though a 351-inch engine was available. A notchback hardtop Sport drew another 17,090 orders.

◄ From this angle, the SportsRoof's rakish lines are most evident. The unique bodywork took its toll in weight however, as the Gran Torino Sport tipped the scales about 300 pounds heavier than the standard Torino coupe. Dominant in the midsize category, the Torino line racked up combined sales of nearly 500,000, a commanding 100,000 more than rival Chevrolet's Chevelle model range. Both Sport models started at $3154.

► Pinto sales continued to rise, though not as sharply as before. The Runabout shown here ran a distant second in the sales race, drawing 150,000 customers, to the wagon's almost 218,000. Another 116,000 buyers chose the sedan. Performance was not an option for Pinto buyers, as engine choices were limited to slow and less slow. Motivation came from either the standard 54-bhp four-cylinder, or an optional 83-horsepower unit.

► Though the F-series cab design was all new, it took a discerning eye to detect the smoother, less-sculpted fenders and more upright grille. Happy campers applauded the introduction of the Super Camper Special, a pickup specifically designed for in-bed camper installations. F-series sales reached a staggering new high, totaling just over 1 million for the first time.

▲ Ford called its dual-purpose Ranchero its "pickup car." A direct competitor for Chevrolet's El Camino, the Ranchero was available in 500, GT, and Squire trim.

▲ First seen in 1972, Ford's Mazda-built Courier served pickup buyers with an eye for economy. Only one engine was available, a 1.8-liter four-cylinder.

► An automatic transmission and power steering were added to the options list on Ford's four-wheel-drive Bronco. Both were available only with the extra-cost V-8, though. A 200-cid six-cylinder engine became standard, replacing a somewhat underpowered 170-cube six as base engine. The slow-selling pickup was dropped from the lineup, leaving only the $3636 removable-top wagon. Ford ads advised that its sport-utility truck was "a popular choice for the outdoor minded." A total of 21,894 found buyers this year.

► This Continental Mark IV coupe featured the Silver Mark decor group. The $400 package included a power sliding glass moonroof and unique trim and badging. Muscle was down again this year, as the standard 460-cubic-inch V-8 now produced only 208 horsepower, a reduction of four from the previous year.

▲ Lincoln sedan buyers looking for that little "something extra" now had the Town Car to turn to. The Town Car package included distinct interior and exterior trim and unique badging. Upgrading to the "TC" cost $467 over the sedan's $7474 base price. Lincoln sedan production totaled slightly more than 45,000 for 1973.

▲ Celebrating success, Lincoln-Mercury Division General Manager William P. Benton proudly poses with four sales record breakers. The Capri, Continental, Mark IV, and Pantera had combined 1973 sales in excess of 1972's record totals. The "exotic" Ford-powered DeTomaso Pantera found almost 1500 buyers, 500 more than the previous year.

MERCURY

► Making its final appearance as a ponycar, a Cougar ragtop would prove to be Mercury's last convertible of the decade. Fewer than 4500 topless Cougars rolled off the lines in '73, with production biased heavily toward the XR-7 version. All of the 60,628 Cougars built for 1973 were powered by some version of Ford's now-ubiquitous 351-cid V-8.

▲ Mercury's poshest midsize offering was the Montego MX Brougham. Shown here in sedan form, the Brougham was also available in hard-top coupe form. The most expensive Montego sedan, Broughams wore a base sticker price of $3189, $273 more than the standard four-door.

▲ As if changing the guard, L-M boss William Benton rests on a sunroof-equipped '74 Cougar coupe while a '73 convertible fades into the background.

► Either a 429- or 460-cubic-inch V-8 moved the big Marquis. This Brougham hardtop sedan cost $424 more than the $4782 standard Marquis.

■ New "downsized" Mustang II shares Pinto mechanicals; sales soar

■ *Motor Trend* tabs Mustang II as its "Car of the Year"

■ Ford remains number two in overall sales but leads the pack in trucks

■ Cougar grows, now firmly entrenched as a personal-luxury car

■ Federal law requires all cars to be equipped with five-mph bumpers

■ Ford President Lee Iacocca proposes moratorium on new federal auto regulations

FORD ▲ Lee Iacocca was a key driving force behind the Mustang II, reprising his role with the original Mustang. The new "miniponycar" was an immediate success, racking up more than 385,000 sales. Mustang II power came from either a 140-cid four-cylinder, or a 170-inch V-6. Starting prices ranged from $3134 to $3674.

▶ The base notchback coupe was the runaway popularity leader of the new Mustang family. This one, with an optional vinyl roof covering, was one of 177,671 built. Mustang shoppers looking for more luxury could opt for the new Ghia. Named for the Ford-owned Italian design firm, Ghias assumed the luxury-Mustang role left open by the former Grandé. A standard vinyl roof and upgraded interior appointments helped justify the Ghia's $346 premium over base models. Roughly 90,000 customers went with the Ghia.

◀ Though not as popular as the base coupe or Ghia, the hatchback still managed to find almost 75,000 buyers of its own. In the face of global competition, American carmakers began to adopt a more international lingo. As a result, instead of being identified by cubic-inch displacement, the Mustang II's engines would soon be better known in their metric 2.3- and 2.8-liter sizes.

▶ Henry Ford II shows outspoken Ford shareholder Anna Muccioli the new Mustang II. Muccioli had been a critic of the previous Mustang's increasing dimensions and actively campaigned for a new, trimmer model. For Ford, its original Mustang II design goals of a shorter wheelbase, smaller engines, and lower weight proved to be the perfect formula for a nation gripped by the oil-embargo energy crisis in force as the Mustang II was entering the market. The new-style Mustangs were 19 inches shorter and 200-350 pounds lighter than the cars they replaced.

◀ The hatchback's European-style rear liftgate was still uncommon on American cars. Mustang IIs shared a number of components with the little Pinto. Though suspension pieces and steering racks were similar, and both vehicles were of unibody construction, the Mustangs were tuned for a sportier feel. Rear-seat passengers were among the first to realize the disadvantages of the newly shortened wheelbase. While front-seat room was about the same as the previous generation, Mustang's rear seat was now suitable only for small children.

▶ Lincoln's 460-cid V-8, optional in Thunderbirds since 1972, became standard this year. Having just gained 320 pounds, the T-Bird needed every one of the engine's 220 horsepower. Prices had risen sharply too, by almost $900 to $7330. Sales retreated to 58,443.

◀ This year's subtle trim changes included a new chrome-outlined taillight with a centrally located single back-up light. Added options included "Autolamp" automatic headlamp control, a power moonroof, and color-keyed exterior/interior decor packages.

A full-size Ford receives final attention before rolling off the assembly line. Big Fords were essentially carry-overs for 1974, except that the 429-cubic-inch engine was no longer offered. All optional V-8s, including the massive 460, were now fitted with solid-state ignition that reduced emissions and lengthened tune-up intervals. Full-size models sold poorly in the wake of the 1973–74 energy crisis, and production sank by almost half.

▲ The big-wagon roster included the Custom 500 Ranch Wagon, this Galaxie 500 Country Sedan, and the optionally wood-grained LTD Country Squire.

▲ A Gran Torino Elite, the new lower-cost entry in the personal-luxury field, meets the press at Ford's Chicago assembly plant in January 1974. Base price: $4437.

► Steel-belted radial tires were now standard on LTD Broughams, which accounted for 17 percent of big-Ford sales. This would be the last year for pillarless hardtops.

LINCOLN

▼ ► At \$10,194, the Mark IV became the first Ford product to break the five-digit price barrier. Despite the stiff price of entry, Marks still comfortably outsold standard Continental coupes almost 8-to-1. Sales plunged nearly 20 percent, to 57,316, in the face of higher prices and fuel economy concerns. Thicker carpeting and added sound insulation kept things quiet inside.

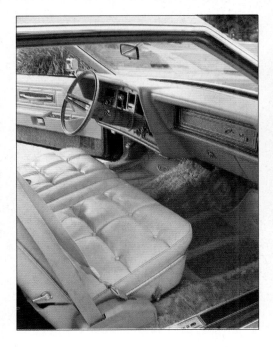

◄ ▲ No trees were harmed in the production of this dashboard, though several were simulated. Additional gold or silver trim elements were available to buyers in the form of the Luxury Group package. The options list also included a power sliding sunroof and a dual-exhaust system. The standard cloth upholstery could be upgraded to velour, or to the leather upholstery shown

◄ Standard Lincoln Continentals received a mild facelift, with a new vertical-bar grille and wraparound turn-signal lights. Rear bumpers were beefed up to match the fronts in meeting new federal impact standards. The four-door sedan was a big beast, riding on a 127.2-inch wheelbase and tipping the scales at just under 5400 pounds. Base price: $8238.

MERCURY

► With its demise as a ponycar, the Cougar XR-7 was reborn as a personal-luxury coupe. Mercury's redesigned big cat got bigger, riding an inch-longer wheelbase and tacking on almost 800 pounds. Cougar now shared chassis and drive-trains with its midsize stablemate, the Montego. Prices started at $4706.

▲ Cougar power came from either of a pair of 351-cid V-8s, a 400-cube job, or a monstrous 460-inch unit. Sales of the "new breed" Mercury caught fire, as 91,670 customers lined up to drive one home. Lower bodyside moldings were made of the same vinyl material as the covering for the standard landau roof.

► Frugal shoppers often chose Mercury's less-dressy Monterey models, which were no smaller than the Marquis, but roughly $700 less expensive. As did large-car sales everywhere, Mercury's full-size numbers plummeted to roughly half their 1973 totals. Slightly more than 61,000 Marquis and fewer than 28,000 Montereys were sold. Monterey prices started at $4367.

◄ Badder, but no bigger, the Marquis Brougham cost more than the similar Monterey, but included a number of meaningful upgrades. Among them was a standard 460-cid V-8 that made 25 more horsepower than the Monterey's base 400-cube engine.

► Perhaps the only Mercury offering that wasn't in need of a diet, the plucky Capri received a bigger V-6 engine and body-colored front and rear bumpers. Though bigger, the emissions-sensitive V-6 engine was slightly down on horsepower, to 105. Sales slipped from 1973's peak to just over 75,000.

◄ The top wagon in the Montego line was this MX Villager with faux-wood trim. Montego wagons were now tipping the scales at more than 4400 pounds, with much of the new weight coming from federal safety equipment. Montego sales were down, though not as dramatically as the big cars, to just under 100,000.

LEE IACOCCA
The "Father" of the Mustang

IN THE **32** YEARS he spent at Ford and 14 more with Chrysler, Lee Iacocca became one of autodom's most colorful figures. Admired by many who know him least, disliked by some who know him best, he is chiefly remembered for having "fathered" the Mustang, being fired by Henry Ford II, and rescuing Chrysler.

The son of Italian immigrants, Lido Anthony Iacocca was born in 1924 in Allentown, Pennsylvania, where his father became a successful businessman. After earning degrees from Lehigh and Princeton, "Lee" joined Ford's sales organization in 1946. Whip smart, ambitious, and hard driving, he rose rapidly through the company's flagship Ford Division. In 1960, he was named divisional vice president and general manager. Five years later, he was vice president of the car and truck group, and a company director. In 1967, he was named executive vice president for North American automotive operations.

Iacocca vaulted into national prominence during the Mustang's 1964 introduction, when he was pictured simultaneously on the covers of *Time* and *Newsweek*. Though lionized as the father of the Mustang, he neither conceived, designed, nor named the ponycar. The vehicle was designed by a team under relatively unsung designer Joe Oros and brought into being by a talented team of product developers: Don Frey, Hal Sperlich, Don Petersen, and Bob Graham, plus a supporting cast.

The name was first suggested by Robert J. Eggert, manager of Ford Division marketing. Lee contributed invaluably to the project, however. First, he knew a brilliant design when he saw one. After seeing a Mustang prototype, he backed the car to the hilt. Second, he sold the Mustang to Henry Ford II and a management reluctant to take risks following the Edsel debacle.

Iacocca was, in fact, a super salesman, one of the best America has ever produced. A "marvelous huckster," as Frey put it, he could sell an idea, a product, or himself. At every meeting, Henry II recalled, he was "selling, selling, selling." Selling was in his blood, and came as naturally as breathing.

Conversely, Iacocca was a poor handler of people, "the worst I ever saw," in the words of Robert W. Hefty, a Ford public-relations executive. "He would sit in a product or design committee meeting and just chew people out right and left, rather than take them into his office afterwards, and chew them out in private. He seemed to delight in embarrassing his underlings. He also always called you by your last name. 'Hey, Hefty, come on in here,' or 'Frey, come on in here.' . . . Not only did these people have first names, but they were all on a first-name basis. It was just his way of doing things." Such behavior reflected Iacocca's enormous ego. Asked to rate his boss' vanity on a scale of 1-to-10, Frey replied, "11, 13, 15."

After promotion to executive vice president, Iacocca assumed that he was next in line for the presidency. Thus, he was staggered in September 1968 when Henry Ford II replaced Arjay Miller with ex-General Motors executive Semon E. "Bunkie" Knudsen. Lee responded by undermining Knudsen at every opportunity in hopes of hastening his early departure. When Bunkie was fired in September 1969, Iacocca again saw himself as company president. Instead, he was named president of Ford North American Automotive Operations. At the same time, Robert J. Hampson was named president of Ford North American Nonautomotive Operations and Robert Stevenson became president of Ford International Operations. Finally, in December 1970, Lee became the company's sole president.

Henry Ford II never warmed to Iacocca. He disliked his arrogance, brashness, and vanity, along with some of his friends. He also resented Lee's proprietary attitude toward the company's most luxurious executive airplane, a Boeing 707. Over Lee's protest, HFII sold the plane to the Shah of Iran.

Henry II also persuaded himself that Iacocca was mismanaging company operations, especially product development. "He got thoroughly confused in his later years by what the hell to do," Ford said in 1982. "He had a new program every two or three months. The organization was totally discombobulated. . . . There is just one hell of a lot of things that got let go that shouldn't have been let go. It was sloppy."

As the Seventies wore on, Henry II came to detest Iacocca more than anyone he had ever known, even his grandfather's satrap, Harry Bennett. In 1976, when the chairman experienced chest pains that alarmed him, he became increasingly concerned about his successor. Ruling out Iacocca, in 1977 he set up a three-member Office of the Chief Executive comprised of himself as chairman/CEO, Philip Caldwell as vice chairman—a new position, and Iacocca as president and chief operating officer. It was made clear in writing that Caldwell, not Iacocca, would lead the company in Henry II's absence.

LEE IACOCCA
Continued

Henry II hoped that Iacocca's wounded pride would prompt his resignation. Instead, Lee hung on. "I was greedy," he states in his autobiography. "I enjoyed being president. I liked having the president's perks, the special parking place, the private bathroom, the white-coated waiters. I was getting soft, seduced by the good life. And I found it almost impossible to walk away from an annual salary of $970,000. . . . I earned more than the chairman of General Motors. I wanted that $1 million a year so much that I wouldn't face reality."

On July 13, 1978, Henry II, out of patience, summoned Iacocca to his office and fired him. He also informed his board that he would resign if he did not have its support. It was an ultimatum the board could not refuse. Director Arjay Miller summed up the board's attitude by observing that, given the tension between Henry II and Lee, it was in the company's best interest for Iacocca to go. Nonetheless, some directors much regretted Iacocca's departure, and also disapproved of the way in which he was handled. "The treatment which [Lee] received from the company was in my judgment not only unfair, but bordered on being cruel," said director George F. Bennett, chairman of State Street Investment Corporation, in 1989. "He was a towering figure in the company's history and was, and is, a master marketer and manager." Enraged by Henry II's power play, Iacocca told NBC, "That's something I won't forgive the bastard for. . . . I told my kids, 'Don't get mad. Get even.' . . . I did it in the marketplace. I wounded him badly. It took five years. I could have spilled my guts and maybe felt good inside if I'd done it in five minutes, but then what have I proved?" Iacocca also expressed bitterness toward the Ford family and its wealth. "I knew how to make money for the company," he said, but, "the Ford family practiced the divine right of kings. They were a cut above even WASPs. I mean, they wouldn't even socialize with you. You could produce money for 'em, but you weren't about to hobnob with 'em. It never bothered me that much, but I knew I had to scratch for what I got. Nobody was going to say, 'There's a nice Italian boy. I'd like to take care of him.'"

Iacocca also sought to get even—in the view of UAW president and Chrysler director Douglas A. Fraser—by accepting 150,000 shares of Chrysler stock worth $4 million, awarded him by Chrysler's directors. "I got into an argument with board members about values in society," Fraser recalled, and said, "That money is I don't know how many times more than I made in 50 years of work, and he makes it in five minutes. . . . When I sat down to lunch, I was still mad, and another board member came up to me and said, 'Don't

be upset, Doug. Wouldn't you like to see the look on Henry Ford's face when he reads about this tomorrow?' And lightning strikes. This has nothing to with money; it's let's get even, show Ford that I'm going to be the richest S.O.B. in the auto industry."

Rated by the *Detroit Free Press* as one of "150 moments that made Michigan," Iacocca's departure paved the way for him to save Chrysler Corporation. When Iacocca accepted the top job at the number-three automaker in 1978, the company was in the throes of one of its periodic tailspins, still reeling from the effects of the OPEC oil embargo earlier in the decade. The company would have gone bankrupt had not Iacocca, previously an ardent free-enterpriser, persuaded Congress to guarantee bank loans up to $1.5 billion. Only Lee, it was generally agreed, could have so swayed the government. At this point, the firm could go only one way—up. It did so thanks to its popular K-cars and minivans, introduced for 1981 and 1984, respectively. In 1983, Chrysler earned record profits and paid off its loans seven years ahead of schedule. Lee helped the cause by appearing in TV ads in which he pointed a finger at the camera and demanded of viewers, "If you can find a better car, buy it."

In the mid Eighties, Iacocca served as chairman of the Statue of Liberty-Ellis Island Centennial Commission, formed by the National Park Service to raise $300 million for restorative work. Having raised the money, Iacocca thought he should have a strong say in how it was spent. Instead, the Park Service thanked and dismissed him. Iacocca was miffed, putting it mildly.

In 1984, with coauthor William Novak, Lee brought out *Iacocca: An Autobiography*, one of the best-selling non-fiction hardcover books in U.S. history, excluding the Bible. Net earnings from the sale of more than 2 million copies went to diabetes research in memory of Lee's wife, Mary, who died of the disease in 1983.

Though riddled with errors, the book was accepted as near-gospel by most readers, while others ventured that Iacocca was overly vindictive toward Henry II. In any event, the book certainly accomplished its primary purposes: downsizing Henry Ford II and glorifying the author. Index subheadings under "Henry Ford II" illuminate Lee's thrust: "arbitrary use of power by," "aversion to putting things in writing," "bigotry of," "drinking habits of," "firings by," etc.

Conversely, the book greatly boosted Iacocca's public image, and contributed to his designation by the *Wall Street Journal* and *Industry Week* as the most respected businessman in the country. He was ranked second in a Gallup Poll survey of representative Americans to name the world's "most admired" persons. The first businessperson to crack the top 10 in the poll's 40-year history, Lee was eclipsed only by

President Ronald Reagan, while outpolling Pope John Paul II, Billy Graham, ex-President Jimmy Carter, and Archbishop Desmond Tutu. Iacocca fantasized about running for president, and the Hammond, Indiana, *Times* endorsed him for the office. In any event, he became the auto industry's first folk hero since Henry Ford. However, unlike Ford, his heroism was fleeting.

Iacocca retired from Chrysler in 1992. Afterward, by his own admission, he floundered. In a *Fortune* article entitled "How I Flunked Retirement," he partially blamed his high life at Ford and Chrysler for his failure. "I wasn't ready for retirement," he explained. "When you're a CEO, you never rub shoulders with the people who make your cars, or buy them, or service them. When I flew corporate, I was alone most of the time. . . . They really treated you like a king." Besides, Lee explained, he never had prior experience with retirement.

Iacocca took some constructive steps, chief among them founding the Iacocca Institute at Lehigh University in Bethlehem, Pennsylvania, to "increase the global competitiveness of American organizations" and "provide a foundation from which great industrial leaders can emerge." He briefly considered teaching at the institute. Instead, he charged off in various directions, including a failed attempt to enter Detroit's casino business. He also supported Chrysler's largest shareholder, billionaire Kirk Kerkorian, in a failed bid to gain control of the company. Iacocca's support of Kerkorian so antagonized Chrysler's management that it backed away from naming the company's new Auburn Hills, Michigan, headquarters for him.

Lee also invested in and served as a spokesman for a number of companies ranging from an electric bicycle manufacturer to a producer of a buttery-tasting olive-oil spread. After Daimler-Benz took over Chrysler, he offered to serve as a DaimlerChrysler advisor, but was rejected by Chairman Juergen Schrempp. He remarried—twice—but his second and third marriages failed.

Iacocca has received honorary doctorates from Lehigh, Michigan State, Duke, and Southern California universities. He was inducted into the Automotive Hall of Fame in Dearborn in 1994. He perhaps was best summarized by the Associated Press at the time of his retirement: "He has dazzled, awed, angered, and alienated colleagues, underlings, and adversaries. Few are neutral about him."

Ford Division chief Lee Iacocca (left) and product planner Don Frey proudly pose with an early Mustang in 1964.

1975

- New "deluxe compact" Granada enjoys strong sales; Mercury adds similar Monarch

- Mustang II sports new V-8 option

- Despite strong new models, Ford sales slip behind Chevrolet

- Ford market share dips below 18 percent

- First F-150 ½-ton pickup appears; new-generation Econoline/Club Wagon vans debut

- Mercury takes the Pinto and turns it into the Bobcat

FORD ▲ With the Thunderbird now listing at well over $7000, Ford needed a lower-priced coupe to go head-to-head with Chevrolet's popular Monte Carlo. The Gran Torino-derived Elite offered many of the big 'Bird's trappings for $4767. While well shy of the Monte's 259,000 sales, Elite found a respectable 123,372 buyers.

► Subtle fender badging was the only clue that this Mustang II Ghia was packing V-8 power. With only 122 emission-controlled horsepower on tap however, the big-engined Mustangs were a mere shadow of the Bosses and Mach 1s of the past. Available only with an automatic transmission, the 302-cubic-inch V-8 was a $470 option.

▲ With the energy crisis gone, but not forgotten, sales of Ford's full-size cars recovered some of their lost popularity.

▲ Concealed headlamps and heavy bodyside molding helped distinguish top-line LTD Landau models from lesser big Fords. The coupe shown here came with standard split bench seats and a walnut-look dashboard for $5484. With the Galaxie retired, all heavily facelifted big Fords now wore some variation of the Custom or LTD name.

► Ford marked the 20th birthday of the Thunderbird with a pair of color-based option packages. The Copper Luxury Group featured Starfire paint, a matching vinyl roof, and copper-toned interior treatments. A similar Silver Luxury Group was also available. Another hefty price increase raised the point of entry to $7701. Sales were down slightly, to 42,685.

▲ Priced at $4837, the Gran Torino Brougham sedan could be ordered with the optional 400- or 460-cubic-inch V-8 engines. Offering little more interior space and a much larger body, Torino became a tough sell when compared to the newer, cheaper Granada. A hardtop-style coupe was the lowest-priced Torino, with a base price of $3954.

▶ Ford president Lee Iacocca stands behind another car that enjoyed his influence, the new Granada. Though its wheelbase was the same as the four-door Maverick it would eventually replace, Granada was a foot longer and up to 400 pounds heavier. Granada came in two- and four-door models, and was available in base and Ghia trim levels. Prices started at $3698.

▲ Granada Ghia interiors were decidedly plush, lending themselves more toward Continental than Maverick. A sporty floor-mounted shifter was available for both manual- and automatic-transmission-equipped models.

▲ A dressier Bronco could be had by ordering the Ranger model. A new Northland Special option package included an 800-watt engine-block heater to aid cold-weather starting. A 200-cubic-inch six was standard.

LINCOLN ▲ The Blue Diamond Luxury package on this Continental Mark IV included Aqua Blue Fire paint, a Normande-grain vinyl roof, and matching velour upholstery. (The glass moonroof was an extra-cost item, however.) A similar "Lipstick-and-White" package was also available. Horsepower was down again, now to 194.

▲ A new "colonnade-style" roof graced the largely unchanged Continental sedan. The elliptical opera windows in the sail panel was a detail borrowed from the Continental Mark IV. The big sedans weighed almost 5300 pounds and had a base price of $9656.

MERCURY ▲ Drawing sales from both the Comet and the Montego lines, the new compact Monarch struck a chord with a newly practical buying public. Top motivation came from a 351-cubic-inch V-8, good for 143 horsepower. Weighing up to 3400 pounds, Monarch performance was tepid, even with the optional V-8 engines.

▲ This photo demonstrates how similar Mercury's new Monarch was to Granada, its mechanical twin. The new compact came out strong, racking up more than 100,000 sales, instantly becoming Mercury's best-selling line. Monarch came in the same standard and Ghia trim levels as Granada, but also offered an uplevel Grand model.

► Montegos returned this year in standard, MX, and MX Brougham trim levels. Competition from sibling Monarch helped limit sales of the Brougham sedan shown here to just 8235, a 40 percent drop. Power steering and power front disc brakes were now standard across the line. Montego prices started at $4092.

◄ Grand Marquis topped Mercury's big-car lineup, which still included the Marquis and Marquis Brougham models. The low-end Montereys didn't return for 1975. This Grand Marquis sedan would have stickered for $6469 without options. A 460-cubic-inch V-8 was the top engine; it provided 216 horsepower.

► Though dubbed a '76, the Capri II arrived fairly early in 1975. Mercury essentially skipped a model year with Capri, selling leftover '74s until the revamped IIs came online. Most easily identified by its bright grille surround, blacked-out headlamp bezels, and new roofline, the Capri II sported stronger engines and a new "S" sport package. For $272, a buyer could have the V-6, now good for 110 bhp. The S package included special exterior trim, racing mirrors, and a beefier sport suspension. Prices rose sharply, now starting at $4117, up $1134 in two years.

◄ Feeling the need for a fuel-efficient subcompact of its own, Mercury created the Bobcat. Available in two-door hatchback and wagon bodies, Bobcat was little more than a dressed-up Pinto. The "woodie" Villager wagon shown here had a base price of $3481, almost $700 more than the similar Pinto Squire wagon. The pricey little Bobcat failed to generate the same enthusiasm as its popular Ford cousin, finding fewer than 35,000 buyers its first year. Canadian buyers had the option of ordering their wagons without a woodgrain appliqué.

■ Granada becomes America's best-selling compact car

■ Pinto and Mustang II rank first and third, respectively, in domestic subcompact sales race

■ Ford considers—but abandons—plan for a compact "minivan"

■ Mark IV designer special editions include Givency, Bill Blass, Pucci, and Cartier

■ Henry Ford II hospitalized after bout of chest pain

FORD ▲ Differences from 1974 to '76 were slight, though Mustang IIs could now be customized with a greater variety of options. Base hatchback sales doubled, but Mach 1 sales declined sharply. Production was almost unchanged, at about 190,000.

▶ This Mustang show car provided fairly accurate foreshadowing of the "T-tops" that would become available next year. Production cars would be spared the heavy black "targa bar" shown here. Horsepower was up across the board, with the optional V-8 receiving the biggest boost, to 134. The list price for a standard coupe was now $3525.

▲ The last of a generation, the Lincoln-based Thunderbird would be "downsized" to merely big for 1977. Proclaimed in advertising to be "one of the world's best luxury car buys," the big 'Bird saw sales recover somewhat, to almost 53,000. The 4800-pound Thunderbird carried a suggested retail price of $7790 without options.

► Hidden headlamps again differentiated the LTD Landau models from lesser full-size Fords. All-disc brakes joined the options list, along with a trendy half-vinyl roof for some two-door models. Production rose by nearly 54,000, after having slipped badly in 1975.

◄ Although the Ford Elite shared its basic sheetmetal with the Torino, it was differentiated by what looked like three full-width triple-section taillights. The center section actually hid the fuel-filler cap. The "twindow" opera windows were an Elite feature throughout its short life. With a base price under $5000, the Elite did an excellent job of acting as Ford's "Thunderbird on a budget." Almost 150,000 found homes.

► Intending to reposition the Thunderbird down-market for 1977, Ford knew in advance the Elite would lead a short life. The Thunderbird badge would essentially be applied to a restyled Elite, leaving no room in the lineup for the latter. The new, less-expensive Thunderbird would now be in a better position to do battle with Chevrolet's hot-selling Monte Carlo.

◄ With memories of fuel-shortage gas lines fading, large-car production totals began to rebound. Big-Ford output totaled around 400,000 (including 35,663 LTD Landau sedans), about 50,000 ahead of rival Chevy. Pricier Oldsmobile ran off a respectable 280,000 full-size cars. Fuel economy for these cars was still dismal however, and all new cars required costlier unleaded gas.

▲ Demand for 1976 Granada Ghias just missed 100,000, with 46,786 being two-doors. A $482 option, the Sports Sedan equipment package, dressed the "precision-size" Granada coupe in special paint, pinstripes, a floor-mounted shifter, and a leather-trimmed steering wheel. A 302-cid V-8 engine was available as an $88 option.

▲ Torino racked up respectable sales numbers its final year. With the Granada stealing sales on one side, and a new midsize LTD II waiting in the wings, Torino sales still approached the 200,000 mark. This Gran Torino sedan sports an optional $120 vinyl roof. Another $100 would have bought deluxe wheel covers. Prices started at $4172.

◄ Riding on the wave of its successful launch, Granada was little changed for its sophomore year. The Ghia shown here started at $4355. This car's $642 Luxury Decor Option group added aluminum wheels, a mandatory black-and-tan paint job, four-wheel disc brakes, and a unique velour-and-vinyl interior. Ambitious Ford advertising compared Granada to the likes of the Cadillac Seville and Mercedes 300-series cars. Despite the Ghias' added finery, the standard Granadas accounted for almost 80 percent of total sales.

▶ If it was named for a horse, it got the package. Ford's Stallion option group was offered on the Mustang II, Maverick, and Pinto. Stallion prices ranged from $72 to $329, depending on the model. The package included special silver paint, darkened hoods and rocker panels, and Stallion badging and decals. The package also included raised-white-letter tires, racing mirrors, and sport suspensions.

◀ Front-disc brakes were now standard on all four-wheel-drive F-Series trucks, including this long-bed Ranger XLT. A new Custom Decor group fitted base trucks with the Ranger XLT's exterior trim pieces. Despite having its second-strongest year ever, Ford was narrowly edged out by Chevrolet in the annual truck sales race.

▶ Simulated wood paneling adorned the flanks of the slow-selling Ranchero Squire, which wore a Gran Torino grille and newly standard radial tires. Buyers on a budget could opt for the more popular base- or 500-model Rancheros. As with the Torino on which they were based, Rancheros would go under the knife for 1977, and reemerge wearing new LTD II skin.

◄ The Bronco looked little different, but enjoyed several mechanical improvements. Stopping power was improved by the adoption of front-disc brakes and self-adjusting rear drums. Handling was augmented by a newly optional front stabilizer bar and heavy-duty shock absorbers. A new Special Decor group added a matte-black grille, bodyside tape striping, additional exterior chrome trim, and bright wheel covers.

LINCOLN

► Lincoln's most exclusive car, the Continental Mark IV, picked up nearly 9000 more customers this year. A total of 56,110 buyers drove home in one of the big personal-luxury coupes. Largely a symbolic victory, the Mark's big V-8 was again producing more than 200 horsepower. Power ratings were climbing as automakers learned to cope with new federal emissions regulations.

▲ At 5100 pounds, the Continental sedan was one of the heaviest cars on American roads. Prices started at $9293. Though little changed mechanically, audiophiles could now order their cars equipped with "Quadraphonic-8" tape players. Other new options included a four-note horn, forged aluminum wheels, and an engine-block heater.

▲ Ford's fondness for special-edition vehicles carried over to Lincoln in a big way for 1976. The Continental Mark IV's designer and "color" cars each came with package-specific paint, trim, and matching interior decor. Among the designer-series cars was this Pucci Edition in Dark Red Moon Dust paint.

▲ This Givenchy Edition Mark IV featured Aqua Blue Diamond Fire paint, a white landau roof, and matching upholstery of leather or velour. Thanks in part to the designer cars, Mark IV sales rose sharply—while the base prices actually declined by a few dollars, to $11,060. A 460-cubic-inch V-8 was still the only engine available.

▲ Dove-gray paint and a "Valino" vinyl roof were mated to form the Cartier Edition package. Each car in the series featured a facsimile of the featured designer's signature on its opera-window glass. Also available was the dark-blue Bill Blass Edition.

► Offered in sedan and coupe form, Marquis Brougham was Mercury's midlevel full-size car. With a starting price of $5955 for the two-door, Broughams slotted between the Grand and standard models. Total Marquis sales reached around 116,000.

◄ With sales on the decline, Mercury made few changes to Comet, now in its second-to-last year. Standard motivation came from a 200-cubic-inch six, good for 81 horsepower. A 250-cube six and a 302 V-8 with 138 horses were more powerful upgrade options. The popular Custom package now cost $496 and included bucket seats, fancier interior trim, tinted glass, a unique vinyl roof, and special wheel covers. Sales came to 15,068 two-doors and 21,006 four-doors.

► Despite strong initial demand, the revised Capri II failed to stem falling sales of "the Sexy European." Unfavorable exchange rates continued to drive the German-built coupe's prices higher. With a base price now over $4100, four-cylinder versions of the Capri could cost as much as V-8-equipped Monarchs. Fewer than 30,000 of the imports were sold.

▲ Offered in base and Colony Park versions, Mercury's big wagons accounted for almost 18,000 Marquis sales. The woody-looking Colony Park shown here claimed the lion's share of those buyers. A 400-cubic-inch V-8 was now the standard engine, but those looking for more punch could order the 460-cid mill. Colony Parks started at $5590.

1977

- Torino gets new lines and a familiar-sounding name: LTD II
- New lower-cost Thunderbird shares LTD II chassis

- A similar transformation turns Montego chassis into new Cougar
- Maverick and Comet ride out one last year virtually unchanged

- New smaller, lighter Mark V sets model sales record
- Luxury-trimmed Granada joins Lincoln lineup as Versailles

- Portholes and bold graphics turn the Pinto into a Cruising Wagon
- Ford market share climbs two points, now 28 percent

FORD

► Mustang II entered 1977 with a bevy of new options. A T-bar roof with lift-off glass panels, a tilt- up/take-out glass sunroof, and a Ghia-only sport appearance package helped spice things up. Mach 1s like the one shown here accounted for only 6700 of 153,000 total Mustang II sales.

◄ Available midyear, the $535 decal-and-cladding Cobra II package was truly "all show and no go." Actual muscle could be added to the mix by selecting the $607 Sport Performance Package. The sport package included a 139-horsepower V-8, sport suspension, power steering and brakes, and a heavy-duty manual transmission.

► While Mustang II sales had slipped about 20,000 cars since 1976, rival Chevrolet Camaro was enjoying increased popularity. Camaro sales climbed almost 36,000 for 1977, to 218,000. Mustang and Camaro were no longer the direct competitors they once were, however. The downsized Mustang II was a now sporty compact, while Camaro clung to its old ponycar roots.

▲ Generations of growth had left the Thunderbird bloated and pricey. The remedy was an edgy redesign and a move to the LTD II coupe chassis. The outcome was a car 900 pounds lighter, $2700 cheaper, and six times as popular as it predecessor. More than 318,000 of the new "Lean 'Birds" left showrooms. Starting price: $5063.

▶ Replacing the Elite in the Ford lineup, the leaner Thunderbird was now better equipped to battle Chevy's Monte Carlo for the hearts of personal-luxury car shoppers. Monte Carlo hung tough, however, racking up more than 411,000 sales. The lighter T-Bird could get by with a smaller engine, so a 302-cid engine replaced the old car's standard 460 V-8.

◀ While the standard Thunderbird's base price had been slashed, its companion, the flossy Town Landau model, actually cost more than the previous year's T-Bird. For $7990, Landaus added a unique grille, an aluminum roof band, and turbine-spoke wheels. The standard coupe shown here features optional sport wheels and a vinyl roof.

▶ Reacting to General Motors' downsized big cars, Ford advertised its LTD, including this Landau coupe, as "the full-size car that kept its size," and touted its "wide stance and road hugging weight." Despite the redesigned competition, the LTD held its own, racking up 445,000 sales, 40,000 more than 1976.

◀ With only a mild facelift, the old Torino became the squarer new LTD II. Mechanically identical, the Torino's nine-car lineup survived the transition to junior LTD intact. Sales surged almost 20 percent, to more than 230,000. Prices started at $4528.

▲ Borrowing an idea from the Econoline van, Ford debuted the Pinto Cruising Wagon. The youth-oriented package added $415 to the cost of a base wagon.

▲ The Pinto Cruising wagon featured full-length rear quarter panels fitted with nautical-looking "portholes," a tape-graphics package, and styled steel wheels.

▶ The custom-van craze of the Seventies saw buyers spending considerable sums of money to personalize their vehicles. The Cruising Van option was Ford's attempt to keep some of that after-market money for itself. Based on the Econoline E-150 panel van, the Cruising Van added porthole side windows, a blacked-out grille and bumpers, forged aluminum wheels, a choice of exterior graphics packages, and a luggage rack. For van lovers on a budget, Ford offered less-comprehensive "Free Wheeling" option groups.

◄ The original Continental (rear left), Mark II (left), Mark III (rear right), and Mark IV (right) joined the newest Mark for this family photo. The new Mark V shed roughly 400 pounds to squeeze into its new, sleeker duds. A modest $336 price increase over the final Mark IV (to $11,396) did little to curb interest in the redesigned luxury coupe. Sales surged 43 percent to a Mark record 80,321.

► For the times when more is not enough, buyers could choose the Williamsburg-edition Town Car. Of course, the Town Car was itself an upgrade on the standard Continental. The package included "Twin Comfort Lounge" seats, luxury wheel covers, and a two-tone paint treatment.

◄ Lincoln responded to the call for better fuel economy by turning the 460-cubic-inch engine into an option and introducing a 400-inch V-8 as the standard powerplant. The new, slightly-less-huge engine was good for 179 horsepower, while the optional 460 made 208 bhp. Sales of the Continental four-door sedan, shown here in Town Car trim, rose sharply, to almost 70,000. Price: $9636.

MERCURY ▲ Mercury's big Marquis carried over from 1976 almost unchanged. The half-vinyl roof shown here was available on Brougham and Grand coupes only, where it was standard. Marquis and Broughams got a standard 400-cid, 173-bhp V-8. A 197-horse, 460-cid engine came with the Grand Marquis.

▲ All Marquis models, including this Grand sedan, were now fitted with DuraSpark high-energy ignitions. Cars ordered with eight-track players could now be equipped with Quadrasonic four-channel stereos. Combined sedan sales came to around 97,000, leading coupes by a margin of three-to-one. Standard sedan prices started at $5496.

◄ The popular Monarch soldiered on with few changes for the new year. The two-door Ghia pictured here started at $4643. Available on Ghias was a new "S" package with upgraded wheels, lower-body cladding, custom exterior trim, bucket seats, and a floor-mounted shifter. A total of 129,057 Monarchs found buyers in 1977.

▲ A 302-cubic-inch V-8 was the only engine for Monarch buyers in California, thanks to that state's stricter emissions laws. Elsewhere, shoppers could also choose from a pair of sixes or a 351-inch eight.

▲ While the Cougar badge was reassigned to the former Montego lineup, the XR-7 retained some distinction. Now sharing a chassis with the Thunderbird, the big cat racked up 124,799 sales. Base price: $5274.

◄ Like the Thunderbird with which it shared its platform, the new XR-7 was lighter than the car it replaced. Power was all V-8, ranging in size from 302 to 400 cubic inches. A fresh look and a new name seemed to be all the line needed. The new Cougar lineup racked up 195,000 sales, 60,000 more than the combined 1976 total for all Cougar and Montego models. Non-XR-7 Cougars—offered in coupe, sedan, and station wagon models—started at $4700.

▲ Riding into its final year unchanged, the compact Comet came only in one trim level. This car wears the Sports Accent Group that added two-tone paint and a unique vinyl-roof treatment. Base price: $3544.

▲ The little-changed Bobcat got a new all-glass rear hatch as a $13 option. Redesigned five-mph bumpers helped reduce weight. A four-cylinder engine was standard, but a 93-horsepower V-6 could add some zing.

1978

- The Ford Motor Company celebrates its 75th anniversary

- Chairman Henry Ford II fires President Lee Iacocca for "insubordination"

- New Fairmont line replaces dated Maverick

- Fairmont-clone Zephyr replaces Mercury's Comet offerings

- A number of Ford and Lincoln models offer Diamond Jubilee editions

- Sporty Capri finally dropped from lineup

- Redesigned Bronco now based on full-size F-Series truck

F O R D ▲ Replacing the compact Maverick, the Fairmont line included two- and four-door sedans, plus a station wagon. Lighter than their predecessors, Fairmonts could get by with smaller engines. A 2.3-liter four-cylinder was standard. More power was available in the form of an optional six and a limited-availability 302-cid V-8.

◄ The extra-large LTD put in its final appearance in '78. Marking time, LTDs made do with subtle trim changes. Lovers of big coupes could step into the $5970 Landau shown here. The LTD's extensive V-8 roster included the buyer's choice of a 302-, 351-, 400-, or 460-cubic-inch engine.

► Attempting to emulate the subtle nuances that made a car "European," Ford created the Granada ESS. The Euro-spiced ESS came with body-color wheel covers, darkened grille trim, black-sidewall tires, and a heavy-duty suspension. Ambitious Granada advertising asked "Can you tell its looks from a $20,000 Mercedes?" Priced at $4962, the ESS sedan cost $186 more than a four-door Ghia.

◄ A carefully placed rib turned this Granada Ghia's rear windows into "twindows." Granada sales were down significantly this year. Impacted in part by the Fairmont introduction, sales slipped to just under 250,000, a plunge of 140,000. Ghia buyers looking for a swankier passenger compartment could order the $475 Luxury Interior package. The group included front bucket seats and velour upholstery. Granada prices started at $4300.

▲ New for Mustang II was the King Cobra. With the standard 139-horsepower V-8 and four-speed manual transmission, *Motor Trend* clocked a 17.7-second quarter-mile time.

▲ A one-off Mustang II IMSA Cobra toured the auto-show circuit. Mustang sales posted a healthy increase this year, reaching more than 192,000.

▲ No sophomore slump for Thunderbird. After a successful first year, the redesigned T-bird racked up more than 352,000 sales for 1978, an increase of 34,000. This car was equipped with both the Sports Decor Group and the removable T-top panels. At $10,106, a Diamond Jubilee Edition cost nearly twice as much as the standard coupe.

▶ Ford's newest import fighter was, in fact, imported. Built by Ford of Germany, the spunky Fiesta arrived on these shores to battle the likes of Chrysler's Omni and Horizon twins, Volkswagen's Rabbit, and a host of other low-cost, fuel-efficient cars that were popping up on showroom floors. Power came from a 1.6-liter four-cylinder engine producing 66 bhp. Despite the modest output, the lightweight Fiestas were considered frisky for the time. Fiesta earned the distinction of being Ford's only front-wheel-drive offering. Though available as a bare-bones commuter car, Fiesta could be dressed up with a Ghia or Sport package. Prices started at $3680.

▲ Ford worked hard to sell its new Fairmont into police and taxi fleets, but the idea never caught on. Fairmont's "Fox" chassis would host a number of cars during its lifespan, including the next Mustang.

▲ Ford's F-series pickups wore a new fascia that closely resembled its heavy-duty models. The new availability of tilt-steering and a luxury-option group reflected the big truck's increasing use as a commuter vehicle.

◀ The Mazda-built Courier continued to sell well. The pioneering small pickup found 70,546 customers in 1978, despite minimal changes. A chrome bumper and full wheel covers were part of this truck's XLT trim level. Ready for work, Couriers had a GVW rating of 4005 pounds, less when equipped with the optional soft-ride suspension.

LINCOLN

▶ Now in its second season, the pricey, compact Versailles was failing to live up to sales expectations. Intended as a rival for Cadillac's Seville, the $12,529 Versailles was priced $2363 higher than the Continental sedan. Too aware of the Versailles' pedestrian Granada roots, buyers weren't swayed by its luxury embellishments. Fewer than 9000 rolled out of dealerships in '78.

◀ Larger rear-wheel openings and a new dashboard spruced up the standard Continentals for 1978. Sales were off slightly this year, but still strong at over 88,000. Standard sedans were outselling coupes more than 3-to-1. The two-tone paint treatment marks this Town Car as a Williamsburg edition. Sedan prices began at $10,166 sans options.

▲ To celebrate its 75th anniversary, Ford issued several Diamond Jubilee editions including this Mark V. The limited-edition coupe came with a Valino-grain roof and the buyer's choice of Diamond Blue or Golden Jubilee paint. Special bucket seats and "Tiffany" carpeting finished the interior. A stiff $8000 premium kept sales to just 5159.

▶ Lincoln's big coupes could be had with the same Town Car package as the sedans. For $1440 over the coupe's $9974 base price, buyers were treated to Twin Comfort Lounge seats, premium bodyside moldings, and contrasting pinstripes. Logging fewer than 21,000 sales, the big coupe was the slowest-selling Continental model.

MERCURY ▲ A new grille surround and rectangular headlamps were part of the Monarch freshening for 1978. The four-door shown here had a starting price of $4457. Buyers looking for a touch of "European" sophistication could opt for the ESS package. The $524 ESS group included black-out trim and a sport suspension.

◀ With sales slowly declining and a replacement on the way, changes to the Marquis line were minimal. All models had smaller standard engines, a 351-cubic-inch V-8 for the base Marquis and Brougham, and a 400-inch mill for the Grand. The Grand Marquis sedan remained the line's top seller, accounting for almost 38,000 sales. The base price of this Grand Marquis coupe was $7290; 15,624 were sold.

▲ This Cougar XR-7 was ordered with the Midnight/Chamois Decor option. The package included a half-vinyl roof, cross-over strap, padded rear deck, trim-colored wheels, and bodyside paint striping. Stripped of wagons, the Cougar line was down to three models, a standard coupe, XR-7, and a four-door sedan. Prices started at $5052.

► Replacing the dated Comet, the Zephyr line debuted with two- and four-door sedan models, a sporty Z-7 coupe, and a wagon. The less-hefty Zephyrs, like their Fairmont cousins, could get by with a standard four-cylinder engine. Borrowed from the Pinto, the base engine was good for 88 horsepower. Two-thirds of Zephyr buyers chose the extra torque of the optional 200-cid six. With just 139 bhp on tap, an available V-8 failed to elevate Zephyrs to hot rod status. Two-door prices started at $3777.

◄ Plagued by recalls and priced a bit higher than the mechanically identical Pinto, Mercury's little Bobcat failed to break out of its sales slump. Available as the hatchback Runabout, standard wagon, and the Villager shown here, Bobcat sales barely cleared 32,000 in 1978. At $3830 to start, the base Runabout cost $86 more than a hatchback Pinto.

- Serious downsizing results in trimmer LTD and Marquis models
- Mustang loses the "II" and gains a chassis shared with Fairmont

- All-new Mustang picked for pace-car duty at Indianapolis 500
- Mustang-clone Capri hatchback puts Mercury back in ponycar field

- Subtle redesign nets Pinto and Bobcat new front end, more room
- Diamond Jubilee T-Bird renamed Heritage, becomes regular model

- Lincoln adds "Collector Series" to Continental line
- Versailles facelift results in temporary bump in sales

FORD ▲ Two years after General Motors began downsizing its big cars, Ford followed suit with its full-size offerings. The LTD's wheelbase was shortened almost seven inches, yet interior room grew. A new all-coil suspension helped the trimmer cars ride as well as their predecessors. Despite average price hikes of $700, sales rose more than 50,000 to 357,000. The outgoing LTD's eight-model lineup carried over intact. Prices started at $6184.

◄ This LTD II coupe was equipped with the newly available Sports Touring Package. The options group included two-tone paint, raised-white-letter tires, and Magnum 500 wheels. Lost in the shadow of the hot new LTD, sales of Ford's old intermediate plunged more than 70 percent, to less than 50,000. Coupes started at $5561.

► Larger inside and out, the new Mustang's 100.4-inch wheelbase was 4.2 inches longer than its predecessor, yet it weighed a couple hundred pounds less. Engines ranged from a standard four-cylinder shared with the Pinto, to a 140-horsepower 5.0-liter V-8. The new Mustangs were available as notchback coupes and slope-roofed hatchbacks, and in standard and Ghia trim levels. Prices started at $4071.

► A turbocharged version of the 2.3-liter four-cylinder engine, rated at 140 horsepower, went into the Mustang Turbo. This car's Cobra trim cost an extra $1173, and included a sportier suspension and TRX wheels. Turbo models were the quickest Mustangs, capable of reaching 60 mph in less than nine seconds.

◄ Ford advertising immodestly referred to Granada as "An American Classic." Ironically, this ESS-optioned sedan was supposed to look and feel European. Base price: $5317. A slow economy and a new LTD helped curb Granada sales. A total of 182,000 found homes, about 68,000 fewer than in 1978.

► A touched-up grille was the big Thunderbird change. Riding out the last year on its current chassis, T-Bird changes were limited to options-list tweaking. Due to the success of the previous year's Diamond Jubilee Edition, the package was carried over for the new year and redubbed the Heritage Edition. Base coupes started at $5877.

▲ Fairmont sales fell as the nation's economy lagged, but the compact remained popular. Two-door sedans found the fewest buyers, while the Futura coupe, four-door sedan, and wagon models divvied up the remaining sales fairly evenly. For an extra $329, a sporty new ES option package added black-out trim and a firmer suspension.

▶ The colorful Cruising package, replete with porthole, added $566 to the Pinto wagon's price. Power front-disc brakes were standard, a V-6 engine was optional. Total Pinto sales improved to almost 200,000.

▲ Ranchero wrapped up its stay in the Ford lineup with respectable final-year sales of 25,000. With a history spanning more than two decades, the Ranchero had been losing buyers to the increasingly civilized compact and full-size pickups with which it shared a showroom. This well-dressed GT started at $6289.

LINCOLN

▶ Replacing the Diamond Jubilee Edition, the Lincoln Mark V Collector's Series coupe wore a gold-tone grille, Midnight Blue or white paint, and Midnight Blue upholstery. Prices started at $21,452. A 159-horsepower 400-cubic-inch V-8 was the only engine.

◀ Lincoln's luxury compact, the Versailles, wore a fresh roofline and wider rear doors for a more formal appearance. A padded vinyl cover now decorated the decklid's simulated spare-tire hump. Sales more than doubled 1978's dismal totals, but still only reached a disappointing 21,007. Versailles came in a single trim level starting at $12,939.

▶ Members of the Lincoln Continental Owner's Club enjoyed a sneak preview of some new product during their 25th anniversary gathering at an Atwood, Ohio, golf course. They are seen here examining a Collector's Edition Continental. Four-door sedan prices began at $11,200.

▲ This Collector's Edition Sedan is parked beside an original collectible Lincoln: a '47 Continental. Compared to the classic, the new Continental rode a wheelbase 2.2 inches longer, packed on 500 pounds, and cost $6500 more. Total sales favored the modern Continentals, however. Only 1569 were sold in 1947, compared to 92,600 '79s.

MERCURY

▶ Sharing mechanical parts with the LTD, Marquis was downsized as well. Distinguishing this Grand coupe from lesser versions was a choice of vinyl roof treatments and a host of interior upgrades. Marquis sedans outsold coupes by nearly 3-to-1. Standard power came from a 5.0-liter V-8.

◀ Marquis sedans were available in the same trim levels as the coupes. This top-of-the-line Grand Marquis was the most popular, narrowly out-selling the base-series sedan. Brougham models anchored the middle of the lineup. According to Mercury advertising, the Marquis was able to reach 50 mph in 10.2 seconds. Sedan prices started at $6387, or $95 more than a coupe.

▶ Standard Marquis wagons were joined by a new high-end model with a name from the past. No longer just a trim package (as it had been the last two years), the Colony Park added power windows, rosewood bodyside appliqué, and additional exterior trim. Wagons accounted for roughly 20,000 Marquis sales. Buyers could opt for a 5.8-liter V-8 and its nine-bhp advantage over the standard engine.

◀ As Monarchs came only in a single trim level, dressing them up required careful use of the options list. This two-door was upgraded with a number of add-ons including cast-aluminum wheels, cornering lamps, the Bumper Protection Group, and two-tone paint. Monarch sales were in a steady decline. Only about 76,000 left showrooms this year, about 15,000 fewer than the year before. Coupe prices started at $4735, sedans from $4841.

► Compared to other Zephyrs, the Z-7 sported unique "basket-handle" side pillars, special striping, and wraparound taillights. The sporty-looking coupe accounted for the lion's share of Zephyr sales, racking up nearly 43,000 buyers. The matching roof and wheel trim were part of the Exterior Decor Group. At $4504, a Z-7 cost $251 more than a base two-door sedan.

▲ Almost as popular as the Z-7 was the Zephyr four-door sedan, which drew 41,316 customers. Prices started at $4370. A new Luxury Interior Option added a sporty four-spoke steering wheel and upgraded interior trim. The standard transmission in six- and eight-cylinder cars was a new four-speed overdrive manual.

▲ The new Mustang-derived Capri included a sporty RS that could be had with a turbocharged four. RS wheels were of a metric size not quite 16 inches in diameter.

▲ A new front-end designed around rectangular headlamps topped the list of Bobcat changes. The aluminum wheels on this car are part of the Sports Package.

The "Me" Decade

THROUGH TWO business-friendly Reagan administrations, corporations and workers flourished. Ford, for instance, had the resources to develop a startling new success, the Taurus. The fortunes of the middle class improved, and the wealthy grew wealthier still. The president was beloved by many. But the poor and dispossessed were left to fend for themselves economically, and civil rights gains of previous decades were scaled back.

U.S. defense spending escalated so dramatically that the Soviet economy was mortally wounded playing "catch-up." In 1985, Mikhail Gorbachev became Soviet premier, and set a reformist course.

Britain trumped Argentina in the TV-friendly—but politically inconsequential—Falklands War in 1982. A year later, a terrorist bomb killed 237 U.S. Marines dispatched to Lebanon.

Vice President George Bush won the presidency in 1988, and harshly criticized China's brutal 1989 crackdown on pro-democracy students.

Other dramatic developments included President Ronald Reagan's wounding by a gunman in 1981; the explosion of the *Challenger* space shuttle, and a disastrous meltdown of a Soviet nuclear reactor at Chernobyl in 1986; and the literal fall of the Berlin Wall in 1989.

■ Philip Caldwell succeeds Henry Ford II as company chairman

■ Donald Petersen now president; for the first time ever, there is no Ford in charge of the company

■ Drastically smaller Ford Thunderbird and Mercury Cougar XR-7 personal coupes debut

■ Full-size Lincoln Continental is downsized, though still a large car

■ New Continental Mark VI includes first four-door in the line's history

■ Ford Pinto and Mercury Bobcat subcompacts enter final year of production

■ Bronco sport utility redesigned along with mechanically similar F-Series full-size trucks

■ Performance-tuning Special Vehicle Operations unit formed

FORD

▶ Downsizing came to the Thunderbird in 1980, with the adoption of a stretched version of the Fairmont "Fox" platform. As a result, the new T-Bird was nearly 16 inches shorter overall, more than four inches narrower, and fully 700 pounds lighter than its predecessor. Thunderbird was once again built with unit-body construction, the first time since 1966.

▲ The eighth-generation Thunderbird sported an electronic instrument panel with a digital speedometer and graphic fuel gauge.

▲ An eggcrate grille and hidden headlamps were continued from the previous T-Bird. Prices started at $6432 for the base model seen here. A 255-cid version of the small-block V-8 was standard.

◀ Full-width taillamps were intended to remind shoppers of past T-Birds. Chassis changes included rack-and-pinion steering and MacPherson-strut front suspension. This Town Landau was the step-up model, but a Silver Anniversary job with a 302 V-8 as standard trumped it during the year. For the first time, a six was optional.

▲ With the demise of the LTD II, Granada was the sole bearer of Ford's midsize-coupe torch. Though technically a compact, Granada was positioned above its Fairmont stablemates. The two-tone paint on this Ghia added $180 to its $5942 base price. Total 1980 Granada sales barely cracked 90,000, not quite half the previous year's total.

► A well-optioned Ghia four-door sedan sports optional aluminum wheels, a $350 alternative to the standard wheel covers. Power upgrades were less expensive. Ordering the 302-cubic-inch V-8 in place of the standard six cost $188, while a smaller 255-inch V-8 added just $38. Production of base, Ghia, and ESS sedans totaled 29,557.

▲ One of the rarest, and quite possibly most garish, Fairmont iterations was the Futura Turbo Coupe. Much of the equipment shown here came as part of the $115 Sport Option Group, which included a blackout grille mesh, black steering-wheel spokes, and rear-fender/bodyside graphics. The turbocharged four-cylinder engine added $480.

► The Mustang Cobra package added $1485 to the cost of a standard hatchback. More show than go, the trim and graphics package did include the buyer's choice of either the turbo-charged four or the 255-cid V-8. Emasculated by emission-control equipment, neither engine could propel the flashy Mustang to 60 mph in less than 10 seconds.

▲ Cobra graphics were keyed to the color of individual cars. Not included in the package was the Cobra hood decal, an $88 option. The TRX wheels included with the package were nice to look at, but problematic. European wheel diameters accepted only metric replacement tires, often at costs three times higher than standard sizes.

◄ For buyers who loved the top-up look of convertibles but hated fresh air, the $625 carriage-roof option was the perfect solution. Actual drop-top Mustangs were still three years away. An alternative roof option was the less-dramatic partial vinyl roof, priced at $188. A standard coupe started at $4884.

▲ Anyone looking to raise the price of their economy car needed to look no further than the Pinto and its Cruising package. Adding $606 to the Pinto wagon's $4622 base price, "Cruisers" received a tri-color graphics package with black accents, porthole-style rear-panel windows, and styled steel wheels. A 2.3-liter four cylinder was standard.

▶ Though less bold than the Cruising package, the Rallye Pack was still more pretense than performance. Comprised mostly of graphics and blackout trim, the package added $369 to this Runabout's $4717 base price. After a long run, the Pinto would soon be out of production. For the final year, buyers snapped up 185,000 of "the cars nobody loved, but everybody bought."

◀ Long before the words "soccer mom" would impugn the potential sportiness of van travel, Ford was tacking portholes and multicolor graphics on its Econoline panel van. Still a functioning truck, a Cruising Van could be had with engines as large as 460 cubic inches for heavy hauling or towing. Often, though, the "cargo" was the sybaritic lounge into which the van's interior had been converted.

LINCOLN ▲ Though still a large car, the new Continental sedan was 800 pounds lighter, and rode a 10-inch shorter wheelbase than its predecessor. The standard 302-cid V-8 was down 30 horsepower from 1979's base unit. An optional 140-bhp, 351-cid engine roughly matched '79 performance in the new, lighter cars.

▲ An all-new downsized Continental Mark—the VI—debuted for '80, accompanied by the first-ever four-door model in series history. Though technically a separate line, Mark VI was, in reality, an upmarket extension of the Continental, and was mechanically identical to its standard-line siblings. Concealed headlamps, unique exterior-trim pieces, and distinct roof treatments set the Mark VI apart. Coupe prices started at $15,424, sedans at $15,824.

▲ Dressed nearly as well as a Mark VI, this standard Continental sports the $1089 Town Coupe roof option and $396 Turbine Spoke wheels. Of the 31,233 standard Continentals that found homes in 1980, just 7177 were coupes. Considerably less expensive than the Marks, these new-style Continentals started at $12,555.

▲ Looking much the same as it did in 1979, the Bill Blass Edition of the Mark VI Signature Series closely mirrored its larger predecessors. Highlighted by a carriage-style white vinyl roof, Blass editions also featured Turbine Spoke wheels and "loose-pillow" leather upholstery. A Signature Series-only option, the Bill Blass package added $2809.

▲ With Signature Series Mark VIs starting at $20,940, a car like this Bill Blass Edition could easily top $25,000 after a not-so-selective tour of the options list. Items from the "options we no longer see" file included the $356 CB radio and the $253 California emissions system. Deleting the electronic instrumentation netted a $707 credit.

▲ The new Lincoln chassis was based on the platform created for the 1979 Ford LTD and Mercury Marquis. The Mark VI coupe even shared their 114.3-inch wheelbase. Other Lincolns were on a 117.3-inch stretch. A full-length vinyl roof covering and opera windows were standard on Marks; a Bill Blass-style carriage roof was a $984 option.

▲ Like the Mark VI coupe, the new sedan was available in standard and uplevel Signature Series trim. Signature Series sedans like this one listed for $21,309. They carried all the expected Mark VI visual cues, right down to the "continental kit" decklid hump. With the exception of the fading Versailles, Lincoln's lineup was all Continental.

► An RS does not a turbo make, at least not in the case of this Mercury Capri. Plastic wheel covers betray this as the trim-only RS package. Comprised of exterior-graphic appliqués and blackout trim, the non-turbo RS package added $204 to the $5250 Capri base price. The turbo RS option group with the sport suspension and TRX wheels cost $1185.

▲ Capri could be equipped with any combination of four engines and two transmissions. The Pinto-sourced standard 2.3-liter four produced 88 horsepower, while a turbocharged version of the same engine was good for 140 bhp. Falling between the two extremes, a 3.3-liter six and a 4.2-liter V-8 produced 91 and 118 bhp, respectively.

► With more than 60 stand-alone options, personalizing a Capri was no problem. The standard steering wheel could be leather wrapped for $44. Adding cloth to these vinyl-trimmed seats was a $21 add-on, while Recaro-brand sport seats were available for $531. Color-keyed seatbelts came only on pricier Ghia models, however.

▲ Cougar was back for 1980, though it took up a lot less space. Again available only in XR-7 trim, the new Cougar rode on a modified version of the Fairmont chassis. Roughly 700 pounds lighter, Cougar was now powered by a smaller 4.2-liter (255-cid) V-8, though last year's 5.0-liter (302-cid) V-8 was still available. Prices started at $7045.

▲ The slow-selling Monarch would make its final pit stop in 1980, when it accounted for approximately 30,000 sales. Mercury would position a variation of the Zephyr to cover for the deleted Monarch the next year. Monarch was at its sportiest as pictured here in ESS guise with optional aluminum wheels. Two-doors priced from $5628.

► Though a convertible was in the works, Mustang roof options were currently limited to the standard solid top, the $228 "flip-up" sunroof, and the $874 T-top. Mustang sales took a dramatic hit in 1981, down approximately 90,000 to 182,000. Street buzz about the upcoming all-new 1982 Chevrolet Camaro may have encouraged some ponycar shoppers to take a "wait and see" attitude.

■ Pinto departure makes room for new front-drive Escort "world car"

■ Escort-twin Lynx replaces Mercury's Pinto-based Bobcat

■ Granada moves to Fairmont chassis; Monarch replaced by new Cougar sedans built on Zephyr underpinnings

■ Lincoln's standard Continental series renamed Town Car

■ Ford advertising asks "Have you driven a Ford, lately?"

■ Corporate market share falls to 16.5 percent, a new low

◄ Though it wasn't a close race, Fairmont placed second in Ford's annual sales derby. Racking up sales of 211,000, Fairmont trailed the new Escort by roughly 90,000. Identified by quad-headlight grilles, the slightly upscale Futura models gave Ford a product to slot between standard Fairmonts and the newly downsized Granada line.

► Ford's full-size LTD returned for 1981 unchanged. With fuel-economy concerns keeping big car sales in a holding pattern, LTD managed to find 131,000 buyers, down slightly from 1980. The best-dressed LTD was the Crown Victoria. The half-vinyl roof on this Crown Vic coupe added $141 to the car's $11,061 base price.

► A seeming contradiction, the new Granada was smaller outside and larger inside. Now riding on a version of the Fairmont chassis, the new Granada was about 400 pounds lighter and two inches shorter than before. Last year's 5.0-liter V-8 was replaced by a 4.2-liter unit as the top engine. New to the lineup was a standard 2.3-liter four, producing 88 horsepower. This GLX two-door started at $7148.

▲ If sales were an indication of how well-liked the downsized Thunderbird was, then the reviews were brutal. Ford sold 86,693 of the slimmed-down T-Birds in 1981, less than one third the number sold in 1979. Looking like a ¾-scale model of its former self, the unloved personal-luxury coupe listed for $11,355 in high-content Heritage trim.

◄ Ford's new Escort "world car" was a startling contrast to the departed Pinto. A completely new design, the front-drive subcompact made more efficient use of space and fuel. Power came from a new 1.6-liter overhead-cam four, good for 69 horsepower. Escorts came in two-door hatchback and four-door wagon models. This GLX wagon started at $6799. An automatic transmission added $344.

▲ With the subcompact Escort, compact Fairmont, and full-size LTD, Ford had a wagon to suit most buyers' needs. The most-expensive model in the LTD line, Country Squire, was essentially a full-size Ford wagon in Crown Victoria trim. LTD wagon starting prices: $7942 for the budget S model, $8180 for the LTD, and $8640 for the Squire.

◄ Though unlikely to strike fear in the hearts of serious criminals, service-ready Fairmonts offered police fleets an efficient alternative to the larger Ford LTDs, Chevrolet Impalas, and Dodge Diplomats most commonly tapped for patrol duty in the early Eighties.

▲ With a catalog that included beefier suspensions, speed-rated tires, and a host of paint colors and schemes, Ford was a serious player in the police-fleet game. Ford, along with Chevrolet and Dodge, had a virtual lock on the police and taxi markets. Keen eyes will spot the Crown Victoria quad-headlamp grille on this standard LTD body.

► A new smaller V-8 was available in Ford's "wind-tunnel tested" F-Series pickups. The 4.2-liter engine slotted between the 5.0-liter eight and the 4.9-liter six in price and performance. Two styles of the Free Wheelin' decor package were continued for 1981. This Custom F-150 Styleside has the Free Wheelin' "A" group, plus optional alloy wheels.

LINCOLN ▲ In an effort to make a clearer distinction between its two remaining lines, Lincoln rebadged the standard Continental. Borrowing a title from a former option package, it was now called Town Car. This sedan, one of 27,904 built, was paired with a coupe that faded from the scene after recording just 4935 assemblies in '81.

▲ The Continental name lived on with the Mark VI. Designer editions returned for 1981, again exclusively for Signature Series coupes. Bill Blass, Cartier, Givenchy, and Pucci packages added between $2160 and $3015 to the $22,463 starting tab. The formerly standard aluminum wheels on this Bill Blass Edition were now a $414 option.

Quality

MEANS BUSINESS
BUSINESS
MEANS YOUR JOB

MERCURY ◄ Wearing suspiciously clean lab coats, assembly line workers looked over a new Lynx, Mercury's version of Ford's new front-drive subcompact Escort. First-year sales neared 122,000.

▲ Not much was new for Mercury's sporty Capri, but options like this $644 Black Magic decor group helped keep things exciting. Capri prices started at $6685.

► Options including chrome wheel trim rings and dual sport mirrors helped identify this Lynx as an uplevel GS. Lynx prices started at $5603 for the standard hatchback and reached $6563 for the sport-trimmed RS wagon. Air conditioning was a $530 option.

◄ Available in standard Marquis, uplevel Marquis Brougham, and top-of-the-line Grand Marquis trim, Mercury's full-size offering was a mechanical twin to Ford's LTD. A 4.2-liter V-8 replaced the 5.0-liter engine as standard equipment, the latter becoming a $42 option. This Grand Marquis' front-bumper rub strips added $46 to its $9459 starting price.

► A long way from the 428-cubic-inch V-8s of a decade before, Cougar XR-7 now came standard with a 200-cid inline six. The once-optional 5.0-liter V-8 was gone, while the previously standard 4.2-liter eight became a $263 extra. Cougar two- and four-door sedans were new additions to the line, successors to the Monarch in the Mercury lineup.

▲ Though Cougar XR-7 prices started at $6835, ordering the automatic transmission, 4.2-liter V-8, air conditioning, flip-top sunroof, and the LS decor group shown here brought the price to $9232. XR-7 sales slumped again, falling to 37,275. The more prosaic Cougar sedans teamed up to attract 53,653 sales, more than the '80 Monarch.

◄ Stretching the woody theme to its potential limit, Mercury added this Lynx wagon clad in faux-wood appliqué to its lineup. The car shown here features the $243 Villager Wagon option with the $74 roof rack. Wagons accounted for a little more than one third of Lynx sales. Regardless of body style, all Lynxes were mounted on a petite 94.2-inch wheelbase. The program that developed the Lynx and Escort involved Ford units from around the world.

- Escort grabs number-one sales spot, edging out aging Chevette

- Escort-based Ford EXP and Mercury LN7 two-seat coupes introduced

- New Escort GT model replaces SS, gets 10 extra horsepower

- Escort/Lynx add four-door hatchbacks; Granada/Cougar field station wagons

- 3.8-liter V-6 debuts in several cars

- Lincoln Mark VI shares Continental badge with new Seville-sized sedan

- New GT model returns 5.0-liter V-8 to Mustang,

makes 175 horsepower

- Economic recession results in lowest industry sales in two decades; Ford losses since 1980 add up to $3.26 billion

FORD ▲ Ford's new "Essex" 3.8-liter V-6 was newly available for standard and Town Landau Thunderbirds. Producing 112 horsepower, the new V-6 was a step up from the standard 3.3-liter six. A 4.2-liter V-8 was standard on Heritage models like the one shown here, a $241 option elsewhere. Thunderbird prices started at $8492.

▲ Escort's lineup expanded by one, as a new four-door hatchback joined the team. An immediate hit, the new four-door accounted for 130,000 sales. Technically a separate model, the new EXP coupe shared its platform and drive-trains with the rest of the Escort line. Also popular, the sporty-looking two-door racked up sales of nearly 100,000.

▶ Testing the water, Ford showed this Mustang convertible concept on the auto-show circuit. Looking production ready, the prototype featured a body-color windshield frame not found on later production versions.

◀ Previously unnamed, Mustang's base model was now dubbed L. Anchoring the Mustang lineup, L models started at $6345 with standard four-cylinder power. New midlevel GL and uplevel GLX models were added to the lineup, replacing the discontinued Ghia.

▶ Ads boldly proclaiming "The Boss is Back," may have mildly overstated the case, but with the introduction of the new GT, the words "Mustang performance" were no longer oxymoronic. With 157 horsepower on tap, the 5.0-liter V-8-equipped GT was capable of reaching 60 mph in eight seconds. In black, a factory project car demonstrates the GT's add-on parts potential. First year GT sales reached 24,000, roughly 20 percent of total Mustang volume. GT prices started at $8308.

▲ In the world of station wagons, Fairmont's loss was Granada's gain. Making little difference in size and shape, the Granada line assumed both Fairmont wagons, redubbing them L and GL. Ironically, this was Granada's last year in Ford showrooms, as a Fairmont-based LTD would assume the uplevel midsize slot in the lineup for 1983.

◄ A relative technical *tour de force*, Ford's big Bronco SUV sported several meaningful advancements. A new four-speed automatic transmission promised improved fuel economy and longer engine life than models equipped with the old three-speed unit. Another Ford exclusive, Ford boasted the only independent front suspension on a full-size sport-utility vehicle. Also new, Ford added two snowplow packages and fuel-saving P-metric radial tires to the Bronco's already lengthy options list.

► Listing for $7094, the F-150 Flareside pickup sported a 78-inch cargo bed and available four-wheel drive. Three optional V-8 engines were available for buyers looking to upgrade from the standard 4.9-liter six. The battle for truck market share was handily won by Ford, taking 42.7 percent, to Chevrolet's second place 34.5.

LINCOLN

▶ The latest car to bear the name, Lincoln's trim new Continental came aboard as fleet flagship. Almost 400 pounds lighter, and more than a foot shorter than the Town Car, Continental was a close match for Cadillac's Seville. Power came from a 126-horsepower V-8.

▲ With the arrival of the compact Continental, Mark VI was now the senior Lincoln in terms of age and size, though not price. With the discontinuation of the Town Car coupe, Lincoln's uplevel Mark series became the sole bearer of two-door models. Designer cars like this Bill Blass were now separate models, not just option packages.

▲ Mark VI sedans were little changed for the new year. A new Pucci designer model joined the carryover Signature Series and standard Marks. For 1982, sedans made up almost 15,000 of the nearly 27,000 Mark VIs sold. This well-chromed Signature Series sedan listed for $22,720. Leather seating and aluminum wheels were standard.

MERCURY ▲ Like the similar Escort, Mercury's little Lynx sprouted an extra set of doors for the new year. The new four-door hatchback brought the Lynx line to three body types, adding to the existing two-door hatch and wagon models. Standard, L, GL, GS, and LS trim levels were available for all body types, while the sporty RS was limited to the two-door hatchback. Lynx prices ranged from $5502 for the base two-door hatch, to $8099 for the LS wagon.

▲ Not fully recovered from the shame of 1981's four-cylinder engine, Cougar would suffer another spiritual blow: a wagon. With the fading Zephyr demoted to an entry-level role, Cougar's uplevel image was better suited to wagon duty. Again, Cougar wagons were a single-year anomaly with the role passing to the new Marquis for 1983.

1983

- Fairmont-based LTD and Marquis replace Granada and Cougar sedans and wagons

- New Thunderbird helps industry establish aerodynamic look

- T-Bird-based Cougar coupe launched; sales rebound

- Mustang revives convertible after 10-year absence

- Homegrown compact Ranger pickup replaces Mazda-supplied Courier

FORD ▲ Sharing a 105.5-inch wheelbase with its predecessor, the new midsize LTD sported a more contemporary look than the outgoing Granada. Though based on aging Fairmont mechanicals, the new midsize Ford sold briskly, finding 155,000 buyers—35,000 more than the previous Granada. Prices started at $7777.

► Filling the slot between the hot-selling Escort and the freshly introduced LTD, the new Tempo was expected to give Ford a weapon in the fiercely competitive compact market. Replacing the dated Fairmont, Tempo featured a front-wheel-drive layout and impressive four-cylinder fuel economy. An early arriving 1984 model, Tempo eked out more than 402,000 sales in its extended first model year.

◄ For year two, the Escort-based EXP returned in three distinct forms. The base EXP boasted 72 horsepower and a four-speed manual transmission. Midlevel cars came with the optimistically named "high-output" 80-horsepower engine and a five-speed shifter. Thrill seekers opted for the 120-horse EXP Turbo shown here, with its TRX wheels and sport-tuned suspension.

▲ A long way from the chromed-box look of recent Thunderbirds, the all-new 1983 was a striking example of modern aerodynamic design. Paving the way for the upcoming Taurus, T-Bird shared its sleek look with the similar Mercury Cougar. Eager buyers nearly tripled Thunderbird sales, snatching up 121,999. Prices started at $9197.

▲ Ford's new "Essex" V-6 served as standard Thunderbird motivation, while an optional fuel-injected 5.0-liter V-8 would spice things up for an additional $383. The Turbo Coupe would arrive midyear, dressed in sportier trim and equipped with a turbocharged 2.3-liter four producing 142 horsepower. The wheels on this car were a $549 option.

▶ The formally dressed Heritage edition returned to top the redesigned Thunderbird line. Priced at $12,228, the Heritage's coachlamps, whitewall tires, and chrome trim seemed at odds with T-Bird's sleek new look. Customers shied away from the strange blending of old and new, preferring the cleaner look of the base model. A designer model would replace the Heritage for 1984.

► With fuel injection entering the mainstream, the days of the carburetor were numbered. By midyear, Escort GT and LX models would be equipped with fuel-injected versions of the standard 1.6-liter four. Boosting horsepower by eight over the carbureted high-output engine, "fuelie" cars were more efficient and smoother running. This facelifted GT started at $7339.

◄ Though its memory would live on in the LTD and Mustang it lent chassis parts to, the Fairmont and its Mercury Zephyr clone would fade away before the end of the year. Over its six-year life, the Fairmont line racked up 1.6 million sales, with Zephyr adding another half million. This last-of-the-breed Futura sedan listed for $6590.

▲ With its distinct "basket-handle" roof pillars, the Fairmont coupe was easily identified from the side. Fairmont power came from either the standard 2.3-liter four, or an optional 3.3-liter six. Coupe prices started at $6666. Frugal buyers could pass on the $199 eight-track tape player and delete the standard AM radio for a $61 credit.

◄ Posing with the soon-to-be-released Mustang convertible, executive vice president Harold A. Poling (left) and president Donald E. Petersen proclaimed that "1983 belonged to Ford." The Mustang convertible was one of 10 new products unveiled by Poling and Petersen during a 22-city satellite news conference for media and dealership personnel. Still several months from production, an out-of-focus Escort Turbo GT is visible in the background.

▲ A four-barrel carburetor helped squeeze 18 additional horsepower from the Mustang GT's 5.0-liter V-8, now making 175 horses. Ford's new 3.8-liter V-6 replaced the available 3.3-liter six. Base price for a GT: $9328.

▲ With a list price of $6727, Mustang L provided buyers with the look of a Mustang for Escort money. Shown here adorned with optional finery, most Ls left the factory with the standard 2.3-liter four-cylinder engine.

▲ For the first time since 1973, Mustang buyers were given the option of lowering the top. Initially offered in GLX trim, the new ragtop accounted for roughly 20 percent of Mustang's 120,000 1983 sales. While fixed-roof GLXs made do with a standard four-cylinder engine, convertibles enjoyed the extra torque of the 3.8-liter V-6.

▲ A design exercise intended to "probe" the limits of passenger-car aerodynamics, the Probe IV concept was a popular attraction on the auto-show circuit. The Probe IV's wind-tunnel-tested coefficient of drag was 0.152, roughly one third that of most contemporary production sedans. A subsequent Probe V concept would reach 0.137.

► With the LTD moniker now applied to two lines, it was the Crown Victoria suffix that differentiated Ford's traditional big cars from the new midsize line. Ford's full-size wagons were still available in standard-body and "wood"-sided Country Squire versions like this one. Big-wagon sales totaled 20,343 for 1983.

▲ Looking to reduce drag, an F-150 undergoes windtunnel testing. With many customers attuned to fuel-economy figures, even full-size trucks were being tweaked for increased efficiency.

▲ Replacing the Mazda-sourced Courier, Ford's new Ranger compact pickup looked much like a scaleddown F-150. Prices started at $7068 for a standard short-bed like this one. A 2.0-liter four was standard.

LINCOLN ▶ Appearing in four-door guise for the last time, the Mark VI line would be exclusively coupes in 1984. This car's coach roof was a $294 option.

▲ This Town Car Cartier Edition was finished in Medium Charcoal Moondust on top, with Platinum Mist flanks. Town Car prices started $16,923 for standard cars, and climbed to $19,601 for Cartiers. An electronic instrument panel was an $804 option. Finding 53,000 buyers, Town Car accounted for more than half of all Lincoln sales.

▲ With a redesigned Mark VII due for 1984, Mark VI changes for '83 were limited. This Midnight Black Bill Blass designer edition featured French Vanilla accents, but a reverse scheme with Midnight Black accents was also available. Bill Blass Editions started at $24,533. An optional power sliding moonroof added another $1289.

M E R C U R Y

▲ Mercury Capri RS's 5.0-liter V-8 experienced the same jump to 175 horsepower enjoyed by the similar Mustang GT. The newly available 3.8-liter V-6 was a $309 option in non-RS Capris.

▲ Mechanically identical to Ford's Escort-based EXP, Mercury's LN7 enjoyed the same upgrades. The previously optional 1.6-liter high-output engine was now standard, as was a new five-speed manual transmission.

▲ The rear roofline was the most significant visual difference between the '83 Thunderbird and Cougar. Mechanically identical, the two cars differed only in style and trim. Cougar's standard 3.8-liter V-6 produced 110 horsepower. This LS started at $10,850.

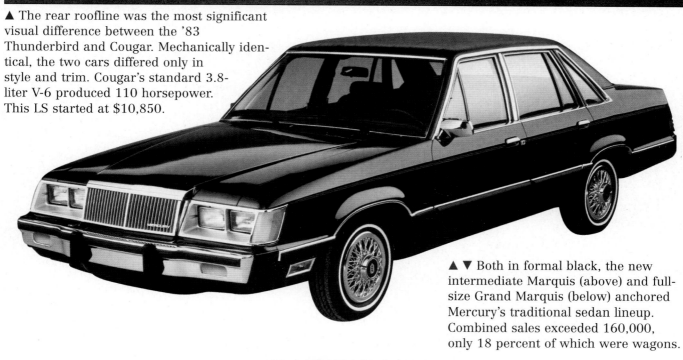

▲ ▼ Both in formal black, the new intermediate Marquis (above) and full-size Grand Marquis (below) anchored Mercury's traditional sedan lineup. Combined sales exceeded 160,000, only 18 percent of which were wagons.

1984

- Ford celebrates 20th Mustang anniversary with GT-350 package, "Euro-themed" turbocharged SVO model

- Compact Ford Tempo, Mercury Topaz debut

- Mercury goes turbo for Capri RS, Cougar XR-7

- Mazda-supplied diesel engine available in Ford Escort and Mercury Lynx

- Ford introduces Ranger-based Bronco II compact sport utility

- Mark VII introduced; features aero styling, "hot rod" Lincoln LSC model

FORD ▲ Marking Mustang's 20th year on American roads, Ford issued this GT-350 anniversary option, available only in "Shelby White." Purely a paint-and-trim package, anniversary cars were mechanically identical to standard Mustang GTs.

◄ The GT-350 package added $145 to the Mustang GT's $9578 base price. The Turbo GT swapped the 175-horsepower 5.0-liter V-8 for a turbocharged 2.3-liter four. Priced higher than the GT and spotting it 30 horsepower, the short-lived Turbo GT appealed to few buyers.

► Mustang's big news was the introduction of the SVO. A European-themed GT alternative, SVOs enjoyed sophisticated upgrades including four-wheel disc brakes, an intercooled turbocharged engine, and articulated sport bucket seats. Matching the V-8 GT in horsepower, the SVO was at a disadvantage in price. At $15,596, the SVO cost 62 percent more than the GT.

▲ Topping the Tempo line, the GLX stickered at $7621 in two-door guise. Though arguably better styled, coupes like this one were outsold by sedans almost three-to-one. Tempo sales broke 400,000 for 1984.

◄ Officially breaking all ties with the past, Ford dumped the high-line Heritage edition Thunderbird in favor of a cleaner-looking Fila model. Named for the Italian sportswear manufacturer, Filas came only in two-tone gray with body-colored wheels. Otherwise well-equipped, Filas topped the T-Bird scale at $14,471. Buyers could upgrade their automatic transmissions to the new four-speed with overdrive for $237 more.

▲ Ford's midsize LTD entered its sophomore year little changed. All-new for 1983, LTD was now Ford's second best-selling line after Escort. The optional 3.8-liter V-6 now featured throttle-body fuel injection, and enjoyed a corresponding 10-horsepower bump to 120. Broughams like this one came standard with a cloth carriage roof.

▲ Fresh on the heels of Chevrolet's compact S-10 Blazer, Ford's Ranger-based Bronco II featured four- and six-cylinder power and a $9998 sticker price.

◄ Ford's ever-popular full-size F-Series trucks were little changed for 1984. All light-duty models were now F-150s, the F-100 moniker having been put to rest. Ford's burly 300-inch six came standard in F-150s, with a 5.0-liter V-8 the next step up. F-Series prices started at $7381 for the F-150 short-bed Flareside.

► Replacing Fairmont as Ford's midsize police offering, LTD found its way into a number of law-enforcement fleets, but not in the same volume as the larger Crown Victoria. At the Fairgrounds in Pomona, this LTD stands ready for testing by the Los Angeles County Sheriff's Department, known for its comprehensive annual evaluations of potential law-enforcement fleet vehicles.

LINCOLN ▲ Shown here in Givenchy designer guise, Continental was again available in Valentino and standard trim as well. Little changed for its sophomore year, Lincoln's compact four-door racked up just over 30,000 sales for 1984. Marking the end of an era, the optional eight-track tape player was no longer available.

▲ Riding the wave of Ford's aero-styling theme, Lincoln's new Mark VII was dramatically sleeker than the blocky Marks that preceded it. Mechanically similar to the year-old Continental, Mark VII used the same 5.0-liter V-8 and automatic transmission. Shown here, the sporty LSC included a handling-tuned suspension and listed at $23,706.

▲ A small "V" emblem on the rear pillar marked this Continental as the $24,217 Valentino. Perhaps taking the drive for fuel efficiency too far, Lincoln made a diesel available in Continental and Mark VII for 1984. The BMW-sourced engine produced only 115 horsepower and cost $1235. The poorly received option would disappear midyear 1985.

▲ With the Mark VI gone, Town Car could lay sole claim to the title "Big Lincoln." Again available in standard, Signature, and Cartier trim levels, Town Car returned little changed. New gas-pressurized shock absorbers helped control the big sedan's ride, while an automatic rear-decklid pulldown spared owners the trouble of slamming.

► Jumping on the diesel bandwagon, Topaz and similar Ford Tempo were offered with the same economy-minded unit found in Escort. A $558 option, the Mazda-supplied 2.0-diesel produced 52 horsepower and returned an EPA estimated 41 mpg. This LS came standard with a digital clock and "luxury luggage compartment trim."

◄ Maintaining its winning ways, Mercury's aerodynamic personal-luxury Cougar was selling vastly better than its square-sided predecessor. Now in the second year of the new design, Cougar racked up 131,000 sales, an eight-fold increase over 1982. A new turbocharged model resurrected the XR-7 moniker, borrowing its 2.3-liter engine from the T-Bird Turbo Coupe.

▲ What price exclusivity? If you were one of the 50 people to take delivery of an ASC/McLaren Capri convertible in 1984, the answer was $25,000. For the price of a well-equipped Continental, buyers got a V-8 powered Capri sporting a hand-built convertible body and a racing-tuned suspension. Only 433 were built over three years.

■ Big Three makers post record profits, but Ford market share slips slightly to 18.8 percent

■ Ford F-Series pickups retain title of nation's best-selling vehicle

■ Donald Petersen named Ford chairman, Harold "Red" Poling now president

■ Escort and Lynx freshened at midyear, get more power

■ Limited-availability anniversary package marks Thunderbird's 30th model year

■ German-built Merkur line imported for sale at Lincoln-Mercury dealers

■ One-year-only LTD LX boasts V-8, sport suspension, and bucket seats

■ Groundbreaking Taurus concept makes auto-show debut

FORD

▶ The year-old Mustang SVO received a number of significant improvements for its second season. Engine tweaking coaxed 30 additional horsepower from the turbocharged four, now up to 205. A competition package deleted non-essentials like air conditioning and stereo equipment for a $1417 credit. Unimpressed, buyers opted instead for the V-8-powered GT and its $5000 lower sticker.

◀ Mustang GT was treated to a bevy of nifty-sounding upgrades, including roller tappets, a quadra-shock suspension, "gator-back" tires, and a hotter cam. Mustang's beefier résumé led to bigger sales, breaking 155,000 for 1985, almost 15,000 more than the prior year.

▶ The SVO enjoyed a number of technical features unique among Mustangs. These included a turbocharged engine with electronic fuel injection and air-to-air intercooling, rear-disc brakes, and adjustable shock absorbers. SVO sales slumped however, accounting for little better than one percent of total Mustang volume.

▲ Celebrating a turbulent 30 years, Thunderbird was offered with a limited-production anniversary package. Essentially a top-line Elan painted Medium Regatta Blue, the newest T-Bird's groundbreaking shape seemed an appropriate homage to the original's fresh design. Sales broke 150,000 this year, ten times the 1955 model's total.

▲ Thunderbird's 30th year was relatively quiet, with a freshened grille and wraparound taillights topping the list of changes. Turbo models received internal changes designed to extend engine life, while all cars were treated to self-propping hoods. Base models finally broke the $10,000 barrier, though only by $101. A 5.0-liter V-8 added $392.

► Midyear, a restyled Escort emerged with aero-style headlamps and a redesigned grille. The big news was under the hood however, where a larger 1.9-liter engine offered as many as 16 horsepower more than the old 1.6. Sales were up by better than 30,000, to just over 400,000.

◄ Tempo's standard 2.3-liter four was treated to electronic fuel injection for the new year, raising output to 86 horsepower in standard tune, a bump of two. Horsepower jumped to an even 100 when Tempo GLs were ordered with the Sports Performance Group. Sales remained brisk, reaching nearly 340,000.

► Ford's big, rear-wheel-drive LTD Crown Victoria now had standard gas-pressurized shock absorbers and an available self-leveling rear suspension. Power came from a 5.0-liter V-8 that produced 140 horsepower in standard tune, 155 when ordered with the optional dual-exhaust system. A low-content fleet-special S model anchored the Crown Victoria line, starting at $10,609. This standard model began at $11,627.

▲ On the way out, plunging sales were making full-size two-door models a rarity. Crown Victoria coupes like this one offered nearly the same interior space as four-door models, but accounted for less than 10 percent of total sales. This well-dressed CV's Brougham roof was a $793 option. Black bumper rub strips added another $60.

▲ Ford's midsize LTD was now comfortably outselling the bigger LTD Crown Victoria. Existing models carried into the new year with only minor trim revisions. A new performance-minded LX model joined the LTD lineup for 1985, sporting a handling-tuned suspension and standard V-8 power. This well-equipped Brougham started at $9262.

▶ Prices for the four-wheel-drive Bronco II rose almost 10 percent, starting now at $10,899. Slotted between the standard base and uplevel Eddie Bauer models, XLTs like this one accounted for the bulk of sales. A 115-horsepower 2.8-liter V-6 was the only available engine. A five-speed manual transmission was standard.

◀ Still available with the massive 460-cubic-inch (7.5-liter) V-8, Ford's Club Wagon was an able worker. When properly equipped, the big van was capable of ferrying up to 15 passengers or 300 cubic feet of cargo. The uplevel XLT was trimmed with a chrome grille and window surrounds, lower bodyside moldings, and rocker-panel accent paint.

▶ Though inherently basic, compact Ranger pickups like this one were often sold well-optioned. Equipped with four-wheel drive, V-6 power, uplevel wheels and tires, and XL trim, this truck stickered for close to $10,000. Ranger's standard 2.3-liter four-cylinder engine was now fuel injected.

▶ Lincoln's Mark VII coupe was treated to a host of exciting new colors for the new year, including Burnished Pewter and Carob Brown. A 5.0-liter V-8 was standard across the line, producing 165 horsepower in LSCs like this one, 25 less in other models.

▲ Somber and serious, the LSC's dashboard reflected the performance orientation of the model. All Marks received a leather center armrest for the new year.

▲ Non-LSC Marks were now fitted with woodgrain instrument-panel appliqué. The speaker-grille "coaxial" badge identifies this car's Premium Sound option.

▲ More than a sophomore slump, sales of Lincoln's personal-luxury coupe dropped by nearly half in its second year. Finding only 18,000 buyers, Mark VII now accounted for only 10 percent of total Lincoln volume. Not since the 1968 introduction of the Mark III had Mark sales slipped below 20,000. Mark VII prices started at $22,399.

► A cutaway rendering reveals the Mark VII LSC's fuel-injected 5.0-liter V-8, rear-wheel-drive chassis, and four-wheel-disc brakes. Technically sophisticated for the time, the Mark's disappointing sales were partially attributable to the buying public's fading interest in large coupes.

◄ Lincoln's big Town Car was slightly more luxurious for 1985. Uplevel Signature and Cartier models now came with newly standard premium sound systems, illuminated keypad entry systems, and power-remote outside mirrors. Other changes included redesigned grilles and thicker passenger-compartment carpeting.

► The bread-and-butter of the Lincoln brand, Town Car accounted for 75 percent of total volume. Sales leapt more than 25,000 in 1985, to 120,000. As with all Lincolns, Town Cars came standard with a 5.0-liter V-8, producing 140 horsepower in standard trim, 155 when equipped with optional dual exhausts. While TC prices started at $19,047, loaded Cartiers like this one could reach $25,000.

MERCURY ▲ A mechanical twin to the Ford Thunderbird, Mercury's sporty two-door Cougar received a revised instrument panel, a new grille and taillamps, and a redesigned rear-seating area for the new year. Carrying a base price of $13,599, this XR-7's 155-horsepower 2.3-liter turbocharged engine was denied to other Cougars.

► Sporting optional TRX wheels and tires, this Topaz LS was a decent handler. Like the similar Ford Tempo, Topaz now enjoyed smoother power from its newly fuel-injected standard engine. With air conditioning, automatic transmission, and cassette, this LS would have listed for $10,379.

◄ Mercury's biggest car enjoyed a smoother ride, compliments of gas-pressurized shock absorbers. Otherwise, Grand Marquis was little changed for the new year. Prices ranged from $12,240 for the standard sedan, and rose to $12,854 for the better-equipped LS four-door. The only available powertrain combination was a 5.0-liter V-8 with a four-speed automatic transmission.

► Like the calm before a storm, Mercury's midsize sedan stood pat for 1985, while the front-drive Sable was readied in the wings. Marquis' last full year was marked by decent sales, reaching more than 90,000. Marquis' sedan and wagon bodies were available in standard and Brougham trim, with no matching model for Ford's new V-8-powered LTD LX. Base price: $8996.

► Outfitting your 1985 Capri RS for performance was a matter of careful study. Value seekers might turn to the standard V-8, now producing 180 horsepower. For an extra $1237 however, a high-output version of the same engine pumped out an additional 30 horses.

◄ Capri RS shoppers could also opt for the 2.3-turbocharged engine, and its challenging-to-master power curve. Though mechanically similar to Ford's Mustang, Capri made exclusive use of a "bubble-back" rear hatch. RS prices started at $10,232, but nudged $14,000 with the high-output V-8, "T"-bar roof, and air conditioning.

► Though hidden in the shadow of Ford's nearly identical Escort, Mercury's little Lynx sold respectably. Buyers drove away in nearly 85,000 of Mercury's subcompacts, a healthy bump of 10,000 over 1984. This four-door was produced prior to a midyear freshening that included a move from 1.6- to 1.9-liter engines.

◄ Looking appropriately foreign, Lincoln-Mercury's newest model was sourced overseas. A new addition to the L-M franchise, the Merkur (pronounced mare-COOR) brand carried select Ford-of-Europe cars. Based on the German Ford Sierra, this XR4Ti sported a U.S.-built 2.3-liter turbocharged four.

■ Ford corporate profits top General Motors' for first time since 1924

■ Daring new Ford Taurus and Mercury Sable intermediates launched

■ Aerostar "midivan" unveiled, competes with Caravan and Voyager

■ Compact Ranger pickup now available with extended "SuperCab"

■ Mercury Capri ponycar puts in final appearance

FORD ▲ Fresh from a midyear restyle, Ford's subcompact Escort stood pat for 1986. Escort GT lost its optional turbocharged engine, sporting instead a 108-horsepower version of the standard 1.9-liter four. Escort production soared to 430,000.

◄ With the exception of four-cylinder models, Ford's renaissance pony-car line was now entirely fuel injected. The previous year's carbureted high-output V-8 was gone, replaced by a nearly as strong 200-horsepower fuelie. This GT convertible started at $14,420. Leather seating added $429.

▲ Named *Motor Trend*'s "Car of the Year," Taurus and Mercury-companion Sable debuted to rave reviews. Taurus's forward-thinking styling and modern front-wheel-drive chassis helped establish a new paradigm in sedan design. Power came from either an 88-bhp 2.5-liter four, or a 140-horsepower 3.0-liter V-6. Prices started at $9645.

▲ Thunderbird returned for the new year down one model. Previously T-Bird's priciest model, Elan was deleted from the model lineup, leaving carryover Fila the sole luxury variant. This Turbo Coupe listed for $14,143 without options, but stickered out at $15,687 with an automatic transmission, air conditioning, and leather seat trim.

▲ The mostly unchanged Ford pickup line still came in F-150, F-250, and F-350 versions. F-Series prices started as low as $8625, but well-equipped SuperCabs could near $20,000. Ready for towing, F-250HD and F-350 models could be equipped with a 6.9-liter diesel. Standard power came from a 4.9-liter six good for 120 horsepower.

◄ New front and rear styling, a revised passenger compartment, and larger standard tires highlighted the changes to Tempo for 1986. A fresh look failed to curb a decline in sales, to 278,000, a drop of nearly 60,000 from 1985. Tempo's entry-level L model was history, raising the cost of entry to the previously midline GL's $7358 base price.

▲ Adding the "Sport" suffix to your Tempo GL coupe was as easy as spending $934. Along with the longer name, buyers got tinted glass, dual power mirrors, cassette stereo, power steering, and bigger tires on aluminum wheels. The unloved 2.0-liter diesel engine was still on the Tempo options list, good for an EPA-estimated 36 mpg average.

► Substantially quicker than contemporary police sedans, this Florida Highway Patrol car likely struck fear in the hearts of habitual speeders. Inexpensive and fast, Mustangs were periodically pressed into interceptor duty by law-enforcement agencies.

LINCOLN

► Mustang and Capri were not the only Ford products to garner the attention of aftermarket tuners. Lincoln's already-sporty Mark VII LSC is seen here in GTC trim as modified by C&C Incorporated of Brighton, Michigan. The GTC was available in standard and Stage II versions.

◄ "As good looking as it is gutsy," said C&C, the GTC had undeniable presence. Apart from the obvious aesthetic alterations, Stage IIs also enjoyed reduced ride heights, improved braking, and massive Goodyear-supplied tires. GTCs were sold on a special-order basis and were priced around $40,000.

▲ A move to port fuel injection resulted in power increases for Continental and Mark VII. LSCs leapt from 165 to 200 horsepower, while the others climbed 10, to 150. Sales rose slightly for 1986, to just over 20,000. The Versace model was discontinued, leaving the $23,857 Bill Blass the sole designer-edition Continental.

▲ Sagging noticeably in the middle, this Gold Wing Limousine was an exercise in wretched excess. With Chrysler's Imperial long gone, Lincoln and Cadillac were the only major competitors battling for the hearts of livery operators. The straight lines on Town Cars like this one made the process of adding new sections a relatively simple affair.

◄ Mercury's Capri RS was available with only one engine for 1986. With the turbo option deleted, RS models were powered by the same fuel-injected 5.0-liter found in the Mustang GT. Other Capris used either a 2.3-liter four, or a 120-horsepower 3.8-liter V-6.

▲ Along for the technology ride, Mercury's full-size Grand Marquis was now port fuel injected. The big Marquis' 5.0-liter V-8 was now making 150 horsepower, up 10 from the previous year. Other changes included upgrading to standard 15-inch wheels and tires, up from the former 14-inchers. Base price for this Grand Marquis LS: $13,851.

► Wearing unique trim and bodywork, Mercury's new midsize Sable was otherwise identical to Ford Taurus. A sedan and wagon were available, both in the buyer's choice of standard GS or uplevel LS trim. Sable prices started at $10,700.

◄ Optional for GS sedans, the 140-horsepower 3.0-liter V-6 in this LS was otherwise standard. The unloved standard 2.5-liter four was relatively uncommon, and would disappear from equipment lists by 1987. A slow production start-up and competition from remaining Marquis held sales under 100,000.

► Possibly a function of their sleek good looks, wagons would account for a major portion of Sable sales. While wagons made up only 10 percent of Marquis sales, they would eventually claim a third of Sable production. This LS wagon began at $13,068.

◄ Cougar's new Mercedes-style grille topped the list of revisions for 1986. As with other Ford V-8s, Cougar's optional 5.0-liter engine was up in power, compliments of port fuel injection. Mercury's midsize coupe was again available in base, uplevel LS, and sporty turbocharged XR-7 trim. The aluminum wheels on this LS added $507 to its $12,696 starting price.

▲ Looking very much like its Ford cousin, this Lynx XR3 was a virtual twin to the Escort GT. A standard 108-horsepower engine gave the little Lynx decent scoot.

▲ The German-made Merkur XR4Ti was unchanged. The turbo engine produced 175 horsepower mated to a manual transmission, 30 fewer with the automatic.

▶ The phantom of 1986, Merkur's Scorpio was scheduled for a July debut, but never arrived. Bowing almost a year late, the first Scorpios finally appeared as '87s. Poor XR4Ti sales had put the viability of the Merkur brand in question, with delays stemming from the potential cancellation of the line.

▲ Approximating a theme established by Sable, Topaz's freshened fascia expanded Mercury's new family look. Frugal buyers had one last chance to order the Mazda-built diesel engine, as it would not return for 1987. Among other changes, the standard wheels grew an inch in diameter to 14, and bumpers were now body color.

1987

- Retired Chairman Henry Ford II dies
- Record profits help Ford outearn GM for second straight year
- Taurus earns nation's best-selling car crown; sales reach 375,000
- Ford lands one-two punch as Escort ranks second in total sales
- New Thunderbird earns *Motor Trend* "Car of the Year" award
- Tempo and Topaz add all-wheel-drive models
- Lincoln-Mercury dealers sell a second Merkur, the Scorpio sedan
- West Coast dealers begin selling Korean-built Festiva minicar
- The carburetor passes on; all Ford car engines now sport fuel injection
- Ford LTD and Mercury Grand Marquis full-sizers offer their final two-doors

FORD

▶ Groundbreaking in 1983, the crisply restyled Thunderbird retained its clean, uncluttered look. Turbo Coupes like this one enjoyed a healthy horsepower bump to 190; 160 in automatic-transmission cars. Not available on other Thunderbirds, Turbo Coupes now came standard with antilock brakes.

◀ New to the nest, the uplevel LX was now the Thunderbird luxury leader. An appropriately named Sport also joined the lineup, featuring V-8 power and a suspension borrowed from the Turbo Coupe. Sports wore blackout trim in place of the chrome window surrounds on the LX pictured here. Sport prices started at $15,079, LX's listed for $304 more.

▶ Very similar to the arrangement found in the now-discontinued Mustang SVO, the Thunderbird Turbo Coupe owed much of its newfound power to intercooling. Essentially a radiator for incoming air, the turbo's intercooler lowered the temperature and increased the density of the air/fuel mixture. Turbo Coupes started at $16,805. Leather trim added $415.

▲ A restyled EXP arrived early in 1986, but the Escort-based two-seater continued to struggle in the market. Two models—Luxury Coupe and Sport Coupe—were available, each with a fuel-injected engine. Sales fell again however, to just over 25,000, down from 31,000 in 1986. Starting at $8831, this Sport Coupe now packed 115 horsepower.

◄ While Mustang's redesign resulted in a generally cleaner look, the GT's heavy application of tack-on body addenda created a blocky, purposeful silhouette. Now packing 225 horsepower, GT's 5.0-liter V-8 could propel the freshened Mustang to 60 mph in as little as six seconds. Base price for this GT convertible: $15,724.

▲ Economy-minded hot rodders might have turned to Mustang's new base LX. Starting at $8043, LXs could be equipped with the new $1885 5.0-Liter Engine Package. The high-content package included the GT's 225-horsepower V-8, as well as its wheels, tires, and suspension. The high-tech low-sales Mustang SVO was discontinued.

▲ Following a mid-1986 introduction, the radical new Taurus earned top-seller honors its first full year in show-rooms. Knocking stablemate Escort to the number-two spot, Taurus found 375,000 buyers during the 1987 model year. The top-of-the-line LX sedan shown here started at $14,613. The styled road wheels were a $113 option.

◄ Loosely based on components borrowed from the Ranger, Aerostar was a bigger, heavier vehicle than Chrysler's hugely popular Caravan and Voyager minivans. Aerostar owners enjoyed ample passenger and cargo room, but the rear-drive layout resulted in handling that was perceived as "trucky." With its standard 3.0-liter V-6, Aerostar prices started at $10,682. This XLT with auto and air would have cost around $14,000.

► The changes to Ford's compact Bronco II sport-utility vehicle were mostly under the skin. Increased use of galvanized sheetmetal resulted in better corrosion resistance. All models also benefited from newly standard rear-wheel anti-lock brakes. Bronco II prices started at $12,587 with four-wheel drive. The only engine was a 140-horsepower 2.9-liter V-6.

► The seemingly unstoppable F-150 chalked up another huge sales year, as 550,000 trucks rolled off dearlership lots. As with Bronco II, rear-wheel antilock brakes were now standard. A restyling gave the popular pickups a more aerodynamic look that included flush-mounted headlamps. F-150 buyers could upgrade to a 5.0-liter V-8 for $556.

▲ Though there was technically only one model, option groups could dress Ranger up. Packages included the luxury XLT, sporty GT, and the off-road STX pictured.

▲ This Super Van was actually an E-250 Econoline with a 20-inch stretch. Its monstrous storage area could swallow up to 300 cubic feet of cargo.

LINCOLN ▲ Lincoln's personal-luxury coupe stood pat for the new year. Mark VIIs like this LSC now had more powerful batteries and upgraded alternators. This was the standard coupe's last year, as only the Bill Blass and LSC would return for '88. Sales slipped to 15,000, down 5000 from 1986.

PHILIP CALDWELL
A man of few words, but big ideas

PHILIP CALDWELL WAS ONE of the three most effective executives in Ford history, James Couzens and Ernest R. Breech being the others. Chief executive officer from 1979 to 1985, he held 17 jobs during his 32 years with the company, and left each in better shape than he found it. His career deserves a book-length biography, better yet an autobiography, inasmuch as he's retired with his wife, Betsey, in New Canaan, Connecticut.

Born in 1920 in Bourneville, Ohio, and reared in South Charleston (between Dayton and Columbus), Caldwell graduated in 1942 from Muskingum College, in New Concord, Ohio, and earned an MBA from Harvard. He served as a naval officer from 1942 to 1946, and was the top civilian employee in the Bureau of Naval Procurement before joining Ford Division's purchasing staff in 1953.

After managerial stints in purchasing, engineering, product planning, and general parts, Caldwell served as a truck executive from 1964 to 1970. During these years, perhaps the happiest of his career, he laid a solid foundation for Ford's enduring truck leadership. His work earned him a vice presidency in 1968 and a further "reward"—a posting in 1970 to Ford's equivalent of Siberia: Philadelphia-based Philco-Ford, regarded by Henry Ford II as the company's worst managerial mess. Told that Philco-Ford had chewed up three general managers in the previous 18 months, Caldwell's 13-year-old daughter, Desiree, asked, "Daddy, if it doesn't work out, will Mr. Ford throw you on the scrap heap?"

"Actually," Caldwell later mused, "it was a pretty appropriate question."

During 19 months at Philco-Ford, Caldwell eliminated unprofitable consumer-products operations, thus paving the way for its aerospace business to prosper. having enhanced his reputation as a problem solver, he was given charge of manufacturing in 1971, made chairman of Ford of Europe in 1972, and named executive vice president of international operations in 1973.

As Caldwell's star ascended at Ford, Lee Iacocca's declined. In 1973, Caldwell was named a company director. Three years later, when HFII suffered an angina attack, he decided that Caldwell would succeed him. In 1977, the heir-apparent was named vice chairman; in 1978, president and deputy CEO; in 1979, CEO; and in 1980, chairman as well. One secret of her husband's success, Betsey Caldwell said, was that he focused on the job at hand, rather than think about promotions "as some did."

Caldwell was the logical choice to succeed Henry II, most observers agreed. He even looked and acted the part of a chairman, some said. "The way his hair had silvered was almost artistic," recalled speechwriter Bonnie Thompson. "With a light behind him, he looked as if he had an inner radiance, intelligence, and capability. I thought he made a remarkable picture." A tough government safety regulator, Joan Claybrook, described the executive as "a very charming guy, very stately . . . a really gracious human being."

Caldwell had no vices. "He wouldn't lie or tell a half-truth, and he never swore," said his secretary, Ruth H. Thomas. "When he was really frustrated or angry, the worst he would do was to say 'Christ' preceding a statement." A nonsmoker and teetotaler, Caldwell toasted audiences with nonalcoholic champagne. "Drinking is not a moral issue," he said. "I simply feel the better for not doing so. I've seen so much damage from all that stuff."

A workhorse, Caldwell was said by a Ford president, Robert J. Hampson, to have "no hobbies except work." When Betsey suggested that he should rest or take a nap, he would reply, "When the house is burning down you don't have time to take a nap," or "When there is a storm, the captain is up on the bridge, not down below taking a nap."

Caldwell's inordinate attention to detail was discounted by Henry Ford II. "He drives people crazy about staff work," Ford acknowledged in 1982. "But that's all right. He's very meticulous about staff work, and he wants a hell of a lot of it. Well, so what? Better to get all the answers before you need them, rather than not having the knowledge that you ought to have when you are put on the spot. I think that's what one should do."

When handing the reins to Caldwell upon his retirement, Henry II apologized for the company's poor condition. As Ford knew, North American automotive operations, traditionally the company's big breadwinner, had problems masked by the company's overall profitability. In 1979, thanks largely to Ford of Europe's fine performance, the firm reported earnings of $1.2 billion, third highest in its history. That same year, U.S. automotive operations posted a deficit of $1 billion, and the third and fourth quarters of 1979 were disastrous, with worse times to come.

The highly successful 1986 Ford Taurus, and related Mercury Sable, came about because Philip Caldwell was willing to risk funds for their development.

To resuscitate Ford, Caldwell focused on quality improvement, manufacturing and labor-cost reductions, and new-product development. Quality, long a stepchild, was made an integral part of the business, and by 1982 the company's new advertising slogan, "Quality Is Job One," was becoming believable.

Caldwell's biggest product gamble was the Taurus/Sable program. Although "aero" styling appeared on the redesigned 1979 Mustang and '83 Thunderbird, many considered it risky to apply it to the company's new flagship intermediate sedans. "Frankly," manufacturing executive Louis R. Ross recalled, "I wondered if I'd have had the guts to spend that much money [$3 billion] on our product program. He was betting the company." Added manufacturing executive John A. Betti, "He's the guy that had the [confidence] to make the decision to do the Taurus when we were deep in the red. . . . He's the guy who said that we've got to keep putting money into product, we can't cut back on product."

Executive vice president and director Thomas C. Page concurred. "I don't know of any gamble bigger than the Taurus/Sable program, and Caldwell firmly pushed it," he said. "He was willing to spend money at a time when the rest of us would have been willing to slide a year or two, conserve some cash, and upgrade the other cars." Caldwell was, however, simply living up to his credo: "For good ideas, we have unlimited resources. For bad ideas, we have none at all."

"When we started on the Taurus/Sable program," recalled design chief Jack J. Telnack, "Caldwell really pushed it. He said, 'Are you sure you're reaching far enough?' I couldn't believe him. None of us could believe him. We'd heard such questions before and thought this was just another top executive saying, 'I want to reach.' But when you really reach, they never buy it.

"But he said, 'Look, I'm serious. I really want us to make a strong statement and have our own unique identity on the road. How can you do that?'" Telnack replied, "'I'd like to show you.' And that's when we started developing Taurus and Sable."

The twin cars, introduced as '86 models from Ford and Mercury, were immediate hits. General Motors first disparaged their "jellybean" styling, then copied it.

Caldwell's reforms and product program took time to pay off (the Taurus and Sable contributed nothing to the bottom line during his tenure). Passenger-car market share fell from 23.6 percent in 1978 to 16.6 percent in 1981. The company lost $3.5 billion during 1980–82, and no dividends were paid in 1981–82, or the first half of 1983. "Maybe we're using slow-release fertilizer," Caldwell explained to critics, some of whom speculated that he was losing favor with Henry Ford II. Not so, insisted Henry II, whose faith in the chairman was vindicated by the company's splendid comeback. Car market share increased to 19.2 percent by 1984, and the company earned $1.8 billion in 1983 and a record $2.9 billion in 1984.

Almost everyone close to the scene credited Caldwell for the turnaround. "He really was a rock during that time," said future chairman Alex Trotman. Certainly Ford's outside directors were aware of Caldwell's fine work. For his 63rd birthday, they, with the Ford brothers, gave him an enlarged reproduction of the well-known painting "Washington Crossing the Delaware." Caldwell's head was superimposed over that of Washington's.

At age 65 in 1985, Caldwell was not ready for retirement. But retirement was mandatory, and the Caldwells moved from Bloomfield Hills, Michigan, to their Connecticut home, about 70 miles from New York City. He became a senior managing director of investment banker Shearson Lehman Brothers. A chair in manufacturing and technology was established in his honor at the Harvard Business School. In 1990, Caldwell was elected to the Automotive Hall of Fame.

Betsey Caldwell deserves a word. In Henry Ford II's view, she and her husband were a "man-and-wife team." Secretary Ruth Thomas described her as "absolutely the perfect mate for Mr. Caldwell because she knew the company came first. She never called me once to say, 'But when is he finally coming home?' She shared his job enthusiasm, conscientiousness, and dedication. . . . She was never a hindrance; she was always a support."

The Caldwells live quietly in New Canaan, enjoying the warmth and beauty of the 18th century American furniture they have collected through the years.

MERCURY

► . . . And then there were two. Slow sales would force the cancellation of the Grand Marquis coupe at the end of 1987, leaving only the wagon and sedan.

▲ With its once-severe roofline softened somewhat, Cougar emerged from refreshening sporting a somewhat subtler silhouette. Perhaps in keeping with Cougar's image of sleek refinement, the XR-7's raucous turbocharged engine was pulled, replaced by the otherwise-optional 150-horsepower V-8. XR-7 prices started at $15,660.

▲ Having earned "European Car of the Year" status in 1986, the sporty Scorpio seemed a sure bet for the U.S., but the newest Merkur almost failed to show at all. Slow sales of the companion XR4Ti stalled the sedan's American debut for more than a year. Scorpios started at $16,361, $1300 more than top-line showroom-mate Sable LS.

- Ford wins sales race with first-place Escort, third-place Taurus, and fifth-place Tempo

- Ford outearns General Motors for third straight year, takes in $5.3 billion

- New Continental is Taurus-based; has V-6 power, front-wheel drive

- Mercury goes it alone: loses Escort-clone Lynx, introduces Mazda-built subcompact Tracer

- Tempo reskinned to more closely resemble Taurus, gets new uplevel GLS model

- Ford cuts T-Bird Turbo Coupe, two-seat EXP at end of model year

- Topaz line freshened; gets XR5 and LTS models, loses GS Sport sedan

- Ford acquires majority stake in Hertz Rent-a-Car, creates Taurus-heavy rental fleet

FORD

▶ An aero-themed front-end freshening seemed at odds with the LTD Crown Victoria's still slab-sided flanks. Two-door models were now history, leaving only sedans and wagons to carry Ford's big-car banner. This LX started at $16,134. Two-tone paint added $117.

◀ The adoption of port fuel injection gave Thunderbird's standard 3.8-liter V-6 a 20-horsepower boost. Likewise, the optional 5.0-liter V-8 enjoyed a 15-horse supplement, courtesy of a new dual-exhaust system. This $16,030 Sport could be dressed up with aluminum wheels for $89.

▶ Additional torque was the big Taurus news for 1988. A newly available 3.8-liter V-6 was added to the options list, replacing the still-available 3.0-liter as top engine option. Though the new engine produced no additional horsepower, its 55 pound-feet of torque advantage over the 3.0-liter engine resulted in a substantially snappier Taurus. The wheels on this LX added $140.

► A midyear model change saw the GL badge pulled from the Escort lineup, replaced by the slightly more upscale LX series. Positioned like the departed GL, between the entry-level Pony and sporty GT, LXs accounted for most of total Escort sales. This LX three-door hatch started at $7127.

▲ Only one year past a freshening, Ford's performance-bargain Mustang rolled into 1988 virtually unchanged. This LX hatchback is equipped with the $1885 5.0-Liter V-8 Package, bringing its sticker to $11,106. A Preferred Equipment Package including air conditioning, tinted glass, and power windows brought the total to $11,713.

► Now port fuel injected, Mustang's 5.0-liter engine produced a healthy 225 horsepower. Producing most of its torque at fairly low rpm, the muscular V-8 was well-suited for the kind of stoplight racing enjoyed by Mustang enthusiasts.

◄ Previously available only as a single, standard model, Aerostar returned for '88 sporting three distinct trim levels. Previously packages, the XL and XLT badges were now the entry-level and midline models. A completely new Eddie Bauer edition topped the range, sporting additional equipment and Bauer-specific color combinations. This XLT started at $14,602.

▲ Ford's L-Series trucks topped out with the L9000 Aeromax. A class-8 tractor, the dual-axle L9000s were rated for loads in excess of 33,000 pounds. Cummins diesels were popular engine choices.

▲ Wedged between the ultrapopular F-Series pickups and chassis cabs, and the big over-the-road tractors, Ford's medium-duty L-Series trucks worked quietly, without fanfare. Commonly dressed for specific vocational tasks after purchase, these middle-weight Fords saw duty in jobs as diverse as fire truck and snowplow.

◄ A five-speed manual transmission and a Sport Equipment Package were new additions to the Bronco II résumé for 1988. Replacing the previously standard four-speed manual, the new five-speed transmission gave the little Bronco a small bump in highway mileage, now 24 mpg. The wheels, tires, and stripes on this truck were part of the $1213 Sport Appearance Package.

LINCOLN ▲ With half the cylinders and all the weight, the newest Continental seemed a mere shadow of its classic ancestor pictured here. In truth, the new Taurus-based Lincoln mustered 140 horsepower from its 3.8-liter V-6, 20 more than the vintage V-12 under the hood of this 1941. Continental prices started at $26,078.

▲ Lincoln's biggest car returned for 1988 sporting cleaner lines and new interior fabrics. A mild freshening helped smooth the best-selling Town Car's sharp edges, while new taillamps helped soften the rear view. Unchanged under the hood, a 5.0-liter V-8 remained the standard, and only, power option. This Signature Edition started at $26,179.

► A simplified lineup and a significant power infusion did wonders to boost sales of Lincoln's personal-luxury coupe. Now with 225 horsepower on tap, the newly fleet Mark VII rung up more than 38,000 sales, better than double 1987's total. Available in both the Bill Blass and LSC models, the 5.0-liter V-8 was a close cousin to the Mustang GT's powerplant. Both Mark models started at $25,016 with standard antilock brakes.

▲ Dressed in somber black, this Continental Signature Series was all-new for 1988. Based on Taurus architecture, the front-drive luxury sedan featured a Lincoln first: V-6 power. Though roughly the same size outside, the new Continental offered more interior space than its rear-drive predecessor. The Signature Series started at $26,078.

◄ Lincoln's sales leader, Town Car accounted for more than 70 percent of total sales. Stationed in the middle, this Signature Series was pricier than the standard Town Car, but less expensive than the top-line Cartier. Town Car competed most closely with Cadillac's Brougham, also V-8 powered and rear-wheel drive.

MERCURY

▼ ▶ As with Ford-twin LTD, Mercury's big car was given a more aerodynamic-looking fascia for the new year. The previously available two-door was history, leaving only sedan and wagon versions of the full-size Grand Marquis. Ford's ubiquitous 5.0-liter V-8 coupled to a four-speed automatic transmission was the only available powertrain option.

▶ Going it alone, Mercury abandoned the Escort-based Lynx in favor of the truly international Tracer. Based on the Australian Ford Laser, the Mexican-built Tracer used Mazda drivetrain components and was sold in the U.S. and Canada. The plucky subcompact was offered in hatchback and wagon versions.

▲ Tracer power came from an 82-horsepower Mazda-designed 1.6-liter four-cylinder engine. Slightly more frugal than the departed Lynx, a manual-transmission Tracer was rated at 35 mpg on the highway. With air conditioning and a three-speed automatic, the Tracer five-door hatchback pictured here would have stickered for $9901.

► A different grille and a boost in power topped the Topaz highlight list for 1988. GS and LS models now packed a 98-horsepower punch, a gain of 12. Higher-output XR5 and LTS engines gained only six horses, now boasting an even 100. Topaz prices started at $9166. A driver's-side airbag was an $815 option.

◄ Despite a spacious cabin, fuel-injected V-6, antilock four-wheel-disc brakes, and a Autobahn-bred suspension, Americans were shying away from Merkur's newest model in droves. Scorpio prices topped out at $27,063 including an automatic transmission, leather seats, power sunroof, and trip computer.

- Thunderbird again earns *Motor Trend* "Car of the Year" title

- Cougar redesigned too; XR7 is Mercury's version of supercharged T-Bird Super Coupe

- High-performance Taurus SHO debuts, features V-6 engine designed by Yamaha

- Ford launches Probe; sporty coupe jointly designed with Mazda

- Aerostar minivan available in roomier extended-wheelbase "stretch" models

- Ranger and Bronco II come in for modernizing facelifts

- Premium European Merkur brand fades; Scorpio and XR4Ti sold through end of 1989

- Ford purchases Britain's Jaguar for a reported $2.5 billion

FORD ▲ Prior to its mid-1988 debut, Ford product planners had meant for Probe to be the new Mustang. In sharp contrast, Probe's front-drive layout and four-cylinder power offered buyers a more Japanese interpretation of the sports coupe than the rear-drive, V-8 Mustang. Prices for Probe GTs like this one started at $13,794.

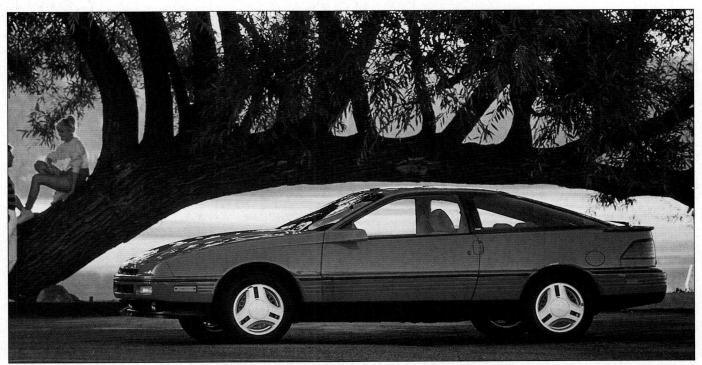

▲ Base GL- and midlevel LX-model Probes were powered by a Mazda-designed 2.2-liter four. A 145-horsepower turbocharged variant of the same engine was standard on GTs. Built alongside the similar Mazda MX-6, all Probes were assembled in Flat Rock, Michigan. Unique tuning gave the Probe and MX-6 distinct handling characteristics.

▲ Despite a nine-inch wheelbase stretch, the redesigned Thunderbird was actually more than three inches shorter than its predecessor. Base and LX models returned for 1989, joined by this sporty new supercharged Super Coupe. Powered by the standard 3.8-liter V-6, an LX started at $16,817. Antilock brakes added $1085.

► The cornering lamps on this base Thunderbird were part of a $1235 Popular Equipment Package. Standard and LX models accounted for the lion's share of T-Bird sales, finding 102,000 buyers. With its limited enthusiasts-only appeal, the pricey Super Coupe sold only 13,000 copies.

◄ With a V-8 engine missing from the options list, the 210-horsepower Super Coupe had sole claim to the Thunderbird performance crown. Sporting a supercharged version of the standard T-Bird's 3.8-liter V-6, manual-transmission SCs could reach 60 mph in as little as seven seconds. Super Coupe prices started at $19,823. Antilock brakes, aluminum wheels, and lower bodyside cladding were standard.

► Full-size Fords, like this $16,767 Crown Victoria LX sedan, saw little change after 1988's freshening. Technically imports, the Crown Victoria and sister-ship Grand Marquis were built at Ford's St. Thomas assembly plant in Ontario, Canada.

▲ With most of the attention on the racy 220-horsepower SHO sedan, other Taurus models went little changed for the new year. Minor styling tweaks were evident in the grille plate, headlamps, taillamps, and interior door panels. This $16,524 LX wagon came standard with a torquey 3.8-liter V-6. Production fell just shy of 400,000 in 1989.

► Destined to be Ford's second best-selling model for 1989, the subcompact Escort returned relatively unchanged for the new year. Pony and GT models were again available only in two-door hatchback form, while the LX added a wagon and four-door hatchback to its lineup. This LX wagon started at $8280. Optional air conditioning and an automatic transmission added $1103.

▲ Though released midyear 1964, the original Mustang was badged a '65. Ford acknowledged the anniversary of its ponycar's debut, but would hold off on a special package until 1990. The introduction of the Probe seemed to have little effect on Mustang sales, which held level at about 210,000. A flip-up sunroof was a $355 option.

▲ New Bronco II front-end styling provided the public with an excellent foreshadowing of the nearing Explorer. The junior Bronco's only engine was a 2.9-liter V-6, good for 140 horsepower. The two-tone paint, white-letter tires, and wheel trim rings on this truck were part of the XLT package that added $622 to its $14,704 base price.

▲ Ford's rear-drive minivan returned for 1989 sporting several significant changes. The original standard-wheelbase Aerostar, shown here in Eddie Bauer trim, was joined by a new extended-length body boasting 15 additional inches of legroom and cargo space. Other changes included a new grille and a larger fuel tank. Base price: $11,567.

► Ford's popular F-Series pickups received a number of minor changes for 1989. A switch to electronically controlled automatic transmissions meant less expressway "hunting" between gears. Two years from its most recent freshening, trim tweaks kept Ford's big pickup looking new. Optional on heavy-duty models, a 7.3-liter diesel provided extra torque for serious towing. A four-speed automatic transmission was now available on some models.

◄ With sales of the practical SuperCab on the rise, long-bed regular cab pickups like this one were becoming less common. This 4×4 started at $10,844. Equipped with the XLT package shown, a 5.8-liter V-8, and automatic transmission, the sticker rose to $14,020. Ford took the total truck sales title again in 1989.

► Like the rest of the truck line, Ford's big vans "cleaned up good." Dressed in XLT trim, this Club Wagon was ready to transport up to 12 passengers to Sunday services. As with other big Ford trucks, a four-speed manual was now available with some engines. A 145-horsepower 4.9-liter six was standard in E-150 and E-250 models.

LINCOLN

▶ Fresh from 1988's powertrain and trim upgrades, Lincoln's big coupe went unchanged for 1989. Sold "fully loaded," Mark VIIs were available with only a handful of stand-alone options. LSCs like this one had firmer suspensions and larger wheels and tires than the luxury-oriented Bill Blass.

◀ Looking much as it might under the hood of a Mustang, Lincoln did little to disguise the Mark VII's engine. Rated at 225 horsepower and an even 300 pound-feet of torque, the little 5.0-liter V-8 transformed Lincoln's personal-luxury car. Seemingly more at home under the hood of the sporty LSC, Bill Blass Editions came with the same engine, but wore smaller wheels and tires.

▲ All new for 1988, Continental returned little changed for the new year. Lincoln's only front-drive model, Continental also made exclusive use of a V-6 engine. After more than doubling for 1988, sales rose again in 1989 to nearly 58,000. This top-of-the-line Signature Series started at $29,334. A CD player was a $617 option.

MERCURY ▲ As with Ford-twin Thunderbird, Cougar was redesigned for 1989. Again available only in LS and sporty XR7 trim, Cougar sales slid slightly for 1989, to just over 80,000. Improvements in ride quality and noise reduction took their toll in weight. Mercury's new coupes were 200 pounds heavier than the '88s.

▲ Similar to Thunderbird's brash Super Coupe, the new Cougar XR7 enjoyed the thrust of a supercharged 3.8-liter V-6. With 210 horsepower on tap, the sportiest Cougar was capable of reaching 60 mph in just over seven seconds. Along with a sport-tuned suspension, XR7 came standard with antilock brakes and a Traction-Lok rear axle.

1990–1999

One Superpower

REAGAN-BUSH POLICY climaxed in 1991, when the Soviet Union collapsed and fragmented into loosely linked independent states, liberating itself (and the Eastern Bloc in Europe) from communism. Outspoken, hard-drinking Boris Yeltsin pulled Russia toward democracy and a free-market economy.

Bloody ethnic and tribal conflict swept across the former Yugoslavia and much of Africa. In the Middle East, a UN coalition led by the United States went to war with Iraq in 1991, following Iraq's invasion of Kuwait. The Iraqi military was crushed in less than a month, but dictator Saddam Hussein retained power.

The coalition victory was a great win for President George Bush, but a year later, voters felt he was out of touch. A young Arkansas Democrat, Bill Clinton, defeated Bush in the '92 presidential race, and easily won reelection in 1996.

In a developing "world economy," companies based overseas undercut American prices, and Ford was just one of many corporations to feel the hot breath of foreign competitors.

Unemployment was low, and the federal deficit nearly nonexistent during the Clinton years, but the president's personal behavior would bring his impeachment in 1998. He was not convicted.

1990

- Harold "Red" Poling replaces Donald E. Petersen as chairman

- Taurus ranks second in sales race, Accord claims top spot

- Ranger becomes best-selling compact pickup in America

- Bronco II replacement arrives midyear in form of all-new Explorer

- Lincoln introduces all-new Town Car

▶ Mustang convertibles offered a rare combination of top-down motoring, V-8 power, and an asking price below $20,000. In addition to the folding top, convertibles came with larger wheels and tires, and a rear-deck luggage rack. Just under 27,000 Mustang convertibles were produced in 1990.

FORD ▲ Mustang GT relied largely on additional exterior trim to justify its cost premium over bargain-priced LX 5.0 models. GTs and LX 5.0s shared the same V-8 engine, good for 225 horsepower. A five-speed manual transmission was standard, a four-speed automatic was a $539 option. GT prices started at $13,986.

◀ The LX 5.0 was the value leader of Mustang's performance lineup. Equipped with all the power of the GT, but with a sticker price as much as $1800 lower, LX 5.0 was the ideal car for gearheads on a budget. Unlike the GTs, the LX models were available in notchback and hatchback form. Fast for the money, V-8 Mustangs were among the least-expensive cars capable of finishing the quarter mile in under 15 seconds.

◄ With an all-new Escort on the way, changes to the existing line were few. Bolder looking than ever, this GT was an early '91 arrival. With a rev-happy twin-cam engine good for 127 horsepower, the little GTs had no problem reaching 60 mph in under nine seconds. Escort slipped to fourth in the annual sales race, giving the first-place spot to Honda's Accord.

► To honor the Thunderbird's 35th anniversary, Ford issued 500 commemorative editions based on the Super Coupe. All featured two-tone black and titanium paint, blue striping, and black wheels. The supercharged V-6 engine produced 210 horsepower.

▲ Though still popular, Ford's subcompact Escort line badly needed an overhaul. Relief would arrive midyear, when an all-new design would be introduced. A shortened selling season helped limit sales to just under 200,000. The LX four-door hatchback in the foreground was the most popular Escort, accounting for over 70,000 sales.

▲ Now the second most popular car in the land, Taurus soldiered into the new year with few changes. Wagons came with either a 3.0- or 3.8-liter V-6, both good for 140 bhp. Wagon prices started at $14,272.

▲ The Probe GT pictured here was again powered by a turbocharged 2.2-liter four. A 140-horsepower V-6 was added to the engine roster for exclusive use in midlevel LX models. Base GL hatchbacks started at $11,470.

◄ Though low on horsepower, Bronco's big base engine, a 4.9-liter six, provided sufficient torque for most situations. The majority of buyers opted for the available 5.0- and 5.8-liter V-8s, however. New this year was an optional electronically controlled four-speed automatic, replacing the old three-speed unit. Bronco prices started at $16,795, but could reach $24,000 when equipped with the Eddie Bauer Package.

► The popular Ranger received a welcome gift: more power. With its newly available 160-bhp, 4.0-liter V-6, Ranger could be quite the sprinter. Standard motivation came in the form of a 2.3-liter "Twin Plug" four, good for 100 horsepower. Rangers started at $7856.

▶ Despite hefty price increases, sales of the trim, Taurus-based Continental continued to rise. Stately elegance again took precedent over performance, as the only available engine produced a middling 140 horsepower. Prices started at $29,258; the uplevel Signature Series seen here began at $31,181.

▲ Lincoln's biggest car was also its best-seller. A major redesign smoothed the previous Town Car's sharp creases, producing a shape that would soon become a favorite of limousine drivers everywhere. Nearly 130,000 were sold, with prices starting at $27,315.

▲ Available in designer Bill Blass and performance LSC versions, Lincoln's personal-luxury Mark VII returned for 1990 almost unchanged. The BBS alloy wheels on the LSC pictured here were now standard. Sales continued to slide, reaching just 22,313. All Marks were snappy performers, enjoying the same 225-horsepower 5.0-liter V-8.

MERCURY ▲ This was an awkward year for Mercury's plucky, Mazda-sourced Tracer. Slow sales and passive-safety-equipment requirements prompted the decision to skip the 1990 model year completely. Leftover 1989s, like the one shown here, were sold well into the new year. A new Escort-based car was waiting for 1991.

► Ford's most international car made its debut in 1990 wearing Mercury clothes. Based on Mazda mechanicals, the Capri was built in Australia for sale in the U.S. Unlike the Miata, the little Capri was a front-drive four-seater.

◄ Taurus-twin Sable was still a strong seller, but down about 30,000 from last year's record numbers. Antilock brakes were now available as a $985 option. Buyers had a choice of two 140-horsepower V-6 engines, a 3.0 and a 3.8, the latter of which provided substantially more torque. The LS wagon was the most-expensive Sable, starting at $16,789.

▲ The compact Topaz entered its third year little changed. Shown here in coupe form, the Topaz line also included Mercury's least-expensive sedan. The only engine offered was a 2.3-liter four. All-wheel drive was offered as a $1466 option; a driver-side airbag cost $815 extra. The base GS started at $10,027.

▲ Though Grand Marquis looked the same, much was new under the skin. Inside, updates included a revised dashboard, new rear shoulder belts, a standard tilt steering wheel, and a driver-side airbag. As with most of the Mercury line, prices were up and sales were down. A base GS sedan was now $17,633, up $932 from a year ago.

1991

- All-new Escort debuts; sales exceed 300,000

- Escort-based Tracer replaces Mazda-built model in Mercury lineup

- Thunderbird and Cougar now available with 5.0-liter V-8

- Five of top-10-selling cars in America are now Ford products

- F-Series trucks rank first in sales for tenth consecutive year

- Big Bronco celebrates 25 years with Silver Anniversary Edition

FORD ▲ The Mazda MX-6-based Probe carried over into the new year largely unchanged. Probe buyers were treated to an interesting selection of trim-level-specific engine choices. GLs came with an economical 110-horsepower four, LXs a torquey 145-horsepower six, and GTs a free-revving 145-horsepower turbocharged four.

▶ Leapfrogging its existing engines, Ford introduced a new overhead-cam V-8 to sit under the hoods of its big cars. The 4.6-liter engine was significantly smoother and more economical than the engines it replaced. The powerplant would serve as a foundation for a family of new engines.

◀ Supercharging was the most significant component of the aggressively styled Thunderbird Super Coupe. The T-Bird's pumped-up six was good for an impressive 210 horsepower and 315 pound-feet of torque. A five-speed manual was standard. The 3600-pound coupe was surprisingly agile for its size and heft. Price: $20,999.

◄ A more powerful base engine and a few safety upgrades led the list of changes to the Mustang lineup. Base cars now came with the same "twin plug" engine as did Ranger, bumping standard horsepower to 105, a jump of 17. This Mustang GT sports new 16-inch wheels, replacing the previous 15 inchers. GTs started at $15,034, a $1048 jump.

▲ For almost $1000 less, this LX 5.0 offered all the GT's V-8 muscle without the added trim. Crosstown rival Chevrolet Camaro dropped its IROC models, reinstating the Z28 badge after a two-year hiatus.

▲ Though perceived by many as cheap looking, Mustang's interior was clean and functional. The manual shifter's goose-neck bend took some getting use to. For an extra $489, V-8 models could be spruced up with leather interior trim.

► For the budget minded looking for a good time, the Mustang LX 5.0 convertible was without rival. Starting at $19,242, the open-air V-8 Mustangs offered serious go for relatively little cash. Combined Mustang sales were down for the year, falling just short of 100,000. Ford's sporty front-wheel-drive Probe sold nearly as well, reaching almost 94,000.

▲ Ford worked with Mazda on the redesigned '91 Escort, which gained four inches in wheelbase, to 98.4. The standard 1.9-liter, 88-bhp four was carried over; GTs got a Mazda-built twincam 1.8-liter with 127 bhp.

▲ Escort adopted Ford's aero styling theme and was offered in three body styles: two-door hatchback, four-door hatchback, and four-door wagon. Base prices ran from $7976 for the two-door to $9680 for the wagon.

▲ This was one of Ford's last full-size wagons. An aerodynamic, redesigned Crown Victoria would arrive midyear in sedan form only. Prices for this last-of-the-breed Country Squire LX started at $19,085.

▲ Attempting to stretch the meaning of the word as far is it might go, Ford added a "Sport" appearance package to the Aerostar options list. The $1285 option included aero-look body cladding and bodyside stripes.

▲ Ford's work-ready F-Series lineup included three cab sizes to suit individual needs. The standard "regular cab" included a single bench or two bucket seats. SuperCabs added interior storage or short-distance seating for additional occupants. CrewCabs added a second pair of doors and a full-size bench seat. F-Series prices started at $10,455.

▲ Shown here in top-of-the-line Eddie Bauer trim, the new Explorer redefined the sport-utility segment and quickly became a sales leader. Two-wheel-drive prices started at $15,406, four-wheelers at $17,219.

▲ Two-door Explorers came in XL, Sport, and Eddie Bauer trim levels. This Sport carried a base price of $17,255 with four-wheel drive. All Explorers were powered by the same 155-horsepower 4.0-liter V-6 engine.

LINCOLN

▶ As sales continued to fall, Lincoln erased all functional differences between its Mark VII models. The LSC's sporty suspension and aggressive wheel-and-tire package were now standard on Bill Blass coupes as well, making the cars mechanically identical. For $74 over the cost of a Bill Blass, LSC buyers got fog lights, sport seats, and analog instruments.

▲ Mark VII LSCs got sporty, articulated bucket seats and an analog dashboard. With 225 horsepower on tap, the sportiest Lincoln could move with authority.

▲ The big Town Car news this year was under the hood. Gone was the old pushrod engine once shared with Mustang, replaced by a new 190-horsepower 4.6-liter overhead-cam V-8. The new engine was both stronger and quieter, and as a bonus, used less fuel.

◄ The all-new Tracer shared major mechanical parts with Ford's hot-selling Escort. Tracer was now available in base sedan and wagon trim, as well as sporty LTS sedan guise. The standard 1.9-liter engine produced 88 horsepower and helped Tracer return almost 30 mpg in the city.

► Less popular than its sedan stablemates, the Tracer wagon accounted for fewer than 14,000 sales. Wagon prices started at $10,407. Not yet available with airbags, Escort and Tracer buyers were forced to contend with motorized shoulder-belt "mice" that ran along the door frames and pulled belts snug across front-seat occupants.

◄ The front-wheel-drive Capri convertible returned this year unchanged. Though the base Capri shown here was available with an optional four-speed automatic transmission, the sporty XR2 models came only with the standard five-speed manual.

► This Capri's decklid spoiler tags it as an XR2. Cold-climate driving was made more palatable with the addition of the $1224 hardtop shown here. All Capris came with a driver-side airbag and disc brakes.

► Though a pricey option, Cougar's newly available V-8 transformed the car from a luxury commuter to a sporty GT. With the required Luxury Trim Package, the V-8 added almost $1900 to the Cougar LS's $15,629 base price. The 200-horsepower V-8 was now standard in XR7 models, replacing the super-charged V-6. A four-speed automatic transmission and bucket seats were standard on all Cougars. Antilock brakes were a $985 option.

◄ Biding time until a 1992 redesign, Mercury's Grand Marquis returned unchanged. Available only with a 150-horse-power V-8, the Big Merc was a fairly motivated performer. Sedans came in GS and LS trim lev-els. Grand Marquis sales reached 82,000 for 1991.

► The big Colony Park was a dead man walking. Next year's redesign of the big Mercurys would not include wagons, or wood-look appliqué. Wagon prices started at $18,918 but climbed quickly as options were added. Wagons accounted for less than four percent of all Grand Marquis sales.

- Taurus edges past Accord for nation's top-seller honors

- Crown Victoria and Grand Marquis undergo aero-themed redesign

- Passenger airbags now in Taurus, Sable, Crown Vic, Marquis

- Tempo and Topaz now available with optional 3.0-liter V-6

- Taurus four cylinder disappears, V-6 now standard engine

- Full-size Ford vans receive first major restyle since 1975

- Average domestic car now sells for $17,070

FORD ▲ A new Sport option package for the Probe LX coupe closely echoed the GT's appearance, including its 15-inch aluminum wheels. To keep prices down, formerly standard tinted glass and power mirrors were moved to the options column. Probe LX now carried a base price of $13,257, up only $28 from 1991.

▲ The Crown Victoria Touring Sedan was part of Ford's newly redesigned big-car lineup. With the new look came a new engine, a 4.6-liter overhead-cam V-8 shared with Lincoln's Town Car. An optional dual-exhaust system lifted horsepower from 190 to 210. Touring Sedan models came with antilock brakes and traction control.

▲ While a 3.0-liter V-6 was standard in Taurus sedans, wagons came with the added torque of a 3.8. Like the sedans, wagons came in base L, midrange GL, and uplevel LX trim levels. A major restyle stretched the Taurus three inches outside and made room for an optional passenger airbag inside. Wagon prices started at $16,013.

► The previously standard 2.5-liter four-cylinder engine was gone from the Taurus sedan roster, replaced by a 3.0-liter V-6. Sedans started at $14,980. Safety seekers could add the passenger-side airbag for $488, and the antilock brakes for $985. Buyers drove home nearly 370,000 Tauruses, making it the nation's best-selling car.

◄ Not for U.S. consumption: The all-new midsize Mondeo was about to take Europe by storm. The GLX sedan pictured here was available with five different engines including a 1.8-liter turbocharged diesel. A later Mondeo would be the basis for the American-market Ford Contour and Mercury Mystique.

▶ A lack of sophistication was offset by Tempo's modest prices. Always a top seller, the bargain-priced compact returned this year with a new V-6 option, but without all-wheel drive. The 3.0-liter six borrowed from the Taurus produced 135 horsepower in Tempo form, enough to give it snappy acceleration. This high-line LX four-door started at $11,115.

◀ A discreet fender badge was the only visual cue identifying this Tempo as member of the V-6 club. The six-cylinder engine added $685 to the $12,652 base price of this two-door GLS. Four-door Tempo sales exceeded 300,000 for 1992, more than three times the number of two-doors sold. This would be the last year any Tempo model would fall under the magic $10,000 line.

▶ A bold restyling gave Ford's big F-Series trucks a purposeful, aerodynamic look. The annual sales race with Chevrolet was close, but the Blue Oval crowd nudged the Bow Tie boys by just 8000 trucks. Though a six-cylinder engine was standard, one diesel and three gasoline V-8s were available. A price-leader S model anchored the line, starting at $10,336.

▲ Few changes marked the sophomore year of Ford's hot-selling Explorer. Promptly rising to the head of the sales class, dealerships found themselves with more buyers than trucks. Mazda dealers were able to get in on the action, selling rebadged two-door Explorers as Navajos. This four-wheel-drive Eddie Bauer two-door started at $21,918.

◄ Ford's midsize Aerostar was offered in passenger and cargo versions. Power came from either a 3.0- or 4.0-liter V-6, good for 145 or 155 horsepower, respectively. Though prices started low, they could climb quickly. This extended all-wheel-drive Eddie Bauer was the priciest Aerostar, starting at $24,384.

▶ A fresh face was part of the first full-size van restyle since 1975. Interiors were spruced up as well, making room for the line's first driver-side airbag. Club Wagon passenger versions with a six-cylinder engine started out at $16,740. Econoline cargo models priced from $14,960.

LINCOLN

▶ The man and his namesake: Golf legend Jack Nicklaus poses with a limited-edition Town Car that was named for him. Mechanically identical to lesser TCs, the Nicklaus edition featured a simulated convertible top, custom bodyside striping, gold trim, and special badges. Born for the job, the Town Car's 22-cubic-foot trunk could manage a foursome's clubs.

▲ The sun was setting on the Mark VII which returned this year unchanged. Though dated, the big coupe was hip enough to offer an optional CD player for $299.

▲ Airbags were now standard for both front occupants in the 1992 Continental sedan. This well-equipped Signature Series sedan carried a base price of $34,253.

MERCURY

◀ Selling about half as well as its Thunderbird cousin, Cougar rolled into its 25th season little changed. A midyear anniversary edition would include trim upgrades and special badges. This XR7 came standard with a 200-horsepower V-8. Also standard on XR7s were antilock brakes that were otherwise a $985 option.

◀ Living in the shadow of the more popular Taurus, Mercury's Sable offered the same utility in slightly nicer trappings. This LS wagon now included a passenger-side airbag. All Sables came with four-speed automatic transmission coupled to either a 3.0- or 3.8-liter V-6 engine. Slightly less than 140,000 Sables found new homes in 1992, roughly one third the number of Tauruses sold during the same period.

▶ Introduced early in 1991 as a '92 model, the Grand Marquis was technically still in its first year. Apart from the midseason addition of a passenger-side airbag, the big Mercury was unchanged. The $1952 Handing and Performance Package spiced things up a bit, adding a sport suspension and dual exhausts. Base price for this LS: $20,644.

▲ A Tempo by any other name, Topaz was Mercury's entry into the compact arena. Topaz buyers could now opt for the same V-6 engine found on Tempo. The V-6 and a sport suspension were standard on this XR5.

▲ A little car with big luxury, the top-of-the-line Topaz LTS returned this year with a standard V-6 engine. For $14,244, LTS buyers also got a leather-wrapped steering wheel, sport suspension, and an upgraded stereo.

1993

- Freshened Probe picks up new V-6, earns enthusiasts' praise

- Redesigned Lincoln Mark VIII features 32-valve V-8 engine

- Special Vehicle Team issues Mustang Cobra, F-150 Lightning

- Escort and Tracer receive subtle facelifts

- Slow-selling Crown Victoria Touring Sedan dropped from lineup

- Alex Trotman named chairman and CEO

FORD ▲ A sloping windshield and hidden rear-roof pillars were features of a complete redesign of the sporty, front-wheel-drive Probe. As with the last generation, Probe was designed in conjunction with Mazda, which offered the similar MX-6 through its own dealerships. The new Probe was introduced at the Detroit auto show.

◄ The racy Probe GT replaced its raucous turbocharged four with a free-revving 24-valve V-6. The new 2.5-liter engine produced 164 horsepower, a bump of 19 over the outgoing turbo. Base Probes made do with a 114-horsepower 2.0-liter four. Probe GTs started at $15,174, a $317 bump over the previous model.

▲ Built by Kia of Korea, Ford's tiny Festiva was the answer to a question few Americans seemed to be asking. Despite a $6914 price of entry, sales were slow. This car's $366 sport package didn't make it faster.

▲ A freshened front end and revised trim were the big changes to the popular Escort line for 1993. This GT came with low-mounted fog lights and spunky 1.8-liter dual-overhead-cam engine. Escorts started at $8355.

◄ Though the Mustang GT shown here was down 20 horsepower for the new year, a new Cobra model gained that and 15 more. Going out with a bang, the special-edition Cobra commemorated this generation Mustang's last year with special trim and a performance bump. GT coupes proved to be rare, with buyers opting for the less-costly LX 5.0s.

► Though the new Cobra was available in coupe form only, other V-8 Mustangs were open to going roofless. This LX 5.0 carried a sticker price of $20,293, plus options. Though down 20 horsepower on paper, the V-8s felt little different in actual use. The following year's redesigned lineup would not include the budget-priced LX V-8s.

◄ In a bow to convention, the Crown Victoria added a traditional grille to its rakish front end. Other changes included the addition of cup holders and the deletion of the unloved Touring Sedan. Prices started at $19,972.

► Lineup trimming left the Thunderbird with only LX and Super Coupe models. Some content shuffling helped the newly base LX wear an entry-level price tag, now just $15,797, a $2800 drop from 1992.

▲ The heavy-breathing Taurus SHO enjoyed the use of a 24-valve V-6 with Yamaha-designed cylinder heads. Quick for the day, the slick SHOs could reach 60 mph in under eight seconds. Prices started at $24,829.

▲ Changes were minimal to the popular midsize Taurus line. The optional antilock brakes were now almost $400 less expensive, adding only $595 to the sticker. The base GL sedan now started at $15,491.

▲ Ranger was given the corporate "aero" look in a complete redesign. SuperCabs again offered center-facing rear seats. Top engine option was a 4.0-liter V-6.

▲ Introduced midyear was the sporty Splash, with monotone trim and the first fenderside bed on a compact pickup. Two- and four-wheel drive were offered.

▲ Still the king of the SUV hill, Explorer was finally available with four-wheel antilock brakes. Though otherwise unchanged, buyers snapped up nearly 330,000 of the roomy, rugged-looking Fords. This four-wheel-drive Eddie Bauer four-door started at $24,066.

▲ More than just a pretty face, the blacked-out F-150 Lightning packed a respectable 240-horsepower punch. Available only in standard-cab form, the Lightning package included a lowered suspension and huge tires on unique alloy wheels. Only 10,000 were built.

LINCOLN ▲ Adding I to the storied line made the new Mark an VIII. Still a big, rear-drive, personal-luxury coupe, the new Mark was otherwise completely new. Wearing modern clothes, Lincoln's big two-door was better prepared to do battle with the Cadillac Eldorado and popular Lexus SC 300/400 cars.

▲ Vestiges of the Continental spare-tire "bump" survived the redesign, though the tire itself was long gone. Available only in a single trim level, the new Mark started at $36,640. A center-console-mounted cellular telephone added another $706.

▶ While naming engines was becoming fashionable, the Mark VIII's Intech V-8 was well worth the special attention. The 32-valve, 280-horsepower mill was capable of launching the big Lincoln to 60 mph in less than seven seconds.

▲ The straight lines and boxy dash elements of the Mark VII gave way to the gentle contours of the VIII's new interior. Considered stark by some, later versions of the cabin would feature liberal doses of wood and wood-look trim. Brightening up the interior was as easy as adding the optional $1550 power moonroof.

▲ Strikingly different in design, and no longer wearing a Continental badge, the new Mark VIII had little in common with the Mark II in the background. With roughly 36,000 1993s in the hands of buyers, sales of the new Mark were tepid by contemporary standards, but still strong enough to handily trump the Mark II's two-year total of 3000.

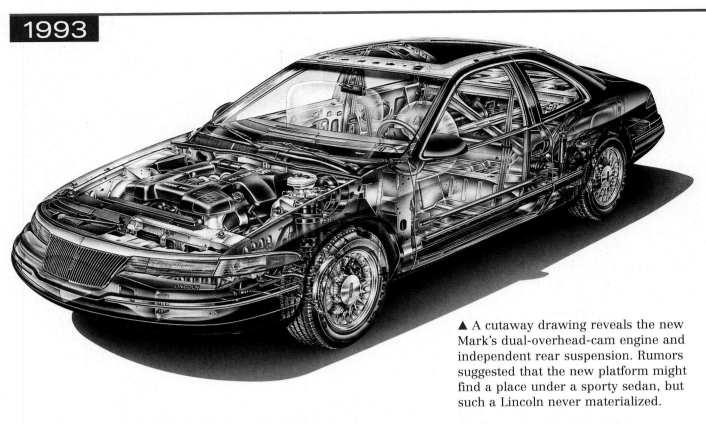

▲ A cutaway drawing reveals the new Mark's dual-overhead-cam engine and independent rear suspension. Rumors suggested that the new platform might find a place under a sporty sedan, but such a Lincoln never materialized.

▶ The addition of an overdrive-lockout button was the big news for Lincoln's biggest car in 1993. Base prices now ranged from $34,190 for the Executive to $37,581 for the high-zoot Cartier. Aspiring limousine drivers could add the livery package for only $417.

MERCURY ▲ The new front-drive Villager minivan shared its design with Nissan's Quest, and could seat up to seven. A 150-bhp, 3.0-liter V-6 was the only engine offered. The LS came with standard air conditioning and a two-tone paint treatment.

▲ This Villager concept vehicle that appeared at auto shows was a near clone of the Nautica edition that would appear for '94. Named for the sportswear manufacturer, Nautica was designed to tempt brand-conscious high-end buyers.

▲ Luxury seekers were well-served by the Sable's $515 leather seating option. Adding the leather-wrapped steering wheel raised the tab another $96.

▲ The previously optional passenger-side airbag was now standard for Sable. Otherwise, Mercury's Taurus twin soldiered on with a pair of available V-6 engines and two trim levels. This LS is shod with the $270 aluminum wheels.

▲ Ford experimented with a one-price "no dicker sticker" on some Tracer models. This sedan, when equipped with an automatic transmission and air conditioning, listed at $11,665 including destination.

▲ Mercury's big car now came with a standard passenger-side airbag. Like the big Lincolns of the Seventies, it could be equipped with "Twin Comfort Lounge" seats.

▲ Like the sedan, Tracer wagon also came in one-price trim. For the "no dicker" price of $11,665, buyers got an automatic transmission and air conditioning.

▶ A hefty price cut and an all-XR7 lineup helped prop up Cougar's sagging sales. The now-base XR7 was $1600 cheaper than the previous LS, but the standard V-8 had become an option. Value-hungry buyers grabbed up more than 80,000 Cougars, 30,000 more than in '92.

1994

- Mustang gets new body, but mechanical parts are carried over; Cobra convertible paces Indianapolis 500

- Ford Aspire replaces mini Festiva; it is also tiny and built in Korea

- Slow-selling Capri enters last year, receives only minor changes

- Continental undergoes mild freshening; leather upholstery is standard

- Automakers begin phaseout of R-12 Freon in favor or environmentally friendlier R-134A

FORD ▲ Receiving its first major redesign since 1979, the new Mustang employed a number of styling cues borrowed from the 1965 original. Notable among them were the side air scoops, three-element taillights, and galloping-pony logo. The former LX trim level was gone, replaced by an unnamed standard model.

◀ The Mustang Cobra returned wearing feisty new sheetmetal and boasting five additional horsepower. Other Cobra features included standard antilock brakes, 17-inch wheels and tires, and unique trim.

▲ Though the Mustang looked new from the outside, the platform underneath was little changed. Base Mustangs now came with a 145-horsepower V-6.

► With the Mustang's new clothes came additional equipment—and higher prices. Base cars started at $13,365, a healthy $2646 increase over the last generation's standard LX model. Gone, however, was the base car's Pinto-sourced four-cylinder engine, replaced by a smoother, quieter, 3.8-liter V-6. Potentially larger monthly payments didn't keep buyers away, as almost 140,000 lined up to drive the new ponycars home.

▲ Putting the pony back on the ponycar, the galloping logo returned to grilles across the line after an exclusive tour-of-duty on the front of the '93 Cobra.

▲ Available in several less-than-discreet colors, the new Mustangs certainly demanded attention. This GT convertible started at $21,970 and boasted 215 horsepower from its 5.0-liter V-8. A preferred equipment package and antilock brakes raised the tab to almost $24,000.

◄ A pricey option, the $1545 convertible hardtop was passed over by most shoppers. Ragtop sales were strong however, accounting for more than a third of total Mustang sales. This six-cylinder convertible with the hardtop listed for $21,705.

▶ With the spotlight on Mustang, Probe carried over into 1994 largely without alteration. A passenger-side airbag was now standard and prices were up slightly. This GT coupe started at $16,015. Selecting an automatic transmission would have added $790.

◀ Wagons accounted for roughly 20 percent of all Taurus sales. This LX came with a 3.8-liter V-6 similar to that found in Mustang. Equipped with antilock brakes and a popular equipment package, this wagon listed for about $22,000.

◀ Still charging hard, Taurus clung to its top-seller title for the third year running. Little-changed for the new year, Taurus continued to lure buyers with practical dimensions and reasonable prices. Sedans like this one accounted for 239,000 of the 311,000 Tauruses sold in 1994.

▶ For buyers reluctant to embrace the Taurus's front-wheel-drive layout and modern silhouette, Crown Victoria was a logical alternative. Though not nearly as popular as Taurus, almost 110,000 buyers opted for the big Vic's traditional six-passenger cabin and standard V-8 power.

◄ Introduced in mid 1994 as a 1995 model, the Windstar (foreground) was Ford's first front-drive entry into the exploding minivan market. Powered by a 155-horsepower, 3.8-liter V-6, Windstar was a direct competitor for Chrysler Corporation's immensely popular Dodge Caravan and Plymouth Voyager offerings. Ford's other van offerings included the rear-wheel-drive Aerostar (left), the Nissan-designed Mercury Villager (right), and Ford's full-size Club Wagon. Windstar prices started at $19,455.

▲ Ford's F-Series pickups had been the best-selling vehicles in America since the early Eighties, and that streak continued for 1994. This four-wheel-drive XLT Supercab started at around $19,000 with a V-8.

▲ The Explorer saw only minor changes for the new year, but continued to rack up huge sales numbers. Almost 400,000 buyers made it America's most popular sport-utility vehicle. Four-door base price: $18,130.

LINCOLN

◄ Launched a half year early, the freshened '94 Continental sported a smoother-looking front end and standard leather upholstery. A well-equipped Signature Series neared $40,000.

► The previously optional dual-exhaust system was now standard, giving Lincoln's Town Car an additional 20 standard horsepower. A $215 Traction Assist system helped launch the big Lincoln in slippery conditions. The top-of-the-line Cartier Designer Series was up $519, to $38,100.

► The once-Spartan interior of the Mark VIII was now accented with real wood trim. Also new was a keyless entry system that recalled individual drivers' power seat and mirror settings. Sales fell however, down 5000 from 1993, to 28,000.

◄ Though prices started at less than $39,000, a Mark VIII equipped with a power moonroof, chrome wheels, and an upgraded sound system neared $43,000. Steep prices may have been one reason Lincoln sold nearly five times as many Town Cars as Mark VIIIs.

MERCURY

◄ Grand Marquis managed to do something in 1994 that no other Mercury could hope to achieve: sell virtually as well as its mechanical twin at Ford. Mercury moved 108,000 of its big sedans this year, only 1600 fewer than the total of Crown Victorias sold.

◄ Only minor cosmetic changes marked the 1994 edition of Mercury's slow-selling convertible. Now in its last year, the Mazda-based ragtop failed to generate the kind of showroom traffic Mercury had hoped for. Mid-1993 price cuts lowered the cost of the sporty XR2 by $2200, but didn't boost sales.

► Fresh from its 1993 value-price adjustment, Cougar entered the new year almost unchanged. Prices rose moderately, but Cougar still cost less than it did in 1992. Sales dipped slightly, down about 5500 to near 76,000.

◄ While the Cougar's standard V-6 went unchanged, the formerly optional overhead-valve V-8 was bumped in favor of the modern overhead-cam engine powering the Marquis. The new 4.6-liter V-8 was smaller than the engine it replaced, but its 205 bhp were five more than before.

▲ Again in 1994, Sable edged out big-brother Grand Marquis for the title of best-selling Mercury. Though only a fraction of Taurus's numbers, Sable's 116,000 sales beat Marquis by 8000.

▲ Tracer's experimental "no dicker sticker" pricing policy returned for 1994, but didn't seem to help sales much. Despite the "no-haggle" price of $11,665 with an automatic transmission and air conditioning, only 46,000 buyers opted for the little Tracer. Not included in the no-dicker program was the sporty LTS sedan, which started at $12,560.

- Europe's Mondeo becomes America's Contour and Mystique

- The new Mondeo-based cars replace dated Tempo and Topaz

- Restyled Explorer gets new instrument panel, passenger-side airbag

- Despite a strong showing by Accord, Taurus remains top-selling car

- Ford sells 2 million trucks, wrests sales title from combined General Motors brands for first time since 1970

- Trucks now account for 49 percent of Big Three vehicle production

FORD ▲ Europe's popular Ford Mondeo was now America's Ford Contour. Replacing the aged Tempo, the modern compact featured a MacPherson strut suspension, multivalve engines, and four-wheel disc brakes. Similar to Contour, Mystique replaced the Topaz in Mercury's lineup. The base Contour GL started at $13,310.

▲ A Ford wearing the FFV (Flexible Fuel Vehicle) badge was equipped to burn fuel with an alcohol content as high as 85 percent. Popular in agricultural regions, FFVs were designed to run cleaner and use less petroleum than standard vehicles.

▲ Though not quite as popular as big-brother Taurus, subcompact Escort sales exceeded 300,000 for the third consecutive year. Base and LX models were available only with an 88-horsepower four, while GTs came with a dual-overhead-cam 1.8-liter engine good for 127 horsepower. Like the Mercury Tracer, Escort was again available with high-value "one-price" packages, "eliminating the haggling that can make car buying unpleasant." A one-price LX sedan or wagon listed for $12,810.

▶ For its final year of the current design, Taurus returned little changed. Pictured here is an LX sedan (left), an LX wagon (center), and a sporty SHO sedan (right). Sales of 395,000 kept Taurus the nation's number-one-selling car, just ahead of Honda's Accord.

◄ The recently restyled Mustang was little changed for the new year. A value-priced V-8 GTS model debuted midyear but sold poorly, and failed to reappear for '96. This 215-horsepower GT started out at $17,905.

▲ Rare and race ready, this limited-edition Cobra R was designed for the track. Replacing the standard Cobra's 240-horsepower engine with a 300-horse, 5.4-liter unit, Rs covered the quarter mile in 13.5 seconds and reportedly reached 151 mph. Just 252 were made.

▲ Mustang's value leader was the base coupe. Starting out at $14,330, the entry-level Mustang's 145-bhp six was strong enough for buyers looking for style over substance. For an additional $670, the Mach audio system added an equalizer and 460 watts of power.

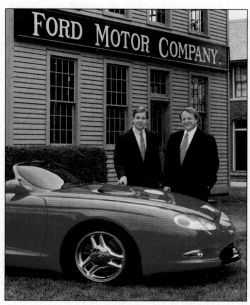

▲ Ford scions Bill Ford Jr. (left), Edsel Ford II, and the Mach III show car. The building replicates the first Ford plant.

▲ Early Thunderbird designers Alden "Gib" Giberson (left) and William Boyer (center) pose with Ford's then-current vice president of design, Jack Telnack. Suggesting that it "sounded strong," Giberson is commonly credited with being the source of the Thunderbird name.

▲ Taurus (left) never caught on for police or taxi use. The Crown Victoria (right) however, battled with Chevrolet's Caprice for the allegiance of departments across the county. Though the CV was not an especially swift pursuit vehicle, its roomy interior and rugged body-on-frame chassis were popular with the law-enforcement community.

▼ A fresh face and a new dashboard topped the list of changes to the Explorer line. Base prices ranged from $18,895 for the two-wheel-drive XL two-door, to $33,395 for the four-door Limited with four-wheel drive.

▲ Clearly pleased, racing giant A. J. Foyt gives his approval to the GT-90 concept car. A modern interpretation of Ford's popular GT-40 race car of the Sixties (in which Foyt competed), the new GT sported fresh angular styling and a quad-turbocharged V-12 engine. Performance claims for the GT-90 included reaching 60 mph in just 3.1 seconds.

◄ Windstar rolled into its first full year on the market unchanged. Midyear, a 3.0-liter V-6 replaced the 3.8-liter engine as standard on GL models. Unlike Chrysler's minivans that came in long and short versions, all Windstars rode the same wheelbase.

LINCOLN

▼ Town Car's new adjustable-steering system allowed drivers to select the steering-effort level that suited them best. A redesigned front end help smooth the big Lincoln's looks. The top-rung Cartier Designer Series started at $41,200.

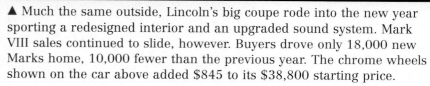

▲ Much the same outside, Lincoln's big coupe rode into the new year sporting a redesigned interior and an upgraded sound system. Mark VIII sales continued to slide, however. Buyers drove only 18,000 new Marks home, 10,000 fewer than the previous year. The chrome wheels shown on the car above added $845 to its $38,800 starting price.

▶ Though still front-wheel drive, Continental no longer shared its platform with the midmarket Taurus. Borrowing the Mark VIII's twincam V-8 engine, the 260-horsepower Continental easily outperformed its V-6 predecessor. Prices rose steeply, now starting at $40,750, a $5150 increase over the previous year's Signature Series model.

▲ ▶ With its softly sculpted lines, the new Continental's interior had a more organic feel than that of the previous model. A cutaway drawing reveals the sedan's transverse-mounted 4.6-liter V-8 and its front-wheel-drive layout.

◄ Taking a breather before its upcoming redesign, the Sable family rolled into 1995 much the same as last year. Though aged, the Sable line continued to be a strong seller, accounting for more than a third of combined Mercury sales.

► Making a single-year stop on top of Sable's model roster was this fully equipped LTS. Available in sedan form only, LTS came with unique bodyside cladding and wheels, leather seating, and a host of otherwise optional items. At $21,715, the LTS cost $1245 more than an LS.

◄ A new grille and redesigned headlamps helped clean up the Grand Marquis' appearance for the new year. New Special Value editions added features for little or no additional cost. A GS Special Value started out at $20,990, $340 less than 1994's GS.

► At $16,860, Cougar seemed like a bargain, but the standard V-6 wasn't quite up to the task of propelling the heavy coupe. The available 4.6-liter V-8 added a hefty $1130 to the tab, but was well worth considering. Cougar sales slipped again, now just topping the 60,000 mark.

◄ As with Ford's Contour, Mercury's new Mystique was based on the European-market Ford Mondeo. The front-wheel-drive compact was a welcome replacement for the tired and unloved Topaz line. Contour and Mystique rode a 106.5 inch wheelbase. Production of the Mercury version came to 66,742 cars—about 112,000 behind the Contour total.

▲ The sedan-only Mystique came in GS and uplevel LS trim. Power came from either the "Zetec" 2.0-liter four, or the "Duratec" 2.5-liter V-6. The LS pictured here started life at $15,230, but equipped with a popular equipment group, V-6 engine, antilock brakes, and an automatic transmission, it would have cost around $19,000.

◄ The addition of a new model was the big news for Mercury's minivan lineup. The new $25,305 Nautica edition topped the Villager roster by adding exclusive exterior trim and wheels, leather upholstery, and a Nautica-brand duffel bag. The pictured LS started at $23,825 and came with aluminum wheels, contrasting lower-body trim, and a luggage rack.

1996

- Taurus and Sable receive first major facelift
- Redesigned F-150 rolls out in January as a '97
- Explorer now available with 210-horsepower V-8
- Mustang drops old V-8 for overhead-cam unit
- Supercharged T-Bird dropped from lineup
- One-third stake gives Ford control of Mazda

▶ Wagons were back, extending the oval theme to the rear and side windows. The previous 3.0-liter V-6 returned five horsepower stronger, while the 3.8-liter engine was dropped in favor of a new 24-valve 3.0-liter six producing 200 horsepower. The base GL Wagon started at $19,680.

▶ After its '95 redesign, Crown Victoria rolled into the new year with little new to talk about. A natural-gas conversion option, ordered mostly by fleet buyers, was newly available. Approximately 5000 of the big Fords were equipped with the alternative-fuel systems.

FORD ▲ The new-look Taurus took the "jelly bean" look a step farther, with prominent ovoid shapes inside and out. The wheelbase was stretched by 2.5 inches, and curb weight rose by about 200 pounds. A new entry-level G model anchored the line, while the GL, LX, and SHO models carried over intact. Prices started at $17,995.

◀ Rounded shapes dominated the interior of the new Taurus as well. The oval radio-control housing may have been aesthetically pleasing, but it seriously complicated the installation of aftermarket audio equipment.

► Mustang's age-old overhead-valve 5.0-liter V-8 was replaced by a pair of new 4.6-liter powerplants. The new V-8s were similar to those found in the Thunderbird and Crown Victoria. This GT was equipped with the single-overhead-cam V-8 producing 215 bhp. Cobras were treated to the dual-overhead-cam version good for an extra 90 horsepower.

◄ The new Cobra powerplant came with impressive numbers: four cams, eight cylinders, 32 valves, and 305 horsepower.

► While its new engine failed to make the Mustang GT quicker, it was smoother, quieter, and more willing to rev. With air conditioning and an automatic transmission, this GT would have stickered for slightly less than $20,000.

▲ Neglected again, the front-wheel-drive Probe drove into the new year unchanged. While Mustang was getting the attention with its new engines, Probe got only a new appearance package. The SE group gave base cars a GT-like look, without the GT-like horsepower.

▲ Cobra's new engine was enough to transform the otherwise unchanged car. With 65 more horsepower on tap than in '95, the newly energized Cobra covered the quarter mile in about 14 seconds. Price: $24,810.

▲ Ford's least-expensive car, the "minicompact" Aspire, was reduced to a single trim level for 1996. With the SE models gone, the hatchback Aspire now came only in base two- and four-door versions. The frugal Aspire was rated to return up to 42 mpg on the highway.

▲ The Thunderbird lineup was also pared to a single model for the new year. The slow-selling supercharged SC was dropped, leaving the lower-priced LX to fend for itself. Though prices increased only slightly, sales plummeted nearly 30,000, to just over 86,000.

▲ Ford's Ranger made headlines as the first compact pickup to offer an optional passenger-side airbag. Because some versions came without rear seating, a switch allowed drivers to disable the new airbag, allowing children to safely ride in the passenger seat.

▲ One of the original sport-utility vehicles, Ford's big Bronco was finally saying goodbye. With the Expedition in the wings for '97, Bronco's crude truck chassis and two-door layout were inconsistent with the needs of a new generation of family oriented SUV shoppers.

▲ Equipped with an onboard charger, the Ecostar Electric delivery vehicle had limited range, but found use in local delivery fleets. The purely electric Ecostars were based on the European Escort van, but designed for U.S. use. Payload capacity topped 1000 pounds.

▲ Packing on some middle-aged flab, Explorer's increasing weight challenged the SUV's 4.0-liter V-6. The injection of V-8 torque quickly ended any power shortages. Borrowed from the F-Series, the 5.0-liter engine produced 210 horsepower.

▲ Also in need of some additional muscle, Windstar was treated to a horsepower infusion for the new year. While the standard 3.0 liter stood pat, the optional 3.8-liter V-6 now produced 200 ponies, 45 more than before. This top-of-the-line LX started at $24,465.

LINCOLN ▲ The Mark VIII pictured here was powered by a 280-horsepower, 4.6-liter V-8. A new LSC (Luxury Sport Coupe) option package bumped the power rating by 10, firmed up the suspension, added bodyside moldings, and hiked the price $1300.

◄ Town Car base prices ran from $36,910 for the Executive to $41,960 for the Cartier. Lincoln commissioned the Diamond Anniversary Edition of its popular Town Car to celebrate its 75th year. The $1565 package was available only on the Signature Series and added a power moonroof, leather upholstery, an upgraded sound system, and unique interior and exterior trim. Heated front seats added $290.

► After a decent first season, Continental sales slipped 35 percent in its sophomore year, to just under 30,000. Among other things, a Diamond Anniversary package included a voice-activated cellular phone and raised the Continental's $41,800 base price by $1750.

MERCURY

▶ Mechanically identical to the Taurus, Sable logically underwent surgery at the same time. Like Taurus, the fresh-looking Sable was now longer, slightly heavier, and available with a new 24-valve V-6. This LS sedan started at $21,295.

◀ Replaced in many showrooms by the SUV, the increasingly rare station wagon continued in the redesigned Sable lineup for 1996. The new 200-horsepower V-6 was standard on the LS wagon, while a 145-horse unit carried over to power the less-expensive GS. Wagons accounted for 12 percent of the 121,000 Sables sold.

▲ The facelifted Cougar XR7's 3.8-liter V-6 now produced 145 bhp, a bump of five. The added power came from a series of design changes intended to smooth the coupe's standard engine. The optional 4.6-liter V-8 was still rated at 205 horsepower, but performance tweaking resulted in added torque. The extra muscle did little for sales, which continued to languish. Just under 40,000 Cougars drew orders, 20,000 fewer than the year prior. This Cougar listed for $17,935 with alloy wheels.

◄ As proof that Americans were growing larger, the European-designed Mystique's rear seating area was deemed cramped by many shoppers. By hollowing out the backs of the front seats and repositioning the rear bench, Mercury hoped to create the illusion of greater space. By year's end, 62,207 buyers found the revised interior acceptable and roomy enough for their needs.

► Returning in base GS and upmarket LS trim levels, Mercury's full-size Grand Marquis saw little change for '96. The standard 4.6-liter V-8 was good for 190 horsepower in standard trim, 20 more with the optional dual exhausts. This LS started at $23,385.

◄ What do you get when you take an Explorer, give it a toothy grille, and call it a Mountaineer? Mercury's first SUV, of course. Arriving as an early '97, Mountaineer came only with the Explorer's optional 5.0-liter V-8. Unlike Explorer, Mercury's sport-ute was not available in two-door guise.

► A new face and a passenger-side airbag topped the list of Villager changes for the new year. Villager's Nissan-built 3.0-liter V-6 produced 151 horsepower, low compared to stablemate Windstar. This midlevel LS started at $24,300.

1997

- Escort and Tracer receive fresh new skins, bigger engines

- Thunderbird flies for last time; rumors suggest name will return

- Rear-drive Cougar also goes extinct

- Full-size four-door Expedition replaces two-door Bronco

- Aerostar and Explorer now available with five-speed automatics

- All early '98s, Contour, Mystique, and Windstar enjoy modest makeovers

- Based on "Modular" V-8s, new V-10 powers full-size trucks and vans

FORD ▲ The redesigned Escort went on sale in May 1996 as an early '97 model. Riding on the same 98.4-inch wheelbase as before, the new cars stretched nearly four inches longer. The slightly larger standard engine now produced 110 horsepower, for a gain of 12. The LX sedan in the foreground started at $11,515.

▲ A new $745 GTS sport-appearance package dressed the already racy Probe GT in chrome wheels and a rear spoiler. The GT's 2.5-liter V-6 produced 164 bhp and propelled the trim Probe to 60 mph in less than eight seconds. Leather front bucket seats cost $500 extra.

▲ Without hatchbacks or a GT, the Escort's six-model lineup had been pared to three. Sedans came in standard and LX trim, wagons only as an LX. A base sedan with an automatic transmission and air conditioning stickered for $11,015. Antilock brakes added $570.

▶ The little car that couldn't, Aspire failed to find buyers who favored economy over power and comfort. With only half the Escort's-power, the Korean-built mini cost almost as much, a two-door with automatic and air listed for $10,680. At the end, just over 37,000 Aspires were sold.

▲ For its last year-in four-seat form, Thunderbird received a freshened interior with a revised instrument panel. Thunderbird sales declined by about 13,000 to 73,814. This LX started at $17,885, but probably stickered for closer to $20,000 with popular options.

▲ Selling below expectations, Contour received a lower-cost base model to help stimulate interest. Starting at $13,460, the new entry-level Contour was $825 less expensive than the GL, but lacked some of its interior refinements. This sporty V-6 SE started at $16,615.

◄ Mustang Cobra trumped the lesser GT by making exclusive use of a "power-bulge" hood and round fog lamps. The Cobra's standard 17-inch aluminum wheels were a $500 option on GT. A preferred equipment package that included leather seating and an upgraded stereo added $1335 to the Cobra's $25,335 base price.

► Producing 305 horsepower, Cobra's 32-valve, 4.6-liter V-8 gave it street credentials as bold as its looks. Hardcore enthusiasts applauded the engine's willingness to rev smoothly past 6000 rpm.

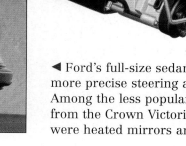

◄ Ford's full-size sedan was back with more precise steering and fewer options. Among the less popular items removed from the Crown Victoria's accessory list were heated mirrors and memory seats.

▲ Though down one Bronco, the Ford truck family was up the new Expedition sport-ute (front, left). Despite flat sales, Ford profits soared 59 percent as buyers continued their defection from automobiles to higher-margin trucks. Redesigned F-150s (front, center and right) remained the top sellers in Ford's truck and SUV line.

◄ There's no substitute for cubic inches—or extra cylinders. Ford's newest Triton engine featured 10 cylinders and 265 horsepower. More importantly, the tow-worthy V-10 generated a diesellike 410 pound-feet of torque. The new engine would become available in Ford's heavy-duty pickups, vans, and commercial chassis.

► With Expedition, Ford finally had competition for Chevrolet's perennially strong-selling Suburban. Borrowing engines and chassis parts from the F-Series pickups, the new full-size sport-utility came in XLT or Eddie Bauer trim. Prices started at $27,270.

▲ With the availability of two more cylinders than other full-size vans, Ford's Club Wagon and Econoline were serious workers. Equipped with the newly optional V-10 engine, they were capable of towing up to 10,000 pounds. This seven-passenger XLT Chateau Heavy Duty started at $27,540.

◄ Rumors of the Aerostar's death were greatly exaggerated. Reportedly in its final year, Ford's midsize van looked the same, but boasted a new five-speed automatic transmission. With Chevrolet's similarly sized Astro van still selling well, Ford brass opted to keep the rear-wheel-drive "midivan" around until 2000.

► Anxious to focus on its core light- and medium-duty trucks, Ford sold its heavy-truck division to Daimler-Benz early in 1997. D-B, in turn, assigned the new property to its Freightliner division, which began marketing the former Fords under the Sterling name. This L-Line Sterling was a virtual twin of the Ford Louisville from which it was descended. It was available with a 370-bhp Cummins diesel engine and an eight-speed transmission.

LINCOLN

▶ A steep price cut was the big news for Mark VIII. Despite the addition of high-intensity-discharge headlamps, Lincoln slashed the big coupe's base price six percent, to $37,280. Sales rose slightly to about 16,000. Extra-shiny "tri-coat" paint added $300.

▲ A new full-width neon bar illuminated the Mark VIII rear view. The fresh styling failed to boost sales, which were 4000 lower than archrival Cadillac's Eldorado.

▲ With Cadillac's Fleetwood having entered retirement, Lincoln's Town Car was America's last traditional rear-wheel-drive luxury sedan. Sales reached 93,616.

▶ In an effort to spur sales, Lincoln trimmed the base price of the Continental by more than $4500 to $37,280. Traction control was added to the standard-equipment list, and the previous front air-springs were replaced by conventional coils.

MERCURY ▲ Like its Escort cousin, Tracer was dressed in fresh sheetmetal. Introduced in May 1996 as an early bird '97, Mercury's smallest car was still available in thee models, though the names and content had been shuffled. The base and LTS models were gone, replaced by better-equipped GS and LS sedans and wagons.

◄ In addition to a new look, Mercury Tracer was treated to a new engine as well. An upgrade of Tracer's previous power-plant, the 2.0-liter four was slightly larger and 22-horsepower stronger. Economy-minded buyers might have chosen the five-speed manual trans-mission, which helped the little Mercury return as much as 30 mpg. This LS priced from $11,145.

◄ The slow-selling Mystique line was bolstered by a new entry-level model. Prices ranged from $13,960 for the base car to $16,150 for an LS like this one.

◄ The addition of map pockets was the big news for Sable following its '96 redesign. The 24-valve 200-bhp engine was still limited to LS sedans and wagons, leaving the GS to make do with the standard "Vulcan" V-6 and its 55-horse deficit. Optional daytime running lights cost $40.

► Sales retreated in the sophomore year of the redesigned Sable. Mercury's midsize sedans and wagons found 114,000 buyers, down about 24,000 from 1996. This LS sedan carried a sticker price of $22,080. While Sable sedan sales declined by 32,000 from 1996, calls for wagons increased by about 8000.

◄ Now in its 30th year, Cougar celebrated its birthday with a redesigned interior and a bargain-priced anniversary package. New white-on-black instruments spruced up the gauge cluster, while a revised center console added new cup and coin holders.

► Though only available in Toreador Red, 30th-Anniversary Cougars could be had with either the standard V-6 or optional V-8. The group included a sport suspension, upgraded wheels and tires, and unique interior and exterior trim. With sales down, the Cougar name would skip the 1998 model year, then return on a smaller, front-drive sporty coupe.

◄ Like its Crown Victoria cousin, Grand Marquis received mechanical tweaks designed to improve steering feel. Rarely ordered options, including the 12-volt power outlet and secondary sun visors, were stricken from the order sheet. Base price for this LS: $23,905. Leather upholstery added $646.

▲ Explorer-clone Mountaineer was technically still in its first model year. Introduced in 1996 as a '97, Mercury's first sport-ute found 46,000 buyers for whom an Explorer was not luxurious enough. Available only with a 5.0-liter V-8, Mountaineer could be had in either rear-wheel- or permanent all-wheel-drive trim. Prices started at $27,240.

▲ The running boards and roof rack on this Mountaineer were part of a $230 package that also included floormats. With a power moonroof, all-wheel drive, leather upholstery, and a luxury equipment group, Mountaineer's sticker climbed to $32,980.

▲ Possibly losing customers to stablemate Mountaineer, Villager sales slid by 10,000 to 55,000. The base GS was now available with quad captain's chairs. This top-of-the-line Nautica listed for $26,915. An option group including electronic instruments added another $1500.

1998

- New sporty ZX2 coupe extends Escort line

- Contour receives face-lift, sport-tuned limited-edition "SVT"

- Lincoln enters burgeoning SUV market with full-sized Navigator

- VIII is enough: Lincoln Mark series counted out

- Big Fords, Mercurys, and Lincolns redesigned

- Cost-cutting wizard Jac Nasser rises to Ford president and CEO

FORD ▲ Ford's traditional big car received a fresh look and revised chassis for the new year. The Crown Victoria also enjoyed a little more horsepower bringing the standard 4.6-liter V-8 to 200 horsepower, 215 with dual exhausts. Production hit about 111,000. This LX cost $24,070 with the Handling and Performance Package.

◀ Sharing mechanical parts with the less-exciting Escort sedan and wagon, the sporty ZX2 wore unique two-door sheetmetal and sported the Contour's Zetec powerplant. Though of the same 2.0-liter displacement as the standard 110-horsepower Escort engine, the dual-overhead-cam Zetec produced an additional 20 horses.

▲ Escort's carryover sedan and wagon changed little for 1998. A perennial top-ten seller, Escort again racked up big sales numbers, finding 292,000 buyers. This SE listed for $12,580. Keyless entry added $135.

▲ ZX2 came in two trim levels, standard Cool and better-equipped Hot. Best identified by its 15-inch aluminum wheels, this ZX2 Hot listed for $14,490 with the optional Sport Group. Antilock brakes added $400.

◄ Always looking for more muscle, Mustang fans applauded the GT's 10-horsepower nudge to 225. Though quick, Mustang GT was still no match for Chevrolet's thumping 305-horsepower Z28. This GT convertible listed for $23,970.

► This midline Contour SE came with a 125-horsepower 2.0-liter four. The fog lamps were standard, and the eight-spoke 15-inch aluminum wheels were a $425 option. The new high-performance SVT enjoyed the benefits of a 200-bhp, 24-valve, 2.5-liter V-6.

◄ Caught off guard by the dual-sliding side doors offered on Chrysler, Dodge, and Plymouth minivans, Ford lengthened the Windstar's left door to permit rear compartment access from the driver's side of the van.

► This Windstar Limited now topped Ford's minivan lineup. Priced $3300 higher than the LX, the $29,505 Limited came standard with rear air conditioning, quad captain's chairs, and leather upholstery. Equipped with the 200-horsepower 3.8-liter V-6, Windstars were among the quickest minivans available.

▲ The NASCAR F-150 jointly marked the 50th anniversaries of the stock-car racing circuit and the F-Series truck. The dual side pipes on this prototype moved to a traditional rear location on production models. All came with the 4.6-liter V-8 and started at $19,995.

▲ Having received a fresh grille and a new range of engines for '97, Ford's big-van lineup stood pat for the new year. The E-Series Econoline and Club Wagon vans accounted for a commanding 48 percent of the full-size van market.

◄ An impatient Ford introduced its redesigned Super Duty trucks in '98 as early 1999s. This F-250 features the 6.8-liter V-10. A 5.4-liter V-8 and a 7.3-liter turbodiesel V-8 were also available. The Super Dutys' brawny frontal styling would set the tone for the appearance of future Ford truck models.

► For a portrait spanning 50 years, a '48 Ford F-1 poses behind the contemporary F-150. Enjoying its 16th-consecutive year as the best-selling vehicle in America, Ford's big pickup was largely unchanged in the wake of the previous year's thorough redesign. Trim levels now included the entry-level standard, XL, XLT, and high-zoot Lariat models. Heavy haulers could order the 5.4-liter V-8, good for 235 horsepower.

▲ Still winning a fourth of the SUV market, Ford had to offer incentives in the face of slightly sagging Explorer sales. As a result, Explorer sales rose more than 12 percent, to more than 430,000. This Explorer Sport started at $19,880 with standard rear-wheel drive.

▲ Now sporting a larger regular cab and a revamped four-wheel-drive system, Ranger rode into 1998 looking to extend its sales title. The best-selling compact pickup for 11 straight years, Ranger had something for everyone among its 16 models. Prices started at $11,385.

◀ This two-wheel-drive Ranger XLT was ordered with an option package that included raised-white-letter tires mounted on "deep-dish" alloy wheels. Ranger accounted for 328,000 Ford sales in 1998, a full 100,000 more than Chevrolet's similarly sized S-10 pickup. Youth-oriented Splash models featured chrome wheels and body-colored bumpers.

LINCOLN ▲ By the late Nineties, off-road vehicles had become major status symbols. Hence, the Navigator, America's first full-size luxury SUV. Lincoln's $39,310 big rig tipped the scales at 6000 pounds.

▲ Navigator ranked second in Lincoln sales its first year out. Making exclusive use of a 32-valve version of Ford's 5.4-liter V-8, Navigator was reasonably quick. These 17-inch chrome wheels cost $950 extra.

◄ A slumping coupe market helped seal the fate of Lincoln's understated big cruiser. Despite heavy incentives and a new model, final-year Mark VIII sales totaled just over 10,500, a 35-percent decline from 1997. Base models continued to be powered by a 280-horsepower version of Lincoln's 32-valve V-8, the others had 10 additional horsepower.

▲ Visible to the keen eye, the script on the door veneer identifies this car as a Collector's Edition. The most-expensive 1998 Mark VIIIs, they had wood trim on the steering wheel and shift knob.

▲ Otherwise identical to the LSC from the outside, this Mark VIII Collector's Edition was discreetly badged in gold on the driver's door rub strip. Each Collector's Edition came with a set of commemorative gold ingots marking the end of the Mark VIII run. Collector's Editions started at $40,890. These chrome wheels were a no-cost option.

► A major restyle resulted in a slightly sleeker-looking Continental. Mechanically unchanged, the new Continental featured a revised interior with bird's-eye maple trim. To keep prices down, the previously standard driver-selectable electronic suspension was now a $595 option. Prices started at $37,830.

◄ As if back from spring training, Lincoln's big Town Car entered the new year leaner and meaner. A major redesign pared 200 pounds and three inches of length from Lincoln's top-selling cars. Newly optional dual exhausts raised the horsepower ante to 220, ten more than last year's only engine. The Executive, Signature, and Cartier trim levels all returned intact, while prices rose only slightly.

► Dual-exhaust outlets jutting discretely from under the bumper help identify this Town Car as a Cartier. With better leather and heated front seats, the Cartier was the Town Car flagship at $41,830. Stand-alone options included a power moonroof and a voice-activated cellular phone.

MERCURY ▲ Wearing what appears to be a sly smile, the redesigned 1998 Mystique was a mid-'97 arrival. Hoping to bolster disappointing sales, Ford rushed Mystique and similar Ford Contour changes to market only two years after the cars' debuts.

▲ Subtle driveline tweaking resulted in a slightly quicker Sable, which was otherwise unchanged. All wagons now wore the LS badge, with the GS label now applied only to a single, entry-level sedan. A premium LS wagon listed for $22,285.

► Like its Crown Victoria twin at Ford, Mercury's Grand Marquis was given a fresh face and a revised chassis for the new year. The new-look Marquis was also treated to upgraded brakes and a small boost in horsepower. This top-of-the-line LS started at $23,790. Leather upholstery was a $735 LS-only option.

◄ While competitors such as Buick LeSabre and Oldsmobile Eighty-Eight were now riding smaller, front-wheel-drive chassis, Mercury's full-size rear-drive Marquis remained a haven for more traditional big-car buyers. Though not a luxury car, the large Mercs could be well-appointed. A $2400 Ultimate package added antilock brakes, traction control, electronic instrumentation, and an upgraded sound system.

▲ Mechanically similar to Nissan's Quest, Mercury's minivan was unique in offering a designer model. The Villager Nautica featured unique trim and striping as well as quad captain's chairs. A firm-ride suspension and bigger wheels and tires were also included. Base Villagers started at $20,450; Nauticas added $6455.

▲ The Explorer-clone Mountaineer was little changed, entering its second year in the Mercury lineup. Mountaineer came in just one trim level, but with a choice of rear-wheel, four-wheel, or full-time all-wheel drive. The previously standard 5.0-liter V-8 was now a $465 option, replaced by the Explorer's 4.0-liter V-6.

■ A Ford—William Clay Jr.—becomes company chairman

■ Mustang marks 35th Anniversary with more power, special badges

■ F-150 SuperCabs now available with reverse-opening rear doors

■ Sport-truck fans tempted by supercharged F-150 Lightning pickup

■ Cougar returns as front-drive sports coupe

■ Ford acquires Volvo's automotive operations for a reported $6.45 billion

FORD ▲ With little direct competition except from in-house, America's last homegrown rear-drive full-size sedan rode into 1999 almost unchanged. Antilock brakes were now standard; otherwise Crown Victoria and the related Mercury Grand Marquis rested in the wake of 1998's reworking. This LX had a $23,925 base price.

◄ A victim of its own fleet-sales success, Ford's Crown Victoria was easily imagined in the paint schemes of numerous police forces and taxi companies. Crown Vic power came from a 4.6-liter V-8 producing 200 horsepower; 215 with optional dual exhausts. This car's Handling and Performance Package was a $740 option.

► Higher-end interior trim and a power driver's seat were part of the LX model upgrade. Though not on this Crown Victoria, LXs could be equipped with leather upholstery for $735.

► Ford's ponycar celebrated the 35th anniversary of its introduction in 1999 with new styling and more power. The base model's 3.8-liter V-6 gained 40 horsepower, to 190, while the GT's 4.6-liter V-8 added 35 horses, to 260. A new, wider rear track helped handling, while four-wheel disc brakes were now standard across the board. This GT convertible listed for $24,870.

▲ Buyers could join in the celebration by ordering the 35th Anniversary package. Apart from the wheels, the $2695 package was purely cosmetic.

▲ Usually thought of for pickups, Ford's F-Series Super Duty chassis also played host to a number of commercial applications. Though shod with familiar pickup sheetmetal, the F-450 and F-550 chassis-cabs carried gross vehicle weight ratings as high as 17,000 pounds.

▲ Introduced in mid 1998, the redesigned '99 F-Series Super Dutys featured newly available driver- and passenger-side airbags, as well as four-wheel antilock disc brakes. New overhead-cam V-8 and V-10 engines replaced overhead-valve V-8s.

◄ A new look, dual-sliding side doors, and a dose of luxury highlighted the new year for Ford's front-wheel-drive minivan. Creased edges and sharper lines helped freshen Windstar's previously rounded look. A luxury-laden SEL model now topped the line, adding leather upholstery and a premium audio system. While Windstar prices started at $20,220, a well-equipped SEL could top $32,000.

LINCOLN ▲ America's last big rear-drive luxury car added standard front side airbags for 1999. Though seemingly old-tech, Town Car came with an electronically controlled four-speed automatic transmission, traction control, and antilock brakes. Midlevel Signatures started at $40,325.

◄ Smaller than the Town Car and with front-wheel drive, Continental entered 1999 with little that was new. Now rated at 275 bhp, Continental's 4.6-liter V-8 enjoyed a 15-horsepower increase. The single-model lineup started at $38,325. A power sunroof added $1515.

◄ Based on Contour/ Mystique mechanicals, the new Cougar bore little resemblance to its rear-drive predecessor of the same name. The new Cougar was available with four- and six-cylinder power, but in only one trim level. Reasonably priced, the new Mercury came to $18,245 with V-6, automatic, antilock brakes, and traction control.

► Intersecting lines and sharp angles were part of Ford's "new edge" design philosophy. Though small in appearance, Cougar's dimensions were actually nearly identical to the Contour's. Technically separate models, the four- and six-cylinder Cougars differed only in the engine compartment. The "Zetec" four was good for 125 horsepower, while the "Duratec" V-6 put out an additional 45.

◄ Cougar interiors were easily spruced up with the $895 leather-upholstery option. Trendy black-on-white gauges gave the instrument panel a sporty, serious appearance. Just over 56,000 Cougars found new homes in 1999.

◄ Living largely in the shadow of the popular and mechanically similar Escort, Tracer sales fell dramatically in 1999. Down 10,000 to just 23,000, Mercury's little subcompact was no longer drawing the crowds it once did. Ford Escort sales were also down, though not as dramatically. Base price for this LS sedan: $13,070. An additional $815 was required for an automatic transmission.

▲ These illustrations demonstrate the function of front side airbags. Designed to cushion the body and reduce side-to-side head travel, the new active safety devices were standard equipment in the Cougar and would become increasingly available across other Ford lines.

▲ Villager added a driver's-side sliding door, and a 3.3-liter V-6 was substituted for the previous 3.0. Replacing the discontinued Nautica was a pair of less-expensive new models, the Estate and Sport. Both new Villager versions started at $25,015.

► Sharing the top-of-the-line role with the Sport, this Villager Estate featured aluminum wheels, two-tone paint, and upgraded interior appointments. Sport models were equally well-equipped, but lost the gold exterior trim and gained a sporty black-on-white instrument panel. The new models helped boost Villager sales by almost 7000, to 45,000.

A New Millennium

THE THIRD MILLENNIUM got off to a turbulent start in 2000. George W. Bush defeated Al Gore in a presidential election so tight, it wasn't decided until five weeks after balloting. Then, on September 11, 2001, al-Qaeda terrorists steered hijacked jet planes into the Pentagon and New York's World Trade Center killing nearly 3,000 people. The U.S. responded with tightened homeland security as well as invasions of Afghanistan and Iraq, two wars that would last the rest of the decade and beyond.

On Wall Street, a dot-com bubble burst coupled with the 9/11 attacks sent the market tumbling in 2001. Seven years later, soaring oil prices, a housing bubble burst, and Wall Street greed resulted in the worst recession since the Great Depression. America's first president of color, Barack Obama, could not stop the bleeding after taking office in 2009.

GM and Chrysler couldn't handle the triple blow of high gas prices, the recession, and foreign competition (including the emergence of South Korean giant Hyundai). They filed for bankruptcy and endured the indignity of government bailouts. Of the Big Three, only Ford remained solvent, thanks to drastic cost-cutting and the leadership of Alan Mulally.

2000

- Subcompact Focus debuts; wins 2000 North American Car of the Year award

- Ford and tiremaker Firestone squabble over responsibility for Explorer rollover accidents; massive recalls begin

- Ford makes offer to buy Korean automaker Daewoo, but pulls out of bidding in September

- Land Rover purchased for $2.7 billion from BMW AG; luxury SUV brand added to Ford's Premier Automotive Group

- Ford Contour, Mercury Mystique discontinued

- Mercury announces, then cancels, plans for a 200-bhp Cougar S model

- Lincoln LS debuts; shares Jaguar platform

FORD ▲ Ford's Focus "world car" debuted in North America as a 2000 model, after being voted the 1999 European Car of the Year. Two 2.0-liter four-cylinder engines of 107 and 130 bhp were offered. ZX3 two-door hatchbacks, SE four-door wagons, and four-door sedans in LX, SE, and ZTS trim levels were available.

▶ The race-bred 2000 Mustang Cobra R was available only through selected Special Vehicle Team Ford dealers. A mere 300 were built, all in red, starting at $54,995. Power came from a 385-bhp 5.4-liter V-8 teamed with a beefy Tremec T-56 six-speed gearbox. Radio, air conditioning, and back seat were all removed for weight savings.

◀ The Taurus shed its controversial oval styling for more conventional lines in a major revamp. Exterior dimensions were little changed, but headroom and trunk space increased slightly. The slow-selling Taurus SHO performance sedan didn't return for 2000. Newly optional adjustable gas and brake pedals powered fore and aft about three inches to adjust for varying driver heights.

◄ Four-wheel disc brakes were exclusive to the wagon, but all Tauruses got new 16-inch wheels. SE wagons started at $20,090. Base engine was the 155-bhp Vulcan V-6, with the 200-bhp Duratec twincam V-6 optional. Given the Taurus's family truckster status, safety features were an important selling point. A new Personal Safety System featured "smart" airbags that deployed at different energy levels depending on crash severity.

▲ ► Highlight of the 2000 auto-show season was the design concept for a resurrected Thunderbird. Ford dipped into T-Bird's legendary past to come up with a two-seat convertible with a removable hardtop. This show car provided the first glimpse of the new T-Bird, which would change little for its 2002 debut.

► Ford and motorcycle manufacturer Harley-Davidson teamed up to unveil a special-edition F-150 with Harley-inspired styling touches. The black-only SuperCab featured a billet grille, special badges, and—naturally—an all-black leather interior. Polished 20-inch wheels differed slightly from the proto-type set shown. Production reached 8197 units.

▼► The gigantic Excursion SUV was 7.4 inches longer, six inches taller, and almost 2000 pounds heavier than a 2000 Chevrolet Suburban, making it the largest SUV sold in America. Two- and four-wheel-drive versions were available. A 6.8-liter V-10 was standard on the 4×4 and optional on the 4×2. The rear view shows off the top-hinged hatch and "Dutch" tailgate doors. A 44-gallon fuel tank was standard.

► The Windstar minivan got a $1295 rear-seat video entertainment sys-tem for '00. The setup utilized a VCR and a 6.4-inch LCD screen that flipped down from the ceiling for back-seat passenger use. Two sets of headphones enabled viewing without driver distraction. Power-adjust-able foot pedals were another new option.

◄ Big SUVs like the Excursion came under fire from environmental groups critical of the vehicles' thirst for fuel. Increasingly congested urban driving conditions also prompted exploration of alternative transportation methods. Ford bought the TH!NK program from a Norwegian maker of zero-emissions electric vehicles in January 2000. The Th!nk *city* could go about 53 miles on an eight-hour charge.

► The TH!NK *neighbor* was targeted at residents of gated communities, industrial customers, and, not surprisingly, golfers. The driver could choose between a top speed setting of 15 or 25 mph, and the batteries could be recharged in six to eight hours from a standard 110-volt household outlet. The *neighbor* was legal on streets with posted speeds of 35 mph or less. Production models differed slightly in detail from the prototype unit shown here.

LINCOLN

◄ Developed in tandem with Ford subsidiary Jaguar, the Lincoln LS shared its rear-drive platform with the Jaguar S-Type. A 220-bhp 3.0-liter V-6 or 252-bhp 3.9-liter V-8 were available. A five-speed manual transmission was exclusive to the V-6.

► The LS had ample room for four adults inside, with the expected leather and wood trim. Automatic models had standard traction control, with the $725 AdvanceTrac antiskid system optional. A power sunroof ($995), heated front seats ($290), and Lincoln's RESCU cell phone/satellite assistance system ($960) were also on the options list. LS production topped 60,000 units in its first year.

▶ Less flamboyant than its English cousin, the LS brought to market a conservative but handsome shape, with a long wheelbase, short front and rear overhangs, and an airy greenhouse. The signature Lincoln grille was the only retro element in a classic, muscular design. The base model listed for $30,915, nearly $10,000 below equivalent Jaguar models.

◀ LS suspension commendably blended crisp handling with a smooth ride. An available Sport Package (standard on stickshift cars) replaced 16-inch wheels with 17s wearing high-performance tires. Thanks to its mix of low price, excellent build quality, and European-style performance and handling, the LS rapidly became a welcome and profitable presence in Lincoln showrooms.

MERCURY

▶ The reincarnated Cougar sports coupe was little changed for 2000. It faced stiff competition from rival import models like the Volkswagen New Beetle and Mitsubishi Eclipse, and sales plummeted a worrisome 29 percent over the calendar year. An available Sport Group option package added four-wheel disc brakes, 16-inch wheels, upgraded sport seats, rear spoiler, and other amenities to V-6-equipped Cougars.

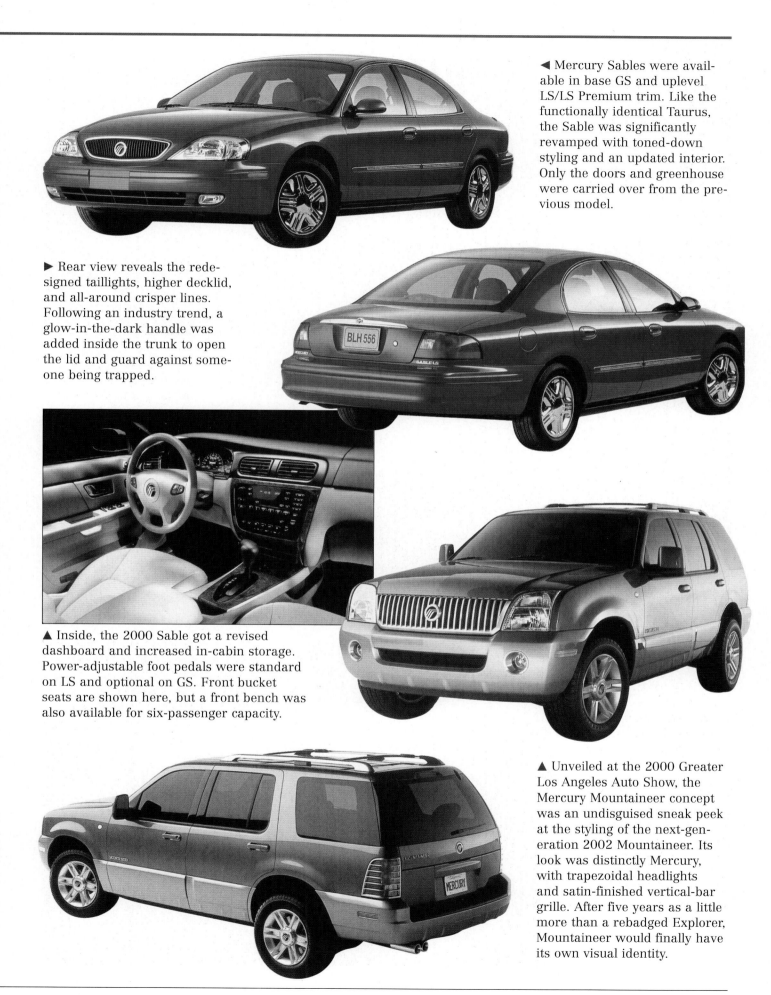

◄ Mercury Sables were available in base GS and uplevel LS/LS Premium trim. Like the functionally identical Taurus, the Sable was significantly revamped with toned-down styling and an updated interior. Only the doors and greenhouse were carried over from the previous model.

► Rear view reveals the redesigned taillights, higher decklid, and all-around crisper lines. Following an industry trend, a glow-in-the-dark handle was added inside the trunk to open the lid and guard against someone being trapped.

▲ Inside, the 2000 Sable got a revised dashboard and increased in-cabin storage. Power-adjustable foot pedals were standard on LS and optional on GS. Front bucket seats are shown here, but a front bench was also available for six-passenger capacity.

▲ Unveiled at the 2000 Greater Los Angeles Auto Show, the Mercury Mountaineer concept was an undisguised sneak peek at the styling of the next-generation 2002 Mountaineer. Its look was distinctly Mercury, with trapezoidal headlights and satin-finished vertical-bar grille. After five years as a little more than a rebadged Explorer, Mountaineer would finally have its own visual identity.

- Ford CEO Jacques Nasser is fired on October 30 after 34 months at the helm
- Chairman Bill Ford Jr. takes over as CEO, marking the first time a Ford has run the company since 1979, when Henry Ford II resigned as CEO
- Ford posts $5.45-billion net loss for the year
- Mustang Cobra back in lineup after one-year hiatus due to complaints over horsepower of '99s
- Historic Ford/Firestone ties cut amid acrimony over Explorer rollovers
- F-150 adds four-door SuperCrew cab style
- Lincoln-Mercury management completes move to Premier Automotive Group headquarters in Irvine, California
- Retro Ford Forty-Nine concept car shown

FORD ▲ ▶ After a successful run on the auto-show circuit as a concept car, Ford approved the Mustang Bullitt GT for a limited production run of 6500 units. The special edition was inspired by the 1968 movie *Bullitt*, which featured actor Steve McQueen behind the wheel of a '68 Mustang fastback in one of the greatest car chases in cinematic history. A larger throttle body, cast-aluminum intake manifold, smaller accessory drive pulleys, and a free-flowing exhaust system added 10 horses to the regular GT's 260, while broadening the torque curve noticeably. The Sixties-inspired five-spoke wheels debuted on the Bullitt, but soon became available on other Mustang GTs.

▲ The Crown Victoria soldiered on with no major changes. A Sport Appearance Package added handsome 17-inch aluminum wheels, unique suspension, front bucket seats, and improved handling. The monochromatic paint treatment shown here was optional when the Sport Appearance Package was ordered.

◄ The Escape compact SUV was developed jointly with Ford partner Mazda, which got its own version called the Tribute. XLS and uplevel XLT models were available in two-wheel- or all-wheel-drive versions. A 2.0-liter inline four cylinder was standard, but the optional 200-bhp 3.0 V-6 set the Escape apart from its competition. V-6 models could accelerate from 0-to-60 mph in 8.9 seconds.

► The Escape's optional Control Trac II all-wheel drive was a "driver-friendly" system that automatically proportioned more torque to the rear wheels when the front wheels began to slip. The driver could switch to full-time "locked" 4WD by turning a switch on the dash. All models came with a rear liftgate incorporating a separate-opening glass window.

▲ With a switch from overhead-valve to overhead-cam design, Explorer's standard 4.0-liter V-6 gained 50 horse-power for 210 total. A five-speed automatic transmission was now standard with the V-6. Though the four-door wagon was by far the most popular, a Sport two-door wagon and Sport Trac four-door crew cab were also offered.

◀ The best-selling Ranger gained a gutsier 4.0-liter overhead-cam V-6 that put out 207 horsepower, 47 more than the previous 4.0. A mild facelift brought slightly blockier lines and a honeycomb mesh grille. XL and XLT models were supplemented by youth-targeted "Edge" models (shown) with color-keyed bumpers, bed-rail covers, "Edge" decals, and raised ride height. The Ranger pick-up platform was shared with Mazda B-Series compact trucks.

▶ The Harley-Davidson F-150 switched to the four-door SuperCrew body for 2001, and side strip-ing moved from the beltline to the lower body. The sticker price jumped to $33,780. A novel, cage-like bed extender could pivot out over a dropped tailgate to add about two feet of cargo space. Options included a moonroof, slid-ing rear window, and six-disc CD changer. Ford claimed that the H-D F-150's exhaust note was tuned to approximate the sound of a Harley-Davidson motorcycle.

LINCOLN

► The $39,380 Continental was Lincoln's sole front-wheel-drive car. The lengthy list of standard equipment included programmable variable-assist power steering, wiper-activated headlights, and heated power mirrors. An optional Driver Select System enabled the driver to switch between three levels of suspension firmness.

▲ The Town Car could be had in a luxurious Cartier L version, which added an upgraded interior, 240-horsepower 4.6-liter V-8, and six inches of wheelbase. Rear legroom was 47.1 inches, tops among factory-built automobiles.

◄ The upscale Navigator started out $10,000 more expensive than a base-model Ford Expedition, but offered a host of luxury accoutrements as standard equipment. Its 5.4-liter V-8 made 300 bhp to the Expedition's 260. Cargo volume was a cavernous 109.9 cubic feet with second- and third-row seats folded, but the EPA fuel economy rating was a meager 12 mpg in the city, 16 on the highway.

MERCURY

▶ Mercury pulled the wraps off a sinister-looking Marauder sedan at the 2001 Chicago Auto Show, announcing that the car would go on sale in the summer of '02 as a 2003 production model. First seen in concept form at the 1998 Specialty Equipment Market Association (SEMA) show, the Marauder was a factory hot rodded Grand Marquis with retro muscle-car appeal.

◀ The '01 Mountaineer was unchanged save for rear-child-seat tether anchors. Optional was a $255 Reverse Sensing System that audibly warned of obstacles when backing up. The 2001 model year was a short one for Ford Explorers and Mercury Mountaineers, since the redesigned 2002 models went on sale in the spring of 2001.

▶ A lengthy list of safety features helped the Sable receive a double five-star crash-test rating from the National Highway and Traffic Safety Administration for the third year in a row. Mercury sold 97,366 Sables in the 2001 calender year, less than a third of its sibling Ford Taurus's sales in the same time frame.

WILLIAM CLAY FORD JR.
A Work in Progress

WILLIAM CLAY FORD JR. had a rather placid career before becoming chairman of his family's firm in January 1999. That month, however, the worst accident in Ford history occurred at the Rouge Plant. The following year, the company was wounded by a massive recall of Firestone tires mounted on Explorer SUVs. Then came more reverses: a decline in market share, severe financial loss, and the sacking of president/CEO Jacques Nasser.

A company poised in 1999 to overtake General Motors was in free-fall by 2001. Bill's world was turned upside down.

Born in 1957, Bill prepped at Hotchkiss School in Lakeview, Connecticut, also attended by his father and his uncle, Henry Ford II. Midway through Princeton, he decided to join Ford after graduating.

After earning a B.A. degree in history in 1979, Bill joined the company as a product-planning analyst in Advanced Vehicles Development. Then—in "Fordspeak"—he went "through the chairs," being assigned a series of "summer jobs," as he later described them, in Automotive Assembly and Ford divisions, the Labor Relations and Finance staffs, North American Automotive Operations, and Ford of Europe. In 1994, he was promoted to vice president for the Commercial Truck Vehicle Center. Resigning this job on January 1, 1995, he ceased being a company employee. Simultaneously, he replaced his father as chairman of the Board's Finance Committee.

Over the years, Bill also became increasingly involved with the Detroit Lions football team, owned by his father since 1964. While in Switzerland, he ran up huge phone bills listening to Lions games. Named team treasurer, then vice chairman, he spearheaded passage of a stadium referendum in Detroit. His phone was rigged to ring simultaneously in his Ford and Lions offices, but, he stoutly insisted, "My job at Ford comes first."

When Alex Trotman retired as Ford chairman/CEO on January 1, 1999, Lebanon-born, Australia-reared Jacques Nasser was named president and CEO. Bill, backed by his family, but not by Trotman, became chairman. Bill "had the education, the intelligence, the family loyalty to be chairman," declared Charlotte Ford, Henry II's eldest daughter.

For a time, the Nasser/Ford duo seemed a match made in heaven. The tough, hard-driving Nasser had ably served the company in the Americas, Asia, and Europe. Nicknamed "Jac the Knife" because of his reputation as a cost cutter, he was delegated to run the company. Bill was to preside at Board meetings and have ample opportunity to pursue his favorite cause, environmentalism, and enhance the company's reputation as a good corporate citizen.

Nasser immediately set out to transform Ford "into a leading consumer company for automotive products and services," and more. A whopping $6.4 billion was spent to acquire Volvo's carmaking operations, and billions more were invested in Land Rover.

Although Ford's market share and profits declined significantly during 2000–01, its Board, in Bill's words, was "lulled by the record profits of 1999." "Besides," he added, "it wasn't so much a gradual decline as a massive implosion." (The company made $3.4 billion in 2000.) However, even before the crisis stage, Ford was upset by some of Nasser's actions and poor communication between the CEO and himself. In July 2001, he created an "Office of the Chairman and CEO" to formally monitor the actions of his chief executive. To backstop Nasser, Bill installed a trusted lieutenant, Nick Scheele, architect of Jaguar's turnaround, as group vice president of the North American Group.

The new office generated endless rumors that Bill and Jacques were at odds, and had engaged in shouting matches. The press correctly predicted that Nasser's days were numbered. On October 7, the Board axed Nasser and made Bill Ford CEO. "One of the great things about having me as CEO," he joked, "is that it eliminates all speculation about who else might take the job."

The chairman's best asset being his name, Bill was trotted out to rebuild confidence in the company, appearing in a series of television and print advertisements invoking his family's automaking legacy. He perhaps found comfort in a 2001 public-opinion survey revealing that family controlled firms have twice the respect of nonfamily owned enterprises.

One of Bill's successes was the Ford Escape Hybrid, the world's first hybrid-electric SUV, which was named North American Truck of the Year in 2005. Nevertheless, the company was losing market share, as Ford was not producing vehicles that were right for the changing times. Bill admitted in 2005 that the company needed a new business model, and that "I [have] too much to do." Selflessly, he relinquished his CEO crown in 2006 and hired Alan Mulally for the position—arguably the smartest move he ever made.

2002

- Company announces extensive revitalization plan in January; restructuring includes layoffs and plant closings

- CEO Bill Ford stars in heritage-themed television ad campaign

- Ford holds unprecedented factory concept car/automobilia auction on June 16; raises $4.4 million for charity

- Two-seat Thunderbird returns

- Lincoln discontinues Continental

FORD ▲ Zippy, sport-compact "tuner" cars skyrocketed in popularity around the turn of the millennium. Ford's entry into this booming market was the Focus SVT, a three-door hatchback with many performance and appearance enhancements.

▶ Contributing to the SVT Focus's outstanding handling characteristics were 17-inch wheels on low-profile tires and well-tuned suspension components. The 2.0-liter Zetec engine was tweaked to produce 170 horsepower at a dizzying 7000 rpm, and was mated to a Getrag six-speed manual transmission. Base price was $17,505.

◀ Base Crown Victorias came standard with a 220-bhp 4.6-liter V-8 and 16-inch wheels, but choosing the LX Sport model netted a slightly hotter 235-horse 4.6, plus 17-inch alloy wheels, front bucket seats, leather upholstery, and performance suspension. Traction control was a $175 option on LX and Sport models. Ford also introduced a long-wheelbase Crown Victoria, with an extra 7.7 cubic feet of rear-seat space, built exclusively for taxi use.

▲ ▼ Two hundred specially trimmed Thunderbirds were sold through upscale department-store giant Neiman Marcus. Exclusive features included a black and silver interior with Neiman Marcus logos on the dash and floormats.

▲ The reborn Thunderbird was built on a shortened version of the rear-wheel-drive platform developed for the Lincoln LS and Jaguar S-Type sedans. The sole engine choice was the LS's 252-bhp 3.9-liter V-8.

▲ A Thunderbird started at $34,965 in Deluxe trim. The Premium model added traction control and chrome alloy wheels for $1000. The removable hardtop was another $2500. Evoking classic T-Birds were such "heritage" cues as fender vents, bright script, eggcrate grille, and hood scoop. This late prototype lacks side-marker lights.

▶ The Taurus was carried over with no major changes. With the proliferation of minivans and SUVs of all sizes, traditional station wagons faded into the background of domestic car offerings. In 2002, only Saturn offered a similarly priced, midsized rival to the Taurus and Sable wagons.

◀ New subseries models called Value, Sport, Choice, and Premium were added to base XLS and uplevel XLT Escapes for '02; each had escalating levels of equipment. A topline "Midnight" option package was also available for the XLT. It included ebony Nudo leather-trimmed seats, 16-inch aluminum wheels with black accents, a Mach in-dash six-disc CD changer with MP3 player, and special all-black paint scheme.

▶ The redesigned 2002 Explorer went on sale in spring 2001 as an early 2002 model. The top-selling SUV retained body-on-frame construction, but got new styling, a wider stance, longer wheelbase, independent rear suspension, and an available third-row seat for seven-passenger capacity. Front- and second-row curtain-side airbags were a $495 option; sensors that deployed them in a rollover accident were phased in at midyear.

► The rugged Super Duty F-350 4×4 pickup could be equipped with a burly 6.8-liter Triton V-10 engine that put out 310 bhp and 425 pound-feet of torque. Equipped with a 4.30 rear axle ratio, an F-350 4×4 could pull 12,500 pounds. A six-speed manual transmission and a number of interior convenience upgrades were new for 2002.

◄ A new FX4 premium off-road model was built on the four-door Ranger XLT SuperCab chassis. The $24,830 truck included Alcoa aluminum wheels on 31×10.5-inch BF Goodrich T/A KO tires, Bilstein off-road shock absorbers and heavy-duty springs, two easy-access stainless-steel tow hooks mounted in the front bumper, and FX4 decals.

► The GT40 concept car was an obvious homage to Ford's LeMans-winning racer of the Sixties, but was four inches taller and 18 inches longer than its Ferrari-fighting namesake. The rear canopy concealed a supercharged and intercooled 5.4-liter dohc V-8 putting out 500 horsepower and 500 pound-feet of torque. Plans for a production version were announced just 45 days after the show car's debut at the 2002 North American International Auto Show in Detroit.

► When Chevrolet dropped the Caprice after 1996, Ford's Crown Victoria was the only V-8, rear-wheel-drive police package available. Ford showed this rugged-looking Interceptor concept car at the 2002 New York Auto Show. Crush-resistant bumpers, reinforced steel push bars, and 18-inch wheels were a few of its heavy-duty features.

LINCOLN ▲ Steadily declining sales led Lincoln to drop the Continental—2002 was its final production year. Regular models like this one were unchanged, but about 2000 commemorative Collector's Editions featured "CE" logos, unique 10-spoke chrome wheels, and exclusive interior trim.

► The luxury SUV craze was spreading unabated, and posh, profitable Navigators were selling well. But the related Blackwood pickup was a dismal failure in the marketplace. Its limited cargo versatility, lack of four-wheel drive, and $51,785 price tag likely outweighed any potential snob appeal. Lincoln had hoped to sell 18,000 Blackwoods in 2002–03, but total production was well under 4000 units when Lincoln opted to pull the plug.

MERCURY

► Mercury was playing with variations on the Marauder theme before the production version even went on sale. Unveiled at the 2002 Chicago Auto Show, the Marauder convertible concept packed a supercharged, 335-bhp version of the 4.6-liter V-8. Mercury asserted the Marauder would "deliver a 1960s muscle-car experience with contemporary driving dynamics, comfort, and safety."

◄ Cougar sales continued to slide, and in January 2002, Mercury announced the sporty coupe would be discontinued at the close of the model year—four years after its introduction. A bittersweet $1195 35th Anniversary package included a Jack Roush spoiler and hood scoop, chromed 17-inch wheels, an in-dash CD changer, and special logos. Four-wheel disc brakes were now standard.

► The Mercury Villager shared its design with the Nissan Quest. The sole engine choice was a 170-bhp 3.3-liter V-6. Villager sales dropped 40 percent in the 2001 calender year to 16,344, and the model was dropped after 2002. Mercury didn't expect to be out of the minivan market for long, however—it announced the Monterey name would be resurrected on a new Ford Windstar-based minivan set to debut in the fall of 2003 as a 2004 model.

◄ In addition to its expressive new styling, the Mountaineer's slightly sharper handling feel and exclusive all-wheel-drive option distinguished it from the Ford Explorer. Like the Explorer, the Mountaineer offered a standard 210-bhp 4.0-liter V-6, or optional 240-bhp 4.6-liter V-8. Mercury's designers considered contemporary building architecture as a styling theme in an effort to attract urban, cosmopolitan buyers. Satin-finished body trim and wheels were echoed by matching interior trim details.

- Ford plans five-day celebration in June to commemorate 100th anniversary
- Ford unveils new ad campaign with Randy Newman song and tag line, "If You Haven't Looked at Ford Lately . . . Look Again"
- Lincoln debuts new Ford Explorer-based Aviator midsize SUV and redone Navigator
- Lincoln-Mercury headquarters returns to Michigan, but L-M design studio remains in California
- Special Centennial Edition Taurus, Mustang, Focus, Explorer, and Super Duty F-Series truck models announced
- Grand Marquis-based Marauder muscle sedan joins Mercury lineup

FORD ▲ The Mustang Cobra ragtop started at a stiff $37,370, but its supercharged V-8 delivered 390 bhp and 390 pound-feet of torque. A six-speed gearbox and independent rear suspension were standard.

▲ The nostalgic, limited-production Mach I recalled Mustang's past with a functional "shaker" hood scoop and Magnum 500-like 17-inch wheels. Its 4.6-liter V-8 produced 300 bhp, 40 more than the Mustang GT.

◄ Crown Victoria gained a redesigned frame and front suspension intended to improve ride and handling. A new speed-sensitive rack-and-pinion system vastly improved steering response. One of the few remaining body-on-frame automobiles, the Crown Victoria accounted for more than 80 percent of U.S. police pursuit vehicles and more than 90 percent of the taxicabs on New York streets.

► Other than the addition of a four-door hatchback version, the SVT Focus was virtually unchanged for '03. Only four colors were available: Sonic Blue, Infra-Red, CD Silver, and Pitch Black. Special front and rear fascias with honeycomb grilles, rear spoiler, "smoked-glass look" headlamps, and 17-inch five-spoke wheels distinguished it from lesser Focuses. Interiors featured titanium-look gauges, metal-trimmed foot pedals, and an optional 290-watt Audiophile Sound System.

▲ Independent rear suspension and an industry-first power fold-down third-row seat highlighted the redesigned Expedition. The wider body featured new styling inside and out, and Ford's AdvanceTrac traction-control/antiskid system was a new option. A base rear-drive XLT started at $31,275, while a 4×4 Eddie Bauer model cost $41,315.

▶ F-Series pickups celebrated 25 years as America's best-selling trucks in 2003. A $1200 Heritage Edition package was available on the SuperCab XLT. It included special badging and a two-tone paint scheme with a black upper body and choice of Burgundy Red, Arizona Beige, or Dark Shadow Gray lower body colors.

▲ The 260-horsepower, 5.4-liter V-8 engine was standard in the F-250/F-350 trucks and Excursion, optional in F-150s and Expeditions.

▲ F-750 Super Duty trucks, Ford's biggest, were available in regular-cab, extended SuperCab, and four-door crew-cab versions. A 5.9-liter Cummins diesel was the base engine.

LINCOLN

► The Town Car was updated with more formal styling, revamped frame and suspension, restyled dashboard, and standard front side airbags. Trim levels escalated through Executive, Signature, and Cartier models, each with higher levels of standard equipment. New 17-inch "Euroflange" wheels replaced the previous 16-inchers. Prices started at $40,270.

◄ Both LS sedan engines got a horsepower boost in '03; the V-6 was up 12 bhp to 232, and the V-8 gained 28 to 280. The V-6's manual transmission was no longer available. Minor styling changes included a new front fascia, new taillights and decklid, and restyled wheels. Chrome dual exhaust tips were standard, and a touch-screen DVD navigation system was a $2995 option.

► The new-for-'03 Navigator boasted independent rear suspension and power-retractable running boards, which automatically extended when a side door opened and retracted when it closed. Power-adjustable pedals, leather upholstery, walnut interior trim, heated power-fold door mirrors, and a CD changer were all standard features. Luxury, Premium, and top-line Ultimate models were offered, all with a 300-bhp, 5.4-liter V-8.

◀ The Sable received no major changes for 2003. Base model GS sedans started out at $20,280. With the cancellation of the slow-selling Cougar sports coupe and Villager minivan, Mercury's lineup dwindled to just three lines in 2003: the Sable, the Grand Marquis/Marauder, and the Mountaineer. Ford remained committed to the brand, however, promising six new models by 2008.

▲ Marauder sedans came in black only, with three-inch polished exhaust tips and 18×8-inch aluminum alloy wheels on BF Goodrich g-Force T/A tires. The 4.6-liter V-8 put out 302 bhp and was good for mid-seven-second 0-60 sprints and mid-15-second quarter-mile times. "Step on the gas and forget what year it is," ads urged buyers.

▲ Console-mounted Auto Meter gauges, a 140-mph speedometer, and "dot-matrix" carbon-fiber-look trim lent a racy appearance to the Marauder's interior.

▲ An optional rear-seat DVD entertainment system and a longer list of standard equipment were '03 additions to the Mountaineer.

2004

- Mustang marks its 40th anniversary

- Full-size F-150 pickup is redesigned

- F-Series and Escape see record sales

- Escape Hybrid named "North American Truck of the Year"

- Ford says it increased per-unit revenue in North America by $745

FORD ▲ With an all-new Mustang scheduled for 2005, Ford marked the Mustang's 40th birthday with a special 40th Anniversary package that could be ordered on all 2004 models. Available in white, black, or exclusive Crimson Red colors, the $895 option included special stripes, a beige-leather interior, "Bullitt" wheels with beige painted spokes, floor mats, and special badging.

◄ ▼ The SVT Focus was still available with the "European" appearance package. In addition to unique Competition Orange and Screaming Yellow paint colors, this $3410 option package included Recaro-brand front seats, a black leather interior, upgraded audio system, power sunroof, HID headlamps, and unique alloy wheels.

► Focus models were little changed for 2004, but there was some news under the hood of the ZTW wagon. A 2.3-liter four became the standard engine, replacing the 2.0. The larger mill was also standard on ZTS sedan and Premium-model hatchbacks.

◄ Ford redesigned America's best-selling pickup, the F-150, for 2004 with roomier cabs, more power, and new styling and features. Regular-, extended-, and crew-cab body styles returned. All cabs, even the "regular," had four doors and were about six-inches longer and four-inches wider than their predecessors. Two engines were offered, both V-8s. The base 4.6 liter had 231 bhp, and the optional 5.4 300, up from 260. A four-speed automatic was the only transmission choice. Five trim levels were offered: work-oriented XL, sporty STX, mainstream XLT, off-road FX4, and luxury Lariat. The previous-generation F-150, renamed F-150 Heritage, was available too.

► The two-door Explorer Sport was dropped for 2004, but the Explorer Sport Trac continued to be available. Still based on the previous-generation Explorer, Sport Tracs combined the passenger compartment of a traditional SUV with a four-foot-long pickup bed. A base rear-drive version started at $23,710.

◄ Ford revamped its minivan for 2004, giving it new styling and features, and changing the name from Windstar to Freestar. Freestar came in a single body length that was similar in size to such rivals as the Toyota Sienna and Dodge Grand Caravan. The 3rd-row bench could fold into the floor—a first for a Ford minivan.

► Ford's full-size cargo and passenger vans saw a new diesel engine option and other minor changes for 2004. The base V-6 engine was dropped, making a 4.6-liter V-8 standard in E-150 and E-250 models. Optional on those, and standard on E-350, was a 5.4-liter V-8. Also available on the E-350 was a 6.8-liter V-10. New was a 6.0-liter turbodiesel V-8 that made 235 horsepower.

◄ Lincoln added a second SUV for 2003, a gilded version of the Ford Explorer/Mercury Mountaineer. Little changed for 2004, Aviator's styling mimicked Lincoln's Navigator and differed from its brothers in engine power, suspension tuning, and cabin decor. Aviator had a 302-bhp version of the V-8 that was optional in the Ford and Mercury. It had a five-speed automatic transmission and either rear- or all-wheel drive. A Kitty Hawk Edition with special trim was added midyear.

► Lincoln's Town Car carried on as the lone American-brand full-size rear-drive luxury sedan. Satellite radio was available for the first time in 2004, and rear-obstacle detection became standard. Three trim levels were available: Signature, Ultimate, and the limousine-like Ultimate L, which added six inches to the wheelbase to create more rear leg room. The previous entry-level Executive model was dropped.

MERCURY

◄ Mercury's midsize Sable sedans and wagons received minor appearance changes for 2004. Sedans received a new rear fascia and taillights, and both body styles wore a new grille and front fascia. GS and LS Premium models were offered.

► Ending a one-year hiatus, Mercury returned to the minivan market for 2004 with a nameplate it last used in the 1970s. Monterey shared its design with Ford's Windstar replacement, the Freestar. Both were based on an update of the 1999–2003 Windstar platform. Convenience, Luxury, and Premier trim levels were offered, each with seven-passenger capacity. All were equipped with a 201-bhp 4.2-liter V-6 and four-speed automatic transmission.

- All-new Mustang debuts

- Ford Focus receives facelift in U.S., but all-new second-generation Focus hits the market in Europe

- Ford GT sports car enters limited production

- Ford sells Hertz Corporation rental-car business

- Company reports net income of $2 billion, despite losing money in North America

- Ford gains market share in the United States for the first time since 1993

- F-Series sells more than 900,000 units for the second year in a row

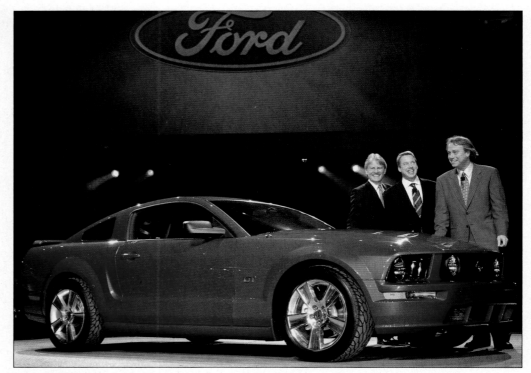

FORD ▲ Ford's big news for 2005 was the first all-new Mustang since 1979. Heritage-inspired styling and stronger engines helped make the new 'Stang a big hit. Shown with a GT at the 2004 Detroit auto show are VP of Product Creation Phil Martens (left), Chairman and CEO Bill Ford Jr. (center), and Group VP of Design and Chief Creative Officer J Mays.

◄ Mustangs used a new underbody structure replacing one that dated from 1979 but retained a solid rear axle rather than adopting independent rear suspension. The base V-6 became a 210-hp 4.0-liter. GTs reprised a 4.6-liter V-8, but with 300 bhp instead of 260. A five-speed manual remained the standard transmission. The optional automatic had five speeds rather than the previous four. The lack of grille-mounted fog lamps help identify this coupe as a V-6 model.

▶ At introduction, the 2005 Mustang was only available in a coupe bodystyle. During the year, a convertible joined the line. The new cars gained some six inches in wheelbase and overall length vs. the 1999–2004 generation. Weights rose about 100 pounds on coupes, 275 pounds on convertibles. Before options, a V-6 coupe with five-speed manual transmission listed for $19,215; convertibles $23,940.

▶ Ford's smallest car was revamped for 2005, getting more power and revised styling inside and out. Focus came as a two-door hatchback called the ZX3, and with four doors as the ZX4 sedan, ZX5 hatchback, and ZXW wagon. All had a 136-horsepower 2.0-liter four-cylinder except the ZX4 ST version of the sedan (shown), which had a 151-horse 2.3. The ZX4 ST was also equipped with sport suspension, four-wheel disc brakes, traction control, and mandatory manual transmission.

▲▶ For 2005, Ford debuted the new Five Hundred, a full-size four-door sedan with available all-wheel drive. The Five Hundred accommodated five passengers on seats Ford said were mounted about four inches higher than in other sedans. SE, SEL, and Limited models were offered, all with a 203-bhp 3.0-liter V-6 and a choice of front-wheel drive or AWD. The Five Hundred shared its basic design and powertrain with the Mercury Montego sedan and Ford's Freestyle crossover SUV.

▶ Ford launched its first crossover SUV for 2005, the Freestyle, a wagon that sat up to seven. SE, SEL, and Limited trim levels were available, each with front-wheel drive or optional AWD. The sole powertrain was a 203-horsepower 3.0-liter V-6 linked to a continuously variable automatic transmission. The CVT provided variable drive ratios vs. a conventional automatic's preset cogs. Like Five Hundred, Freestyle was based on a platform developed by Volvo, then owned by Ford.

◀ A 50th Anniversary Thunderbird joined Ford's two-seat convertible line for 2005. Thunderbird came with a power-folding soft top with heated glass rear window or an available removable hardtop with trademark porthole windows. The only powertrain was a 280-bhp V-8 with five-speed automatic transmission; a manual-shift feature was available for the automatic. Thunderbird was discontinued after 2005.

▶ Ford revived a classic name and shape with the 2005 Ford GT. Styling and powertrain layout were based on the Le Mans-winning GT40s of the '60s. Like the original, the GT was a mid-engine, two-seat sports car. The '05 sported a mid-mounted supercharged 5.4-liter with dual overhead camshafts and 32 valves. This all-aluminum V-8 made 550 horsepower. Power was delivered to the rear wheels through a six-speed manual transmission and limited-slip axle. No automatic transmission was available. The body was constructed mainly of aluminum and carbon fiber. Base price was $139,995.

◄ A new engine and transmission highlighted the 2005 updates to Lincoln's Navigator SUV. The revised 5.4-liter V-8 provided the same 300 horsepower but delivered more low-range grunt. Also, a six-speed automatic transmission replaced the old four-speed unit. The antiskid system added Ford's Roll Stability Control, which was designed to detect an impending tip and activate the system to reduce the risk of a rollover.

MERCURY

► The new Montego was the first Mercury car in more than a decade to offer all-wheel drive. Montego came in Luxury and Premier models with a 203-bhp 3.0-liter V-6. Both offered front-wheel drive with six-speed automatic transmission or AWD with a continuously variable automatic transmission. All Montegos were equipped with antilock four-wheel disc brakes and traction control, but no antiskid system was offered.

◄ Mercury cataloged its first compact SUV for 2005. The Mariner was a five-passenger wagon based on Ford's popular Escape. Mariner had its own styling details and interior decor but used Escape's 153-bhp four-cylinder and 200-bhp V-6 engines. Prices started at $21,425.

- "Way Forward" restructuring plan is launched in January

- Ford Motor Company has over 280,000 employees and more than 100 plants worldwide

- Bill Ford Jr. becomes Executive Chairman and Chairman of the Board

- Ford mortgages nearly all of the company's assets to raise $23.5 billion to finance restructuring

- Alan Mulally leaves Boeing to become President and CEO of Ford Motor Company in September

- Once the nation's best seller, Taurus is dropped

- New midsize sedans Ford Fusion, Mercury Milan, and Lincoln Zephyr debut

- Losses for the year total $12.6 billion

▼ The new Fusion effectively replaced the aging Taurus as Ford's midsize sedan. It shared a basic architecture with the Mercury Milan and Lincoln Zephyr. All were based on the Mazda 6 from Ford's Japanese affiliate. Fusion offered S, SE, and SEL models, in a lone four-door sedan body style. Four- and six-cylinder engines were available, and a five-speed manual transmission was standard with the four.

FORD ▲ Focus didn't change much for 2006, following the previous year's refreshing. One new item was a Street Appearance Package that added sporty visual cues like a rear spoiler, lower-body cladding, fog lamps, and a chrome exhaust tip. The year's least-expensive Focus was the ZX3 S hatchback, starting at $13,450.

◄ In June 1966, Ford GT40 Mark II racecars swept the first three places in the running of that year's Le Mans 24-hour endurance race. The winning car was the #2 machine driven by Bruce McLaren and Chris Amon. This win started Ford's four-year domination of the legendary event. This historic machine served as the inspiration for the modern day Ford GT supercar.

▲ For 2006, the Ford GT supercar could be ordered as a no-extra-cost 40th anniversary special edition to commemorate the company's 1-2-3 finish at Le Mans in 1966 with the original GT40 Mark II. The 40th anniversary model came only in Tungsten Grey.

◄ Over time, Taurus lost much of its sales magic, and by 2006 it had the reputation that it was mostly found in rental-car fleets. Ford dropped the wagon and the optional V-6 for 2006, along with Mercury's Sable. Sedans were offered in SE and SEL trim only. Taurus did not return for 2007.

◄ ▲ For 2006, Ford's Explorer SUV was redesigned and boasted more V-8 power and additional safety features. America's best-selling SUV, Explorer used a truck-type body-on-frame design and offered rear-wheel or four-wheel drive. Most models were available with a 3rd-row seat for seven-passenger capacity.

► The F-150, America's best-selling vehicle, added a few options and a new Harley-Davidson model for 2006. Ford's F-150 pickup came in regular-cab, extended SuperCab, and SuperCrew models. The new Harley-Davidson was a specially trimmed SuperCab with 5.4 V-8, 2WD or 4WD, and a 6.5-ft Styleside box.

◄ Ford's compact Ranger pickup wore a mild facelift for 2006. Styling changes involved modest revisions to bumpers, grille, fenders, and lights. Rangers came in regular-cab and extended SuperCab models spanning six trim packages. SuperCabs came with two rear fold-down jump seats as standard or optional, depending on trim, and back-hinged rear-access doors were available.

2006

▶ The Mark LT was Lincoln's second attempt at a luxury truck, following the poor-selling 2002–2003 Blackwood. It was a more-conventional pickup, and unlike Blackwood, offered both two- and four-wheel drive. With four doors and a 5.5-foot cargo bed, Mark LT was essentially a dressed-up Ford F-150 SuperCrew crew cab. The lone powertrain was a 300-bhp V-8 and four-speed automatic transmission. Prices started at $38,680.

▲ The rear-drive Lincoln LS was in its last year for 2006. Only a V-8 Sport model was listed. It had a 280-bhp V-8, five-speed automatic transmission with manual-shift capability, ABS, and traction control. In *Consumer Guide®* testing, a V-8 Sport ran 0-60 mph in 6.8 seconds, on par with V-8-powered rivals.

▲ New for 2006 was the front-wheel-drive Lincoln Zephyr, a luxury version of the Ford Fusion and Mercury Milan. Sized and priced below Lincoln's rear-wheel-drive LS sedan, it was Lincoln's smallest car ever. Zephyr's only engine was a 221-bhp V-6 mated to a six-speed automatic transmission. Options included xenon headlamps, sunroof, cooled front seats, and a navigation system. Zephyr priced from $28,995.

MERCURY ▲ Milan replaced Sable as Mercury's midsize sedan. Milan could be ordered in base or uplevel Premier models. Premiers came with leather upholstery and a choice of metal or wood interior trim at no extra cost, and were available with heated front seats.

▲ For 2006, Mountaineer was redesigned with more V-8 power, freshened styling, and front side airbags. Convenience, Luxury, and Premier models were offered. Mountaineer's performance and accommodations mirrored those of similarly equipped Explorers.

ALAN MULALLY
The Man with the Plan

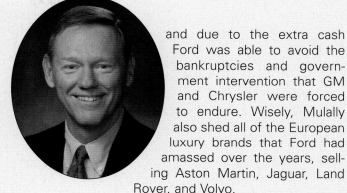

In 2006, with Ford losing about a billion dollars a month, an employee asked new CEO Alan Mulally a critically important question: Would Ford Motor Company survive?

"I don't know...," Mulally replied. "But we have a plan, and the plan says we are going to make it."

Mulally had not just a plan—and a darned good one—but the vision, resolve, and leadership skills to carry it to fruition. Not only was Ford hemorrhaging money in 2006, but an oil crisis and a horrific recession lay ahead. Mulally skillfully led the company through all three crises, and by 2010 Ford was making a multibillion-dollar profit. When *Fortune* magazine asked its readers to pick its Businessperson of the Year for 2010, out of 32 candidates, Mulally and Steve Jobs were the top two picks. In a head-to-head matchup of the two, Mulally prevailed—with 96 percent of the vote!

The "savior" of Ford was an unlikely candidate. A native of Kansas with an aw-shucks grin, Mulally more resembled a neighborly car salesman at a Topeka Ford dealership—or perhaps even a Toyota dealership, for he was driving a Lexus when Bill Ford hired him as CEO. Mulally not only wasn't a "Ford man," but he had never even worked in the auto industry. He had spent 37 years at Boeing, where he rose from engineer to CEO of Boeing Commercial Airplanes.

While a brilliant engineer (he headed the development of the 777 airliner), Mulally proved even more remarkable as a corporate leader, once earning "Person of the Year" honors by *Aviation Week.* Bloomberg News praised Ford for acquiring Mulally, but they added that his hiring "may be too late" to save the company.

Mulally, though, embraced the challenge. The first thing he did was learn about the company and the industry from top to bottom, interviewing scores of employees and analysts. Arriving at work at 5:15 every morning, he brought positive energy and a fierce determination to Ford World Headquarters—traits that would resonate throughout the corporate offices.

Under Mulally, the company credo became "One Ford: One Team, One Plan, One Goal." According to the company, this concept "encourages focus, teamwork and a single global approach, aligning employee efforts toward a common definition of success and optimizing their collective strengths worldwide."

Showing remarkable foresight, Mulally in 2006 took out a company loan of $23.5 billion against FoMoCo's assets. Should a recession hit, he reasoned, Ford would have the money to weather it. Four-dollar gas prices and a massive recession arrived in 2008, and due to the extra cash Ford was able to avoid the bankruptcies and government intervention that GM and Chrysler were forced to endure. Wisely, Mulally also shed all of the European luxury brands that Ford had amassed over the years, selling Aston Martin, Jaguar, Land Rover, and Volvo.

Within the company, internal rivalries became a thing of the past as Mulally blew open the channels of communication. At his Thursday board meetings, *every* department was represented. Everyone knew the plan and was expected to follow it. Mulally also refused to let old ideas get in the way of his vision. "Everybody says you can't make money off small cars," he said. "Well, you'd better damn well figure out how to make money, because that's where the world is going."

Under Mulally, Ford would offer fewer models of vehicles, but extra care would be put into each. He successfully pushed for better fuel efficiency across the Ford line. Ford EcoBoost engines produced substantially better fuel efficiency and reduced greenhouse emissions. In addition, Mulally brought to the U.S. two high-mileage cars that had been big sellers in Europe: the Fiesta and the Focus (which replaced the dated U.S. car of the same name).

"Mulally...is the reason that Ford is about two to three years ahead of GM and Chrysler regarding their product cadence," asserted auto industry analyst Erich Merkle of Autoconomy.com in 2010. "Ford's product is some of the best on the market. Not only is this backed up objectively through numerous quality study comparisons, but they are delivering with most every product launch—products that are best in segment."

Mulally expected Ford to turn a profit by 2011, but the company exceeded expectations. In the first half of 2010, Ford sales rose by a stunning 28.2 percent over the same period in 2009, making the gains of GM (14.3 percent) and Chrysler (11.0 percent) seem paltry. While improving market share, Ford earned more than $6 billion in profit in the first three quarters of 2010. That fall, the company paid down its total debt to $22.8 billion (from $33.6 billion a year earlier) and had more than $20 billion in cash on hand.

While Ford stock floundered at under $7 a share in mid-2006, and plummeted to under $2 in January 2009, it shot up to more than $16 in late 2010. Moreover, the company was set to take advantage of exploding markets overseas, particularly in China, India, and Brazil.

"Alan was the right choice," said executive chairman Bill Ford, "and it gets more right every day."

2007

- Implementation of Mulally's "One Ford" plan proceeds

- Aston Martin is sold

- Ford opens new Nanjing assembly plant in China to produce small cars for Chinese market

- New Ford Edge and Lincoln MKX crossover SUVs are introduced

- Jim Farley leaves Toyota to join Ford as Vice President of Marketing and Communications

- Company creates a single global product development organization

FORD ▲ High-performance Shelby GT500 coupe and convertible variants joined the base and GT models in Mustang's stable for 2007. The Shelby GT500s packed a supercharged 500-horsepower V-8 backed by a six-speed manual transmission. Also new was a California Special Package for GT Premiums that added unique trim and 18-inch wheels.

◀ The 2007 Edge was Ford's new car-type mid-size SUV. It was a five-passenger wagon based on the same platform as the Fusion sedan and came in front- and all-wheel-drive guises. The sole powertrain was a 265-bhp V-6 and a six-speed automatic transmission. Optional for dressy SEL models was Ford's Vista Roof, a glass roof with a sliding section over the front seats.

▶ Explorer Sport Trac was redesigned for 2007, adding safety features, available V-8 power, and an independent rear suspension. Like the 2001–2005 Sport Trac, it was based on Ford's Explorer SUV, but with a four-by-five-foot open cargo bed. Wheelbase grew by five inches vs. the previous Sport Trac and was 16.8 inches longer than Explorer's. The cargo box, made of dent-resistant composites, had three in-floor covered bins with drain plugs.

▲ Expedition, Ford's largest SUV, gained fresh front and rear styling and an extended-wheelbase model for 2007. The Expedition EL rode a 12-inch-longer wheelbase and was 14.8 inches longer overall. Either sat seven or eight with available three-place 2nd-row seating. An available front bench seat increased seating capacity to nine. The sole engine remained a 300-bhp V-8, but a six-speed automatic transmission replaced a four-speed unit.

▶ Ford's heavy-duty pickup trucks wore several new trim packages for 2007. This Outlaw package for Lariat crew cabs included front captain chairs, console, color-keyed bumpers and grille, chrome tubular side steps, unique interior and exterior trim, and chrome exhaust tips. It added $1580 to a F-250 Lariat four-wheel-drive crew cab's $37,450 base price.

◀ Ford's brawniest 2007 F-Series trucks were the F-650 (shown) and F-750. Aimed at businesses and municipalities, these chassis-cab trucks could be outfitted for a variety of tasks. Regular Cab, SuperCab, and Crew Cab styles were offered, along with nine different frames. Engines were from three different diesel engine families, with the top choice a Caterpillar 7.2-liter I-6 with 300 horsepower and 860 pound-feet of torque.

◄ What's in a name? Lincoln decided to rechristen the one-year-old Zephyr MKZ for 2007. It also received revised styling, more horsepower, and available all-wheel drive. MKZ's 3.5-liter V-6 was good for 263 horsepower.

▲ ► Lincoln's first car-type SUV, the MKX, was a five-passenger wagon that shared its basic design with Ford's Edge. The MKX had different styling and came with some features unavailable on Edge. MKX offered front- or all-wheel drive. It was only available with a 265-bhp 3.5-liter V-6 and six-speed automatic transmission.

► Lincoln revamped its Navigator large SUV for 2007, giving it fresh styling and an extended-wheelbase Navigator L model. The L had a 12-inch-longer wheelbase and was 14.7 inches longer overall. Both versions could seat up to eight. Luxury and Ultimate trims were offered on standard-length versions. L came in a single trim, though the standard-length Ultimate's features were available as part of an option package.

MERCURY

◄ For 2007, Mercury Mariner came in gasoline and gas/electric-hybrid versions. The Hybrid had AWD and teamed a four-cylinder gas engine with a battery-powered electric motor. It used a continuously variable automatic transmission (CVT). Mariner's hybrid system would automatically run on one or both power sources to balance acceleration and fuel economy. Mariner Hybrid started at $27,950.

► Not much changed on the 2007 Mercury Mountaineer, but the model lineup was pared down, and a heated windshield joined the options list. For 2007, curtain side airbags with rollover deployment became standard; these covered the 1st and 2nd seat rows.

2008

- Sync system, developed with Microsoft, debuts in updated Focus

- Jaguar and Land Rover are sold to Tata Motors

- Record run-up in gas prices followed by worldwide financial crisis

- Ford loses $14.7 billion, including $6 billion in fourth quarter

- General Motors and Chrysler need financial assistance from U.S. and Canadian governments

- In December, Ford presents U.S. Congress with the company's business plan in case it requires bridge loans from the government

▲ Ford debuted its Sync voice-activated in-car communications and entertainment system in the redesigned 2008 Focus. Developed with Microsoft, Sync allowed wireless access to Bluetooth-enabled cell phones by pressing a button on the steering wheel. Digital music players were connected through a USB port on the dashboard. Once connected, SYNC allowed voice control of these devices via predetermined vocal commands. After the Focus debut, Sync quickly spread throughout the Ford, Lincoln, and Mercury product lines.

FORD ▲ For 2008, Ford substantially updated the Focus with new styling inside and out, and some new features. The new Focus was available only as a two-door coupe and as a four-door sedan; the old hatchback and wagon models were no longer available. A lone 2.0-liter four was on offer, mated to a five-speed manual or four-speed automatic.

▲ Bullitt was a new Mustang model that paid homage to the classic Steve McQueen film of the same name. The 2008 Bullitt Mustang packed a 315-horsepower 4.6-liter V-8 mated only with a five-speed manual transmission. Mustang GTs had to make do with an even 300 ponies. The Bullitt also used unique interior and exterior trim, as well as a performance suspension and brakes.

◄ Ford's Five Hundred was renamed and became the 2008 Taurus. Along with the name change, this large sedan received more power, freshened styling, and revised suspension tuning. A 260-horsepower 3.5-liter V-6 replaced Five Hundred's 203-bhp 3.0 V-6 as the only engine. A six-speed automatic became the sole transmission; the CVT was dropped.

► For 2008, Ford's Freestyle crossover morphed into the Taurus X. Along with the name change, this SUV received freshened styling and more power. Taurus X was essentially a wagon version of the Taurus sedan. Front-wheel-drive and all-wheel-drive models were available in SEL, Eddie Bauer, and Limited trims.

◄ The 2008 Ford Escape was updated with freshened exterior and interior styling, new features, and lower prices. This compact SUV was nearly identical in size and had the same powertrains as the 2001–2007 version. Prices started at $19,140.

► The 2008 Ford Econoline wore a redesigned front end, and also benefited from revised braking, suspension, and steering systems. Also new was increased cargo capacity and an exclusive double locking system on the cargo doors to secure valuables stored inside.

LINCOLN ▲ The 2008 Lincoln Town Car remained the only American-brand premium large sedan with rear-wheel drive. Available models were Signature Limited and limousine-like Signature L with a six-inch-longer wheelbase for more rear legroom. All used a 239-horsepower 4.6-liter V-8 engine and four-speed automatic transmission. Among the few available options were xenon headlamps and chrome alloy wheels.

► The 2008 Lincoln MKX came with more standard equipment. Previously optional heated and ventilated front seats and a driver-seat memory system became newly standard. Also standard was Ford's Sync voice-activated control for cell phones and MP3 players. A new Limited Edition Package included specific trim, 20-inch wheels, and upgraded leather upholstery.

◄ The 2008 Lincoln Mark LT was basically unchanged. Two versions were available, one with a 138.5-inch wheelbase and a 5.5-foot cargo bed; the other a 150.5-inch wheelbase with a 6.5-foot bed. A navigation system and 20-inch wheels joined the option list.

MERCURY

► The 2008 Mercury Milan received a few new features. Offered in Base and fancier Premier models, both were available with a 160-horsepower 2.3-liter four-cylinder engine or a 221-bhp 3.0-liter V-6. The four-cylinder mated with a five-speed manual or five-speed automatic transmission. V-6 versions used a six-speed automatic. Newly available features included rear obstacle detection and Ford's Sync.

◄ For 2008, Mercury Sable returned as a more-powerful, restyled version of Mercury's Montego large sedan. Base and uplevel Premier models were cataloged with front- or all-wheel drive. Available safety features included ABS, traction control, antiskid system, front side airbags, and curtain side airbags. A navigation system and DVD entertainment were optional.

- "One Ford" plan producing positive results

- Ford reduces automotive structural costs by $5.1 billion

- Ford manages to avoid a government bailout

- General Motors and Chrysler go through government-sponsored bankruptcies

- Company announces net income of $2.7 billion, an improvement of $17.5 billion compared to 2008

- Gas/electric hybrid versions of Ford Fusion and Mercury Milan go on sale

- Ford F-Series best-selling truck in U.S. for 33 years, in Canada for 44 years

FORD ▲ Mustang saw no major changes for 2009, as an updated 2010 model was expected during calendar '09. Still, a fixed glass roof panel became a new option for Mustang coupes. Base, GT, Bullitt, and GT500 models returned, as did the "Warriors in Pink" edition. Part of the proceeds from the latter went to benefit breast cancer research.

▶ The Flex was a new midsize SUV that sat six or seven. Unlike some recent Fords that were long on function and short on style, Flex had both, in spades. Flex came in three trim levels: base SE, midlevel SEL, and top-line Limited. Front-wheel drive was standard. All-wheel drive was available on the SEL and Limited. Flex's distinguishing visual features were its squared-off shape, contrasting roof and body colors, and use of exterior chrome accents. Power was supplied by a 262-bhp 3.5-liter V-6 mated to a six-speed automatic transmission.

► For 2009, Focus coupe appearance was updated with new front and rear fascias and a dark-finished grille. Top-line SES coupes (shown) also received a roof-mounted spoiler and "Dark-Chrome" 17-inch aluminum wheels. The SE coupe used a decklid spoiler; 2008's price leader S coupe was no longer available.

▲ ► The Edge lineup gained another new model for 2009. After adding a dressy Limited version in 2008 (above), a stylish Sport model (right) arrived for '09. Sport boasted standard 22-inch wheels, unique body panels, dual exhaust, specific seats, and unique interior trim.

► The F-150 was redesigned for 2009, gaining power, passenger room, and numerous new features. A 248-horsepower 4.6-liter V-8 replaced the V-6 as base engine and came with a four-speed automatic transmission. The regular-cab model deleted its rear access doors. Also new was an SFE (Superior Fuel Economy) package for 2WD models with the 292-bhp 4.6 V-8 and six-speed automatic transmission (shown). The package included low-rolling-resistance tires and a different axle ratio for a 1-mpg increase in the EPA highway fuel economy rating.

◄ With the demise of the Lincoln Mark LT after the 2008 model run, Ford added a new top-dog F-150 Platinum model for buyers who were looking for a luxurious truck. Platinum models featured a satin-chrome grille with fine mesh inserts and 20-inch, 16-spoke alloy wheels. Inside, specific leather interior trim with "tuxedo" stitch details, along with LaCrosse Ash wood accents and real brushed-aluminum trim added extra class. F-150 Platinum pricing started at $40,910.

LINCOLN ◄▼ Lincoln's new flagship sedan was the 2009 MKS. It used the basic chassis from the Ford Taurus and Mercury Sable but was clothed in unique sheet metal. MKS had a 3.7-liter V-6 engine under the hood that was good for 275 horsepower. Front- and all-wheel drive was offered. Standard was Ford's new "EasyFuel" capless fuel-filler system (left), which allowed owners to fill their fuel tanks without removing a gas cap.

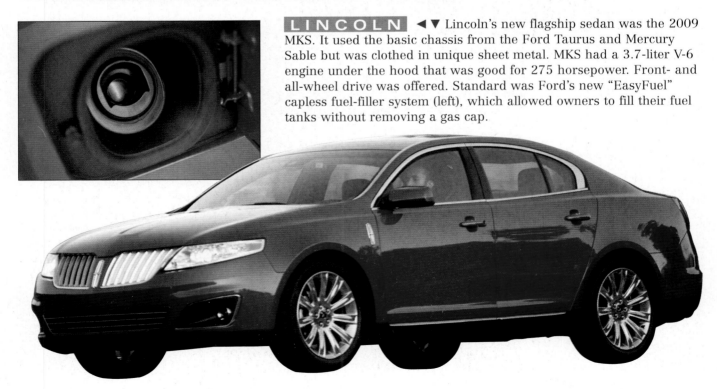

▼ ▶ Lincoln's MKT crossover SUV arrived in summer 2009 as an early 2010 model. It shared a basic seven-passenger layout with Ford Flex but used completely different styling. The base model had a 270-horsepower 3.7-liter V-6 engine and front- or all-wheel drive. The top-line EcoBoost model was AWD only and boasted a 355-horsepower twin-turbocharged 3.5-liter V-6. The sole transmission was a six-speed automatic. Prices started at $44,200 for a base front driver; EcoBoost at $49,200 before extras.

MERCURY

▶ Mercury's Milan benefited from a series of small changes for 2009. A five-speed automatic was now available with Milan's 2.3-liter four-cylinder engine. A new VOGA appearance package added cashmere leather interior trim, a special color palette, and unique trim. Premier models, like the one shown, started at $23,410.

◀ The large Sable sedan returned with few changes for what proved to be its last model year. Like Mariner and Milan, a VOGA appearance package was available. The package listed for $995 and added chrome alloy wheels and unique interior and exterior trim.

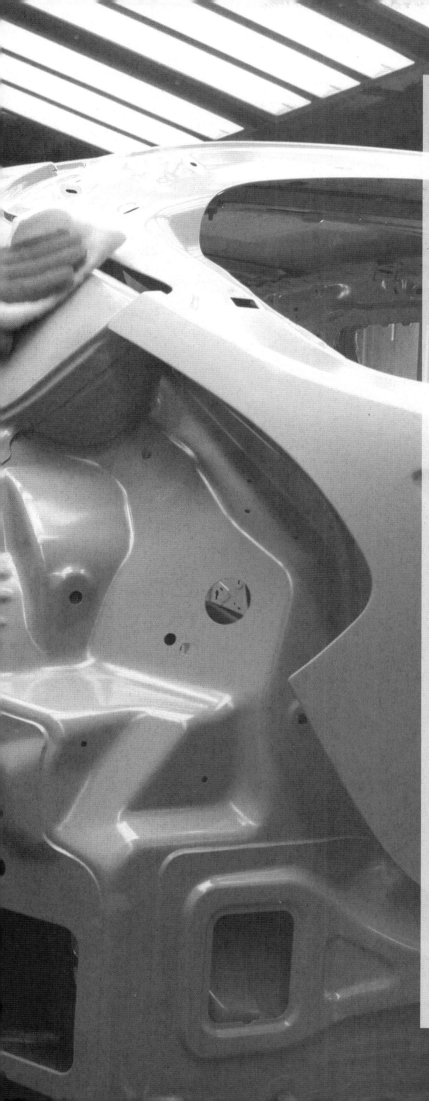

Renaissance

While Wall Street recovered from the great recession in the early 2010s, severe problems continued to plague the American economy. The U.S. annual budget deficit hovered around $1.5 trillion, and unemployment—caused in part by corporate outsourcing of American jobs—remained unsustainably high. Meanwhile, state and local governments faced budget crises of their own.

The Republican Party consistently banged heads with President Barack Obama and the Democrats in Congress, challenging such Democratic initiatives as the massive 2010 health care reform act.

An oil spill in the Gulf of Mexico, a tsunami in Japan, and revolutions in North African and Middle Eastern countries, added to the turmoil.

Thankfully for the U.S. auto industry, car sales roared back after horrendous years in 2008 and '09. GM and Chrysler, both recovering from bankruptcy and government intervention, began to spin profits. Ford enjoyed the greatest renaissance of all, turning a $6.6 billion profit in 2010—its biggest since 1999.

With oil prices and reserves a global concern, automakers pushed forward with alternative-fuel vehicles. They rolled out new hybrids and even all-electric cars, including one by Ford: the 2012 Focus Electric.

- New Focus unveiled at the Detroit Auto Show in January
- Fiesta and Turkish-built Transit Connect commercial van go on sale in America

- In June, company announces Mercury brand will be phased out by year's end
- In November, U.S. government sells a portion of its General Motors stock

in country's largest-ever IPO
- Ford completes sale of Volvo to China-based Zhejiang Geely Holding Group

- Company reduces automotive debt by $14.5 billion, or 43 percent. Lowers annual interest expenses by more than $1 billion
- Net income for the year is $6.6 billion

FORD

▶ Mustang received an effective update for 2010. Revised styling, upgraded interior trim, and additional V-8 power were some of the most notable changes. The 4.0-liter V-6 remained the base engine, but GTs now had the 315-horsepower 4.6 V-8 previously reserved for the Bullitt. The high-performance Shelby GT500 packed a supercharged 5.4 V-8 good for 540 ponies. A new option for GT Premium coupes with manual transmission was the "Trackpack." It added a limited-slip differential, uprated brakes, sport suspension, 19-inch wheels, and a special antiskid system.

◀ Fusion was reworked for 2010 as well. New styling and more power were on tap, as was a new Sport model with a 263-horsepower 3.5-liter V-6. Fusion Sport started at $26,180 for a front-drive version, and $28,030 with all-wheel drive.

◄ Fusion also added a gas/electric hybrid model for 2010. The Hybrid paired a 2.5-liter four-cylinder gas engine with an electric motor for 191 horsepower total. It was able to run on one or both of its power sources to balance acceleration and fuel economy and required no plug-in charging. It used a continuously variable (CVT) transmission that behaved much like an automatic. The Fusion Hybrid boasted EPA-estimated fuel-economy numbers of 41 mpg city and 36 mpg highway.

► Ford also gave its Taurus large sedan a substantial makeover for 2010. It retained the basic platform and powertrain of the 2008–2009 model, but with all new interior and exterior styling. Front- and all-wheel-drive versions were offered.

▲ The high-performance SHO model was reprised for 2010, after last being available in 1999. It used Ford's "EcoBoost" twin-turbocharged 3.5-liter V-6, rated at 365 horsepower. A six-speed automatic transmission and all-wheel drive were standard on every SHO. An available "Performance Pack" added better brakes and 20-inch summer-only tires.

► Ford introduced Americans to the company's Transit Connect small van for 2010. The front-drive people or cargo hauler was already sold in many global markets and was assembled in Turkey. The sole powertrain was a 136-horsepower 2.0-liter four-cylinder engine.

◄ Transit Connect could be outfitted to seat between two and five people, and various combinations of glass windows and steel panels were available to suit different needs. All had minivan-like sliding rear-side doors on each side and large rear "barn doors," like a commercial cargo van's in the back.

LINCOLN

► Lincoln's big MKS sedan added an optional engine; the same EcoBoost V-6 found in Ford's Taurus SHO. It came packaged with all-wheel drive and 19-inch wheels. The EcoBoost's extra grunt added $5000 to the cost of an AWD MKS, raising the starting tab to $47,760.

► Lincoln's MKZ was updated with freshened styling inside and out and a few new features. It shared the 263-horsepower 3.5 V-6 with the Ford Fusion Sport. A Sport Appearance Package was new for 2010. It included a retuned suspension, 18-inch tires, and some specific trim bits.

◄ The big Navigator SUV soldiered on virtually unchanged. It was still available in standard and extended-length "L" versions.

MERCURY

► The Mercury Milan was updated for 2010, closely following the improvements made to the Ford Fusion. This included the debut of a Milan Hybrid. The brand's biggest news was released June 2; Ford announced Mercury production would end during the year's fourth quarter. Mountaineer was dropped at the end of 2010. Milan, Mariner, and Grand Marquis were retired after short runs of 2011 models.

2011

- Mustang gets new engines, including a 5.0-liter V-8

- Popular F-150 line gets four new engines. The 3.5-liter EcoBoost V-6 receives the highest trailer-tow rating

- Updated Edge crossover SUV is first vehicle available with company's "MyFord Touch" control interface; early reviews are mixed

- New Focus compact goes on sale in the U.S., Europe, Africa, and the Asia-Pacific region

- Ford unveils an electric version of the Focus at the Detroit Auto Show, along with several variants of the Focus-based C-Max small van

FORD ▲ After a substantial rework for 2010, Ford's Mustang was treated to even more improvements for 2011. The biggest news was two new engines; a 3.7-liter V-6 with 305 horsepower, and a 5.0-liter V-8 with 412 ponies for GTs. Suspension and steering upgrades arrived too, as did restyled front and rear fascias.

▶ Though it had been on sale in some markets for a couple of years, the subcompact Fiesta went on sale in the U.S. as a 2011 model. Two body styles were sold here, this four-door hatchback and a four-door sedan. The lone engine in the states was a 1.6-liter four-cylinder.

◀ Fiesta sedans came in S, SE, and SEL trim; hatchbacks were SE and SEL only. Fiestas could be loaded up with options including Sync, sunroof, keyless engine start, leather upholstery, and heated front seats.

◄ There was an old-style 2011 Focus, but early in the year an all-new Focus went on sale as a 2012 model. Like its little brother the Fiesta, Focus offered Americans the choice of four-door sedan and hatchback body styles. An all-new 2.0-liter four-cylinder engine came with direct injection and put out 160 horsepower.

► Focus had lots of options on offer too, including the latest MyFord Touch interface that allowed many vehicle systems to be controlled via a centrally mounted touchscreen or by voice commands. Atop the Focus range were new Titanium models.

▼ The 2011 Ford Edge was the first vehicle available with the new MyFord Touch interface that replaced much of the traditional audio and climate switchgear with a touchscreen, touch-sensitive pads, and voice activation. There were two variations available, with this Sony-branded version a standard feature on Limited and Sport.

▲ The Edge SUV received a major freshening for 2011. There was a new interior, new engines, and revised styling. This Sport used a 305-horsepower 3.7-liter V-6.

▲ Ford's best-selling F-150 full-size pickup trucks received several new engines for 2011. The extensive F-150 lineup included three cab styles, a like number of bed lengths, and four different engines. Trim levels included base XL, sporty STX, off-road-oriented FX4, volume XLT, uplevel King Ranch and Lariat, and line-topping Platinum. F-150 also offered special-edition models including limited-production Lariat Limited, sporty Harley-Davidson, and off-road SVT Raptor.

▲ One of the F-150's new engines was the EcoBoost 3.5-liter V-6. Completely reworked for truck duty, it was good for 365 horsepower and 420 pound-feet of torque. Properly equipped, a F-150 with the EcoBoost V-6 could tow 11,300 pounds.

▲ Ford's Explorer was completely redesigned and switched from truck-type body-on-frame construction to crossover-style unibody design. It now shared some basic structural elements with Ford's Taurus sedan. Front- and all-wheel-drive versions were available.

► The standard Explorer engine was a 290-horsepower 3.7-liter V-6. A turbocharged EcoBoost 2.0-liter four-cylinder was slated to arrive for 2012.

LINCOLN

◄ ▲ Like the related Ford Edge, Lincoln's MKX crossover was heavily revised for 2011. Updated styling, more power, and new features were part of the deal. MKX was the first of the marque's products to be available with MyLincoln Touch control interface.

► The MKZ sedan added a gas/electric hybrid version for 2011. It was available only as a front-drive model and started at $34,330. The conventional V-6 powered MKZ cost the same; with all-wheel drive the tariff was $36,220.

INDEX